Luther in English

Princeton Theological Monograph Series

K. C. Hanson, Charles M. Collier, and D. Christopher Spinks,
Series Editors

Recent volumes in the series:

Neal J. Anthony
*Cross Narratives: Martin Luther's Christology
and the Location of Redemption*

Philip Ruge-Jones
*Cross in Tensions: Luther's Theology of the Cross
as Theologico-social Critique*

Caryn D. Riswold
Coram Deo: Human Life in the Vision of God

Paul S. Chung
Martin Luther and Buddhism: Aesthetics of Suffering, Second Edition

Chris Budden
Following Jesus in Invaded Space: Doing Theology on Aboriginal Land

Lisa E. Dahill
*Reading from the Underside of Selfhood: Bonhoeffer
and Spiritual Formation*

Ryan A. Neal
*Theology as Hope: On the Ground and Implications
of Jürgen Moltmann's Doctrine of Hope*

Luther in English

The Influence of His Theology of Law and Gospel on Early English Evangelicals (1525–35)

Michael S. Whiting

☙PICKWICK *Publications* • Eugene, Oregon

LUTHER IN ENGLISH
The Influence of His Theology of Law and Gospel on Early English Evangelicals
(1525–35)

Princeton Theological Monograph Series 142

Copyright © 2010 Michael S. Whiting. All rights reserved. Except for brief quotations in critical publications or reviews, no part of this book may be reproduced in any manner without prior written permission from the publisher. Write: Permissions, Wipf and Stock Publishers, 199 W. 8th Ave., Suite 3, Eugene, OR 97401.

Pickwick Publications
An Imprint of Wipf and Stock Publishers
199 W. 8th Ave., Suite 3
Eugene, OR 97401

www.wipfandstock.com

ISBN 13: 978-1-60608-900-2

Cataloging-in-Publication data:

Whiting, Michael S.

    Luther in English : the influence of his theology of law and gospel on early English evangelicals (1525–35) / Michael S. Whiting.

    Princeton Theological Monograph Series 142

    xviii + 360 p. ; 23 cm. Includes bibliographical references.

    ISBN 13: 978-1-60608-900-2

    1. Luther, Martin, 1483–1546—Theology. 2. England—Church history—16th century. 3. Reformation—Great Britain. 4. Tyndale, William, d. 1536. 5. Frith, John, 1503–1533. 6. Barnes, Robert, 1495–1540. 7. Wycliffe, John, d. 1384. 8. Lollards. I. Title. II. Series.

BR375 W50 2010

Manufactured in the U.S.A.

Dedicated to
the memory of Professor Emeritus Nigel Yates, DD
(1944–2009)

Contents

Preface / ix

Acknowledgments / xiii

List of Abbreviations / xv

INTRODUCTION: Luther and the English Evangelical Reformers in Retrospect / 1

1. "*Lex Sola Accusat*"? Modern Appraisals of Law, Gospel, and the *Tertius Usus Legis* in the Theology of Luther / 17

2. Law and Gospel in Luther's "Breakthrough" Years and Early Lectures on the Bible (1515–1520) / 41

3. Combating Legalism and Lawlessness: Law and Gospel in Luther's Writings of the 1520s / 71

4. Law and Gospel in Luther's Later Years and His Dispute with the Antinomians (1530–1540) / 124

5. After Lollardy and Humanism: Luther's Writings in England and the Beginnings of "Evangelical" Reformation / 146

6. Law and Gospel in the Theology of William Tyndale / 170

7. Law and Gospel in the Theology of John Frith / 273

8. Law and Gospel in the Theology of Dr. Robert Barnes / 309

CONCLUSION: Reassessing the Influence of Luther's Theology of Law and Gospel on Early English Evangelicals / 338

Bibliography / 345

Preface

THIS BOOK IS A REVISED VERSION OF MY DOCTORAL DISSERTATION, "Luther in English: Law and Gospel in the Theology of Early English Evangelicals (1525-1535)," written between 2004-2009 under the supervision of Dr. Eva De Visscher and the late Nigel Yates, Professor Emeritus of Ecclesiastical History, at the University of Wales, Lampeter.

While I do agree with recent scholars that the singular title of "Reformation" to describe the period of the sixteenth century tends to underemphasize the rich national diversity that characterized the historical reality, affirming the complex tapestry of theological emphases and political and social realities does not deny that there were various factors that knit that web together. Thus, the concern of this book is to trace theological influences through an international connectedness, in this case between Germany and England, that contributed to a certain solidarity meriting the title of the "Reformation." Of course, there is also some ambiguity in establishing when the "Reformation" actually begins (and ends) that depends upon how "Reform" is being defined. Thus, as was the case in a course I taught on the Reformation at Wheaton College in the Spring semester of 2008, beginning a discussion of the Reformation well before the famous posting of the 95 theses in 1517 and extending it well into the seventeenth century has its merits. It acknowledges that "reform" did not begin with Luther but was in some form characteristic of the Church throughout the Middle Ages, and that the "new reforms" of the sixteenth century in all their diversity were still being worked out in Church, State, and European society well into the next century. However, this does not underestimate the critical importance of Luther.

It is my assumption that theological ideas as much as the forces of political, economic, and social-cultural dynamics shaped the story of the Reformation. On the other hand, I realize that theological ideas are themselves constructed within historical contexts. Therefore, this book incorporates a substantial amount of historical and biographical background, mainly for the purpose of establishing literary context as well as to identify the precise historical, cultural, and social conduits upon which writings and their influence were passed from one person (and nation) to another. Nevertheless, this is less of an historical narrative than a work of intellectual history and theological interpretation concerning the complex and much disputed issue of Law and Gospel in the Christian life.

Little did I realize when I first proposed my research topic in 2004 what a complex conversation and debate I was joining that has lasted for over a half a century. Early twentieth-century historians identified early English evangelical reformers of the 1520s and 30s as basically "Lutheran" in reforming outlook (of course, with the obvious exception that most rejected the doctrine of the Real Presence of Christ in the Eucharist). Two works in the middle of the twentieth century, however, challenged this view with the conclusion that Luther had some influence but was surpassed (even contradicted) by the early English evangelicals in stressing the Law and good works in the Christian life. The most recent work by Carl Trueman, *Luther's Legacy: Salvation and the English Reformers* (1995) has become widely accepted by the scholarly community and indeed offers an important revision of revisionist interpretations by at least stressing a greater implicit continuity with the theology of Luther. Nevertheless, the prevailing opinion, including that of Trueman, is that Luther had a very real, but quite measurably limited, influence on the developing theology of Early English evangelicals. Yet, an even more recent monograph on the theology of William Tyndale denies Luther even a limited role in favor of the influence of native English dissent in Lollardy. It is my conviction that Luther is still central to any discussion of the theology of early English evangelicals and that previous scholars have not devoted enough time and study to Luther himself. Therefore, these scholars have not proven beyond doubt the premise upon which their conclusions are based. Therefore, this is my attempt to build a more solid bridge between Luther studies and scholarship on the early English evangelicals.

Though not confessionally a Lutheran, I have for a long time been fascinated with the theology and personality of Luther, who I consider to be the most interesting figure to study in the entire history of Christianity other than Jesus Christ. Although many scholars now downplay any significant relationship between Luther's "discovery" and the whole complex development of the Reformation, I am still amazed at the extent to which his anxious, some might even say narcissistic, quest for his own assurance of salvation did so dramatically impact religious thought and culture in Germany and beyond. Of course, it was Luther's pastoral goal to provide all Christians with real assurance of God's grace in Jesus Christ, but he was also very much aware of the dangers of an assurance that cheapens grace and muffles the call to repentance and to warfare against sin.

Michael S. Whiting, PhD
October 17, 2009

Acknowledgments

WITHOUT THE SUPPORT OF MANY WONDERFUL PEOPLE IN MY LIFE NEIther my PhD thesis nor this book would ever have seen the light of day. First of all, I want to thank my wife, Julia, for the incredible sacrifices she has endured since this journey began five years ago. Without her willingness to temporarily set aside her own calling so that I could pursue mine, none of this would have been possible. I am grateful to her for her faithful commitment and patience over the years even through times of rejection and uncertainty. Secondly, my parents have been incredibly generous and supportive over the years and I want to especially thank them for funding my numerous trips back and forth to England and Wales. I also want to thank my mom for all the time she has spent with her granddaughter so that I could escape away to the library or coffee shop for much needed study time. Jaylin, I want to thank you for providing Daddy with a playful escape from his obsession with Luther and the Reformation and the pressures and stresses of life as an academic. I am truly blessed by the bond we have developed over these last five years and I would not trade it for anything else in the world. To our new baby boy Chase Christopher, I look forward to beginning our own adventure, and I hope that you and your sister will one day understand something of my fascination with the history of Christianity.

I also want to thank Dr. Jeff Greenman, Dr. Kathryn Long, Dr. Dennis Okholm, and Dr. Tim Larsen for all their continued encouragement and support for my academic career over the years. I am extremely humbled and privileged to now call former professors my colleagues and friends and grateful to those who gave me the surreal opportunity to teach the history of Christianity and the Reformation as a guest adjunct professor at Wheaton College in the Spring semesters of 2007 and 2008.

I want to thank Richard Rex for kindly responding with his expertise to my many questions about Lollardy and the technicalities of citing early printed materials, Rev. Dr. Ralph Werrell for our few but valued email discussions on Tyndale, and Robert Kolb for reading my entire thesis and for his kind support and keen insight on Luther. Thanks to all those who have been so accommodating at Wycliffe Hall, Oxford University and the Bodleian Library, and Peterwell House. I am humbly grateful to my two learned doctoral examiners, Dr. Simon Oliver and Dr. George Newlands, for their overwhelming affirmation of my PhD thesis and gracious support to see it published. Many thanks to Christian Admonson and Dr. K. C. Hanson at Wipf and Stock Publishers for guiding the editorial process and providing me with the opportunity to publish my thesis. Finally, the thesis on which this book is based would not have been possible without the encouragement and insightful guidance of my two erudite advisors, Dr. Eva De Visscher and the late Professor Nigel Yates, who sadly passed away just a few months after my doctoral defense and before my graduation. This book is dedicated in his memory. As is commonly said in works of this kind, I take full credit for the flaws that remain.

SOLI DEO HONOR ET GLORIA

Abbreviations

A&M [1563]   Actes and monuments of these latter and perillous dayes touching matters of the Church, wherein ar comprehended and decribed the great persecutions [and] horrible troubles, that haue bene wrought and practised by the Romishe prelates, speciallye in this realme of England and Scotlande, from the yeare of our Lorde a thousande, vnto the tyme nowe present. Gathered and collected according to the true copies [and] wrytinges certificatorie, as wel of the parties them selues that suffered, as also out of the bishops registers, which wer the doers therof, by Iohn Foxe., Imprinted at London: By Iohn Day, dwellyng ouer Aldersgate. Cum priuilegio Regi[a]e Maiestatis, [1563 (20 March)]. Henry E. Huntington Library and Art Gallery.

A&M [1570]   John Foxe. The first volume of the ecclesiasticall history contaynyng the actes and monumentes of thynges passed in euery kynges tyme in this realme, especially in the Church of England principally to be noted : with a full discourse of such persecutions, horrible troubles, the sufferyng of martyrs, and other thinges incident, touchyng aswel the sayd Church of England as also Scotland, and all other foreine nations, from the primitiue tyme till the reigne of K. Henry VIII., At London: Printed by Iohn Daye, dwellyng ouer Aldersgate, these bookes are to be sold at hys shop vnder the gate. 1570. Harvard University Library.

BSLK	*Die Bekenntnisschriften der evangelisch-lutherischen Kirche: Herausgegeben im Gedenkjahr der Augsburgischen Konfession 1930.* Zwolfte Auflage. Göttingen: Vandenhoeck & Ruprecht, 1998.
CR	*Corpus Reformatorum* [microform]. Philippi Melancthonis. *Opera quae supersunt omnia.* Volumes 1-28. Edited by C. G. Bretschneider and H. E. Bindsell. Halle, 1834-1860; Ioannis Calvini. *Opera quae supersunt omnia.* Vols. 29–87. Edited by Guilielmus Baum, Eduardus Cunitz, and Eduardus Reuss, et al. Braunchsweig-Berlin, 1863–1900.
DNB	*Dictionary of National Biography.* 22 vols. Founded by George Smith. Edited by Sir Leslie Stephen and Sir Sidney Lee. Oxford: Oxford University Press, 1885–1901; reprint, 1917.
EM	*Ecclesiastical memorials, relating chiefly to religion, and the Reformation of it, and the emergencies of the Church of England, under King Henry VIII. King Edward VI. And Queen Mary I.: with large appendixes, containing original papers, records, &c.* 4 volumes. Edited by John Strype. Oxford: Clarendon, 1822.
Ep	*Epitome* of the *Formula of Concord*
Kolb and Wengert	*The Book of Concord: The Confessions of the Evangelical Lutheran Church.* Edited by Robert Kolb and Timothy J. Wengert. Minneapolis: Fortress, 2000.
Institutes	John Calvin. *Institutes of the Christian Religion.* 2 volumes. Library of Christian Classics 20. Edited by John T. McNeill. Translated and Indexed by Ford Lewis Battles. Philadelphia: Westminster, 1960.
LC	*Large Catechism*

L&P	*Letters and Papers, Foreign and Domestic, of the Reign of Henry VIII, preserved in the Public Record Office, the British Museum, and elsewhere.* Second edition. Revised and greatly enlarged by R. H. Brodie. 21 volumes. London, 1920; Vaduz Kraus reprint, 1965.
LW	*Luther's Works: American Edition.* [CD-ROM]. 55 vols. Edited by Jaroslav Pelikan and Helmut T. Lehmann. St. Louis: Concordia Publishing House; Philadelphia: Fortress Press, 1955–1986.
ODNB	*Oxford Dictionary of National Biography.* 60 vols. In Association with the British Academy. From the Earliest Times to the Year 2000. Edited by H. C. G. Matthew and Brian Harrison. Oxford: Oxford University Press, 2004.
Preus	Philipp Melancthon. *Loci Communes* 1543. Translated and Edited by J. A. O. Preus. St Louis: Concordia, 1992.
SC	*Small Catechism*
SD	*Solid Declaration* of the *Formula of Concord*
Tappert	*The Book of Concord.* Edited by Theodore G. Tappert. Philadelphia: Fortress, 1959.
WA	*D. Martin Luthers Werke: Kritische Gesamtausgabe.* 63 volumes. Weimar, 1883–1987; Verlag Hermann Böhlaus Nachfolger Weimar, 2001.
WA Br	*Briefwechsel* volumes of *WA*
WA DB	*Die Deutsche Bibel* volumes of *WA*
WA Tr	*Tischreden* volumes of *WA*

Whole Works   John Foxe. *The vvhole workes of W. Tyndall, Iohn Frith, and Doct. Barnes, three worthy martyrs, and principall teachers of this churche of England collected and compiled in one tome togither, beyng before scattered, [and] now in print here exhibited to the church. To the prayse of God, and profite of all good Christian readers.* At London: Printed by Iohn Daye, and are to be sold at his shop vnder Aldersgate, An. 1573. Henry E. Huntington Library and Art Gallery.

Introduction

Luther and the English Evangelical Reformers in Retrospect

ACCORDING TO ONE WELL KNOWN BRITISH HISTORIAN, "WITHOUT Luther, we can be reasonably certain that there would have been no Reformation, or not the same Reformation."[1] While some scholars might concede this point with respect to the Reformation in German lands,[2] its inclusiveness of all European nations is no longer taken for granted, and the extent and originality of Luther's actual impact continues to be a contested issue in Reformation historiography. This is especially true with regard to his influence on early English evangelical reformers living during the Henrician period of the English Reformation in the 1520s and 30s.

Although mindful of the heroic importance of Luther, historical chroniclers beginning with John Foxe in the middle of the sixteenth century rooted the Elizabethan Reformation in an earlier tradition of native English dissent going back to the fourteenth and fifteenth centuries.[3] It was not until the late nineteenth and early-to-mid twentieth centuries that historians even began to take a more intent look at the actual extent of the continental legacy, first and foremost in its Lutheran forms,[4] leading one historian to describe the English Protestant Reformation as an essentially "Lutheran Reformation."[5] More recently, the emphasis has shifted to broaden the study of influences beyond that of Luther and

---

1. Collinson, *Reformation*, 6.
2. Dixon, *The Reformation*, 44.
3. Elton, "England and the Continent," in Baker, *Reform and Reformation*, 9; Hudson, *Premature Reformation*, 60; Mullet, *Luther*, 6–7.
4. Jacobs, *Lutheran Movement in England*.
5. Tjernagel, *Henry VIII and the Lutherans*, 188–89, 248, 250, 252–54.

the Lutherans in Germany, but most scholars do agree that England was significantly influenced by continental currents of reform, an example of how truly international the Reformation was and how it all "remained recognizably part of the same movement."[6] Diarmaid MacCulloch goes so far to argue that the English context contributed nothing theologically unique to the Reformation, and that "to chronicle the theological story of the English Reformation" involves mostly observing how English theologians reacted to continental developments.[7]

Many historians indeed now acknowledge an increasing awareness of the "European dimension" and "international-mindedness" of "pre-Elizabethan Protestantism."[8] E. G. Rupp even encouraged nationally conscious English Protestants to not be "ashamed or afraid to acknowledge the full indebtedness of the English reformers to their brethren on the Continent." Elsewhere, however, he qualifies this by also stating that "the history of the English Protestant tradition cannot be explained according to Continental categories. In England we have gone our own way, in religion and in theology as in our political history."[9] G. R. Elton adopted a moderate approach as well, arguing that England "culturally and intellectually . . . was, to all appearance, very much a part of Europe," while at the same time stressing that Henry VIII's break with the papacy allowed for the creation of something unique in English religion and politics.[10] More recently, Christopher Haigh argues that the traditional use of the singular term "Reformation" itself undermines not only the recognition of the various stages of "reformation" within the English story itself (as indicated by the title of his work) but the reality of geographical diversity despite obvious international connectedness between "reformations." With regard to the English context in particular, he stresses that undue exaggeration on this interconnectedness wrongly relegates English religious history to mere imitation of continental happenings.[11]

6. Pettegree, "Early Reformation in Europe," in Pettegree, *Early Reformation in Europe*, 22.

7. MacCulloch, "England," in Pettegree, *Early Reformation in Europe*, 169.

8. Elton, "England and the Continent," in Baker, *Reform and Reformation*, 10–11; Marshall and Ryrie, *Beginnings of English Protestantism*, 10; Marshall, *Impact of the Reformation in England*, 9.

9. Rupp, "Luther in English Theology," 12; Rupp, *Studies in the Making*, 47.

10. Elton, "England and the Continent," in Baker, *Reform and Reformation*, 4–6, 14–15.

11. Haigh, *English Reformations*, 12, 14. See also Buechner, "Luther and the English Reformation," 799–805; Lindberg, *European Reformations*.

Whether one prefers to use the term "Reformation" or "Reformations," then, seems to largely depend upon whether the interconnectedness or diversity is being emphasized.

This broader question of the relationship between national reformations relates more narrowly to ongoing debates surrounding the particular influence of Martin Luther's theology upon the career of three leading English evangelical reformers who lived during the 1520s and 30s in the Henrician period of the early English Reformation.[12] Where Luther was once a central figure in any study of Reformation theology in general, recent works have redefined the extent of his pan-European influence with respect to other, perhaps even lesser known, personalities.[13] As it relates to the English context and the period leading up to the "Act of Supremacy" (1534) and the official course of the early English Reformation, Luther's influence on the theology of early English evangelicals, especially William Tyndale, has even been somewhat diminished as of late in favor of humanist, Reformed, and even Lollard legacies. One recent scholar goes so far to say that "Anyone who reads Tyndale's writings theologically realises that Luther had virtually no influence on Tyndale's theology."[14]

The particular influence of Martin Luther on English evangelical reformers of the early sixteenth century has certainly received a fair share of attention by scholars in the past, especially with regard to Tyndale. For the last few decades, however, most historians of the English Reformation have focused on the complex years following the Elizabethan Settlement and the Protestantization of the English people. Thus, as some historians have noted, there has been a comparable absence of scholarly studies interpreting the life and work of the early generation of evangelical reformers.[15]

That Martin Luther had some degree of influence on early English Reformation theology is agreed upon by most scholars. Renowned historian G. R. Elton states that "the English Reformation and its advance-

---

12. By "English Reformation," I mean to refer both to the reformation "from below" as well as the more officially sanctioned reformation "from above." See Marshall, *Reformation England*, 27.

13. Dixon, *Reformation in Germany*, 20; Steinmetz, *Reformers in the Wings*.

14. Werrell, "John Trevisa and William Tyndale," 22–26.

15. Marshall, *Impact of the English Reformation*, 9; Marshall and Ryrie, *Beginnings of English Protestantism*, 4.

ments cannot be entirely understood without Luther and his influence."[16] Carl Trueman, in his recent and widely acclaimed work on the English reformers, also claims that it is impossible to understand the English Reformation without some reference to him. However, Trueman also aptly points out that the precise nature and extent of Luther's influence is what has stimulated the most vigorous debate.[17]

Tyndale's earliest major biographer, Robert Demaus, described Tyndale in 1871 as a scholar capable of independent thought but still largely a theological follower of Luther.[18] According to Henry Jacobs pioneering work, *The Lutheran Movement in England* (1890), Tyndale remained "thoroughly a Lutheran."[19] This opinion was echoed later in the writings of E. G. Rupp in the 1940s and 1950s and by J. E. McGoldrick in the 1970s. These scholars all basically describe the first generation of English evangelical reformers, such as William Tyndale and Robert Barnes, as generally "Lutheran," although openly acknowledging the former's wholesale objection to Luther's doctrine of the Real Presence of Christ in the Eucharist.[20] Rupp states with regard to Tyndale that, although he was not a "complete devotee, and certainly no mere mechanic snapper-up of another's considered trifles," he was nevertheless "concerned to make known the teaching of Luther in an English dress." As for Robert Barnes, he is commonly perceived as the one most fully aligned with the opinions of Luther, including his doctrine of the Eucharist.[21]

Groundbreaking and influential studies appeared in the 1960s by W. A. Clebsch and L. J. Trinterud. The most prominent claim arising from Clebsch and Trinterud was that the English evangelicals laid a far greater and more positive stress on the Law and good works in the life of the Christian. Although Trinterud's opinions have tended to be most ac-

---

16. Elton, *Luther in der Neuzeit*, 121. My translation.
17. Trueman, *Luther's Legacy*, 6, 54–56.
18. Demaus and Lovett, *William Tindale*, 154–56, 173–74, 207, 278–80, 397–98.
19. Jacobs, *Lutheran Movement*, 37–38.
20. McGoldrick, *Luther's English Connection*, "Preface," 47, 130–35; Rupp, *Six Makers*, 20–21; Rupp, *Studies in the Making*, 49–51; See also Elton, *Luther in der Neuzeit*, 121.
21. Rupp, *Studies in the Making*, 49–51; Rupp, *Righteousness of God*, 37–55; See also Tjernagel, *Henry VIII and the Lutherans*, viii.

cepted by scholars, both he and Clebsch were quick to identify Tyndale as an indigenous progenitor of later English Puritan moralism.²²

In *England's Earliest Protestants*, Clebsch argues that Tyndale started out his reforming career in more agreement with Luther's supposed emphasis on faith alone in the doctrine of justification, but later departed from him in the 1530s, developing a covenantal theology of salvation and a "works-righteousness" description of the Christian life.²³ Even McGoldrick's study, which is among the more favorable to Luther's influence, admits that Tyndale plainly emphasizes the fulfillment of the Law as the goal of a Christian more than Luther, but prefers to interpret this development as a "logical extension of Luther's position" rather than a complete break from it.²⁴

Trinterud's essay, however, has been more widely accepted by scholars, and even the more recent, penetrating, and enlightening study by Carl Trueman qualifies the legacy of Luther in the light of Trinterud's conclusions. In his essay, Trinterud argues that Tyndale from the very beginning of his career emphasized good works and the Law in the Christian life more positively and significantly than Luther, which shows that he never really embraced Luther's theology centered on faith but only manipulated Luther's writings for his own moralistic purposes. In Trinterud's opinion, Tyndale appears to have been shaped more by Humanism and thus has more in common with Swiss and Rhineland reformers such as Calvin or Bucer than with Luther.²⁵ This debt to Humanism has been explored in most detail by John K. Yost, who argues in an unpublished dissertation that Tyndale's "principal concern" was to reform Tudor England according to a "restoration of the law of Christ" and that this reveals him to be more humanist than Lutheran.²⁶ On the basis of Trinterud's essay, another unpublished dissertation by Paul Alan Laughlin argues that Tyndale adopted a theology of covenant in the 1530s because it expressed his original concern for good works more accurately than Luther's dialectical opposition of Law

---

22. Clebsch, *England's Earliest Protestants*, 167, 174, 197; Trinterud, "The Origins of Puritanism," 39–45; Trinterud, "A Reappraisal," 24; See also Moeller, "Beginnings of Puritan Covenant Theology," 50–54; Knappen, "William Tindale," 201–15.

23. Clebsch, *England's Earliest Protestants*, 146–203.

24. McGoldrick, *Luther's English Connection*, 128–35.

25. Trinterud, "A Reappraisal," 24–45.

26. Yost, "Christian Humanism of the English Reformers," v–vii, 10.

and Gospel.²⁷ Donald Smeeton and Ralph Werrell also fall in line with Trinterud, but argue that Tyndale's theology is rooted heavily in the theology of Wyclif and Lollardy rather than the Reformed tradition. Werrell, in particular, is quite insistent that Tyndale was not influenced in any significant way by Luther. Werrell's work is of importance since it is the most recent work on the theology of Tyndale, is endorsed with a foreword by the current Archbishop of Canterbury Rowan Williams, and is really the first systematic treatment of the theology of Tyndale ever published.²⁸

In his monumental history of the doctrine, McGrath likewise distances the early English reformers from Luther with regard to justification by faith:

> the doctrines of justification circulating in English reforming circles in the 1520s and early 1530s were quite distinct from those of the mainstream continental Reformation . . . it is clear that few of [Luther's] distinctive ideas became generally accepted in England . . . that essentially Augustinian doctrines of justification were in circulation in England independently of the influence of Luther . . . the English Reformers appear to have worked with a doctrine of justification in which man was understood to be *made* righteous by *fayth onely*, with good works being the natural consequence of justifying faith.²⁹

The most widely accepted work on the theology of the early English evangelical reformers to appear since the 1960s is Carl Trueman's *Luther's Legacy: Salvation and the English Reformers* (1994). Trueman agrees that referring to the early reformers as "Lutheran" is indeed a misleading oversimplification that ignores the extent to which other influences, such as Augustine, Humanism, and the Reformed tradition, shaped the theology of English reformers such as Tyndale. In fact, he admits that the title of his book is even a bit misleading given that: "my basic argument is that Luther's thought is considerably modified by the theologians of the English Reformation. My intention in using such a title was to underline the fact that, while Tyndale and his fellow Reformers were not Luther and had differing concerns and emphases

---

27. Laughlin, "Brightness of Moses."

28. Werrell, *Theology of William Tyndale*; Smeeton, *Lollard Themes*; See also Stackhouse, "Native Roots," 19–35.

29. McGrath, *Iustitia Dei*, 285–86, 288.

from him, it was nevertheless contact with Luther's work which radicalized their thinking and changed them from Catholic Humanists to Protestant Reformers."[30]

Trueman agrees that Tyndale develops in the second half of his career an even stronger notion of the ethical dimension of the Gospel, but contrary to Clebsch convincingly argues that this is more accurately interpreted as a change in emphasis rather than a change in the substance of his theological convictions. Trueman falls in line with Trinterud and Laughlin by acknowledging differences in emphases between Luther and Tyndale on the subject of good works and the Law in the Christian life from the very beginning. Yet, in distinction to both Trinterud and Clebsch, Trueman stresses that Tyndale's much stronger emphasis on good works and the Law in the life of the Christian is a theologically consistent extension of his doctrine of justification by faith alone.[31]

Along with McGrath, Trueman argues that there are important differences between Luther and Tyndale on the very nature of justification, which impacts their distinctive approaches to Law and good works in the Christian life. Luther defines "justification" and "justified" in terms of the reckoning or imputation of righteousness in Christ apart from the Law and works and Tyndale in the more Augustinian sense of the renewal or regeneration of the will through the grace of the Spirit in love toward the Law and good works. In a more recent essay, Jeffrey Leininger agrees with Trueman that Tyndale's theology of justification is more Augustinian but that this also reflects Luther's own theology in 1515–1516 and to some degree his theology in transition during the 1520s.[32] Leininger closely follows the work of Lowell C. Green who establishes a definite dichotomy between the early Luther on justification and his more "mature" thought of the 1530s influenced by the forensic-imputation theology of Melancthon.[33]

John Frith was another significant early evangelical reformer, though he has received far less attention than either Tyndale or Barnes.

---

30. Trueman, *Luther's Legacy*, 5–6.

31. Ibid., 292–93; Trueman, "Theology of the English Reformers," in Bagchi and Steinmetz, *Cambridge Companion to Reformation Theology*, 163–65.

32. Trueman, *Luther's Legacy*, 92–94; Leininger, "How Lutheran Was William Tyndale," 61–63, 71; McGrath, *Iustitia Dei*, 286 and n.6.

33. Green *How Melancthon Helped Luther*. For the influence of Melancthon on Luther, see also Greschat, *Melancthon Neben Luther*, 232–42.

N. T. Wright, whose work on Frith over thirty years ago remains the most comprehensive and authoritative thus far, essentially underlines Luther's influence with regard to justification by faith and the obedience of the Christian.[34] Nevertheless, Clebsch earlier had argued that Frith also drifted away from Luther by laying greater positive stress on the Christian fulfillment of the Law through good works.[35] Other scholars have gone even further and argue that Frith developed a concept of "double justification" by faith before God but by works before others, which supposedly places Frith closer to Martin Bucer than to Martin Luther.[36] Carl Trueman distinguishes Frith from Luther mostly on matters pertaining to the nature of justification, as does McGrath, but he does not perceive Frith to have developed any significant emphasis on works or the Law in the Christian life comparable to that of Tyndale's theology of covenant.[37]

Of all the early English evangelical reformers, Robert Barnes is described as the most "Lutheran," and this is because he alone among them adopted Luther's doctrine of the Real Presence.[38] However, Clebsch also pits Barnes against Luther with regard to his more positive emphasis on fulfillment of the Law and good works as the fruit and evidence of justifying faith in the life of a Christian, and that this was most visible in Barnes' embrace of the canonicity of the New Testament book of James.[39] Trueman acknowledges some imprint of Luther on Barnes' theology as it relates to Law and Gospel, but argues that this is tempered by the influences of Augustine and Humanism to the point that Barnes stresses more than Luther the role of the Holy Spirit in enabling the Christian to fulfill the Law.[40]

In light of all the work that has been done on the theology of the early English evangelical reformers so far, what is perhaps most surpris-

---

34. Wright, *Work of John Frith*, 27–33.

35. Clebsch, *England's Earliest Protestants*, 114–15.

36. Trinterud, "Origins of Puritanism," 40; Day, "Tyndale and Frith," in Day, Lund, and O'Donnell, *Word, Church, and State*, 175–76.

37. Trueman, *Luther's Legacy*, 154–55; McGrath, *Iustitia Dei*, 286, and n.7.

38. McGoldrick, *Luther's English Connection*, 15; Rupp, "Luther in English Theology," 13; Rupp, *Righteousness of God*, 39; Anderson, "Robert Barnes on Luther," 35–66; Tjernagel, "Robert Barnes and Wittenberg," 641–53; Trueman, *Luther's Legacy*, 17, 197.

39. Clebsch, *England's Earliest Protestants*, 66–68.

40. Trueman, *Luther's Legacy*, 179, 181–93, 198.

ing is the complete and utter omission of any substantial, contextual, and original interaction with Luther's theology of Law and Gospel that spanned a reforming career of nearly thirty-five years. It is largely assumed by all previous scholars that Luther significantly deemphasizes a positive role for the moral Law in the Christian life of obedience and good works, which also happens to be the interpretation of many, but not all, modern Luther scholars.[41] Despite his acknowledgment of the legacy Luther bequeathed to the theology of the English Reformation, Trueman, writing from the perspective of a Reformed theologian, likewise states that "If Luther teaches a third use of the Law, it is in a very mild and very inconsistent manner" and accuses Luther of being ambivalent toward the Law.[42] Instead, Lollardy, Humanism, Augustine, and Swiss Reformed theology are considered as alternative sources by scholars such as Trueman for this emphasis in their thinking. Yet none of these scholars has seriously reevaluated or challenged the very premise upon which their conclusions are based by a rigorous, thorough, and original analysis of Luther's theology of Law and Gospel in its developing historical context. This important foundation is missing in all previous studies of early English evangelical theology.

There is no doubt that Luther understood the moral Law to be indispensable to the ordering of creation and redemption. The very concept of the "uses of the Law" (*usus legis*) in Lutheran theology arguably originated with him. Though more formally defined in his new *Lectures on Galatians* (1531–1535),[43] and later adopted by Philipp Melancthon and the Lutheran confessions, these uses are also evident in substance in his earliest writings as well. Put simply, Luther used the formal concept of the *usus legis* to refer, first, to the moral Law as an instrument of God's providence to restrain the wickedness of the unregenerate by means of coercion, threats, and temporal and civil punishments (the *usus civilis* or *politicus*) for the sake of upholding social and civic order. Secondly, God uses the Law to accuse consciences of sin and damnation so that reconciliation with God is found by faith alone in the promise of forgiveness in the Gospel of Jesus Christ (the *usus theologicus*).

---

41. Most notably, Bring, "Gesetz und Evangelium"; Bring, "Does Lutheran Theology," 113–18; Elert, *Law and Gospel*; Ebeling, "*Triplex Usus Legis*," 62–78.

42. Trueman, *Luther's Legacy*, 66, 73–75, 108.

43. This is an important point to remember, especially since Frith died in 1533 and Tyndale in 1536.

What many scholars still do not agree concerning, however, is whether there is any emphasis or even a place in Luther's thought for an implicit "third use of the Law," or the Law serving as a normative moral standard and goal guiding the justified Christian in obedience and the exercise of good works. It has become widely accepted that Philipp Melancthon, who first coined the phrase *tertius usus legis* in 1535, was responsible for introducing this use in any such form into Lutheran theology.[44] Contemporaries of Luther, including both Catholics as well as other German reformers like Andreas Karlstadt and Thomas Müntzer, criticized his emphasis on justification as the forgiveness of sins apart from the Law while appearing too soft with regard to regeneration and the need for moral obedience to the Law in the Christian life. Much like the German antinomians of the later 1520s and 1530s, English antinomians of the 1640s enlisted isolated statements from Luther's writings to champion the simple preaching of the Gospel, grace, and freedom in opposition to pieties that also stressed the need for preaching the Law and for moral effort and discipline in the Christian life.[45] The famous evangelical revivalist preacher John Wesley was converted by Luther's preface to the epistle of Paul to the Romans, but, after reading Luther's commentary on Galatians in 1741, blamed Luther for the moral passivity he witnessed in Moravian pietism: "Again, how blasphemously does he speak of good works and of the Law of God; constantly coupling the Law with sin, death, hell, or the devil; and teaching, that Christ delivers us from them all alike. Whereas, it can no more be proved by Scripture that Christ delivers us from the Law of God, than that he delivers us from holiness or from heaven. Here (I apprehend) is the real spring of the grand error of the Moravians. They follow Luther, for better or worse."[46]

No other book thus far on the theology of the early English evangelical reformers has seriously acknowledged or addressed the lack of scholarly consensus that still persists to this day with regard to the Law and the Christian life in Luther's theology nor provided any origi-

---

44. See especially Ragnar Bring, "Does Lutheran Theology," 113.

45. Bozeman, *Precisianist Strain*, 190–91, 197–98.

46. Wesley goes on to describe that "I thought it my bounden duty openly to warn the congregation against that dangerous treatise; and to retract whatever recommendation I might ignorantly have given of it." See *Works of John Wesley*, 1:315–6. See also Lindberg, "Do Lutherans Shout Justification," 2–4.

nal contribution to the conversation through a personal reevaluation of Luther's larger theological corpus in its historical context. What is needed, then, is a complete historical-contextual treatment of Luther's theology of Law and Gospel that spans over twenty-five years of reform, polemic, and pastoral ministry, something that is both entirely and surprisingly lacking in the English-speaking world.[47]

Since the early English evangelicals William Tyndale and John Frith died in the early to mid-1530s, and Robert Barnes in 1540, Luther's writings beyond the early 1530s theoretically apply only, if at all, to Robert Barnes, and those beyond the year 1540 are obviously irrelevant as far as any discussion of influence is concerned. Luther's published works from 1517 to the mid-1530s, and especially those of the 1520s, are the most relevant for assessing his influence on the thought of the English evangelical reformers. Nevertheless, it is important to see these works against the backdrop of Luther's pivotal lectures on the book of Romans (1515–1516), which, though not published until the twentieth century, are the capstone of a theological shift in his understanding of the role of Law and Gospel in justification and the Christian life. Furthermore, since Luther's discussion of the "uses of the Law" becomes most fully developed in controversy with antinomians in the 1530s, and although the Lutheran formula of "*usus legis*" itself post-dates the careers of Tyndale and Frith, the study of his writings dating to this decade shows how elements that perhaps took more definitive shape and emphasis later on were already latent in his thought of the late 1510s and throughout the 1520s.

William Tyndale, John Frith, and Robert Barnes are fitting to any study of the evangelical theology of the early English Reformation, who together Trueman aptly describes as constituting "the first significant English expressions of Reformation theology and . . . the focal point of any study of English soteriology during this time."[48] John Foxe, in his "Epistle or Preface to the Christian Reader" introducing the first edition of their collected works printed by John Daye in 1573, also describes them as the "chiefe ryngleaders in these latter tymes of thys Church of England" who: "in one cause, and about one tyme, sustayned the first

---

47. The only other comparable treatment I am aware of that is so singularly devoted is Bridston, "Law and gospel." On the importance of situational context in interpreting Luther's statements on Law and Gospel, see also Kolb, *Martin Luther*, 54–55.

48. Trueman, *Luther's Legacy*, 2.

brunt, in this our latter age, and gaue the first onset agaynst the enemies: as also for the speciall giftes of fruitfull erudition, and plentifull knowledge wrought in them by God, and so by them left vs in their writings."[49] Tyndale has naturally received the bulk of attention over the centuries due to the literary prolificacy of his reforming career and, more recently, because of the amount of controversy generated by his adoption of a theology of covenant in the 1530s.

Referring to Tyndale, Frith, and Barnes as "evangelical" rather than "Lutheran" or "Protestant" reformers is also purposeful and important. After 1520, the derogatory title of "Lutheran" was being used without qualification to scorn anyone with a perceived connection to the ideas of the recently condemned heretic.[50] Yet how should historians properly speak of those who show a genuine sympathy toward Luther in the 1520s and 30s but perhaps do not agree with him on every point? As many have argued, only Robert Barnes could be rightly labeled a "Lutheran" since he alone affirmed the doctrine of the Real Presence. Nevertheless, as already discussed, even the extent of Barnes' debt to Luther has not gone unchallenged in recent years. Furthermore, the word "Lutheran" only began to take on its more formal confessional meaning in the later 1530s and 40s.[51]

Similar problems abound in using the word "Protestant" to refer to an English reformer of the 1520s, the word itself having originated out of the Diet of Speyer (1529) after German princes "protested" the imperial revocation of religious freedoms granted to them under the previous Diet (1526). Andrew Hope argues that the word "Protestant" was not adopted outside of a German context before the reign of Edward VI, and Alec Ryrie observes that the word was used in England in the 1540s but only with reference to those on the Continent who had embraced Luther's doctrines and allied together against Emperor Charles V. According to Ryrie, it was only after Henry's death in 1547 that the word "Protestant" was applied at all to religious reformers in England: "by the 1540s no generally accepted term had yet been coined to refer to the emerging religious factions."[52] In order to avoid anachronism, then,

---

49. *Whole Works*, sig. A ii ʳ–A iii ʳ.

50. Jacobs, *The Lutheran Movement*, 35.

51. Ryrie, *Gospel and Henry VIII*, xvi. See also Bray, "Luther's Legacy," 44.

52. Hope, "Lollardy," in Lake and Dowling, *Protestantism and the National Church*, 1; Ryrie, *Gospel and Henry VIII*, xv.

many historians are reluctant to use the term "Protestant" in reference to any English reformer prior to the official demarcations of the later 1540s, so that "we can only talk of Protestants in England after a fully reformed set of dogmas had been promulgated and accepted under Edward VI."[53] If so, then the word "Protestant" should be avoided with regard to Tyndale, Frith, and Barnes, who were all deceased by 1540. Henry VIII's own ground-breaking separation from papal jurisdiction in 1534 did not make England an officially Protestant nation. If anything, it contributed to a doctrinal imprecision that historian Richard Rex argues characterized the entire Henrician period, such as with regard to supporters of the "Act of Supremacy" against papal power who remained Catholic otherwise in doctrine.[54]

Such complexity, states Ryrie, only serves in reflecting "the reality that religious divisions and religious communities themselves were vague and ill-defined during this early period of the Reformation."[55] To what degree did the early English evangelical reformers even perceive themselves to be an organized movement in solidarity separate from the national Church? Due to such complexity and in order not to sacrifice historical accuracy even for the sake of simplicity and generalization, "evangelicals" is a far more appropriate term to identify Tyndale, Frith, and Barnes (although Barnes could also arguably be tagged a "Lutheran"). The word "evangelical" is general enough to incorporate both continuities and discontinuities and yet specific enough to distinguish these reformers from "humanists" or "Lollards." In modern phenomenology, it has become common to associate "evangelical" and "evangelicalism" with a form of Protestantism that emerged out of the trans-Atlantic revivals of the early eighteenth century and emphasized the instantaneous experience of conversion and assurance of salvation. There is some dispute as to whether sixteenth and eighteenth century Protestants had more or less in common on this subject, but the fact stands that the words "evangelical" and "gospeller" were already in use in the 1520s and 30s as a way of identifying those who confessed the

---

53. Davis, "Lollardy and the Reformation," in Marshall, *Impact of the Reformation*, 50; Marshall and Ryrie, *Beginnings of English Protestantism*, 5–6.

54. Ryrie, *Gospel and Henry VIII*, xv; Rex, "English Campaign Against Luther," 94, 106.

55. Ryrie, *Gospel and Henry VIII*, xv–xvi.

doctrine of justification by faith in Christ alone with the perception that Scripture alone possesses ultimate doctrinal authority.[56]

In studying theological influences from a consciously historical perspective, it is never enough to simply identify conceptual and linguistic similarities between individuals. This is true in the case of Luther and the early English evangelicals. Trueman has astutely stated that "similarity does not necessarily prove influence," a temptation that troubles every historian who traces theological influences.[57] To argue for influence solely on the basis of chronological precedence and theological similarity is to succumb to the logical fallacy of *post ergo propter hoc*. It is also necessary to establish some direct historical connection by locating individuals in their contexts and identifying a conscious use of others' theological material. This is provable with particular ease in the case of Tyndale and Frith's use of Luther's writings, although this does not necessarily prove that they remained entirely faithful to his line of thinking.

Furthermore, though good works and the Law in the Christian life has dominated the most vigorous debate thus far among historians, this issue cannot be adequately understood without looking at wider theological factors requiring a broad treatment of Law and Gospel and other associated themes, including interpretation of the Old Testament, the nature of repentance, theological anthropology, the role of the Holy Spirit, assurance of salvation, and the nature of justification by faith.

No standard, critical work of the complete writings of these three evangelical reformers has yet appeared in print. The original sixteenth century printings and editions held mostly by the British Library and the libraries of Oxford and Cambridge University (see also *Early English Books Online*) remain the best for the serious historian. The writings of Tyndale, Frith, and Barnes were first published together in Foxe's *Whole Works* printed by John Daye in London in 1573. Despite the quantitative scope of the writings included, this collection is not at all suitable for a historical analysis of first and consecutive editions. In the early nineteenth century, the works of the three reformers appeared

---

56. Ibid., xv; Marshall, "Evangelical Conversion," in Marshall and Ryrie, *Beginnings of English Protestantism*, 22; Rupp, *Studies in the Making*, 171; MacKenzie, "Evangelical Character," and Null, "Thomas Cranmer," in Haykin and Stewart, *Emergence of Evangelicalism*, 171–98, 226–33; MacCulloch, *Reformation*, xx.

57. Trueman, *Luther's Legacy*, 107, 122, 124, 137, 183.

together again, although only the article on justification was included from Barnes' *Supplication* of 1534.[58] The works of Tyndale and Frith were also printed in a separate edition,[59] and the writings of Tyndale were published independently for the Parker Society.[60] Select passages compiled from Tyndale's writings were edited in the twentieth century,[61] modern spelling editions of his Old and New Testament translations appeared in the late 1980s and early 1990s,[62] and now a critical series of his works is just beginning to be published.[63] With regard to John Frith, N. T. Wright published a critical edition thirty years ago,[64] and a critical edition of Barnes' 1534 *Supplication* has recently been published by Douglas Parker.[65]

The importance of these three reformers as significant players in the religious history of early sixteenth century England makes a regular revisitation of their life and writings a supremely worthwhile enterprise. Their relationship to Luther, however, remains controversial, as does the nature and extent of Luther's contribution to the English Reformation as a whole. Without a rigorous study of Luther's own theology of Law and Gospel in his own context, however, there is simply no justification for so swiftly diminishing or even disregarding his influence on this subject matter as many scholars have done in the recent past, and there is sufficient evidence to establish that Luther indeed remained a principal influence on early English evangelical understandings of Law and Gospel and as it pertained to critical matters of reconciliation with God and the life of Christian obedience. This is why it is necessary to start this book with Luther himself and then to establish the historical context in which his writings first made their impact upon English theology before embarking on an individual appraisal of his influence on the first generation of English evangelicals.

58. *Writings of Tindal, Frith, and Barnes.*
59. Russell, *Works of the English Reformers.*
60. Walter, *An answer to Sir Thomas More's Dialogue*; Walter, *Doctrinal Treatises*; Walter, *Expositions and Notes.*
61. Greenslade, *The Work of William Tindale*; Duffield, *Work of William Tyndale.*
62. See *Tyndale's New Testament* and *Tyndale's Old Testament.*
63. The first in the series is *An answere vnto Sir Thomas Mores Dialoge.*
64. Wright, *Work of John Frith.*
65. Parker, *A Critical Edition of Robert Barnes' A supplication.*

1

"Lex Sola Accusat"?

Modern Appraisals of Law, Gospel, and the Tertius Usus Legis *in the Theology of Luther*

PREVIOUS SCHOLARSHIP HAS FOCUSED HEAVILY ON THE RELATIONSHIP of the Law to the Christian life in comparing the theology of Luther and the early English evangelicals. Yet the question of whether or not Luther himself ever even taught an implicit "third use of the Law" has been the subject of much controversy ever since the middle of the twentieth century.[1] While the formal development of an explicit "third use of the Law" in Lutheran theology actually post-dates the reforming careers of Tyndale and Frith, addressing the issue with regard to Luther's theology is extremely relevant and needs to be explored in the light of reassessing the influence of his theology of Law and Gospel on early English evangelicals. No other scholar of the early English evangelicals has so far seriously acknowledged or addressed the lack of consensus even among Lutherans concerning Luther's theology of Law and Gospel nor integrated an assessment of the different sides of the debate into their argument. The premise of a single opinion has been largely taken for granted, yet not one of these scholars gives any impression of a firsthand, comprehensive understanding of Luther's theology of Law and Gospel in its historical context.

It is important to state upfront that the evidence indicates that the explicit formula of a "third use of the Law" did not originate with Luther but rather with Melancthon in the mid-1530s. However, the question remains unsettled whether Melancthon's numbering of a "third use" was consistent and even derivative of Luther's own theology. To understand

---

1. A good summary of the major studies over the last century on the question of the "third use of the Law" in Luther and Melancthon can be found in Schurb, "Philip Melancthon," 22–88.

the nature of the debate with regard to Luther, it is important to first identify what came to be known as a "third use of the Law" in the theology of Melancthon as well as the later Lutheran *Formula of Concord*.

There does seem to be a consensus among many modern scholars that during the middle to late 1520s a shift occurred in Melancthon's theology in which he emphasized in new and significant ways the relationship of the Law to good works in the life of the Christian. Ken Schurb points out that many scholars since the 1940s have argued that Melancthon's formulation of a distinct "third use of the law" adopted by Lutheranism is actually an aberration from Luther's faith and Gospel centered thought.[2] Jeffrey K. Mann importantly identifies attempts made to "rescue Luther from Lutheranism,"[3] which is reminiscent of debates within the Reformed tradition concerning the continuity between Calvin and the later Calvinists.[4]

Some have attributed this shift to Melancthon's background in Humanism, which was characterized by a strong emphasis on renewing Christian moral piety. Jeffrey K. Mann, however, has argued that it naturally emerged from his growing concern over moral apathy in the German churches in the late 1520s, and that abuse of the doctrines of *sola fide* and the forensic imputation of righteousness in justification by libertines "made it impossible that he would not explicate a use of the Law for redeemed sinners."[5]

It is incontestable that Melancthon was the first to speak explicitly of "three offices of the law" (*Tertium officium legis*) and a "third use" (*tertius usus*) in his *Loci Communes* of 1535, and later he refers to a "three-fold office of the Law" (*triplex usus legis*).[6] According to Mann and Wengert, however, the substance of the doctrine of a "third use" actually originates earlier in Melancthon's 1534 *Scholia* on the book of Colossians. Wengert adds that the roots of this use go back even further to Melancthon's earliest insistence on the necessity of obedience in the life of the Christian, but that its more formal development emerged out of Melancthon's stronger clarification of justification in 1532–34 as

---

2. Schurb, "Philipp Melancthon," 22, 26–7.
3. Mann, "Melancthon's Response," 305.
4. Clark, "Calvin versus the Calvinists," 16.
5. Mann, "Melancthon's Response," 307–8, 312, 319. See also Osslund, "*Imputatio iustitiae Christi*," 6–7, 21; Wengert, *Law and Gospel*, 195–96.
6. CR 21: 405–6; Ebeling, "*Triplex Usus Legis*," 65.

the forensic declaration of righteousness through faith in Christ.[7] Ken Schurb believes Melancthon was consistent on his teaching of the "third use" even since 1521.[8] According to Gerhard Ebeling, Melancthon's first formal reference to a *usus legis* or a *duplex usus legis* probably did not occur until his *Commentary on Romans* in 1532, but he observes hints even of a "third use" as early as Melancthon's *Instructions for Visitors* (1528) and the *Augsburg Confession* (1530). While it was Luther who coined the concept of the "*usus legis*" for the Lutheran tradition, Ebeling argues that it was Melancthon who eventually refashioned this into a more polished "scholastic schema of the *triplex usus*." For Ebeling, the substance of the *triplex usus legis* is apparent in Melancthon in 1535, although this particular formula itself appears only much later in the *Catechesis puerilis* of 1540 and the *Loci Communes* of 1543.[9]

Of course, disagreements about *when* Melancthon actually began teaching a "third use of the Law" hinge on how it is defined.[10] An adequate place to look for such a definition is Melancthon's own *Loci Communes*, which he personally favored among his other writings as a definitive expression of his theological convictions. Schurb argues that the outline of Melancthon's *Loci* of 1543 is basically the same as that of the edition of 1535, and Osslund claims that there is little development of the *Loci* after 1535. With regard to Melancthon's explicit teaching of a "third use," this remained unchanged between its introduction in the *Loci* of 1535 and the final edition of 1559.[11]

In the *Loci Communes* of 1543, Melancthon defines the Law as the "eternal and immovable rule of the divine mind and a judgment against sin." Schurb argues that this definition is not explicit in the previous 1521 and 1535 editions of Melancthon's *Loci*. In 1521, the emphasis is on the freedom of the Christian from the Law, whereas in 1535 the emphasis shifts to moral Law as a reflection of the universal natural

---

7. Mann, "Melancthon's Response," 319; Mann, *Shall we Sin*, 17; Wengert, *Law and Gospel*, 177–200. See also Richter, *Gesetz und Heil*, 378.

8. Schurb, "Melancthon," 153, 203–4; See also Lund, "Luther's Third Use of the Law," 86.

9. Ebeling, "*Triplex Usus Legis*," 65–69, 73–74.

10. Forde, *Law-Gospel Debate*, 191–94; Forde, "Forensic Justification and the Law," 301.

11. Schurb, "Melancthon," 211, 246; Osslund, *Imputatio iustitiae Christi*, 19.

Law.[12] This will for humanity is revealed not only through Scripture but also through the natural Law written on every human heart. The laws of the Old Testament apply only to the Christian in so far as they agree with natural Law. Whereas the moral Law of the Decalogue reflects the eternal mind of God and is universally valid, the civil and ceremonial laws are not binding for any other nation other than Israel under the Old Covenant. Yet any Old Covenant civil law in harmony with natural moral Law remains equally valid, and Melancthon recommends that Gentile nations study the civil code of Israel for many useful laws.[13]

The moral Law of the Decalogue is restated throughout the whole of Scripture and reflects the natural moral Law given to the first humans. The moral Law given to Israel by Moses was really only a reiteration of the Law implanted within the hearts of the first humans by nature. As a consequence of the Fall, however, this moral Law was clouded by sin and is not readily embraced as are the natural laws of mathematics. Furthermore, moral laws of an outward social orientation, such as laws against murder, are more obvious to the natural person than is the commandment to love God from the heart and to worship Him alone.[14]

According to Melancthon, the proper work of the Law is to be distinguished from the proper work of the Gospel. Law and Gospel form the "chief teaching of Scripture, to which all parts of Scripture must be wisely compared," and their proper distinction is "a light to the entire Scripture." This distinction between Law and Gospel is not equivalent to a distinction between the Old and New Testament canon, as if Law is only found in the former and Gospel only in the latter. The promise of the Gospel was preached immediately after the Fall, and the Law is found in the teachings of Christ. The promises of the Gospel must also be distinguished from promises of the Law. The material promises contained in the Law are conditioned by obedience, whereas the spiritual and eternal promises of the Gospel are free through faith in Christ alone. The Gospel broadly understood does contain the preaching of repentance and good works, but its primary purpose is the assurance of forgiveness through Christ.[15] Melancthon does believe that the Old Covenant, understood in its "most proper sense," was primarily

---

12. Preus, 57; *CR* 21: 685–86; Schurb, "Melancthon," 246–48, 286–87.
13. Preus, 57–58, 123–24; *CR* 21: 687–88, 814–15.
14. Preus, 57–59, 70–71; *CR* 21: 685–89, 711–15.
15. Preus, 57, 81–82, 84, 117–18; *CR* 21: 685–87, 732–34, 738, 801.

characterized by the preaching of laws, while the New Covenant is "the proclamation of the remission of sins and eternal life." Under the Old Covenant the Law was given to Israel to preserve the social order of a community carrying the promise of the Messiah, but God's principal purpose for giving the Law was to reveal the need for the Messiah by declaring God's eternal judgment upon all who failed to keep the Law.[16]

The preaching of the Law must always precede the preaching of the Gospel so that the promise of the Gospel is rightly appreciated. Once the promise of forgiveness is embraced in Christ, the Christian is now liberated from the condemnation of the Law to delight in the Law and to obey it freely in love rather than in fear: "the beginning of keeping the commandments is the acknowledgment of Christ." The works of the other commandments are not even pleasing to God if not flowing from obedience to the First Commandment, which is to believe and worship the one true God. Even after justification by faith, and though obedience to God increases, the Christian still cannot fully satisfy the Law through good works for they remain imperfect and are only accepted by God on account of faith in Christ.[17]

If the preaching of obedience to the Law does not imply that people have the natural power to fulfill it, and if justification is by faith alone in Christ, as Melancthon believed, then for what reason does God give the Law? To answer this common question posed to the evangelical reformers, Melancthon proceeds to define "three uses or duties for the Law" (*tria esse Legis officia seu triplicem usum*). Melancthon defines the first use of the Law as the "pedagogical" or "civil use" (*paedegogicus seu politicus*) found in 1 Timothy 1:9 ("the law is laid down for the unrighteous"). This describes the power of the Law to restrain the rebellion of the unbeliever for the sake of public peace and order. God administers temporal punishments for disobedience to His Law through governments, plagues, war, and famine. Not only do these restrain evil but they keep the moral conscience intact for the work of the Holy Spirit in the Gospel. Melancthon describes this discipline of the Law as a "schoolmaster to Christ" (*paedagogia in Christum*). According to Wengert, Melancthon restricts this pedagogical use of the Law to its civil use, whereas Luther also identified it with the theological, or second, use

---

16. Preus, 117–19; *CR* 21: 802–6.
17. Preus, 60–61, 63; *CR* 21: 692–94.

of the Law.[18] Melancthon acknowledges that God even allows true Christians to experience sufferings, though these are "mitigated for the godly," which keep them humble toward their sins.[19]

Melancthon then defines the second use of the Law as its power to "show our sin and to accuse, to terrify, and to condemn all men in this misuse of human nature."[20] This use of the Law, commonly known as the *usus theologicus, spiritualis,* or *elenchticus,* is what disposes the conscience toward the gift of the Gospel, for a knowledge of sin and the fear of God's wrath is necessary for desiring the salvation promised in the Gospel. Melancthon considered this early on to be the Law's primary use.[21] He states that the Law is a "perpetual judgment which condemns sin in the entire human race" and that "there is no doubt that the voice of the law condemning sins must constantly be set forth and taught in the churches, and indeed it would be a monstrous crime to conceal God's judgment and His voice which announces His wrath against sin." This advice was obviously meant for the sake of unbelieving parishioners and follows the antinomian rejection of the preaching of the Law in the later 1520s.[22] In his earlier *Apology to the Augsburg Confession* (1531), Melancthon stated that the "law works wrath; it only accuses; it only terrifies consciences."[23] Yet true Christians no longer stand under the condemnation of God's wrath. Although the Law continues to reveal their imperfections, it no longer possesses authority to condemn them.[24]

Melancthon then defines "the third use of the law" (*Tertio quaeritur de usu Legis*) as applying only to the "regenerate" who are "free from the Law" and justified by faith. This freedom is from "the curse and condemnation" of the Law, but the Law is to still be preached to the Christian with the Gospel on account of the flesh for the increase of repentance and faith in the mercy of Christ. The Law also teaches

18. Preus, 72–3; *CR* 21: 716–17, 806–7; Wengert, "Luther and Melancthon," 62 (n. 38).
19. Preus 104, 119–20, 122; *CR* 21: 775, 806–7, 810.
20. Preus, 73; *CR* 21: 718.
21. *CR* 21: 152; "the proper work of the law is the revealing of sin, or, to put it more clearly, the bringing about of a consciousness of sin." Melancthon, *Loci Communes Theologici* (1521), in Pauck, *Melancthon and Bucer,* 77–82.
22. Preus, 73; *CR* 21: 718.
23. Tappert, 144; Kolb and Wengert, 160; *BSLK,* 210.
24. Schurb, "The Law Always Accuses," 199–200, 347–49.

Christians what kind of works God says are good so that they, influenced by the flesh, do not create works of idolatry.[25]

According to Melancthon, the "third use of the Law" applies only to the justified and regenerate Christian, but only on account of his or her sinful nature. The "third use" in the life of the regenerate is distinct from the other two uses in the unregenerate since it only applies to those who have the Spirit of God, are free of the condemnation of the Law through faith, and have the earnest desire to fulfill it from the heart. In other words, the "third use" is not for the purpose of restraining the unbridled evil of the wicked nor is it concerned with disposing the unregenerate conscience towards repentance and faith for justification, but with preserving in an ever increasing manner a heart of repentance, faith, and earnestness to mortify sin in the life and spiritual battle of the Christian. In his *Apology to the Augsburg Confession* (1531), Melancthon even stated that "the keeping of the Law should begin in us and increase more and more."[26] Wengert also argues that what sets the third use apart is the active use of the Law by the believer to please God in obedience, whereas the former uses are passive and used by God upon the unbeliever.[27] This is true in a sense, since only the justified Christian has the heart to truly keep the Law, yet it is important to stress that for Melancthon this very willing and walking is born of the Spirit of God by faith in the Gospel. Yet Melancthon also admitted that perfect obedience was not possible on account of the flesh. In the "third use," then, God also continues to use the Law with regard to the weaknesses of the Christian for the renewal of repentance and faith and, through the Spirit, to light the path of godly obedience and resistance to sin on account of the opposition and corruptions of the flesh.

Next to the writings of Melancthon, the *Formula of Concord* (1577) is another critical place to look for a formal definition of a "third use of the Law" in Lutheran theology. However, there is actually some debate whether the *Formula of Concord* even teaches a "third use of the Law" in the same manner as Melancthon. The *Formula of Concord* emerged out

---

25. Preus, 74; *CR* 21: 719. See also Melancthon's discussion of the "third use of the Law" in his 1555 German edition of the *Loci*, which does not reveal any significant changes from his 1543 Latin edition. Manschreck, *Melancthon on Christian Doctrine*, 127–28; *CR* 22: 255.

26. Tappert, 126; *BSLK*, 187.

27. Wengert, *Law and Gospel*, 196, 199–200.

of doctrinal divisions within Lutheranism in the 1550s as an effort to unify and consolidate the Lutheran churches in the face of both Catholic and Reformed theologies. A series of conferences led to the drafting of the *Formula of Concord* in 1577 made up of the shorter *Epitome* and longer *Solid Declaration*. Religious leaders in various German territories signed the Declaration, and in 1580 the *Book of Concord* containing the *Formula of Concord* and other major Lutheran confessional documents was available for distribution.[28]

Werner Elert and Ragnar Bring argue that the *Formula of Concord* does not define a "third use of the Law" in a Melancthonian sense. According to Bring, the novelty of Melancthon's introduction of a "third use of the Law" was its distinctive application to the Christian as "new man," whereas the *Formula of Concord* defines the "third use" in terms of the first and second uses applied to the believer on account of the flesh, which he argues is actually more consistent with Luther's theology.[29] Ken Schurb, on the other hand, argues that the *Formula of Concord* is indeed "Melancthonian" on the issue of the "third use" but that it reflects a particular phase in his thought, namely the *Augsburg Confession* of 1530 and the *Apology* of 1531.[30] Gerhard Forde believes the *Formula of Concord* to be largely ambiguous on the question of the "third use," and Scott Bouman observes that such ambiguity opens it to interpretation. This lack of consensus, of course, results from differences in defining the "third use."[31]

The *Formula of Concord* does agree with Melancthon in defining the proper tasks of Law and Gospel. According to "Article V," the "Gospel" strictly defined is the promise of forgiveness in Christ, although understood more broadly incorporates "the entire doctrine of Christ which he proclaimed personally in his teaching ministry and which his apostles also set forth."[32] Understood in their proper senses, the Law accuses and condemns whereas the Gospel declares forgive-

---

28. See introductory comments in Tappert, 463–64.

29. Bring, "Gesetz und Evangelium," 60–66, 88–89. See also Braaten, "Reflections," 80–81.

30. Schurb, "Melancthon," 99, 284, 287–89.

31. Forde, "Forensic Justification and the Law," 302; Bouman, "The Concept of the 'Law,'" 418.

32. *Ep*, Tappert, 478; Kolb and Wengert, 500; *BSLK*, 791. See also *SD*, Tappert, 558–59; Kolb and Wengert, 582–84; *BSLK*, 951–54.

ness. Yet the "Gospel" broadly understood also acts like Law in the sense that the sufferings of Christ are an "earnest and terrifying preaching and advertisement of God's wrath." In this instance, however, those sufferings are functioning as Law, which is the "alien work" of the Gospel broadly understood leading to its more proper task of promising comfort and forgiveness in those same sufferings.[33] "Article V" of the *Sold Declaration* adds that the word "repentance" also possesses a dual meaning in Scripture. Sometimes it refers to "the entire conversion of man," but when distinguished from faith refers simply to contrition for sin. Repentance in the second sense comes by the preaching of the Law or the Gospel broadly understood, but repentance in the first sense includes the preaching of both Law and Gospel in their proper senses, for without the promise of the Gospel there is only delusional self-righteousness or hopeless despair.[34]

The "third use of the Law" is addressed in "Article VI." The *Epitome* states that the reason for its inclusion is the result of disputes over "whether or not the law is to be urged upon reborn Christians."[35] The article states that the Law has been given by God for three reasons. The first agrees with Melancthon's "*usus civilis*," or the Law extorting outward obedience from unbelievers by means of prohibition, threats, and punishments. The second agrees with the "*usus theologicus*," which is the accusation of the conscience on account of sin and the deserving of the wrath and condemnation of God leading toward repentance and justifying faith in the Gospel. The third reason is defined as the following: "after they are reborn, and although the flesh still inheres in them, to give them on that account a definite rule according to which they should pattern and regulate their entire life."[36]

The article explicitly affirms that the Christian is free from the condemnation and compulsion of the Law with regard to the new man but that the goal of redemption is the keeping of the Law. Even Adam and Eve in their innocence had the Law written on their hearts and the Christian who is justified by faith lives in the Law.[37]

---

33. *Ep*, Tappert, 478–79; Kolb and Wengert, 501; *BSLK*, 792. See also *SD*, Tappert, 560; Kolb and Wengert, 583; *BSLK*, 955.

34. *SD*, Tappert, 559; Kolb and Wengert, 582–84; *BSLK*, 954.

35. *Ep*, Tappert, 479–80; Kolb and Wengert, 502; *BSLK*, 793.

36. *Ep*, Tappert, 479–80; Kolb and Wengert, 502; *BSLK*, 793.

37. *Ep*, Tappert, 480; Kolb and Wengert, 502; *BSLK*, 793–94.

The *Epitome* clearly states that the Law is for believer and unbeliever alike. With regard to the believer, this is on account of the incomplete renewal of the Christian here and now and the desires of the flesh, "which clings to them until death," which make it necessary "for the law of God constantly to light their way lest in their merely human devotion they undertake self-decreed and self-chosen acts of serving God." Furthermore, the preaching of the Law is required because the "old Adam" ("*alte Adam*") remains opposed to the new desires of the Spirit, makes the believer sluggish, and needs to be persuaded by threats and punishments to surrender to the Spirit in obedience to God.[38] The *Epitome* distinguishes, however, between unbelievers and "the regenerated according to the flesh" since the latter, in so far as they possess faith and the Spirit, do have a new desire to obey "as if they knew of no command, threat, or reward."[39]

The *Solid Declaration* expands on this point in the *Epitome* by stressing that the Law makes demands but cannot provide the means for them to be fulfilled. Truly good works are only empowered by the renewing work of the Spirit who is received through faith in the Gospel of Jesus Christ. While the Spirit instructs Christians in the knowledge of the Law, He also rebukes them as often as they "stumble." According to the *Solid Declaration*, reproof of sin is the "real function of the law," and this is true for believers as well on account of their remaining weaknesses and imperfections.[40]

Like the *Epitome*, the *Solid Declaration* defines "Law" as the "immutable will of God." While the Christian delights inwardly in the Law and in the Spirit obeys willingly and freely, he or she is also at war with the old nature that remains at complete enmity with the Law. The coercion and force of the Law are needed, then, for the Christian only with regard to his or her old nature. The "*alte Adam*," like an "unmanageable and recalcitrant donkey," still needs the club of the Law through instructions, threats, punishments, and miseries. This is remarkably similar to a statement made by John Calvin with regard to the Law's third use:

---

38. *Ep*, Tappert, 480; Kolb and Wengert, 502–3; *BSLK*, 794. See also *SD*, Tappert, 564–65; Kolb and Wengert, 588; *BSLK*, 964–65.

39. *Ep*, Tappert, 480–81; Kolb and Wengert, 503; *BSLK*, 794–95.

40. *SD*, Tappert 565–66; Kolb and Wengert, 589; *BSLK*, 966.

"The law is to the flesh like a whip to an idle and balky ass, to arouse it to work."[41]

The *Solid Declaration* reiterates that Christians also need the Law in order that they might not, under the deception of being led by the Spirit, establish rules of piety without the authority of Scripture. Furthermore, the teaching of the Law is needed to keep the Christian humble toward his or her own works, and the Law acts as "a mirror" revealing the impurities even of the believer's works. Yet the believer is reminded in the Gospel that all his or her works are acceptable to God only through Christ and that God is pleased with the inward willingness to obey through the Spirit.[42]

The *Formula of Concord* is mostly in agreement with Melancthon on the teaching of the "third use of the Law." Both link the task of the "third use" to the justified Christian in terms of his or her "old Adam." Where the *Formula of Concord* stands in more direct contrast with Melancthon is in its explicit rejection of good works as necessary for salvation. In his 1535 *Loci Communes*, Melancthon stated that good works in the Christian life are necessary for salvation. In the 1543 edition, however, he did change his wording to emphasize that good works are necessary for "retaining our faith," stating that "the Holy Spirit is driven out and grieved when we permit sins against conscience . . . faith is cut off through sinful works." Ken Schurb suggests that this modification was made to satisfy criticisms of Luther but only to make more explicit what he meant in 1535.[43] Indeed Melancthon had became implicated in a controversy in the 1530s between Conrad Cordatus (1476?–1546?) and Caspar Cruciger (1504–1548) over the necessity of good works with regard to salvation.[44] This debate flared up again as the subject of intra-Lutheran strife in the 1550s and provides the backdrop for the carefully worded statements of the *Formula of Concord*.

To Melancthon and the *Formula of Concord*, then, goes the credit for the formal definition of a "third use of the Law" in Lutheran theology.

---

41. *SD*, Tappert, 567–68; Kolb and Wengert, 590–91; *BSLK*, 966–69; Calvin, *Institutes* 2.7.12; *CR* 30: 262.

42. *SD*, Tappert, 567–68; Kolb and Wengert, 590–91; *BSLK*, 968–69.

43. Preus, 103–4; *CR* 21: 775–76; Schurb, "Melancthon," 231–32, 246, 255–60, 268–73. See also Mann, *Shall we Sin*, 57.

44. Wengert, *Law and Gospel*, 206–10. See also Greschat, *Melancthon neben Luther*, 217–30.

Yet it is quite important to note that Martin Chemnitz (1522–1586), a Lutheran theologian and principal author of the *Formula of Concord*, in a commentary published posthumously in 1591 on Melancthon's *Loci Communes*, actually ascribes the origin of the threefold division of the Law to Luther in context of his discussion of the Law and the justified Christian in his Galatians commentary: "Luther in a very learned way sought the foundations of this doctrine in the Epistle to the Galatians, and divided the use of the law into one aspect which was civil and one which was theological. Likewise in Galatians 5 there is one use of the Law in justification and another for those who have been justified. From this Luther constructed the threefold division of the uses of the Law."[45] This comment has been overlooked by modern scholars who dismiss the possibility that Luther himself was behind the origins of the "third use of the Law," a use that is more readily associated with the Reformed tradition.

It is important to acknowledge, however, that Chemnitz's treatment of the "third use of the Law" is polemically charged, particularly as it relates to defending the preaching of the Law against antinomians and with the purpose of wanting to demonstrate his faithfulness to Luther's theology. Therefore, this comment cannot simply be taken at face value, for it is at least possible that his interpretation was skewed by an apologetic and rhetorical agenda. It must be compared with Melancthon, the Formula of Concord, and ultimately Luther.

Chemnitz opposes those who appeal to the freedom of faith and the Holy Spirit to justify their own subjective inclinations. Rather, he states that the "apostles everywhere preach about the new obedience of the regenerate and clearly seek the description of this new obedience in the Decalog." Chemnitz then delineates three separate causes for the "third use of the Law" (*Tertius usus*) in the life of the believer. First, he states that the Law of the Decalogue adequately prescribes the good works that please God. Secondly, the Law continues to humble the Christian by revealing remaining imperfections. Although this has to do with the continuing function of the Law to reveal sins, it is extremely important to note that Chemnitz refrains from equating this with the "second use of the Law" (*Secundus usus Legis*), which he identifies as applying to the justification of the unregenerate.[46] Thirdly and lastly,

---

45. Chemnitz, *Loci Theologici*, 2:439; Chemnitii, *Loci Theologici*, 99.
46. Chemnitz, *Loci Theologici*, 2:440; Chemnitii, *Loci Theologici*, 100.

the Law is important on account of the fact that the believer is not yet fully spiritual, but is paradoxically both an "old" and "new man." It is on account of the flesh and the fact that faith does not possess full power and spiritual renewal is not complete that the Christian still benefits from a certain amount of compulsion: "For we experience that the new obedience is not so voluntary a thing as a good tree which brings forth its fruit without any command or exhortation."[47] These statements of Chemnitz are essentially the same as those found in the *Formula of Concord* and the later editions of Melancthon's *Loci Communes*. Whether or not Chemnitz is right to ascribe the origins of the "third use of the Law" to Luther has been a matter of great debate since the mid-twentieth century.

In response to Karl Barth's lecture "Gospel and Law" ("*Evangelium and Gesetz*," published 1935),[48] a series of reactionary works appeared by Lutheran theologians Werner Elert, Paul Althaus, Gerhard Ebeling, and Ragnar Bring to defend the paradigm of "Law and Gospel." In the lecture, Barth purposefully shifts the order of the paradigm to stress the goodness of the Law as inherent to the covenant Promise, "that the Law is nothing else than the necessary *form of the Gospel*, whose content is grace."[49] For the Lutheran theologians, this turned the Gospel into Law and made the good news a matter of works. This resulted in a surge of scholarship devoted to the interpretation of historic Lutheran texts and documents.

According to one such scholar, John Calvin was the one responsible for the "leveling out" of the "contrast between law and gospel" in his stress on the role of the Law as a normative rule for Christian conduct.[50] Indeed, in the *Institutes* Calvin does identify the primary function of the Law to be that of instructing and exhorting the believer to good works,[51] which Elert identifies as the Gospel serving the Law within a covenantal framework. Elert even suggests that this statement is a polemic against Luther who always identified the primary purpose of the Law as its "*usus*

47. Chemnitz, *Loci Theologici*, 2:440–41; Chemnitii, *Loci Theologici*, 100.
48. Barth, *Community, State, and Church*, 41–43, 71–80.
49. Ibid., 80.
50. Elert, *Law and Gospel*, 7.
51. "The third and principal use, which pertains more closely to the proper purpose of the law, finds its place among believers in whose hearts the Spirit of God already lives and reigns." *Institutes* 2.7.12; *CR* 30:261–62.

theologicus," or the revelation of sin.[52] Scholars such as Elert argue that the "third use of the Law" is un-Lutheran, that it was an aberration introduced by Melancthon, but given even greater prominence by Calvin and Reformed Protestantism. This Reformed emphasis on the Law in the Christian life is blamed for tendencies toward legalistic moralism in later Puritanism.[53] It is precisely this emphasis that Barth seemed to reaffirm in his lecture and that was believed by his Lutheran critics to be detrimental to the integrity and priority of the Gospel.

Elert's most significant contribution to the discussion of the "third use" in Luther is his essay exposing a forgery in the Weimar Edition of Luther's works. In Luther's *A Disputation Against the Antinomians* (1538), three uses of the Law are clearly described in detail.[54] However, Elert argues that this passage appears in only two of the existing nine manuscripts of the disputation and was probably interpolated later by an unknown author. In fact, no actual minutes of the entire series of disputations exist. Prior to the nineteenth century, Luther's theses were the only source of knowledge regarding the antinomian disputations. Even when discovery was made of the earliest known record of the disputations, this could not be dated any earlier than 1553. One clue for Elert that the "third use" text does not belong to Luther is the association of the pedagogical use of the Law with the civil use, or *usus politicus*, rather than with the *usus theologicus*. Elert proposes that this association is more akin to Melancthon and was probably inserted as if they were the words of Luther by an unknown editor. Of the only two texts that do contain the "third use" passage, one author has been identified as Israel Alectriander, a student of the University of Wittenberg beginning in 1550, twelve years or so after the actual event of the disputation. Elert considers this text, then, to be a cornerstone proof inappropriately used by many previous scholars to argue for a *triplex usus legis* in the theology of Luther.[55]

Gerhard Ebeling agrees with Elert, though with some modifications. Ebeling observes that Luther only ever formally spoke of a "*duplex usus legis*." Ebeling agrees with Elert that the one text mentioned

---

52. Elert, *Law and Gospel*, 7–8, 44.

53. Hesselink, *Calvin's Concept of the Law*, 218.

54. "Tertio. Lex est retinenda, ut sciant sancti, quaenam opera requirat Deus, in quibus obedientiam exercere erga Deum possint." WA 39¹: 485.

55. Elert, "Eine Theologische Falschung," 168–70; Silcock, "Law and Gospel," 2 (n. 6).

above is pseudopigraphal. Ebeling enlarges on Elert's forgery thesis, however, and actually pinpoints three of nine manuscripts that contain the disputed "third use" text, although in the third manuscript it falls in a place remotely distinct from the other two. That these texts all appear in different places with no textual variations may suggest a common editorial origin. Ebeling also importantly notes that the oldest manuscript (Helmst. 773, dat. 1553) does not contain the interpolation of the "third use" passage.[56]

One other "third use" passage in Luther is found in his exposition of Galatians 3:23-29 in the *Weihnachtpostille* of 1522, which does refer to a "threefold use of the Law" and was translated by Martin Bucer in 1525 as *triplex usus legis*. Ebeling argues, however, that upon closer examination Luther is referring to something completely different from what is commonly identified as a "third use of the Law." Luther is distinguishing here between complete disregard for the Law, outward compulsion by the Law, and inward desire for the Law. Ebeling convincingly demonstrates that this is not how Luther elsewhere even formally defines the "*usus legis*."[57]

One noteworthy attempt has been made to defend the "third use" text in the antinomian disputations. In an unpublished dissertation, Norman Lund argues that Melancthon's formulation of a *tertius usus legis* was commensurate with Luther and may even have been a reiterating of Luther's position.[58] He acknowledges along with Ebeling that only three of the nine manuscripts of the disputation contain the text, but argues that there are "wide divergences" beyond whether or not the text is included. Lund actually suggests a "deletion" thesis, that this text was in fact removed from the other six manuscripts. Contrary to Elert and Ebeling, Lund argues that only four of the nine manuscripts could really be used to deny the authenticity of the text (Goth. 264; Helmst. 773; Pal. 1827; Rig. 242). Of the three that do contain it (Helmst. 722; Aug. 67; Monac. 940), two manuscripts place the text at variable locations after the closing of the disputation while the remaining manuscript (Monac. 940) places it several pages earlier in a previous argument. Lund suggests that the probable reason for this discrepancy is due to the appearance of an "M. Georgius" whose impertinence dur-

---

56. Ebeling, "*Triplex Usus Legis*," 62–63 (see n. 2).
57. Ibid., 63–64.
58. Lund, "Luther's Third Use of the Law," 156, 227–46.

ing the disputation caused him to be completely omitted in three of the manuscripts. Therefore, the single copyist of Monac. 940, probably for polemical reasons, decided to move the words of Luther made after the formal closing of the disputation into this earlier section. Two of the six manuscripts that do not contain the text (Helmst. 688b; Homb. 74) end the recording of the disputation well before any of the others so they cannot even appropriately be used to argue in support of the forgery thesis of Ebeling and Elert.[59]

Lund proposes that remarks made by Luther himself after the formal closing of the disputation were obviously not included by every copyist. The manuscripts that do not contain the questionable text also continue the dialogue after Luther's formal word of dismissal, but Lund argues that there is "no need to allege falsification because of the fact that three of the copyists record one final remark which the others omit" since the copyists were under no obligation to continue recording the discussion.[60]

Lund also criticizes Elert for banking his argument too much on the fact that the disputed text aligns the *usus paedogogicus* of the Law with the *usus politicus*. Lund agrees that Melancthon does diverge from Luther by restricting the *usus paedigogicus* to the *usus politicus*, but argues that Luther himself associates the two on occasion.[61]

Lund does admit that the disputed text seems out of place in the disputation and that a reference to "exercise in obedience" is out of character for Luther. Nevertheless, Lund postulates that Luther borrowed from Melancthon's *Loci Communes* of 1535, a possibility he points out Ebeling and Elert never consider. Whereas H. Fagerberg argues that differences between Luther and Melancthon over the *usus legis* possibly existed, though there is "no recorded difference of opinion" between them,[62] Lund highlights the fact that Luther in his *Table Talk* praises Melancthon's treatment of the Law in the later 1530s.[63]

59. Lund, "Luther's third use of the Law," 229.

60. Ibid., 231.

61. Ibid., 236–38. On the "*usus paedigogicus*" in Luther and Melancthon, see also Wengert, "Luther and Melancthon," 62 n. 38; Ebeling, "Triplex Usus Legis," 77.

62. Fagerberg, *A New Look at the Lutheran Confessions*, 83.

63. LW 54 (*Table Talk*, No. 3554: "A Blast Against Agricola's Antinomianism. March 21, 1537") 233; WA Tr 3:405; Lund, "Luther's third use of the Law," 240–44. See also Wengert, "Luther and Melancthon," 70 n. 61.

The controversy involving this disputed text is complicated but critical. If Luther was indeed the author of these words, the debate surrounding the "third use of the Law" in Luther would appear to be finally settled, at least with regard to his theology of the later 1530s. However, since none of these manuscripts can be dated earlier than 1553, and due to the fact that the earliest extant manuscript does not contain the text in any form and it is missing from six of the nine manuscripts, it would be difficult to ever build a case alone on such a questionable text. For now, it seems safe to conclude that Luther never formally referred to a "third use of the Law." That does not automatically mean, however, that the substance of a "third use" cannot be discerned in his theology. For example, Helmut Thielicke acknowledges that the disputed text is not found in the most reliable manuscripts, but he argues that it is not necessarily in conflict with Luther's theological intentions. He believes Elert's accusation of the text as a "blatant falsification" is an exaggeration based on faulty assumptions and that other texts of Luther besides this one can be shown to infer a "third use of the Law."[64]

Ragnar Bring has been very influential in providing theological objections to a "third use of the Law" in Luther on the basis of its lack of coherence with the general tone of his thought. While he admits that certain isolated statements of Luther could in fact be interpreted in agreement with a "third use of the Law," these interpretations contradict Luther's basic presuppositions. According to Bring, the "third use of the Law" upsets Luther's dialectic of Law and Gospel and imposes upon him definitions and meanings that are foreign to his thinking.[65]

Furthermore, Bring argues that by its very definition a "third use" must be unique to the life of the believer as "new man." To say that the "first" and "second uses of the Law" continue to apply to the "regenerate" (*pii*) in a way that is distinct from the "unregenerate" (*impii*) does not even constitute a "third use."[66] According to Bring, the Christian as "new Man" needs no such Law to govern his conduct because he is ruled inwardly by the Spirit of Christ through love and obeys the Law freely without any need of command, instruction, or coercion. Bring does acknowledge that the Law is still needed for the Christian with

---

64. Thielicke, *Theological Ethics*, 1:133.
65. Bring, "Does Lutheran Theology," 113; Bring, "Gesetz und Evangelium," 49.
66. Bring, "Gesetz und Evangelium," 55, 66. My translation.

regard to the flesh, but the enduring task of the Law with regard to its first and second uses is not a "third use."[67]

Lauri Haikola similarly objects to a "third use" in Luther, for the simple reason that Luther always objects to the Law as having any positive function with regard to Christian obedience. The Law demands obedience but provides no "strength" necessary for doing good works. The Christian as "new man" is not ruled by the Law, but rather becomes its master. In Christ, the Christian rules over the Law and has the authority to challenge it if for some reason it conflicts with showing love to others. Love guides the believer in every situation and by its very free nature is prohibited from ever becoming bound to a fixed form. Each new situation presents the Christian with a fresh way to respond in love. However, Haikola points out that experience does show a certain degree of universality in the way love is applied, and this is how Luther can affirm the usefulness of the Ten Commandments. Yet the new obedience of the Christian motivated by love extends above and beyond the minimum requirements of the Law. A "third use of the Law," then, is incompatible with Luther's thought on the basis that it circumscribes the freedom of love. Haikola only allows for one to speak of a "third use" in Luther when this applies to Christian vocation and civic service.[68]

Gerhard O. Forde personally objects to a "third use" in Luther, since the Law functions for the Christian as a citizen under the old age and not the age to come that has already dawned through faith, but has stated that scholars for the most part now agree that a "third use" in Luther is at most implicit rather than explicit in his writings. Forde and others have made the important observation, however, that the crux of the whole argument centers on how the "third use of the Law" is defined.[69]

Paul Althaus, in his classic work on the theology of Luther, admits that the formal expression of the "third use of the Law" never appears in Luther's writings, though he suggests it is there "in substance." According to Althaus, Luther indeed understands the Christian to be a new creature free from the Law with regard to justification and the gift of the Spirit, but there is still a sense in which the Christian in the

---

67. Ibid., 56.

68. Haikola, *Usus Legis*, 145–50, 152. My translation.

69. Forde, *Law-Gospel Debate*, 191–94; Forde, "Forensic Justification and the Law," 301.

flesh needs both the continuing, though mitigated, theological use of the Law to reveal sins and, depending upon the level of the increase of the Spirit, the positive ethical imperatives of the Bible to guide him in good works. However, Althaus prefers to describe the ethics of the New Testament as apostolic "commands" and imperatives of the Gospel rather than "law" to distinguish the positive instruction in good works from the negative work of revealing sins, though he admits that the New Testament exhortations fall under Luther's more general definition of "Law" and are in agreement with the Ten Commandments.[70] Althaus also makes the distinction between "commands" ("*Gebot*") and "Law" ("*Gesetz*") in his work *The Divine Command*. He observes that the justified Christian is free from the condemnation and coercive nature of the Law, but is nevertheless expected to abide by the evangelical "commands" implicative of the Gospel. Thus, whereas "Law" is more negatively associated with revealing sins in both the condemned and the justified, the "command" is positive and affectionately instructs the Christian with regard to the doing of good works.[71] However, Althaus admits again that Luther himself never makes such a formal distinction between "command" and "law."[72]

Wilfried Joest asks whether or not Luther's emphasis on evangelical freedom leaves room for "an exhortational office of the Law" that agrees with the "sense" of a "third use of the Law."[73] According to Joest, "Law" in Luther is not equivalent to any abstract notion of the will of God or to specific ethical commandments, but rather is defined existentially according to the experience of guilt. "Law" lays the burden of salvation on the human person, and "Gospel" unconditionally declares that salvation to have been accomplished by Christ.[74] Joest argues, however, that "Luther knew a command that—only truly in with, and under the Gospel—gives concrete directives, and an obedience of faith that is united to the freedom of faith."[75] These commands do not confront the believer in the same manner that Law confronts the unbeliever. As

---

70. Althaus, *Theology of Martin Luther*, 271–73.

71. Althaus, *Divine Command*, 2, 6–7, 12–21.

72. Althaus, *Theology*, 271–72 (see also n. 123). For a criticism of Althaus, see Klug, "Third Use of the Law," in Preus, *Formula of Concord*, 201–2.

73. Joest, *Gesetz und Freiheit*, 14–16. My translation.

74. Ibid., 195.

75. Ibid., 195. My translation.

a result of being saved it says "you can, because" rather than "you must." According to Joest, Luther's emphasis on evangelical freedom does not absolve the need for commandment, but rather provides liberation to obey without the fear or burden of having to merit salvation.[76] Rather than looking for an implicit "third use" in Luther, since this disturbs the purity of the Law-Gospel dialectic, Joest argues instead for a "practical use of the Gospel" (*usus practicus evangelii*) that applies to the Christian with regard to his or her freedom and not in the character of condemning Law.[77]

Similarly, according to Otto Pesch, "a third use of the Law" is "*unlutherisch*" if it is assumed that the Law inhibits or diminishes Christian freedom. Yet Pesch, like Joest, agrees that Luther still reserved a place for Biblical "directives" and "exhortations" to guide the Christian life, though these are in complete harmony with the nature of Christian freedom.[78]

Ole Modalsi agrees that the "evangelical" or "Gospel exhortations" are heartily embraced by the Christian with regard to his or her faith, but emphasizes the duality of the Christian as *simul justus et peccator* and points out that these exhortations are "required" for the believer on account of the "old man."[79] In one sense then, the commandments of God are welcomed by the Christian much as they were by Adam in the innocence of paradise, as "a friendly admonition," but at the very same time the Christian as "old man" continues to encounter them as "driving and damning Law." Even the accusing force of the Law persists in the conscience of the Christian throughout his or her earthly life, although this is to be overcome by the consistent comfort provided in the Gospel.[80] According to Modalsi, Luther's doctrine of a *duplex usus legis* should not be misinterpreted as dismissing the reality of a "use of evangelical [or Gospel] precepts" (*usus evangelicus praecepti*) and that Luther's emphasis on the obedience of faith is actually consistent with the sense of a "third use." Furthermore, since the obedience of faith surpasses that of the unbeliever's outward obedience to the Law, this could

---

76. Ibid., 196.

77. Ibid., 197. This point is argued by Gerhard Heintze on the basis of Luther's sermonic material in *Luthers Predigt*, 258.

78. Pesch, "Gesetz und Evangelium," 328–29. My translation.

79. Modalsi, *Das Gericht Nach Den Werken*, 172. My translation.

80. Ibid., 173–74.

also suggest a "third use of the Law." Yet Modalsi contends that Luther never used *"lex,"* but rather *"praeceptum,"* when speaking of the obedience of faith. Therefore, he suggests that it is more accurate to speak of a "third use of precepts" (*tertius usus praeceptum*) rather than a "third use of the Law."[81]

Much of the work that argues for an implicit "third use of the Law" in Luther has focused on his *Small* and *Large Catechism*, particularly his exposition of the Ten Commandments. Eugene Klug is one scholar who considers it surprising that "in spite of Luther's clear support of the concept of the third use of the Law there is a strange opposition on the part of many ranking Luther scholars to the idea that he taught it or supported it."[82] In his report on the Fifth International Congress for Luther Research (1993), Klug described a "strange, really antinomian opposition" on the part of many delegates to the idea of a "third use" in Luther. According to Klug, "Luther is so explicit in upholding the concept of the Law's special use for the Christian as a guide and norm for godly living," and that "Brilliantly plain is his use of the concept in his catechisms and the Galatians commentary."[83] Klug argues that Luther's teaching on the "third use" is thoroughly consistent with the Lutheran confessions, including the *Formula of Concord*. Contrary to the opinion of scholars such as Elert who believe that Melancthon and later theologians polluted Lutheranism with works-righteousness, legalism, and moralism, "he [Elert] closes his eyes arbitrarily against the voluminous evidence in Luther's writings in support of the third use of the law." Although the Christian as "new man" theoretically requires no commandment, the Law is still needed as a guide because of the "continued presence of the old man."[84]

David P. Scaer has published widely on Lutheran theology, particularly as it relates to the theme of sanctification and the Law. He affirms that sanctification in Lutheranism comes not from the Law but from faith and that the Law in its condemning, threatening, and coercive function can never produce truly good works. The Law is simply the

---

81. Ibid., 177–78.
82. Klug, "The Third Use of the Law," in Preus, *Formula of Concord*, 200.
83. Klug, "Luther in Lund," 35.
84. Klug, "Luther on Law," 162, 164–66; Klug, "The Third Use of the Law," in Preus, *Formula of Concord*, 202.

embodiment of what faith does naturally.[85] However, like Klug, Scaer sees in Luther's exposition of the Ten Commandments a description of what would only later be more formally termed the "third use of the Law." Scaer argues that Luther's positive augmentation of the negative prohibitions of the Decalogue suggests that the Law has a function in the life of the Christian *qua* Christian other than that of prohibition and threat.[86]

Other scholars who agree that a "third use of the Law" is at least implicit in the theology of Luther include H. H. Kramm,[87] Jeffrey K. Mann,[88] and Armin W. Schuetze. In his essay, Schuetze attempts to demonstrate the substantial agreement of Luther with the *Formula of Concord* and asserts that Luther simply neglected to number the Law's continuing function in the life of the believer as a "third use."[89] Walter H. Wagner answers "an unequivocal but non-Calvinist 'yes'" to the question of a "third use" in Luther and contends that more attention should be given to the catechisms as Luther himself would have desired.[90] This point has been challenged, however, by Bernard Lohse, who argues that Luther never taught a "third use of the Law" even in the catechisms, but only an implicit "pedagogical use."[91]

More recently, Jeffery Silcock has argued in an unpublished dissertation that to impose a "third use of the Law" on Luther fails to do justice to his teaching that the "*usus legis*" always functions in the life of the Christian insofar as he or she is still a sinner. Silcock argues that it is best to speak of "faith's use of the law" rather than even an implicit "third use."[92] Similar to Bring, Silcock argues that whenever Luther speaks of the Law in any normative sense, this more accurately refers to an enduring "*usus theologicus*" rather than a new and independent "third use."

85. Scaer, "Sanctification in Lutheran Theology," 183–84; Scaer, "The Law and the Gospel," 174–76.

86. Scaer, "Sanctification in Lutheran Theology," 183–84; Scaer, "Formula of Concord," 154.

87. Althaus, *Theology of Martin Luther*, 61.

88. Mann, *Shall we Sin*, 17–19.

89. Schuetze, "On the Third use of the Law," 207–27.

90. Wagner, "Luther and the Positive Use of the Law," 55–56, 61–2. See also Hendrix, "Luther," in Bagchi and Steinmetz, *Cambridge Companion to Reformation Theology*, 52–53.

91. Lohse, *Martin Luther's Theology*, 183–84, 275.

92. Silcock, "Law and Gospel," 24.

The Law always confronts the Christian existentially with sin and never merely as a neutral commandment,[93] although this was also certainly true for Melancthon. According to Silcock, the Law acts "in service to the Gospel" and guides the Christian in good works against the deceptions of the flesh. Yet the Law does this only by arousing Christians to battle against the flesh by reminding them of their sins so that good works can be performed freely through the gracious indwelling of Christ through faith. The Law then becomes a servant of the Christian, which allows Luther to speak of creating "new decalogues."[94] Like Althaus and Joest, Silcock acknowledges a distinction in Luther between the harsh preaching of the Law and the preaching of "*paranesis*," or "gospel imperatives," which are more like gentle coaxes and invitations. While Silcock praises Joest's "laudable attempt to explain the evangelical character of the law" by identifying a *usus practicus evangelii* rather than a "third use of the Law," Silcock points out that even the preaching of "*paranesis*" acts like Law and thus leads the Christian back to the Gospel so that good works may come freely and spontaneously from faith. On this account, Silcock suggests an "evangelical use of the law," or "faith's use of the law," even though, technically speaking, the Law really ceases to be "Law" when made a servant of faith and the Gospel.[95]

The issue of the "third use of the Law" in Luther's theology has become somewhat of a tired, though still unsettled, debate. Two recent interpretations of the theology of Luther by leading scholars do not even explicitly address the dispute.[96] The lines have been drawn between those who essentially deny it, those who argue for its substantial but implicit presence, and those who fall somewhere in between but who prefer to name it something else. In some sense the debate is really a moot point when considering that the formal development of the "*usus legis*" in Lutheranism really postdated the major works of the English evangelical reformers. However, the issue of what the "third use of the Law" essentially means and whether or not it can be found in Luther

93. Ibid., 697–700, 703. See also Richter, *Gesetz und Heil*, 378.

94. Silcock, "Law and Gospel," 691, 702–10, 729. For Luther's comment on the "new decalogues," see *LW* 34 ("Theses Concerning Faith and Law: The Theses for the Doctoral Examination of Hieronymus Weller and Nikolaus Medler, September 11, 1535," trans. Lewis W. Spitz): 113 (Thesis 58); *WA* 39^1: 47.

95. Silcock, "Law and Gospel," 716 n. 202, 719–20, 730, 734, 737–38, 740 (see also n. 233).

96. Bayer, *Martin Luther's Theology*; Kolb, *Martin Luther*.

is an important one because it asks whether or not Luther emphasized a positive role for the Law with regard to the life of good works and Christian obedience. This point is the hinge on which much previous scholarship on the early English evangelicals has turned in its identification of a significant contrast with the theology of Luther.

2

Law and Gospel in Luther's "Breakthrough Years" and Early Lectures on the Bible (1513–1519)

IT IS IRREFUTABLE THAT LUTHER ALWAYS RECOGNIZED THE NEED FOR the preaching of the Law, and this was true of his earlier as well as later writings. However, the precise function of the Law in relation to the true Christian is far more complex and has generated the most vigorous debate. In fact, confusion over how the Law relates to the Christian who is both righteous and sinner explains why scholars such as Carl Trueman can understandably interpret Luther as being ambivalent towards the Law.[1] The harsh words Luther has to say about the Law in one place compared with the adulation he expresses for the Law in another place can seem duplicitous, but Luther's statements must be interpreted in their historical and polemical context, or "situational nature," whether he is arguing with medieval Catholics or with antinomians and enthusiasts.[2] Furthermore, Luther's stress on the Christian as both righteous and sinner and its relationship to his theology of Law and Gospel cannot be overstated.

Luther's theology of Law and Gospel first took form during his lectureship on the Bible at the University of Wittenberg between the years 1513 and 1519. By the time the lectures began, Luther had been wrestling for years with the unsettled state of his soul before God (*Anfechtung*) nurtured by the dissatisfaction of his conscience in obtaining peace with God through the austere ascetic piety of the Augustinian cloister at Erfurt. Much to the displeasure of his father, Luther terminated his path to a legal profession and entered the Erfurt monastery in 1505 to seek the favor of his eternal Father by a strict adherence to the laws of the

---

1. Trueman, *Luther's Legacy*, 66, 108.
2. Kolb, *Martin Luther*, 53–55.

Augustinian Order. It is possible that Luther had been considering the life of a monk long before 1505, and that the infamous thunderstorm on the way back to Erfurt one summer night merely made more urgent the calling of God he had been sensing for a long time.[3] Ironically, having entered the monastery to placate God with a higher dedication to mortifying the flesh, Luther, transferred to the Augustinian House in Wittenberg in 1511, found in his university lectures on the Bible the necessary tools to attack the theological training that had caused him so much angst and had impressed upon him the need to rely on the contribution of his own merit in justification. By the time of the publication of *The Freedom of a Christian* in 1520, Luther was concerned above all to oppose what he perceived was essentially a false doctrine of justification by meritorious works in the late medieval Church. Therefore, quite understandably, how Law and Gospel relate to the justification of the sinner before God takes center stage in the development of his early theology. Yet Luther was never so naïve as to not recognize the implications in a doctrine of justification by faith alone for Christian obedience and he always made room to discuss the value of good works.

In the preface to an edition of his Latin writings published in 1545, it seems that Luther identifies the breakthrough in his interpretation of the "righteousness of God" (*iustitia dei*), the righteousness not by which God punishes or rewards human effort but that which is given freely through faith in Christ alone, as occurring early on in his second lectureship on the Psalter (late 1518 or early 1519). Yet this autobiographical statement can also be read to indicate that it was precisely his formulation of that breakthrough between 1515 and 1518 during his lectures on Romans, Galatians, and Hebrews that prompted him to return to the Psalms.[4] Scholars such as Alister McGrath have argued that, while Luther's new understanding of the righteousness of God pertaining to justification has culminated by 1519, it is accurate to identify his "breakthrough" as a development beginning as early as 1514 or 1515.[5]

At the instigation of his Augustinian superior Johann von Staupitz (c.1460–1524), who hoped to divert his attention away from soul-gazing, Luther went on to receive a doctorate of theology in 1512 and to

---

3. Mullett, *Martin Luther*, 28–44.

4. LW 34 (*Preface to the Complete Edition of Luther's Latin Writings*, 1545) 336–37; WA 54: 185–86.

5. See McGrath, *Theology of the Cross*, 141–47; McGrath, *Iustitia Dei*, 190–97.

lecture on the Bible at the newly established University of Wittenberg.[6] Between 1513 and 1515, Luther delivered his first biblical lectures on the Psalter (*Dictata super Psalterium*) and also performed pastoral duties in the city church. In the Psalms lectures, Luther distinguishes Law and Gospel, but not yet in a way that sets him remarkably apart from presuppositions inherited from late medieval Catholic theology. Law refers more to God's outward rule of the Jews under the Old Covenant replaced by the rule of Christians inwardly through the Gospel and new Law of Christ rather than the righteous commands of God sentencing judgment upon all sinners to be distinguished from the promise of absolute forgiveness, justification, and acceptance through faith in Christ.[7] In his surviving *scholia*, first published in the early twentieth century,[8] Luther drives a sharp contrast between mere outward obedience in bondage to fear under the rule of the Old Covenant Law and inward obedience to the Law of Christ in a spirit of freedom through the power of grace. The works of the Law are done coercively, outwardly, and only for temporal advantage, and the Jews had become content with keeping the Law only with the hand and not with the heart. The Gospel of Christ, however, reproves the idolatrous pride of the human heart bringing about a desire for forgiveness and the help of grace to enable the Christian to delight in the moral Law and fulfill it from the heart, which is the root of righteous works leading to the merit of eternal reward.[9] Luther speaks even in these early Psalms lectures of justification by grace through the righteousness of faith in Christ who made satisfaction for sins in His death,[10] as well as the receiving of power from God in grace to keep the Law freely for merit without compulsion, but McGrath has convincingly argued that Luther has not yet established against his late medieval theological education that the desiring of grace through humility and faith is itself the result of God's

---

6. For narrative of Luther's early career, see especially Brecht, *Road to Reformation*, 23–128. For the influence of Staupitz on the young Luther, see also Steinmetz, *Luther in Context*, 7–10.

7. Kolb, *Martin Luther*, 50–51.

8. See the introduction by Hilton C. Oswald in *LW* 10: ix-xii. See also Lillback, *Binding of God*, 58–64.

9. *LW* 10 (*Dictata super Psalterium*, 1513–15) 13–14, 30, 102, 109, 213–15; *WA* 3:17–18, 28–29, 97, 107, 256–58; *LW* 11 (*Dictata super Psalterium*, 1513–15) 155–56, 415, 439–40, 514, 517; *WA* 4: 6, 306, 322–23, 377–78, 379–80.

10. See Mullett, *Martin Luther*, 53, 56–57.

selective, prevenient grace working inwardly nor does he stress the Gospel more strictly in contradistinction to Law as the proclamation of forgiveness and the reckoning of righteousness before God through faith in Christ.[11]

In 1515 Luther began his lectures on the book of Romans, which lasted through the summer semester of the following year. As with the *Dictata super Psalterium,* the *scholia* that served as the basis for his actual lectures was not published until the early twentieth century.[12] These lectures are significant for understanding the development of Luther's doctrine of justification by faith, as well as the coinciding maturing of his theology of Law and Gospel.

In his textual glosses on the Latin text of Romans, Luther describes the moral Law as essentially natural Law and that the core of the Decalogue was inscribed on the conscience from the very beginning of time. The Gentiles may not have received the written Law in the manner of the ancient Jews, but they have always had the Law written upon their minds. Thus, the moral Law existed long before the coming of Abraham and Moses. The Jews found it easy to scorn the Gentile peoples for adultery and murder, but Paul rebukes them for failing to keep the spirit of those laws inwardly.[13] According to Luther, this moral Law binds all people and transcends time, geography, and national identity. All other specific laws, whether of a civil or ceremonial character, are culturally contingent. The Gentile nations were never expected to keep all the laws handed down by Moses to Israel. However, devotion to the one true God and love of the neighbor is at the very core of the Decalogue and binds every child of Adam together in moral accountability. Accordingly, unbelieving Gentiles will not be judged according to the laws of Moses, since these laws were never intended for them. However, this does not excuse them from God's wrath for the works of the natural Law were written on their conscience and will be their judge.[14]

---

11. McGrath, *Theology of the Cross,* 72–92, 113–28.

12. A number of student notebooks and copies made of the originals have also been found with some variations from Luther's *scholia.* See Hilton C. Oswald, *LW* 25: ix–xiv.

13. *LW* 25 (glosses on Romans, 1515–16): 18–24 (see also Luther's marginal glosses [m.g.] in nn. 15, 16, 21); *WA* 56:21–29.

14. *LW* 25 (*scholia* on Romans, 1515–16): 180–83; *WA* 56: 197–98.

Luther repeatedly stresses that any good work done to escape punishment or for personal benefit, though perhaps appearing righteous in the eyes of the world, only fulfills the Law outwardly. In fact, if people were brutally honest, they would wish all laws away so that they could obey their lusts without any fear of retribution or penalty. As such, the Law actually arouses hatred of God and His Law since it represses and restrains selfish desires.[15] As in his Psalms lectures, the kind of outward obedience that is elicited forcefully constitutes "works of the Law" (*opera legis*) for Luther. These works do not and can not justify, and they possess no merit because they do not flow freely from a heart of pure love for God. Luther does make a distinction between people who are confident of their righteousness in such "works of the Law" and those whose works are "prepatory" to the receiving of righteousness and justification knowing the inadequacy of their efforts, hating their sins, and desiring that God would show them mercy and make them righteous. In fact, Luther comments that such humility indicates that a person is indeed "already righteous in a certain sense. For a large part of righteousness is the will to be righteous." The knowledge of sin and a heart of repentance that results in prayerful pleas to God for the mercy of forgiveness and the help of His grace to be made perfect and free of all sinful impulses characterizes the entire earthly life of the elect: "he who thus seeks in heart and work, by the very fact that he seeks to be justified and does not think that he is righteous, is doubtless already righteous before God." It is not those who are satisfied in outward works of compulsion for their righteousness but those who work while humbly seeking the grace of God and constantly desiring that He show them mercy and make them righteous whose sins are not reckoned by God for condemnation through faith in Christ. In other words, the presence of sin does not necessarily condemn the sinner, but only the inward consent of the heart and a false trust in outward works of compulsion.[16] Luther's understanding of justification in terms of healing from the power of sin, along with his emphasis on the righteousness that is bestowed from God through the humility of faith apart from works, is evidence of some influence of Augustine on the theology of the Romans lectures.[17]

15. *LW* 25 (*scholia* on Romans, 1515–16): 182–83, 191; *WA* 56: 197–98.

16. *LW* 25 (*scholia* on Romans, 1515–16): 240–41, 251–54, 340, 377–78; *WA* 56: 253–55, 265–66, 350, 387–88.

17. For the close identification of humility and faith (*humilitas fidei*) in the theology of Luther, see McGrath, *Theology of the Cross*, 91–92, 117–31.

Following in the footsteps of Augustine and his ancient dispute with Pelagius, Luther describes how the Law makes demands of people without providing any help to sinners in bondage to sin for the meeting of those demands. Thus, those who live under the condemnation of the Law are under the dominion and power of sin, for they are in bondage to reluctant toil and fruitless effort to fulfill the Law.[18] This foreshadows Luther's later open dispute with Erasmus in the middle of the 1520s. However, even during his lectures on Romans, Luther was aware of how his more Augustinian theology of the Law and original sin set him apart from Erasmus' annotations on the Epistle to the Romans in the *Novum Instrumentum* (1516). George Spalatin (1484–1545), chaplain and secretary to Elector Frederick the Wise of Saxony, speaks of a "friend" (Luther) who disagreed with Erasmus' ambivalence on the issue of original sin as well as his interpretation that *justicia operum* or *legis* in Paul referred only to the ceremonial works of the Law as if justification was still by the moral Law.[19]

According to Luther, Jew and Gentile both stand eternally condemned and helpless under the judgment of the Law, whether the written Law on tablets of stone in the case of the Jews or the natural Law written on the conscience in the case of the Gentiles. Obedience to the works of the Law can never satisfy the justice of God or make one righteous in His eyes. Rather, the Law is fulfilled because the person is already righteous and has come to recognize his or her own natural weakness and reliance upon the grace of God: "For we are not righteous because we act according to the Law, but because we are first righteous, therefore we then fulfill the Law."[20]

Luther describes openly in the beginning of his *scholia* on Romans that the "chief purpose of this letter" is to undermine all pretense of human righteousness before God: "we must be taught righteousness that comes completely from the outside and is foreign."[21] Luther makes clear, then, really for the first time that the precise function of the Law with regard to justification is to humble the sinner by exposing the deep roots of sin, which actually increases by the compulsion of the Law.

18. *LW* 25 (*scholia* on Romans, 1515–16): 316–17; *WA* 56: 329–30.

19. Seebohm, *Oxford Reformers*, 252–55. See also Ozment, *Age of Reform*, 290–93.

20. *LW* 25 (glosses on Romans, 1515–16): 30; *WA* 56: 35–36. See also *LW* 25 (*scholia* on Romans, 1515–16): 242; *WA* 56: 255.

21. *LW* 25 (*scholia* on Romans, 1515–16): 135–36; *WA* 56: 157–58.

To the sinner, the Law is rigorous and its harshness actually expels all personal delight in it, which constitutes the essence of real moral perfection and righteousness.[22]

Therefore, Luther's Romans lectures develop the important emphasis that the Law brings the knowledge of sin, and not only the knowledge of sinful acts but the very bondage of the natural will and disposition of the soul. In his *Disputation Against Scholastic Theology*, theses prepared for a disputation presided over by Luther in 1517 and then printed in 1520,[23] Luther reiterates that the will by original sin is naturally opposed to the Law: "Law and will are two implacable foes without the grace of God." The natural will cannot even desire to do good without grace.[24]

The context of Luther's objections to free-will is the late medieval "covenant" (*pactum*) theology of Gabriel Biel (c. 1420–1495) whose writings Luther studied as a monk under the tutorship of Johann Nathin. Biel was himself influenced by the teachings of the English Franciscan William of Ockham (c.1287–1347) whose philosophical ideas had become firmly entrenched at the University of Erfurt under professors Jodocus Trutvetter and Bartholomaeus Arnoldi von Usingen. Luther as an arts student in 1501–1505 had already encountered Ockham's belief that the absolute freedom of God (*potentia Dei absoluta*) transcends the dictates of human reason and is restricted only by His revelation (*potentia Dei ordinata*). This, along with the progressive vision of European humanists in providing tools for studying ancient texts in their original languages, such as the Hebrew scholar Johann Reuchlin (1455–1522) and the Greek and Latin scholar Desiderius Erasmus (1469–1536), made an influential contribution to the importance of biblical revelation in the thought of Luther.[25] Also following Ockham, Biel taught that the infusion of grace in justification enabling good works that lead to the reward of eternal life is a congruous merit given by God in His own covenant of mercy to those who in their own natural powers, "doing

22. *LW* 25 (glosses on Romans, 1515–16): 48–49 (m.g. in n. 29), 60 (m.g. in n. 14), 61, 67; *WA* 56: 55–56, 67–68, 74–75.

23. See the introduction by Harold J. Grimm, *LW* 31: 5–7.

24. *LW* 31 (*Disputation Against Scholastic Theology*, 1517): 14 (Thesis 71); *WA* 1: 227–28. See also Theses 62–88, *LW* 31: 13–15; *WA* 1: 227–28.

25. Brecht, *Road to Reformation*, 86–87, 172; Mullett, *Martin Luther*, 32–33, 39, 43, 58, 65; McGrath, *Intellectual Origins*, 109–10. For the medieval background of Luther's thought see also Kolb, *Martin Luther*, 26–41.

what is in them" (*facere quod in se est*), desire this grace through repentance.²⁶ Luther had openly spoken of preparation for grace earlier in his Psalms lectures (1513–1515): "Therefore he bestows everything gratis and only on the basis of the promise of His mercy, although He wants us to be prepared for this as much as lies in us. Hence as the Law was the figure and preparation for the people for receiving Christ, so our doing as much is in us disposes us toward grace."²⁷ McGrath argues that the Luther of the *Dictata super Psalterium* is still influenced by this *via moderna* tradition of late medieval scholasticism and points out that it was Luther's reading of Augustine in conjunction with his study of the book of Romans that caused him to openly challenge these popular assumptions as a revival of the ancient heresy of Pelagianism. Luther's response was then to make even the preparation leading up to the grace of justification through the humility of repentance and faith the effect of the internal and prevenient work of God in His sovereign grace.²⁸

In the Romans lectures, Luther does state that between the ungodly and believing Gentile lies the person who: "through some good action directed toward God as much as they were able earned grace which directed them farther, not as though this grace had been given to them because of such merit, because then it would not have been grace, but because they thus prepared their hearts to receive this grace as a gift."²⁹ Peter A. Lillback identifies Luther's initial break with medieval covenant theology in the *Disputation Against Scholastic Theology* (1517) and in his preference for describing the Gospel as an unconditional "testament" guaranteed upon the death of Christ.³⁰ Yet the concept of congruous merit is explicitly excluded in the Romans lectures,³¹ and his conscious use of "testament" must not overshadow the fact that Luther did go on to speak of the baptismal promise and the ongoing battle with sin in the life of a Christian in terms of a "covenant" in 1519 and in later sermons

---

26. Oberman, *Harvest of Medieval Theology*, 131–34. For a helpful discussion of the medieval concept of "merit," see *Iustitia Dei*, 109–19.

27. *LW* 11 (*Dictata super Psalterium*, 1513–14): 397; *WA* 4: 262.

28. McGrath, *Intellectual Origins*, 108–21; McGrath, *Iustitia Dei*, 192–94; Steinmetz, *Luther in Context*, 10.

29. *LW* 25 (*scholia* on Romans, 1515–16): 186; *WA* 56: 202.

30. Peter A. Lillback, "The Covenant in the Theology of Martin Luther," 58–67. See also Kenneth G. Hagan, "The Testament of a Worm: Luther on Testament and Covenant," *Consensus* 8, no. 1 (Jan 1982): 15–16.

31. *LW* 25 (*scholia* on Romans, 1515–16): 496–7; *WA* 56: 502–3.

on baptism in 1528 and 1538.³² Furthermore, although Luther's *anfechtung* in the confessional resulted precisely from his doubts about the sincerity and merit of the contrition in his confessions,³³ he still continued to stress that a sinner must always be moved by God first through repentance under the Law to desire the gift of righteousness in Christ promised in the Gospel and received through faith alone. The significant development beginning in 1515–1516 is in Luther's insistence that the very movement of the conscience to seek justification in Christ is itself the fruit of the prevenient and sovereign grace of God and the proper ministry of the Law in distinction to the proper ministry of the Gospel, which was in objection to the late scholastic understanding of justification as God's covenant of mercy to bestow the infusion of justifying grace as a congruous merit upon the precondition of a natural mind and will disposed to desire grace through its own powers of repentance and humility before God.³⁴

Luther argues in his Romans lectures that the giving of the Law increased rather than decreased sin, yet insists that there is no fault in God's Law and that His ultimate intention was not that sin should increase. Rather, the Law was given and sin necessarily increased because of the utter wickedness of human nature. Even without the giving of the Law in written form, transgressions against the natural Law would have continued. The fact that the Law was given at Sinai simply afforded the Jews the opportunity to see more objectively the contemptible state of their natural depravity.³⁵

At a convention of German Augustinians held at Heidelberg in April of 1518, Luther, at the behest of Staupitz, prepared a series of theses for academic disputation. Luther was told to avoid the issue of the selling of indulgences directly, which his *95 Theses* (1517) had recently made the subject of an intense controversy involving the integrity of the papacy. Instead, the Heidelberg theses expand on the necessity of repentance, which Luther believed had been undercut by

---

32. *LW* 35 (*The Holy and Blessed Sacrament of Baptism*, 1519): 33–37; *WA* 2: 728, 731–38. See also Kolb and Arand, *Genius of Luther's Theology*, 192–93.

33. Mullett, *Martin Luther*, 43–44.

34. According to Steinmetz, Luther was actually much closer to Aquinas on the necessity of prevenient grace than he knew. See *Luther in Context*, 47–58. See also Janz, *Luther and Late Medieval Thomism*, 3–9, 24–25, 56–59.

35. *LW* 25 (*scholia* on Romans, 1515–16): 306–7; *WA* 56: 319–20.

Tetzel in his recent marketing of indulgences beyond the borders of Electoral Saxony.[36] Luther writes of the bondage of the will to sin and reaffirms that this bondage is not on account of any inherent fault in the Law itself. Instead, the Law, seen through the sufferings of Christ on the cross, exposes the deficiency of human works in salvation so as to exalt the works of God. Contrary to "theologies of glory" that rationalize a human contribution, the incredible sufferings of Christ on the cross for humanity reveal the utter powerlessness of the Law, "the most salutary doctrine of life," to make wretched sinners righteous by it. This emphasis on weakness and self-abasement as opposed to the self-confident rationalization of the late medieval scholastics explains Luther's brief sympathy with certain aspects of the medieval German mystical tradition, such as in the sermons of the Dominican Johannes Tauler (c. 1300–1361), exemplified by his own publication of the anonymous *Theologia Germanica* in 1516–1518.[37] Instead, the Law actually kills, condemns, accuses, and utters the wrath of God against the guilt of all mankind. Righteousness, then, is not by the doing of the Law, but by the believing of faith in the revelation of the Gospel. The Law says to men "do this," which has not yet been done, whereas the Gospel says "believe in this," which promises that the whole Law has already been satisfied for sinners.[38] In his *Explanations of the 95 Theses* (1518), Luther explains again that "Through the Law we have nothing except an evil conscience, a restless heart, a troubled breast because of our sins, which the Law points out but does not take away. And we ourselves cannot take it away."[39] Yet the Law is still extremely important with regard to the necessity of cultivating contrition, as Luther explains in the Heidelberg theses: "sin is recognized only through the law."[40] In fact, this cultivation of repentance through the Law is the operative work of God Himself (*opus alienum*) that He might, in turn, make the repentant sinner righteous through faith in Christ (*opus proprium*).[41]

---

36. See Harold J. Grimm, *LW* 31: 37–38. See also Mullett, *Martin Luther*, 66–78.

37. Mullett, *Martin Luther*, 62–64.

38. *LW* 31 (*Heidelberg Disputation*, 1518): 39, 51–56; *WA* 1: 353–54, 361–64. For a discussion of Luther's "theology of the cross," see McGrath, *Theology of the Cross*, 148–52, and Forde, *On Being a Theologian of the Cross*.

39. *LW* 31 (*Explanations of the 95 Theses*, 1518): 231; *WA* 1: 616.

40. *LW* (*Heidelberg Disputation*, 1518), 51–52; *WA* 1: 361.

41. McGrath, *Theology of the Cross*, 151, 154–55.

In the Romans lectures, Luther begins to carefully develop a proper distinction between the Law and Gospel with regard to their intended effects on the human heart. The work of the Gospel he characterizes as "properly" to preach Christ and the forgiveness of sins. This must not be confused with the proper work of the Law, nor must Christ be thought of as only a new and better Moses. If the nature of the Gospel is confused with the giving of commandments, it would then cease to be really "good news." The work of the Gospel is to preach comfort to consciences troubled by the Law with the promise of the One who performed all that the Law demanded.[42] In his earlier Psalms lectures, Luther describes the "Gospel" more as the law of love in the life of Christ that judges all human egotism. By 1519 Luther still describes how the sacrifice and sufferings of Christ in the passion rightly induce contrition. The cross, which was the death of Christ for sin acts first as a reproof of sin for it was the righteous Son of God who endured the punishment. In a sermon by Luther entitled "Meditation on Christ's Passion," a copy which was sent to Spalatin in 1519 and appeared again in Luther's Winter Postil of 1525,[43] Luther goes so far to state that "the main benefit of Christ's passion is that man sees into his own true self and that he be terrified and crushed by this."[44] Augustine also put a heavy emphasis on the role of the Incarnation and the sufferings of Christ as a blow to human pride,[45] yet the "proper" work of the Gospel as Luther begins to emphasize it and distinguish it from the "proper" work of the Law in the Romans lectures is the proclamation of absolute forgiveness of sins in the death of Christ and the gift of complete righteousness in Him.

In his new and revised *scholia* on the Psalms, based on lectures begun sometime in the latter part of 1518 and published as the *Operationis in Psalmos* (Psalms 1–22) in 1519–1521,[46] Luther continues to develop this contrast between "Law" and "Gospel" particularly in light of the distinctive pedagogies characterizing the dispensations of the Old

42. *LW* 25 (*scholia* on Romans, 1515–16): 326–27; *WA* 56: 338–39.

43. A printed copy of the sermon was sent to Luther's colleague Spalatin in 1519 and it later appeared in Luther's Winter Postil of 1525. See the introduction by Martin O. Dietrich, *LW* 42: 5.

44. *LW* 11 (*Dictata super Psalterium*, 1513–15): 147 (and n. 32); *WA* 3: 641 (and n. 2), 650; *LW* 42 (*Meditation on Christ's Passion*, 1519): 10; *WA* 2:138.

45. Kelly, *Early Christian Doctrines*, 393–94.

46. See the introduction by Jaroslav Pelikan in *LW* 14: ix–xii; Mullett, *Martin Luther*, 99.

and New Testaments respectively. The teaching of the Law and works properly belongs to the dispensation of the Old Testament, namely the Mosaic Covenant. The imposition of these laws and threats of punishment, however, only succeeded in bringing about human rebellion and the wrath of God. The teaching of faith and grace, on the other hand, properly belongs to the dispensation of the New Testament ushered in by the death of Christ. The doctrine of faith is more fully revealed and more frequently spoken of in the light of His coming. It is the preaching of forgiveness, the fulfillment of all righteousness in Christ, and the promise of peace and freedom for all who believe. Luther does continue to speak of Christ as a "Lawgiver" (*legislator*) in the revised *scholia* on Psalms, and his stress on the superiority of Christ over Moses as the One through whom is bestowed the needed power to truly fulfill the inward demands of the Law is similar to statements made in his earlier *Dictata super Psalterium* (1513–1515) where Christ is described as a "Lawgiver" (*legislator*) and "Giver of evangelical law." However, in his *Lectures on Galatians*, which were delivered in 1516–1517 following his lectures on Romans and published as a commentary in 1519 and again in 1523, Luther is careful to stress the proper work of Christ in the Gospel not as "a lawgiver" but "the fulfiller of the Law."[47]

Yet Luther never loses sight of the fact that Christ did teach the Law. In his *scholia* on the book of Hebrews, lectures delivered in 1517–1518, Luther describes the preacher of the Word as straddling the two dispensations of "Law" and "Gospel."[48] On the one hand, he states: "Properly speaking, therefore, it is not the office of the new priest to teach the Law but to point out the grace of Jesus Christ, which is the fulfillment of the Law." However, at the same time, Luther maintains that, "since in this time that righteous man for whom the Law has not been laid down makes no more than a beginning," the evangelical preacher, much like John the Baptist, must teach the Law as well as point to Christ the Savior.[49] Luther also acknowledges in his *Lectures on Galatians* (1519) that Christ and the apostles in the New Testament openly preach the

47. *LW* 14 (*Works on the Psalms*, 1519): 331, 336–37; *WA* 5: 61, 64–65; *LW* 11 (*Dictata super Psalterium*, 1513–15): 147 (and n. 32); *WA* 3: 641 (and n. 2), 650; *LW* 27 (*Lectures on Galatians*, 1519): 226; *WA* 2: 494. See also the introduction by Jaroslav Pelikan in *LW* 27.

48. These lectures were delivered in 1517–18. See the editorial comments of Jaroslav Pelikan in *LW* 29:x-xii.

49. *LW* 29 (*scholia* on Hebrews, 1517–18): 193–94; *WA* 573: 192–193.

doing of works, but that the proper definition of their new office is to proclaim the forgiveness of sins.[50] Thus, Luther here already implies that Law and Gospel relate to the Christian as paradoxically a sinner and a righteous person, a member of both the present fallen world and the more perfect world to come.

For all his stress on the powerlessness of the natural human will before the Law, Luther still valued it, not only as that which shows the very need for the Gospel but also as being the very delight of the Christian who has been released from guilt. In his glosses on the book of Romans, Luther states that the Christian is no longer under the condemnation and dominion of the Law and on this account actually becomes a willing servant of Christ and does good deeds from a cheerful heart pleasing to God: "through faith in Christ we satisfy the demands of the Law and through grace are freed and voluntarily perform the works of the Law . . ."[51]

To have the gift of the Holy Spirit is to have the Law living in the heart, and this is different from having the works of the Law written on the heart: "Indeed it is a law without a law, without measure, without end, without limit, and a law reaching beyond everything that a written law commands or can command."[52] The Gospel by no means abolishes the Law, but only the burden of having to merit God's acceptance by keeping it. Instead, by the word of the Gospel is created in the Christian an obedience that is free, spontaneous, even if no law or commandment existed. Despite his later objections to the apostolic canonicity of James, Luther follows Augustine in juxtaposing Paul's stress on justification before God apart from the Law with James' stress on the keeping of the Law as the fruit of faith and a justification already received. Luther differentiates between a state of life under the Law and a state of life under grace. The "works of the Law" condemned by Paul in Romans are any works that are merely outward and produced by the force and compulsion of the Law. Contrary to the medieval commentator Nicholas of Lyra (c. 1270–1349) as well as the more contemporary Erasmus, Luther follows Augustine in interpreting "works of the Law" not only as the ceremonial legislation of the Jews but all works including the moral

---

50. *LW* 27 (*Lectures on Galatians*, 1519): 183–84; *WA* 2: 466.
51. *LW* 25 (glosses on Romans, 1515–16): 58–59 (m.g.10); *WA* 56: 66.
52. *LW* 25 (*scholia* on Romans, 1515–16): 187; *WA* 56: 203.

Law.[53] The works applauded by James, however, are the "works of faith" (*opera fidei*) that are done in a spirit of liberty flowing from justification as the spiritual fruits of a living faith.[54]

Luther is careful, however, to maintain that not even the works of faith possess merit before God, in opposition to what medieval theologians such as Aquinas referred to as "condign merit" rewarded to a faith "formed by love" (*fides caritate formata*). Luther is insistent that neither the works that precede nor the works that follow faith have anything to do with meriting justification or righteousness before God. In opposition to the ethical philosophy of Aristotle,[55] which had been adapted for medieval Christian thinking by Aquinas and was the subject of lectures given by Luther at the University of Wittenberg during the single academic year of 1509-1510,[56] Luther now states emphatically that it is not the habitual practice of virtue that makes one virtuous: "The works which precede do not justify because they prepare for righteousness; those which follow do not justify because they demand a justification which has already been accomplished. For we are not made righteous by doing righteous works, but rather we do righteous works by being righteous. Therefore grace alone justifies."[57] While "justified," "grace," and "made righteous" in the Romans lectures still convey a sanative meaning similar to that found in Augustine, Luther clearly deviates from medieval Thomism's rationalized concept of a supernaturally created "habit of grace." Adapting Aristotelian concepts of motion, substance, and accidents to the process of salvation, this "habit" in scholastic thought was a creative operation of God in the soul, a righteous disposition infused by His grace resulting in the forgiveness of sins and exercised through human cooperation in the performance of good works for the increase

---

53. *LW* 25 (glosses on Romans, 1515-16): 60 (mg. 11); *WA* 56: 67. On different kinds of "works," see also *LW* 27 (*Lectures on Galatians*, 1519): 223-24; *WA* 2: 492-43.

54. *LW* 25 (*scholia* on Romans, 1515-16): 234-35; *WA* 56: 248-49. On justification by faith as only abolishing the Law as a means of righteousness before God, see also *LW* 27 (*Lectures on Galatians*, 1519): 202; *WA* 2: 477.

55. "moral virtue comes about as a result of habit . . . [we are] made perfect by habit . . . but the virtues we get by first exercising them, as also happens in the case of the arts as well . . . so too we become just by doing just acts, temperate by doing temperate acts, brave by doing brave acts." Aristotle, *Ethica Nichomachea*, in Ross, *Basic Works of Aristotle*, 952.

56. Mullett, *Martin Luther*, 45.

57. *LW* 25 (*scholia* on Romans, 1515-16): 242; *WA* 56: 255.

of condign merit and the reward of eternal life. That this grace was perceived as a created habit now belonging to the soul itself was seen to be necessary since "saving charity must be a voluntary act arising from a disposition man could call his own." Luther not only opposes the idea that this created habit of grace is the basis of justification and righteousness before God, but Stephen Ozment also argues that Luther even early on in 1509–1510 falls more in line with the *Sentences* of Peter Lombard (c.1100–c.1160) in believing that the moral regeneration of the Christian is the uncreated and personal presence of the Holy Spirit mysteriously "working internally without [human] aid or volition."[58]

The lectures on Romans are a significant turning-point in the early development of Luther's evangelical theology of justification. Luther stresses throughout the lectures that a sinner is justified purely by mercy and grace, receiving righteousness extrinsically from God in Christ through faith apart from all works. This righteousness is both a full and complete reality reckoned or imputed to the sinner in Christ and a partial reality relative to the renewal of the Christian through the Holy Spirit and the presence of Christ in faith. "Justification" understood more exclusively as "imputed righteousness" through faith alone in union with Christ and His atoning death and resurrection is developed and emphasized even more strongly by Luther in the 1530s. In the Romans lectures, Luther does speak of the "alien righteousness of Christ" (*iustitia Christi aliena*) as a gift from God received through faith alone and also of the exchange wherein Christ takes upon Himself the sins of sinners and in turn bestows upon them His righteousness. However, Luther does not speak explicitly of the "imputation of Christ's righteousness" (*iustitia imputata Christi*), and.he also stresses that righteousness is "imputed" by God proleptically on account of the future eschatological glorification of the Christian. This is illustrated, using an analogy bearing the influence of Augustine, by a sick patient who is assured a full recovery by the physician long before he is ever completely healed. In the eyes of the physician (Christ) he is as good as healthy even though practical treatment is still required to achieve those ends. Likewise, though the Christian continues to require constant treatment for sin in this mortal life, those who desire His mercy and grace to make them whole and healthy are already reckoned as fully righteous by God on account of the future certainty of complete and permanent healing

---

58. Ozment, *Age of Reform*, 31–32.

from sin. Luther does speak of the "imputation" (*reputatione*) of righteousness and defines it here as the forgiveness of sins. The sinner is accounted in the present as righteous on account of the alien righteousness of Christ received through faith alone and with regard to the sure promise of what God will accomplish in the future in the final resurrection of Christians to glorified perfection. God, then, promises to not "impute sins" (*imputans peccatum*) to repentant sinners who desire His mercy in Christ and earnestly yearn for Him to make them perfect by His own grace. In fact, as has already been mentioned, Luther considered such humility and the desiring of the mercy and grace of God in Christ as characteristic of the whole life of the Christian and indicative that the sinner is already justified in righteous standing before God and has the beginnings of renewal in His Spirit. Thus, the Christian is: "both a sinner and a righteous man; a sinner in fact, but a righteous man by the sure imputation and promise of God that He will continue to deliver him from sin until he has completely cured him. And thus he is entirely healthy in hope, but in fact he is still a sinner; but he has the beginning of righteousness, so that he continues more and more always to seek it, yet he realizes that he is always unrighteous."[59] Repentance and reliance upon the mercy and grace of God as a state of mind characterizing the whole life of the Christian is reaffirmed by Luther in Thesis 1 of his *95 Theses* (1517): "When our Lord and Master Jesus Christ said, 'Repent', he willed the entire life of believers to be one of repentance."[60]

Luther rarely throughout his entire career makes the more formal distinction common in later Protestantism between "justification," or the forgiveness of sins through the forensic declaration or imputation of righteousness in Christ, and "sanctification," or the regeneration of the sinner followed by a life of good works.[61] Justification conceived more explicitly in terms of "imputed righteousness" in Christ does become more developed and emphasized by Luther especially in the 1530s,[62] yet

---

59. *LW* 25 (*scholia* on Romans, 1515–16): 254, 260, 335–36; *WA* 56: 267, 272, 347.

60. *LW* 31 (Thesis 1, *Ninety-Five Theses*, 1517): 25; *WA* 1:233.

61. "Sanctification" in Luther's *Large Catechism* refers primarily to the work of the Holy Spirit in drawing the sinner to Christ for the forgiveness of sins. *LC*, Tappert, 415–20; Kolb and Wengert, 654–58; *BSLK* 653–62. For an example of one instance in the later 1530s where Luther does seem to associate "sanctification" more with the regenerative work of the Holy Spirit, see *LW* 41 (*On Councils and the Church*, 1539): 113–14; *WA* 50: 599–600.

62. *LW* 26 (*Lectures on Galatians*, 1531–35): 132; *WA* 40: 233; Although "imputation" language does occur more frequently in Luther's writings in the 1530s, Lowell

Paul Althaus argues that Luther throughout his career continues to use the words "justify" and "justification," although in a secondary sense, in terms of God's inseparable but subsequent work of "making righteous," or healing from the power of sin through the effective presence of the Holy Spirit and the power of Christ in faith only to be perfected at the final resurrection.[63]

Scholars such as McGrath argue that this more formal distinction between "justification" and "sanctification" is really the legacy of Melancthon upon later Lutheran theology, although the origins of "imputed righteousness" could be said to lie within the theology of Luther. McGrath acknowledges similarities between Luther and Augustine on the doctrine of justification but argues that Luther was no mere imitator of the ancient bishop's theology even in 1515–16.[64] It is clear from his early Romans lectures that Luther did not adopt all of Augustine's interpretations of Paul, as he himself later claims in a comment recorded by Veit Dietrich in 1532.[65] Nevertheless, even in the 1530s, Luther continued to quote from Augustine, considered his insights on justification to be the best among all other Church Fathers, and generally praised his writings as second only to the Scriptures.[66]

Luther was in agreement with Augustine that righteousness in justification is not possible by works of human free-will in obedience to the Law but originates entirely outside of mankind in the sovereign grace of God. Luther, much like Augustine, also encompasses progress in

---

C. Green seems to establish too sharp a dichotomy between the "early" and "mature" Luther. See *How Melancthon Helped Luther*, 61–70, 87–88, 239–49.

63. Althaus, *Theology of Martin Luther*, 224–42; Lohse, *Luther's Theology*, 260–64.

64. McGrath, *Iustitia Dei*, 197–213. In his *Apology to the Augsburg Confession* (1531), Melancthon still describes "justification" in both senses of pronouncing righteous and making righteous. See Tappert, 117; Kolb and Wengert, 132; *BSLK*, 174–75. In a comment recorded by Veit Dietrich, Luther praises the *Apology* as better than anything found in the Fathers about justification, including Augustine. See *LW* 54 (*Table Talk*, No. 252: "Church Fathers Judged by the Gospel:" Between April 20 and May 16, 1532), 33; *WA Tr* 1: 106.

65. *LW* 54 (*Table Talk*, No. 347: "Augustine at First Devoured and Then Put Aside." Summer or Fall, 1532): 49; *WA Tr* 1: 140; See also *LW* 54 (*Table Talk*, No. 85: "About Augustine and Justification." Early November, 1531), 10; *WA Tr* 1: 32. Steinmetz provides an example from Romans 9:10–29 that shows Luther's relative exegetical independence from Augustine. See *Luther in Context*, 12–22.

66. *LW* 54 (*Table Talk*, No. 4567: "The Church Fathers and Biblical Interpretation." May 7, 1539. Recorded by Anthony Lauterbach): 352; *WA Tr* 4: 380–81.

the Christian life under "justification" (*semper iustificandus*) but defines this as being "justified anew" through returning to Christ rather than as a process of becoming "more and more righteous" intrinsically through cooperation with the grace of the Spirit as in the theology of Augustine. According to McGrath, Luther interprets the antithesis of "flesh" and "Spirit" theologically rather than in the more anthropological manner of Augustine, and Augustine stresses "faith working through love" rather than "faith alone" as justifying before God and attaining eternal life, defining "justified" and "grace" more in terms of being "made righteous" intrinsically through the healing power of the grace of the Spirit that increases through "participation in the divine life." According to McGrath, this interpretation of Paul is explicitly rejected by Luther on account of his understanding that the Christian in this life always remains intrinsically sinful so that righteousness in justification is entirely and only ever extrinsic in the "alien righteousness of Christ" (*iustitia Christi aliena*). This is true both of the complete reckoning of righteousness in Christ as well as of the moral regeneration and renovation of the Christian in the living presence and power of the Holy Spirit and Christ present in faith. McGrath does acknowledge that Luther's theology of justification has a sanative and proleptic quality, first identified by Karl Holl in the 1920s, and that this shows some affinity with the theology of Augustine. Holl argues that Luther's theology of justification is analytic and that God imputes righteousness on account of the fact that He has already begun and will complete His work of making the sinner righteous. Althaus agrees that there is a proleptic dimension in Luther's theology of justification and that this continues to be reflected even in his later writings as well, but he criticizes Holl for minimizing the importance to Luther of the necessity of imputed righteousness in Christ through faith alone to forgive the guilt belonging to the Christian as still sinner.[67]

In Luther's theology, justification is primarily the reckoning or imputation of righteousness in Christ, which is God's promise (*promissio*) of complete forgiveness for sins in Christ and His atoning righteousness received through faith alone. As scholars have recently stressed, this is

---

67. McGrath, *Iustitia Dei*, 23–36, 182, 198–201, 205, 210–12; McGrath, *Theology of the Cross*, 133–34; Holl, "Die Rechtfertigungslehre in Luthers Vorlesung," 1: 111–58; Althaus, *Theology of Martin Luther*, 234–42. This eschatological dimension in Luther's theology of justification appears to have been overlooked by proponents of the "New Perspective." See Wright, "New Perspectives on Paul," 9–10.

never a mere legal fiction, for this divine Word that promises complete favor with God in Christ possesses the powers of creation, establishes a new reality of being, and through the divine gift of faith and the present Christ and life of the Spirit adds a new orientation of delight in righteousness and hatred of sin in the experience of the Christian.[68]

It is also true, however, that the more carefully developed distinction between "justification" as the imputation of righteousness in Christ and "sanctification" as regeneration to good works in later Lutheranism tended to obscure the union in justifying faith of Christ as both the favorable verdict and renovating power of God in the theology of Luther.[69] Through justifying faith in the Gospel, the Christian not only passively receives the complete reckoning of righteousness before God in Christ but also the righteous desires and affections of the Holy Spirit and the present Christ. Indeed, as Luther will later elaborate, the Christian is healed from the power of sin in this life only as faith increases, because as the old self decreases and faith in Christ increases room is made for the redeeming crucified and risen presence of Christ to rule powerfully without interruption through the Spirit.[70]

Essential to understanding how "Law" and "Gospel" apply to the life of the justified Christian is Luther's concept of the Christian as "*simul justus et peccator,*" which he really begins to develop in the Romans lectures. According to Luther, it is the mind, or conscience,[71] of the Christian that is released from the authority and condemnation of the Law through faith in the promise of forgiveness in the Gospel. By this faith and the inward power of the Holy Spirit, a spontaneous delight for God and His Law is created within the Christian. However, the Christian is still unable to accommodate his or her new desires in the purest sense because he or she also remains a sinner and experiences impulses that are contrary to the very same Law. In his *Explanation*

---

68. Bayer, *Martin Luther's Theology*, 52–53; Kolb and Arand, *Genius of Luther's Theology*, 148–59.

69. This point is stressed by Finnish scholars, though perhaps too far, in associating Luther's theology of justification with the Orthodox doctrine of "theosis." See Peura, "Christ as Favor and Gift (*donum*)," in Braaten and Jensen, *Union with Christ: The New Finnish Interpretation of Luther*, 42–43; Mannermaa, *Christ Present in Faith*, 4–5, 16–17, 19, 21–22, 39–40, 49–57, 66–67, 87–88.

70. See *LW* 26 (*Lectures on Galatians*, 1535): 349–50, 354, 360; *WA* 401: 536–38; Althaus, *Theology of Martin Luther*, 234–35.

71. Ozment, *Homo Spiritualis*, 94.

to Thesis 6 of the Heidelberg Disputation (1518), Luther states that sin is present wherever there is felt the slightest hint of unwillingness, hesitancy, or reluctance to perform God's will. This is experienced to a greater or lesser degree throughout the Christian life. Such a righteous person whose works are always performed in absolute freedom cannot be found this side of heaven.[72] Similarly, there is no Christian on earth who is immune to sinful impulses, even though he or she does not consent to them inwardly by the presence of faith and the Holy Spirit. The Christian in this life has been transformed by the power of God in the Gospel from a sinner once wholly inclined towards sin but restrained outwardly by the Law, into a person now inclined through the Holy Spirit freely towards the good, but opposed by the sinful nature.[73]

To shed further light on Luther's understanding of the Christian as *simul justus et peccator* it is important to understand the distinction he makes between "flesh" (*caro*) and "spirit," or "Spirit" (*spiritus*). Luther clearly recognizes that the Bible often distinguishes between the immaterial part of a person, the "soul" (*anima*) or "spirit" (*spiritus*) and the "body" (*corpus*), and that the former is the animating and determining principle of human action: "For the flesh experiences no desire except through the soul and spirit, by virtue of which it is alive. By spirit and flesh, moreover, I understand the whole man, especially the soul itself."[74]

Many scholars have argued that during his lectures on the Bible Luther broke away from tendencies toward Platonic, dualistic anthropologies inherited by early and medieval Christian asceticism, which interpreted the disparity between "flesh" and "spirit" described by Paul in Galatians 5:14 in terms of the inferior passions and sensualities of the body (*sensus*) in dissonance with the pursuit of God through the higher faculty of the mind or "reason" (*ratio*). Even Augustine, who stressed that sin is essentially a problem rooted in the enslaved will, spoke of the *libido* in human sexual reproduction as a sinful passion and the one that most supplants the godly exercise of reason. Scholars rightly point out that Luther develops an entirely different approach to the antithesis of "flesh" and "spirit" as descriptions of human nature viewed in totality (*totus homo*) before God, with the rational soul at its core. With regard

---

72. *LW* 31 (*Explanation to Thesis 6*, 1518): 60–61; *WA* 1: 367–68.
73. *LW* 25 (*scholia* on Romans, 1515–16): 330–31; *WA* 56: 341–42.
74. *LW* 27 (*Lectures on Galatians*, 1519): 363; *WA* 2: 585.

to the "flesh," this refers to the essential sinfulness of the human soul in all its idolatry, in reason and thought, in values and motivations, and in will and desires inherited by original sin. Luther does not define sin in terms of outward actions so much as the essential disposition of nature that underlies them in the unbelief of the human heart. The idolatrous state of every human soul is a reality even though people can often appear as outwardly decent and rational beings in the eyes of the world. In the light of this contrast, scholars argue that Luther's definition of the antithesis between "flesh" and "spirit" be understood theologically rather than anthropologically and with regard to the whole human person and the fundamental orientation of his or her nature either toward idolatrous self-exaltation or indulgence, obeying the Law of God only by coercion, or perfect communion with God through humility and faith, delighting in His Law and serving others with love in all things.[75]

The existential struggle between good and evil desires in the Christian is a predicate of his or her paradoxical existence possessing both godly and idolatrous orientations. The Christian is both a "spiritual man" and "carnal man" (*spiritualis et carnalis*), "righteous" and "sinner" (*Iustus et peccator*), "good" and "evil" (*Bonus et malus*). Luther defines the doctrine of *simul justus et peccator* in the Romans lectures in terms of the conflicting desires within the Christian and not exclusively as the totality of divine acceptance in Christ over against intrinsic human sinfulness. Althaus insightfully observes that *simul justus et peccator* in Luther's thought "characterizes not only the paradoxical theological and empirical togetherness of the divine verdict and a man's actual condition, but also the anthropological conflict within the Christian man."[76]

According to Luther, this paradox of the Christian life is best expressed by Paul in Romans chapter seven. Paul speaks of himself as a sinner in the first person, yet states that this only constitutes a "part"

---

75. Luther states that a person is "spirit insofar as he savors the things that are of God, but is flesh insofar as he is influenced by the enticements of the flesh; and if he consents to these, he is altogether flesh." *LW* 27 (*Lectures on Galatians*, 1519): 363, 372; *WA* 2: 585–86, 610–11. See also Ozment, *Homo Spiritualis*, 90–93; Althaus, *Theology of Martin Luther*, 153–56; Wicks, "Luther on the Person Before God," Review of *Ontologie der Person bei Luther*, 289–311 (especially 292–3). On support of this point, McGrath cites Schott, *Fleisch und Geist*. See *Theology of the Cross*, 133–34 (n. 116). On Augustine and the sin of concupiscence in sexual reproduction, see Lancel, *Augustine*, 422–25.

76. McGrath, *Iustitia Dei*, 199–201, 205, 209; *Theology of the Cross*, 133–34; Althaus, *Theology of Martin Luther*, 153–55, 242–44, 268.

of him. Luther defines the "inner man" (*interiorem hominem*) as the "spiritual man" and "mind and conscience that is pure and delights in the Law of God," yet for those not yet justified, "the entire man is the 'old man' and only outward."[77] For Luther the unique experience of the Christian is characterized by Paul's own frustrations with sin: "He does not want to lust, and he judges that it is a good thing not to lust, and yet he lusts and does not carry out his own will, and thus he is fighting with himself; but because the spirit and the flesh are so intimately bound together into one, although they completely disagree with each other, therefore he attributes to himself as a whole person the work of both of them, as if he were at the same time completely flesh and completely spirit."[78] Luther alludes to the ancient theological concept of "*communio Ideomatum*" to illuminate the nature of this duality: "Therefore we must note that the words 'I want' and 'I hate' refer to the spiritual man or to the spirit, but 'I do' and 'I work' refer to the carnal man or to the flesh. But because the same one complete man consists of flesh and spirit, therefore he attributes to the whole man both of these opposing qualities which come from the opposing parts of him. For in this way there comes about a communication of attributes, for one and the same man is spiritual and carnal, righteous and a sinner, good and evil."[79]

In the Romans lectures Luther does describe the unique existential conflict of the Christian in terms of a disparity of understanding, will, and desire rather than as a strict conflict of mind and body. Luther indeed later speaks of the Christian battle with sin in terms of fundamental thoughts, beliefs, desires, and attitudes in the conscience.[80] The battle between "flesh" and "spirit" in the Christian life is a battle between the intrinsic sinful soul and the Holy Spirit and effectual presence of Christ in faith. This conflict continues as long as life in a mortal body continues. According to Luther, the struggle of the Christian with sin will only be once and for all resolved at the Final Judgment and future resurrection of the body. This does not mean, of course, that struggle

---

77. *LW* 25 (*scholia* on Romans, 1515–16): 329–36; *WA* 56: 341–47; *LW* 27 (*Lectures on Galatians*, 1519): 363, 372; *WA* 2: 585–86, 592–93.

78. *LW* 25 (*scholia* on Romans, 1515–16): 333; *WA* 56: 344–45. See also Ozment, *Homo Spiritualis*, 135.

79. *LW* 25 (*scholia* on Romans, 1515–16): 332; *WA* 56: 343.

80. See *LW* 26 (*Lectures on Galatians*, 1535): 336–38, 340–41; *WA* 401: 518–21, 524–25.

with sin in the here and now results from the possession of a mortal body. Not only will the body be made new but it will be reunited with the soul ruled by the Spirit when faith is at last perfected and becomes sight in the presence of the glory of Christ.[81] Luther describes the life to come in terms of the Christian finally being able to purely accomplish the good he or she desires without any hesitation or resistance: "Thus the Spirit accomplishes the good that it wishes when without rebellion it does its work in accord with the law of God, which cannot be done in this life, because 'I cannot do it.'"[82] In his *Lectures on Galatians* (1519) Luther identifies "works of peace and perfect well-being" performed without the slightest hint of hindrance or resistance, which are characteristic only of the life to come: "if he consents entirely to the Law, he is altogether spirit; and this will take place when the body becomes spiritual." Not until the future resurrection of the body, what Luther calls the "changing of the flesh," will the Christian be ruled perfectly by the Spirit and finally and entirely freed of all remnants of sin.[83]

Even though all Christians give in to sinful impulses from time to time, Luther reiterates repeatedly that God does not impute sin to the one who does not give full consent to such sin, as if without contrition, having an inward delight for His Law and earnestly desiring His mercy and the power to be conformed more and more to the Law: "But only to those who manfully struggle and fight against their faults, invoking the grace of God, does God not impute sin."[84] Luther stresses this same point in his *The Holy Blessed Sacrament of Baptism* (1519), a treatise that went through sixteen German editions between 1519 and 1523 followed by a Latin translation in 1543.[85]

---

81. Luther still retained a belief in purgatory until 1522 although admitting it was not provable beyond doubt in Scripture. See *LW* 32 ("The Thirty-Seventh Article," *Defense and Explanation of All the Articles*, 1521): 95; *WA* 7: 450, 452. Eventually, by 1522 and after, Luther believed the soul to be asleep in the safekeeping of God until its reunion with the body at the resurrection. See *LW* 48 ("To Nicholas von Amsdorf. Warburg, January 13, 1522"): 360–62; *WA Br* 2: 422–23; *LW* 52 ("The Gospel for the Festival of the Epiphany, Matthew 2[:1–12]," 1522): 180; *WA* 101a: 588–89. For Luther on "soul sleep," see also Althaus, *Theology of Martin Luther*, 414–17.

82. *LW* 25 (*scholia* on Romans, 1515–16): 332–33; *WA* 56: 342.

83. *LW* 27 (*Lectures on Galatians*, 1519): 223–24, 363, 372; *WA* 2: 492–93, 585–86, 592–93, 610–11.

84. *LW* 25 (*scholia* on Romans, 1515–16): 340; *WA* 56: 350.

85. See the introduction by E. Theodore Bachmann in *LW* 35: 26–27.

Not unlike his contemporaries, Luther refers to baptism explicitly as a "covenant" (*vorpinden*), which he defines as the eternal promise of God bestowed upon infants to forgive their sins and to no longer impute sin so long as they believe upon His mercy in Christ and live out their "spiritual baptism" by the daily mortification of sins. This clearly agrees with statements in the Romans lectures with regard to the freedom from condemnation of those who maintain an aggressive attitude against sin through resistance, repentance, humility, and the desire to be forgiven and made righteous, which characterizes a battle with sin that ceases only at death. It is worth quoting Luther at some length to highlight the certain conditionality he describes in connection with the promise of justification in baptism:

> So long as you keep your pledge to God, he in turn gives you his grace. He pledges himself not to impute to you the sins which remain in your nature after baptism, neither to take them into account nor to condemn you because of them. He is satisfied and well pleased if you are constantly striving and desiring to conquer these sins and at your death to be rid of them. For this reason, although evil thoughts and appetites may be at work, indeed even though at times you may sin and fall, these sins are already broken by the power of the sacrament and covenant. The one condition is that you rise again and enter again into the covenant, as St. Paul says in Romans 8[:1]. No one who believes in Christ is condemned by the evil, sinful inclination of his nature, if only he does not follow it and give in to it . . . We must humbly admit, 'I know full well that I cannot do a single thing that is pure. But I am baptized, and through my baptism God, who cannot lie, has bound himself in a covenant with me. He will not count my sin against me, but will slay it and blot it out' . . . He will not count sin against us if only we keep striving against it with many trials, tasks, and sufferings, and at last slay it at death. To them who do this not, God will not forgive their sins. For they do not live according to their baptism and covenant, and they hinder the work of God and of their baptism which has been begun.[86]

This battle with sin is a daily reality for the Christian who is "*simul justus et peccator.*" In his *Works on the Psalms* (1518), Luther describes

---

86. LW 35 (*The Holy and Blessed Sacrament of Baptism*, 1519): 33–37; WA 2: 728, 731-33. See also LW 36 (*Babylonian Captivity of the Church*, 1520): 124; WA 6: 572; Althaus, *Theology of Martin Luther*, 354-56.

the earthly sojourn of a Christian as a life in transition and an overlap between two ages: "There is no one in this life in whom all the completeness of the New Testament has been fulfilled; nor will anyone be found in whom some part of the Old Testament does not remain. For this life is a kind of transition and passage from Law to grace, from sin to justification, from Moses to Christ. But its consummation is the future resurrection."[87]

As the Christian remains a sinner, so the Law continues its function in relationship to sin. The marriage of Law and sin is what many modern scholars have referred to as the "existential character" of the Law. These scholars also argue that "Law" in Luther is never simply equated with any written legislation such as the Decalogue, but rather is defined as whatever evokes guilt in the human conscience (*lex accusans*). This is why the death of Christ in reproving sin is described as functioning like Law rather than Gospel. *Lex accusans* ceases and becomes *lex vacua* only in the age to come, though this can be experienced in the present in a partial sense through faith in the Gospel. Thus, according to these scholars, the dialectic of "Law" and "Gospel" in the experience of the Christian corresponds respectively to the paradoxical identity of the Christian as still a member of this fallen age but now also of the eschatological age to come.[88] It is certainly correct to say that, for Luther, "the moment never arrives in the life of the Christian when the law has nothing more than an informatory significance for him."[89] Nevertheless, Luther could also speak positively of "Law" in terms of the righteous will of God transcendent of the experience of human guilt.

By 1519, Luther had developed a careful distinction between the proper tasks of Law and Gospel and the biblical dispensation peculiar to each according to their emphasis. However, Luther had also intimated that the preaching of the Law continues to function in the present age alongside the priority of the Gospel. In his *Lectures on Galatians* (1519), Luther explains that the apostles as ministers of the Gospel regularly preached good works as "explanations of the Law whereby sin should be recognized more clearly." By the end of 1519, Luther had become

---

87. *LW* 14 (*Works on the Psalms*, 1518): 331; *WA* 5: 61.

88. See Forde, *Law-Gospel Debate*, 177–85, 191–93; Forde, "Forensic Justification and the Law," 295. See also Ebeling, *Luther*, 136; Althaus, *Theology of Martin Luther*, 261.

89. Wengert, *Law and Gospel*, 42.

more reluctant to speak of Christ as a new "Lawgiver" for the obvious reason of wanting to stress the fact that the proper ministry of Christ was the Gospel. Yet he also wanted it to be clear that the works taught by Christ were not a new and different will of God but merely the proper explanation and interpretation of the will of God already given in the Law, although now with much greater stress on its inward fulfillment. Luther also describes the good works taught by the apostles as "aids and observances by which the grace already received and the faith that has been bestowed may be guarded, nurtured, and perfected, just as happens when a sick person begins to receive care."[90] Although Luther does not go into detail to explain what this means or how it precisely works, he clearly differentiates between a role for the apostolic preaching of good works in exposing how deep the roots of sin go so that grace might be sought all the more and another role that applies to the Christian on the other side of having received grace and faith on account of the sickness of sin that remains.

Of course, Luther believes that faith itself does not require any such laws or exhortations to good works. Yet Luther also understands that faith does not always wax strong, that the renewal of the Christian is never complete in this life, and the residual promptings of sin remain opposed to the desires that proceed from faith in the Spirit: "in the flesh there is no one who attains this goal perfectly . . . the description of the fruits of the spirit, against which there is no law, is rather a goal that is set up in front—a goal towards which those who are spiritual must strive. Therefore the Law is not against them insofar as they live in the spirit, but it is against them insofar as they are prompted by the desires of the flesh."[91]

Luther states that the "Ten Commandments are necessary only for sinners," but then quickly adds that "On account of their flesh . . . the righteous, too, are sinners."[92] However, the relationship of the Law to the justified is not like that of those not justified. The justified Christian is free of the condemnation of the Law and through faith and the gift of the Holy Spirit now has the desire to do above and beyond what the Law before could only outwardly extort by compulsion. The Law and commandments of God are now something desirable and, with regard

---

90. *LW* 27 (*Lectures on Galatians*, 1519): 184; *WA* 2: 466.
91. *LW* 27 (*Lectures on Galatians*, 1519): 379; *WA* 2: 596–97.
92. *LW* 27 (*Lectures on Galatians*, 1519): 232; *WA* 2: 497.

to Christians as still sinners, serve an important purpose in directing them in obedience to God in the world and in resistance to the sinful promptings of the flesh: "that as persons who are already righteous we may know how our spirit should crucify the flesh and direct us in the affairs of this life, lest the flesh become haughty, break its bridle, and shake off its rider, the spirit of faith. One must have a bridle for the horse, not the rider."[93] The Christian by faith delights in the Law and uses the commandments of the Law against the promptings and desires of the flesh and to obey God in good works, which in turn have the effect of guarding the integrity of faith from slipping into a false presumption. Luther even says that the "spirit of faith" can be lost if the flesh is not bridled by the Law and commandments. Though Christians through faith have no obligation to the demands of the Law as a means of acceptance before God, neither any need for the Law to instruct them in the right way, the truth is that Christians are also still intrinsically sinful possessing desires diametrically opposed to the Spirit: "the spirit of the righteous man, although through faith it is now without sin and owes nothing to the Law, nevertheless still has a body unlike itself and rebellious, upon which it works and which it disciplines so as to render it, too, without sin, righteous, and holy like itself."[94] In the light of the *totos homo* anthropology developed in his earlier Romans lectures and repeated again in the lectures on Galatians, Luther's reference to disciplining the "body" (*corpus*) cannot be interpreted dualistically, as if the physical body possesses its own rebellious will and desires independent of and contrary to the soul. The Christian life is a battle between the sinful desires of the soul and its indulgence of the body and the righteous desires of the Spirit rendering the body unto the glory of God with thanksgiving in sacrifice and service to others.

As far as faith is concerned, Luther acknowledges: "we are not under a custodian. But the custodian has become our friend and is honored by us more than he is feared."[95] Without understanding the analogy of the "custodian" (*paidagogos*, Galatians 3:24) in the context of Luther's discussion, it can be easily misconstrued to say that Luther disregarded any need for the Law in the life of the Christian. The metaphor borrowed from Roman culture by Paul refers to the practice of a

---

93. *LW* 27 (*Lectures on Galatians*, 1519): 232; *WA* 2: 498.
94. *LW* 27 (*Lectures on Galatians*, 1519): 231; *WA* 2: 497.
95. *LW* 27 (*Lectures on Galatians*, 1519): 278; *WA* 2: 528.

household slave appointed to supervise the education and moral conduct of the firstborn son until his coming of age. Once the child had reached the age of attaining full rights to his inheritance he was free of the supervision and discipline of his custodian and would actually then become his or her master.[96] According to Luther, this image explains why the apostle can often speak so disparagingly about the Law in the context of the doctrine of justification by faith.[97] Obedience to the Law that is compulsory is illustrated by the young child in servile bondage to his custodian. For Luther, this is what it means for a person to live in bondage to sin under the Law. Until he or she comes to believe in the inheritance that is bestowed purely by the promise of God, he or she forever remains burdened by the Law and is a reluctant slave to it much like the child is to his earthly guardian.[98]

To be free of slavery to the Law does not mean freedom to live an immoral life without inhibition or consequence. For Luther, this is to understand Paul's teachings on faith and grace in a "stupid way." On the contrary, freedom from slavery to the Law is only freedom from servile bondage under the Law as if the law were the means to the eternal inheritance. Insofar as the Christian is accounted righteous by faith and renewed in the power of the Spirit of Christ, no such Law is needed to teach or compel a good life: "So a righteous man does not have to live a good life, but he lives a good life and needs no law to teach him to live a good life."[99] However, when Luther speaks of the righteous who have no need of the Law, he is speaking with regard to the faith of the righteous in Christ. However, as was already stated before, Luther acknowledges in these very same lectures that even the righteous have need of the Law on account of the flesh and there is no sinner, justified or not justified, who can be entirely without the Law in this life.

Furthermore, true Christian freedom is precisely the freedom to live in the Law and to do good works from a free and spontaneous desire without any regard to penalty, reward, or "out of slavish fear or childish desire." The Law itself does not change in the Gospel but only the relationship of the Christian through faith to it: "the same Law that was formerly hateful to the free will now becomes delightful, since love

---

96. Brown, *Dictionary of New Testament*, 2: 445.
97. LW 27 (*Lectures on Galatians*, 1519): 286; WA 2: 533.
98. LW 27 (*Lectures on Galatians*, 1519): 291; WA 2: 537.
99. LW 27 (*Lectures on Galatians*, 1519): 378; WA 2: 596.

is poured into our hearts through the Holy Spirit." In fact, the Christian goes from "servitude to servitude, from freedom to freedom," exchanging slavery to sin for willing service to God under the Law and freedom from righteousness to freedom for righteousness.[100] Like the child who has grown into his inheritance, the Christian in the power of faith now freely chooses what was once formerly imposed.

A Christian is truly free from the Law only in the sense of being liberated from the burden to satisfy God with works. Yet the Christian lives in the Law with a genuine love toward the neighbor, which is "truly the sum, the head, the completion, and the end of all laws." The Christian serves the ecclesiastical and civil laws of his or her respective government, not as a means of righteousness and not out of a fear of punishment, but in so far as these laws harmonize with the love that springs from faith: "Thus one must be subject to the laws of emperors, of popes, of towns, of states, and of provinces only, as Christ says (Matthew 17:27), to avoid giving offense to them and in order not to injure love and peace."[101]

By the end of 1519, Luther had developed a solid foundation for his understanding of Law and Gospel, including the role of the Law in the Christian life, and this was only to be later expanded, developed, and worked out in particular contexts. In these early years, as Luther established his theology in opposition to a perceived overemphasis on works in late medieval scholasticism and Catholic piety, Luther came to understand that the Law judges all for failing to fulfill it from the heart. The Law acts importantly as an accuser, revealing the essential idolatry of the human heart and its deserving condemnation by God to bring about humility. To be justified is to receive the reckoning of righteousness from God in Christ through faith alone and through this same faith a righteous orientation through the power and presence of the living God. The Christian by faith in the Gospel and through the power of the Spirit now freely delights to do what was formerly done outwardly with reluctance as compulsory "works of the Law." Yet the Christian always remains a sinner and experiences opposition to the Law in the sinful impulses of the flesh, never ceasing to plead the mercy of God and to yearn for the day when perfection comes. For now, the

---

100. *LW* 27 (*Lectures on Galatians*, 1519): 325–26, 347–49; *WA* 2: 559–60; 576.

101. *LW* 27 (*Lectures on Galatians*, 1519): 347–52; 357–58; *WA* 2: 574–78; 581–82. See also Marty, "Luther on Ethics," in Kadai, *Accents in Luther's Theology*, 206–8.

Christian is called into the thick of battle against the old nature under the banner of God's favor who promises not to impute sin to his soldiers for their victory is secure. Until the moment of the final resurrection, when the struggle of faith will at last become sight, and the body itself completely restored by the power of the Holy Spirit, the Law continues to be necessary in the daily warfare of the Christian pilgrim.

3

Combating Legalism and Lawlessness
Law and Gospel in Luther's Writings of the 1520s

FROM THE VERY BEGINNING, NAYSAYERS ACCUSED LUTHER AND HIS doctrine of justification as the gift of righteousness in Christ received by faith alone as opening the door to presumption upon the favor of God and thus to moral lawlessness. Such criticisms were made by Catholic scholars and clergy as well as by other compatriot German reformers. However, though Luther did stress the Gospel early on in opposition to a predominance in Catholic thinking on the Law and works in justification, even his earliest biblical expositions of the 1520s stress the importance of preaching the Law in the Church for the sake of the not justified and a use of the Law for the life of the justified with regard to ongoing struggles with sin and the flesh. Throughout the following decade of the 1520s Luther would be challenged to develop his biblical theology in the context of very complicated circumstances and by balancing an emphasis on faith alone *coram Deo* with the moral obligation of the Christian *coram mundo*. The revolutionary decade of the 1520s, in which the evangelical reforming theology of Luther began to be implemented and adapted throughout Germany by sympathizers and zealots, is of great importance for observing how Luther's theology of Law and Gospel addressed everyday life in Church and society.[1]

In 1520, just months prior to receiving his official warning of excommunication from Pope Leo X, Luther published an exposition of the Ten Commandments entitled *A Treatise on Good Works* in answer to direct questions posed by Spalatin about the role of ecclesiastical cer-

---

1. The historical narrative of this period is amply covered in Brecht, *Shaping and Defining*. See also Bornkamm, *Luther in Mid-Career*.

emonies and the laws of Church and State in a theology of justification by faith alone in Christ apart from works.[2]

Luther begins the treatise by defining a "good work" according to the revealed commandments of God and states that a person need not look beyond the Decalogue for the definition of a truly spiritual life pleasing to God. Contrary to the opinions of his earliest opponents and even modern stereotypes, Luther never exalts faith to the exclusion or minimizing of good works, and states in this treatise his purpose "to teach the real good works which spring from faith." Such works do not consist of ritual fasts, monastic vows, prescribed prayers, or pilgrimages, which are neither commandments of God nor do they have any goodness in them when performed with the uncertain hope of earning favor from God. Instead, Luther exposits the Ten Commandments, defining them as "a mirror" (*ein Spiegel*) better than any other to "find what you lack and what you should seek." Throughout the exposition, however, it becomes clear that Luther is not merely thinking of the outward prohibitions as they are strictly stated in the Ten Commandments, but, rightly interpreted, of the even higher demands for worshipping God and social responsibility that speak about the human heart. Thus, the prohibition against stealing is fundamentally a commandment condemning all forms of material greed and self-love, including the hoarding of wealth to the neglect of the needs of others. To fulfill these demands in truth is impossible for sinners and results only from the renovative power of Christ in the heart through faith and confidence in the Gospel. The person who obeys the First Commandment to believe in the one true God with faith and confidence has no problem fulfilling what the commandment teaches because he or she relies completely on God who has promised to meet every need.[3] This approach to the Law is not entirely new for Luther and is apparent in his earlier *Dictata super Psalterium* (1513-1515). Of course, his theology of justification has developed much since then, yet in the Psalms lectures Luther similarly defines mere outward obedience to the Decalogue as the "letter" binding the Jews contrasted with the inward "spirit" of the Law interpreted by Christ who gives the power through faith to keep the true intent of the Law.

---

2. See the introduction by James Atkinson in *LW* 44: 17–20.
3. *LW* 44 (*Treatise on Good Works*, 1520): 22, 63, 108–9; *WA* 6: 204–5, 236, 270–73.

Later on in the treatise Luther states that the order of the Decalogue reveals a certain hierarchy to the commandments.[4] This is particularly true when comparing the first (Exodus 20:1–11) and second tables (Exodus 20:12–17). Luther argues that the fourth commandment to honor parents refers also to the respecting of civil and ecclesiastical authorities, but it can be broken if conflict arises with the first three commandments to believe, honor, and worship the one true God.[5] As such, the first table deals with restoring the relationship of the sinner to God apart from which no truly good work can come: "For as their conscience stands in relation to God and as it believes, so also are their works which issue from it."[6] Luther argues that faith alone fulfills the First Commandment and "is the very first of all commandments and the highest and the best, from which all others must proceed, in which they exist and by which they must be judged and assessed..." For Luther, there is no distinction between works that proceed freely from faith in the grace of God in Christ, but Luther does contrast, as in his earlier Romans lectures, between works performed in faith and freedom, including even the most ordinary daily activities, with the many faithless works done in a spirit of idolatry whose false motivation is the hope of earning divine forgiveness and favor. Such works are not and cannot be pleasing to God, since they are the intentions of a heart and conscience that is unbelieving in the God who promises to justify sinners on the basis of His mercy and grace alone. This is a breaking of the First Commandment and by implication all the other commandments that derive their true goodness from obedience to the First Commandment through faith and confidence in the mercy of God.[7]

Yet, if faith in the mercy of God in Christ alone fulfills the First Commandment and all the rest, why then should the State have so many laws and the Church so many laws, rituals, and ceremonies that might tempt people to falsely rely on them for justification? According to Luther, the answer is simply lack of faith in the Gospel: "If every man had faith we would need no more laws. Everyone would of himself do good works all the time, as his faith shows him." Obviously, Luther considered true faith to be a rare commodity in the world. Luther then

---

4. *LW* 44 (*Treatise on Good Works*, 1520): 39–40, 80–81; *WA* 6: 217–18, 250–51.
5. *LW* 44 (*Treatise on Good Works*, 1520): 87–89; *WA* 6: 255–57.
6. *LW* 44 (*Treatise on Good Works*, 1520): 24; *WA* 6: 205.
7. *LW* 44 (*Treatise on Good Works*, 1520): 23, 30–31; *WA* 6: 209–11.

speaks of "four kinds of men." First, there are the righteous who through faith have no need of such laws or ceremonies to inspire them to work. Then there are those who will need laws because they will use the Gospel only to excuse their laziness and indulgence. Then there are the wicked who like "wild horses and dogs" constantly need to be restrained by laws, threats, and punishments. Finally, the last group is still immature in their understanding and only needs to be better educated with regard to the nature of Christian freedom in the Gospel. Thus, for a time they are coaxed along by various ceremonies, rituals, and religious practices.[8] Laws and ceremonies are necessary, therefore, with respect to the common order of Christendom, which is made up of the wicked and the weak or immature in the faith.

Luther does state openly in the treatise that the "Christian man living in this faith has no need of a teacher of good works, but he does whatever the occasion calls for, and all is well done,"[9] but he is certainly not precluding the need for the Law in the Christian life entirely. His theology of the Christian as *simul justus et peccator* developed earlier in his biblical lectures on Romans and Galatians has certainly not changed. Luther was personally aware of the reality that no Christian carrying around the flesh lives in faith so powerfully from moment to moment throughout life and that no Christian can be without the need for some direction with regard to how faith should be applied in the world for others. The fact that Luther uses the Ten Commandments, rightly interpreted according to their inward sense, as the very outline for the whole treatise shows that he understood the "good works" of faith pleasing to God to have an identifiable shape and form with regard to the Christian living in the world for others. It is also important to keep in mind that this statement is made in the context of a treatise whose primary aim is to teach that all works are "good" only in so far as they spring freely from faith and confidence in the mercy of God who reckons righteousness by His grace alone, exposing the fruitless error of trusting in man-made rituals and ceremonial and civil laws as "good works" and the way of righteousness before God. What Luther is essentially stressing in the statement above, then, is that the Christian "living in this faith" and in the confidence of the mercy of God for righteousness does not need to be taught "good works" since faith makes the Christian righteous and

8. *LW* 44 (*A Treatise on Good Works*, 1520): 26, 34–35; *WA* 6: 213.
9. *LW* 44 (*A Treatise on Good Works*, 1520): 26; *WA* 6: 207.

all the works the Christian does good and well-pleasing to Him. As to why Luther does not make more explicit the fact that the righteous who have no need of the Law are also sinners is difficult to explain. However, Luther has made clear before and will do so again in forthcoming treatises that faith, though justifying, never has complete power and sway in the life of Christians who still need the Law on account of remaining weakness and susceptibility to sin through the flesh.

Luther reiterates some of these same themes in his better known *The Freedom of A Christian* (1520), a treatise addressed to Pope Leo X and written within six months after his disputation in Leipzig in 1519 with the Ingolstadt theologian John Eck. It was published in November of 1520 soon after he received the papal bull (*Exurge Domine*) in October warning him of his pending excommunication and was among the works Luther was asked to renounce several months later before Charles V and other nobles and church officials at the Diet of Worms in April of 1521 (followed shortly by the finalization of his imperial condemnation issued on May 26).[10]

Though justification by faith in Christ alone is central to the treatise, Luther balances the utterly passive nature of justification before God apart from works with the expectation of active responsibility on the part of the Christian living in the world for others: "A Christian is a perfectly free lord of all, subject to none. A Christian is a perfectly dutiful servant of all, subject to all."[11]

As he had already come to emphasize before 1520, the commandments of God teach sinners what He justly requires of them while exposing and condemning their own inherent incapacity to fulfill them. Faith alone, then, justifies the guilty sinner because faith leans wholly upon the truth of God's own promise to reckon mercy and righteousness in Christ: "Faith works truth and righteousness by giving God what belongs to him. Therefore God in turn glorifies our righteousness . . . our faith shall be reckoned to us as righteousness if we believe."[12]

Luther refers again to the exchange that takes place through union with Christ by faith, this time using the Pauline analogy of marriage

---

10. See the introduction by Harold J. Grimm in *LW* 31: 329–30; Mullett, *Martin Luther*, 125–28.

11. *LW* 31 (*The Freedom of A Christian*, 1520): 344; *WA* 7: 49.

12. *LW* 31 (*The Freedom of A Christian*, 1520): 351; *WA* 7: 54. See also Watson, *Let God Be God*.

in Ephesians 5:25–32. Just as a husband and wife become "one flesh" and have all things in common, so Christ assumes the sin of the sinner while the sinner assumes the favor of God and all His gifts in Christ. The reckoning of the alien righteousness of Christ through faith first involves the complete imputation of righteousness in Him on account of His death and resurrection but this is inseparable from the additional gift of His own living presence by the Spirit through faith acting powerfully over the intrinsically sinful soul for the moral renovation of the Christian life. On this basis, the divine gift of faith cannot help but be busy in doing good works, and it "only makes the law and works unnecessary for any man's righteousness and salvation." Faith ascribes complete integrity to God as He has revealed Himself, and this is the "very highest worship of God ... When this is done, the soul consents to His will."[13] Having been freed of all debt to the Law before God in Christ through faith alone, the Christian nevertheless lives as Christ to his or her neighbor freely and not for a divine favor already possessed.[14]

Luther states again that faith alone is the fulfillment of the First Commandment and even the "fulfilling of all commandments." God is neither truly glorified nor is the Law truly fulfilled by mere outward compulsory obedience. Faith is the "source and substance of all our righteousness." It contains the seed of all truly good works: "for he who fulfills the First Commandment has no difficulty in fulfilling all the rest."[15]

Luther repeats again his insistence that true Christian liberty does not give license to sin, but it is expected that Christians will be productive in doing good works. Even though the "inner man" (*interiore homine*) on account of faith in the Gospel has all righteousness and freely delights in the will of God, the Christian also has an "outer man" (*externum hominem*) that remains completely hostile to the will of God in the Law. Thus, although works have no value in attaining justification and righteousness, the Christian must nevertheless work to "reduce the body to subjection and purify it of its evil lusts ... our whole purpose is to be directed only toward the driving out of lusts."[16]

---

13. *LW* 31 (*The Freedom of A Christian*, 1520): 348–52; *WA* 7: 52–55.
14. *LW* 31 (*Freedom of A Christian*, 1520): 365–66, 369; *WA* 7: 64–66.
15. *LW* 31 (*The Freedom of A Christian*, 1520): 352–53; *WA* 7: 56.
16. *LW* 31 (*The Freedom of A Christian*, 1520): 358–59; *WA* 7: 59–60.

Earlier in the treatise, Luther describes the Christian as possessing a "soul ... spiritual, inner or new man" (*animem ... spiritualis, interior, novus homo*) and a "bodily nature" (*iuxta corporalem*), or "flesh ... carnal, outward or old man" (*quam carnem dicunt ... carnalis, exterior, vetus homo*). As in his previous biblical lectures and writings, Luther associates the new creation of the "inner man" with the passive righteousness established *coram Deo* through faith alone in the Gospel of Christ, while the "flesh" or "old man" remains subject to the Law and to the doing of works as the active compliment of faith for righteousness *coram mundo*.[17] Luther's *totus homo* anthropology developed earliest in his biblical lectures on Romans guards his definition of the conflict between "flesh" and "spirit" from being interpreted in a dualistic fashion, as if this conflict characterized an enmity between soul and body. The unique existential conflict of the justified Christian results from a tension between the power of the Spirit and the presence of Christ in faith and the intrinsic sinfulness of the soul that only ceases with death. In another treatise dating to the same period, Luther states that the spirit is the "noblest, best and most important part of man," and reassures Christians again that, on account of the righteousness of faith, God "does not charge the sin which remains in the lesser part, the flesh, toward his condemnation."[18] The "flesh" as the "lesser part" refers to the entire old nature and not just the physical body alone. This old nature is destined to die forever when the Christian dies. Until then, God mercifully overlooks the guilt of the flesh with all its sins so long as the Christian is repentant and believes the Gospel for forgiveness.

Even as Adam before the Fall was given the commandment to cultivate the Garden, the Christian does good works as a way of being productive in the world. Luther is quick to point out that, in both cases, the doing of good works is not what "makes him holier or more Christian." Holiness is an entirely new nature and disposition created in Christ who is present in faith, out of which springs pure love for God and others, and which grows in keeping with growth in faith. Faith in Christ alone makes a person good from within and issues forth naturally in righteous deeds. Luther states in another treatise of 1521 that: "Christ as a gift nourishes your faith and makes you a Christian. But

17. See also Kolb and Arand, *Genius of Luther's Theology*, 28–29.
18. *LW* 31 (*The Freedom of A Christian*, 1520): 344; *WA* 7: 50; *LW* 32 (*Defense and Explanation of All the Articles*, 1521): 20–21; *WA* 7: 332.

Christ as an example exercises your works. These do not make you a Christian. Actually they come forth from you because you have already been made a Christian."[19]

Though not original or unique to Luther, he frequently uses the biblical illustration of the tree and its fruit to describe the relationship of faith to good works: "the fruits do not make trees either good or bad, but rather as the trees are, so are the fruits they bear; so a man must first be good or wicked before he does a good or wicked work, and his works do not make him good or wicked, but he himself makes his works either good or wicked."[20] Luther certainly has in mind here a rejection of the medieval scholastic understanding of moral virtue as a "*habitus*" created in the soul by infused grace and increased through cooperation in works for condign merit worthy of eternal life. Luther is also mindful of the familiar scholastic notion of "faith formed by love" (*fides caritate formata*). However, for Luther, instead of love and works making faith complete or perfect for justification, it is faith alone in the Gospel that makes love perfect. Good works of love are the natural fruits of justification by faith. As faith alone justifies, in the sense of righteousness being reckoned on account of union with Christ, the sinner is also made just and has the beginnings of righteousness through the present Christ solely by means of this same faith. Ironically, and counterintuitive to natural reason, Luther stresses that it is not the active exercise of works that makes one righteous but the passive receiving of the promise of God in Christ by faith alone. In another treatise of the same year, Luther observes that the piling of laws and good works on those who lack faith in the complete mercy of God in Christ only increases their condemnation, since without the freedom that comes from the assurance of divine favor and the gift of the Holy Spirit their hearts grow in defiance and are incapable of obeying freely or willingly.[21]

The emphasis of *The Freedom of A Christian* leans toward freedom from the Law before God in the Gospel, although Luther clearly describes how such freedom leads naturally to the keeping of the Law and good works. Yet this is not to imply that the Gospel makes the

---

19. *LW* 31 (*The Freedom of A Christian*, 1520):360–61; *WA* 7: 61; *LW* 35 (*A Brief Instruction on What to Look for and Expect in the Gospels*, 1521): 120; *WA* 10[1a]: 12.

20. *LW* 31 (*The Freedom of A Christian*, 1520): 361; *WA* 7: 61.

21. *LW* 35 (*A Treatise on the New Testament, that is, the Holy Mass*, 1520):79; *WA* 6: 353. See also Wannenwetsch, "Luther's Moral Theology," 128.

Law unnecessary and irrelevant for preaching and teaching in general. Indeed, Luther's early evangelical writings would become resources for the antinomian rejection of the preaching of the Law entirely, but this only suggests that such reforming theologians differed with Luther even from the very beginning.[22] While certain isolated statements in Luther's early writings might appear to call for the demise of the preaching of the Law and works,[23] these must be interpreted alongside other clear and unambiguous statements in Luther's writings concerning the absolute necessity of continuing to preach the Law and works.[24]

Luther makes this point in his *Answer to the HyperChristian, Hyperspiritual, and Hyperlearned Book by Goat Emser in Leipzig* (1521). Jerome Emser (1478–1527), also known as the "Leipzig Goat," was a staunch supporter of Catholic orthodoxy and an early opponent of Luther's theology of justification by faith alone.[25] In the treatise, Luther emphasizes the importance of distinguishing and preserving both Law and Gospel as "two ways of preaching." The preaching of the Law, or "letter," is to urge obedience to the commandments of God without explaining where to gain the power to fulfill them. According to Luther, this was the mode of preaching characteristic of Moses under the Old Covenant, which was never able to make Israel righteous. Instead, it enslaved their consciences to burdensome demands they could never fulfill. Yet, the preaching of the Law nevertheless served the indispensable purpose of leading Israel to seek refuge in the mercy of God, and this ministry of the Law continues even into the present age of the Church. The ministry of the Spirit and the preaching of grace characteristic of the New Covenant properly begin where the office of Moses ends, but the ministry of Moses did not end in an absolute sense, as the antinomians came to believe, with the first advent of Christ and the coming of the Spirit. Rather, Moses' office ends when personal faith in the Gospel begins. This is why the preaching of the Law is necessary even after the historical event of Pentecost: "Therefore, it is impossible for someone who does not first hear the law and let himself be killed by the letter to

---

22. See also Kjeldgaard-Pederson in *Gesetz, Evangelium, und Busse*, 380.
23. *LW* 31 *(The Freedom of A Christian*, 1520): 371; *WA* 7: 69.
24. *LW* 31 *(The Freedom of A Christian*, 1520): 364; *WA* 7: 63.
25. See the introduction by Eric W. and Ruth C. Gritsch in *LW* 39: 139–41.

hear the gospel and let the grace of the Spirit bring him to life. Grace is only given to those who long for it."[26]

Preaching the Law in this way is nevertheless to be distinguished in form and delivery from Jesus' moral teachings in the Sermon on the Mount. While hiding away in Elector Frederick's castle in Wartburg as an outlaw of the state following his trial at Worms and the official issuance of the Edict condemning him in May of 1521, Luther completed a treatise attacking monastic vows as essentially unbiblical, unbinding, and powerless for establishing righteousness before God (including a preface dedicated to his own father who had been opposed to the vows taken by Luther in 1505). While supporting the abandonment of such vows, Luther carefully stresses the importance of doing the good works that God has commanded in Scripture in order that Christian freedom from monastic vows will not be misinterpreted as giving opportunity for fleshly liberty: "Nor can the freedom of the gospel dispense with the commandments."[27] Luther dismisses the common interpretation that the Sermon on the Mount (Matthew 5:25, 39–44) only speaks of the higher "counsels" vowed by monks to be distinguished from the more common "precepts" expected of the general Christian population. Instead, Luther argues that the Sermon on the Mount teaches the works expected of all who profess to be Christian and disciples of Christ. For Luther, the Gospel understood in its proper sense is "simply the promises of God declaring the benefits offered to man," but among these "benefits" Luther includes all the wisdom of the commandments and exhortations of Christ to His disciples.[28] In a work of the previous year, Luther explains that this mode in which Christ exhorts His disciples to do good works is very different than the ministry of the Law preached by Moses: "We see too that unlike Moses in his book, and contrary to the nature of a commandment, Christ does not horribly force and drive us. Rather he teaches us in a loving and friendly way . . . Christ drives and compels no one. Indeed he teaches so gently that he entices rather than

---

26. *LW* 39 (*Answer to the HyperChristian, Hyperspiritual, and Hyperlearned Book by Goat Emser in Leipzig*, 1521): 182–84, 188; *WA* 7: 653–56; 658–59. See also Forde, *Law-Gospel Debate*, 191–93.

27. *LW* 44 (*The Judgment of Martin Luther on Monastic Vows*, 1522): 297–98; *WA* 8: 606–7; Mullett, *Martin Luther*, 133.

28. *LW* 44 (*The Judgment of Martin Luther on Monastic Vows*, 1522): 256–57; *WA* 8: 580–81.

commands."[29] Thus, although Luther believes Christ in the Sermon on the Mount to be simply interpreting the Decalogue truthfully, he does make a distinction between the rhetorical tone of Jesus' moral teaching and that peculiar to the dispensation of Moses under the Old Covenant. The latter is done more with outward threats and compulsion without providing the motivating power to obey them from the heart, whereas Christ exhorts the disciples to good works in the manner of a loving friend.

That Luther did not want to do away with the Law of the Old Testament entirely on the basis of the Sermon on the Mount is clear in his statement in *Monastic Vows* that the Ten Commandments "ought not be dispensed with, but observed (if I may so express it) according to their inner meaning, but not according to the conscience" (that is, as a proper means to justification). In fact, the one who lives by faith is the one who keeps the Law rightfully. Luther even says that the "office of the Law is not to demand works of us," in the sense that the Law gives the power to do good works or to fulfill the Law, "but to show us our sin and our inability . . . Therefore, just as the works of the law are to be given up, so the teaching of the law ought to be given up." As in his earlier Romans lectures, the "works of the Law . . . to be given up" refer to a particular kind of work enforced by compulsion. The works of the Christian living in the Law freely through faith in the Gospel no longer constitute "works of the Law." Ideally, everyone would live as a true Christian through faith without the need for such compulsion. Of course, Luther knew that there would always be people who without faith can only do "works of the Law." Thus, Luther's statements about the "works of the law" and the "teaching of the law . . . to be given up," if taken in an absolute sense, must either be interpreted idealistically as if all became Christians and lived by faith or in the sense that the "teaching of the Law" and "works of the Law" as realistically attainable means of righteousness for justification "are to be given up" in Christendom.[30]

Similar statements are made in a sermon from Luther's *Wartburg Postil* (1522), a series of homilies created for German pastors and also drafted by Luther while in the Wartburg. The *Wartburg Postil* was made

---

29. See *LW* 35 (*A Brief Instruction on What to Look for and Expect in the Gospels*, 1521): 120–21; *WA* 10^{1a}: 13.

30. *LW* 44 (*The Judgment of Martin Luther on Monastic Vows*, 1522): 301–2; *WA* 8: 608–9.

up of Christmas and Advent sermons and was published in German in 1522.[31] In the sermon on the "Gospel for Christmas Eve, Luke 2:1–14," Luther states: "in the church nothing other than the gospel shall be preached," and later on declares that "faith and the gospel, that they and nothing else should be preached in Christendom."[32] First of all, Luther defines the "Gospel" (*Euangelion*) as containing two things: "Christ and His example, two kinds of good works: one kind belonging to Christ, by means of which we in faith, attain salvation, the other kind belonging to us, by means of which our neighbor is helped."[33] Whereas Luther elsewhere defines the proper work of the "Gospel" to be the proclamation of forgiveness promised in Christ, in this context the word "gospel" is used more broadly to refer to the life of Christ as an example to the Christian. Thus, Luther's statements above cannot be interpreted as removing the need for teaching good works altogether. It should also be noted that the context of these statements is Luther's objection to the teaching of compulsory works and ritual piety as pleasing to God and meritorious of His eternal favor. Yet, it still might appear that he is denying the ministry of preaching the Law in its Mosaic sense to evoke the fear of God and expose sin and its righteous condemnation. However, in another exposition of Luke 2 in the very same *Postil*, Luther insists that faith necessarily follows an encounter with the Law: "For without the law no one recognizes himself and what he is lacking; and he who does not know himself, does not seek grace." Furthermore, Luther describes the Christian after justification as still properly remaining "under the Law," that is, "according to the body," and is expected to be active in resisting sin and productive in doing good works for others in the world while passively and wholly trusting in the mercy of God in the Gospel "according to the soul."[34] Luther, then, on the basis of these other contemporaneous statements, cannot be excluding the need for the Law en-

---

31. See the introduction by John W. Doberstein in *LW* 51: xi–xxi, Hans J. Hillerbrand in *LW* 52: ix–xiii, and Gottfried G. Krodel's excursus in *LW* 48: 237–43, 254. See also Brecht, *Shaping and Defining*, 433, and Luther's 1521 correspondence to Spalatin and Melancthon in *LW* 48: 224–25 (also n. 16), 229; *WA Br* 2: 337–38, 347–49.

32. *LW* 52 ("Gospel for Christmas Eve, Luke 2:1–14," *Wartburg Postil*, 1522): 18, 24–26; *WA* 10^{1a}: 75, 85.

33. *LW* 52 ("Gospel for Christmas Eve, Luke 2:1–14," *Wartburg Postil*, 1522): 16–18; *WA* 10^{1a}: 73–76.

34. *LW* 52 ("Sermon for the Sunday after Christmas, Luke 2:33–40," *Wartburg Postil*, 1522): 131–33; *WA* 10^{1a}: 424–26.

tirely, but only the wrong preaching of the Law and the value of works, which is basically to preach the Law without the biblical Gospel. It is important to remember, too, that Luther assumes many of his fellow Germans to be living under the same bondage to the Law in *anfechtung* that he experienced in the monastery, and, thus, what the people needed in the early 1520s was to be less burdened by the preaching of the Law and more comforted through the preaching of the Gospel.

Also completed in the Wartburg, and using the Greek text of Erasmus' *Novum Testamentum* (1519), was Luther's translation of the New Testament into German published in September in Wittenberg (the "September Testament"). Just as Luther had inserted the phrase "only" (*allein*) after "faith" into his translation of Romans 3:28 to reflect his own understanding of justification, much to the ire of his Catholic critics,[35] the *Vorrhede* (*Preface*) to the translation outlines his new evangelical hermeneutic and reiterates his proper distinction between Law and Gospel. The teaching of Law and commandments is predominantly, though not exclusively, associated with the books of the Old Testament canon, and Luther asserts that the Gospel was prophesied long ago in Genesis chapter three. In his *Brief Instruction on what to Look for the in Gospels* (1521), Luther describes the Old Testament as Christ "wrapped in swaddling clothes and laid in a manger . . . all Scripture tends toward him."[36] Yet, the fuller revelation of that Gospel brought to light in the first coming and life of Christ is the property of the teaching of the books of the New Testament canon. Luther defines the "Gospel" more strictly in terms of the promise of salvation in Christ so as not to confuse it with the proper task of the Law to command, as well as to avoid confusing the two distinctive ministries of Christ and Moses.[37] Luther, of course, acknowledges that Christ often taught good works in the gospels, but that it is important to distinguish his rhetoric from that of Moses, as well as to point out that making satisfaction for sins, not teaching works, was the ultimate priority of His coming. In his *Brief Instruction* Luther warns: "Be sure, moreover, that you do not

---

35. Mullett, *Martin Luther*, 148.

36. *LW* 35 (*Preface to the New Testament*, 1546): 357–58; *WA DB* 6: 2–5. The quotations I use from the English translation of the 1546 German edition are identical, except for minor variations in spelling, with the 1522 edition; *LW* 35 (*Brief Instruction on what to Look for in the Gospels*, 1521): 122–23; *WA* 10[1a]: 14–15.

37. *LW* 35 (*Preface to the New Testament*, 1546): 357–62; *WA DB* 6: 2–11.

make Christ into a Moses, as if Christ did nothing more than teach and provide examples as the other saints do, as if the gospel were simply a textbook of teachings or laws."[38]

Although Christ and the apostles do often teach and provide examples of doing good works, Luther argues that Christ is always offered first as the gift of the favor of God to be received by faith alone. Whereas the Mosaic pedagogy of works drives and compels by means of terrifying threats and warnings of judgment, the kindlier entreaties of Christ and the apostles exhort Christians on the basis of the love of God in Christ. On this account, Luther favored the Gospel of John and the epistles of Paul, since they explained the Gospel more potently than any other New Testament books. Luther even states that he would rather do without the record of Jesus' life and deeds than the preaching of the Gospel in His death and resurrection, since it is this proclamation that justifies and saves sinners through faith.[39] This does not mean that the record of Jesus' deeds have no exemplary value for the Christian life, but these are secondary to, even deriving their proper significance and meaning from, the priority of the Gospel.

It is often pointed out that Luther describes the book of James in his preface to the New Testament as an "epistle of straw."[40] However, it is important to stress that this is not simply because it teaches works, for on that account Luther actually praises it and considers it "good." Rather, his disdain for the book results from the fact that it really only teaches works and, although works are spoken of as the fruits of true faith, does not speak explicitly about faith in the Gospel of Christ. Luther also firmly disapproves of James' statement that justification is by faith and works as in the example of Abraham offering up his son Isaac in Genesis 22. Therefore, on account of its utter lack of any explicit discussion of the Gospel of Christ and since it refers to justification by faith and works, Luther could not conceive how the book was properly an apostolic book if the apostles' ministry was first and foremost the preaching of the Gospel of righteousness to be received by faith alone. For Luther, the practical advice of James without the Gospel acts more

---

38. *LW* 35 (*Brief Instruction on what to Look for the in Gospels*, 1521):118–20; *WA* 10^{1a}: 10–11.

39. *LW* 35 (*Preface to the New Testament*, 1546): 360–62; *WA DB* 6: 8–11.

40. *LW* 35 (*Preface to the New Testament*, 1546): 362; *WA DB* 6: 10–11. The 1546 edition omits this statement as well as Luther's hierarchy of New Testament books.

like the Mosaic pedagogy of Law. On the other hand, Luther warmly praises the epistles of John for their stress on the importance of good works, "not by harping on the law, as the epistle of James does, but by stimulating us to love even as God has loved us."[41]

In his New Testament preface to the book of Romans, Luther identifies the structure of the letter in terms of a logical progression from Law to Gospel: "that the law, correctly understood and thoroughly grasped, does nothing more than to remind us of our sin, and to slay us by it, making us liable to eternal wrath."[42] In the Gospel, the Christian is free of all obligations and debts to the Law with regard to justification before God, yet is expected to do good works for the sake of others: "This knowledge of and confidence of God's grace makes men glad and bold and happy in dealing with God and with all creatures. And this is the work which the Holy Spirit performs in faith. Because of it, without compulsion, a person is ready and glad to do good to everyone, to serve everyone, to suffer everything, out of love and praise to God who has shown him this grace."[43] This does not mean to imply that the justified Christian then becomes morally perfect through faith. Luther reiterates his contrast between "flesh" (*Fleisch*) and "spirit" (*Geist*), defining "flesh" in the not yet justified as essentially the entire opposition of his human nature to God, whether "unbelief" or "unchastity." "Spirit" refers to human nature in harmony with God and the will of His Holy Spirit. While the not justified sinner could be said to be only "flesh," only the justified Christian is both "spirit" and "flesh" experiencing an existential tug-of-war that wages more or less within all who possess the Holy Spirit through faith. This tension is not equivalent to a dualistic conflict between soul and body, since the soul or conscience is the very seat of a battle with the Spirit against unbelief, lustful desires, envy, hatred, and greed. Although the Christian daily receives the righteous redeeming presence of Christ through faith, the battle with sin ceases altogether only when the Christian becomes "wholly spiritual," which for Luther occurs at the final resurrection. In the meantime, Luther identifies the

---

41. *LW* 35 (*Preface to the Epistles of St. James and St. Jude*, 1546): 395; *WA DB* 7: 384–87; *LW* 35 (*Preface to the Three Epistles of St. John*, 1546): 393; *WA DB* 7: 326–27.

42. *LW* 35 (*Preface to the Epistle of St. Paul to the Romans*, 1546): 372–77; *WA DB* 7: 12–21.

43. *LW* 35 (*Preface to the Epistle of St. Paul to the Romans*, 1546): 370–71; *WA DB* 7: 8–13.

major task of faith in the present through the rule of the Holy Spirit as to "slay the old Adam and subdue the flesh," daily sufferings and tribulations being the best remedies for preserving a sober consciousness of sin and a continued dependence upon the forgiveness and grace promised in the Gospel. No matter how strong the raging of sin that Christians experience, so long as they hate, resist, and fight against these urgings and promptings, repenting if they should fall, leaning always on the mercy and strength of God through faith, there is no condemnation for the sake of Christ.[44] That God on account of Christ does not condemn the faithful who fight and resist sins, are repentant and seek always after His grace, have delight for His Law and earnestly long for Him to rid them entirely of all remnants of sin echoes earlier statements made by Luther before 1520 in his Romans lectures (1515–1516) and in his treatise on the sacrament of baptism (1519).

Following an earlier visit in December of 1521, Luther came out of hiding from the Wartburg permanently in March 1522 to shepherd the reform movement that was beginning to progress at a volatile pace in his absence, even though many of those liturgical innovations introduced by Karlstadt were theoretically agreeable to him. These included serving the people communion in the form of bread and wine and translating the entire Mass into the vernacular (Luther published his own *German Mass* in 1526). Though not completed until the end of 1522 and published later in the summer of 1523, Luther had already begun some work on the translation of the Pentateuch while in the Wartburg. It was always his intention to translate the whole Bible into German, and, despite the associations of the Old Testament with the Law of the Mosaic Covenant and what Luther perceived was an essentially Mosaic preaching of the Law in the medieval doctrine of justification, Luther highly valued the books of the Old Testament as eminently valuable to the Church.[45]

In response to those Christians who began to antagonize the Old Testament on account of the Gospel, Luther defends its critical importance in his *Preface* as a servant to the New Testament. Among all the laws and judgments, the coming of Christ is prophesied in the Old

---

44. *LW* 35 (*Preface to the Epistle of St. Paul to the Romans*, 1546): 371–72; 377–78; *WA DB* 7: 12–13, 22–23.

45. See the introduction by E. Theodore Bachmann in *LW* 3: 228, 235 (n. 1). See also Brecht, *Shaping and Defining*, 54–5; Mullett, *Martin Luther*, 135–39.

Testament period. The New Testament is merely the declaration that the promised Christ has now come and that all that was formerly promised has now been historically fulfilled in Him. Whereas the Old Testament contains many useful laws and tells stories often of the keeping and breaking of those laws, the New Testament tells the story of Christ, of the grace of God, and of His gift of the power to truly fulfill His will. The distinction Luther makes between the books of the Old and New Testament canons is roughly parallel to his distinction between Law and Gospel in their proper senses, but this is not to say that the Gospel cannot be found in the Old Testament books. Luther describes the book of Genesis as "an exceedingly evangelical book" providing numerous examples of faith and unbelief. Exodus, Leviticus, and Numbers constitute the core of the Pentateuch with the most detailed expositions of the Law, which Luther defines as important for revealing human sins and weakness under the judgment of God apart from His grace. Luther lastly describes the book of Deuteronomy as a summary of the will of God in terms of faith and love, "for all God's laws come to that."[46]

Similarly, the New Testament is not without the teaching of laws and commandments. In fact, Luther states clearly that along with the offer of grace in the New Testament are teachings about laws and commandments, and he adds significantly that this is "for the control of the flesh — since in this life the spirit is not perfected and grace alone cannot rule." As earlier, Luther again exposes a guarded optimism and preserves the need for moral exhortation in the life of the Christian on account of the flesh and the fact that all Christians are still sinners. Nevertheless, Luther defines the "chief teaching" of the New Testament as "the proclamation of grace and peace through the forgiveness of sins in Christ" and the Old Testament as "really the teaching of laws, the showing up of sin, and the demanding of good."[47]

As harsh as Luther can be against preaching the Law as a meaningful way to righteousness, as if justification was achievable by works of compulsion, he argues that Moses' office of preaching works using compulsion is as necessary as it ever was for revealing sin to spiri-

---

46. *LW* 35 (*Preface to the Old Testament*, 1545): 237–38; *WA DB* 8: 12–15. The translation of the American Edition is based on the complete German Bible of 1545. The quotations I am using from this translation are identical, except with regard to minor changes in spelling, from the 1523 German Pentateuch.

47. *LW* 35 (*Preface to the Old Testament*, 1545): 235–37; *WA DB* 8: 12–13.

tual "blindness and hardened presumption." Even the ceremonial laws, though amoral by nature, were commanded by God and thus brought judgment upon Israel because of their disobedience to them. Unlike the ceremonial laws, the moral laws of the Ten Commandments essentially agree with the natural Law of creation written on every human heart. In this case, even before the Decalogue was ever written down, the breaking of these commandments constituted sin and wrongdoing. In Christ, the "law ceases," and this includes all the ceremonial laws of Israel as well as the whole natural-moral Law of the Ten Commandments. However, the cessation of the latter is not to be understood in this way: "in the sense that they are no longer to be kept or fulfilled, but in the sense that the office of Moses in them ceases; it no longer increases sin by the Ten Commandments and sin is no longer the sting of death." The distinction Luther makes here between the cessation of the Ten Commandments (Law) and the cessation of the "office of Moses in them" is critically important. The "office of Moses" is the terrifying of consciences, which increases belligerence against God leading to even greater condemnation. This "office" ceases only when Christ is grasped in the heart by faith. According to Luther, the "*telos*" of this office of the Law was even prophesied by Moses himself in Deuteronomy 18:15, which predicts that another prophet of God would arise. Luther observes that this cannot refer to the later prophets of the Old Testament, since all prophets even unto John the Baptist served the office of Moses by largely urging works and repentance under the Law in the fear of God. The distinguishing feature of this future "Prophet" would be the new emphasis in his message, which is not the teaching of laws or commandments, since "Moses has done that to perfection." Rather, the office particular to Christ is the preaching of grace and the fulfillment of the whole Law. Whereas the Mosaic Covenant was based on works and promised earthly blessings conditioned by obedience, the New Covenant is guaranteed entirely upon the work of the Messiah who is the fulfillment of all the promises of divine mercy, redemption, and eternal blessing. In this way, the office of Moses under the Old Covenant stands in dialectical relationship to the ministry of the Messianic Prophet of the New Testament.[48]

Out of a concern for reforming the Christian piety of the German people, and probably in response to the religious commotion developing in Wittenberg inspired in part by his own protests, Luther published

---

48. *LW* 35 (*Preface to the Old Testament*, 1545): 241–46; *WA DB* 8: 22–27.

his *Personal Prayer Book* in 1522. This was an adaptation of the medieval form of the prayer book already in use by the fifteenth century but now transformed by Luther's evangelical theology. The prayer book predates Luther's more well-known catechisms created seven years later and is actually based on an even earlier work entitled *A Short Form of the Ten Commandments, the Creed, and the Lord's Prayer* (1520). The prayer book went through many editions and printings and was eventually replaced in popularity by his *Small Catechism* in 1529.[49]

Luther purposefully reverses the traditional order of the prayer book. Instead of beginning with the Hail Mary prayer and proceeding from the Lord's Prayer to the Creed and then the Ten Commandments, Luther begins with the Decalogue followed by the Creed and the Lord's Prayer. Luther did include the Hail Mary prayer at the end, but modified it with warnings against false veneration of the Virgin. This ordering reflects his own basic understanding that the Law (Ten Commandments) leads sinners to the refuge and promises of the Creed and to the supplications of the Lord's Prayer. The devotional purpose of the *Prayer Book* itself indicates that Luther perceived Christians to have need of the Law for the daily renewal of repentance, faith in the assurance of forgiveness, and the receiving of power for good works and the mortification of sins. In the foreword of the prayer book, Luther identifies these three articles as "the essentials of the entire Bible." The Ten Commandments reveal the sins of the human heart, the Creed shows people where they can find forgiveness and strength to keep the commandments, and the Lord's Prayer is a petition to God for help to increase in holy devotion to the God who promises all things to them who keep His ways.[50]

Luther prioritizes the two tables of the Decalogue much as he did in his earlier *A Treatise on Good Works* (1520). He asserts that the moral Law of the Decalogue is in fundamental agreement with reason and the natural Law of the created order and elaborates on what real obedience or disobedience to the commandments looks like in the context of daily life in the human community. For example, fraudulent business transactions, greed and lust for money, and refusing to pay off personal debt or loans are all ways of breaking the prohibition not to steal from

---

49. The English translation in the American Edition is made from the third German edition of 1522, which includes also a selection of Psalms and a translation of Titus. See the introduction by Martin H. Bertram in *LW* 43: 6–7, 13 (n. 11), 39 (n. 29).

50. *LW* 43 (*Personal Prayer Book*, 1522): 14; *WA* 10^2: 377.

others. In a statement anticipating his praise for the Law in his later catechisms, Luther exalts the Decalogue as containing: "in a brief and orderly manner all precepts needful for a person's life. Anyone wishing to keep them all will find enough good deeds to do to fill every hour of the day; he need not hunt for other things to do, running here and there to do things which are not commanded."[51] Luther again has in mind a rejection of fasts, prescribed prayers, pilgrimages, and monastic vows as good works commanded by God. The Decalogue, interpreted correctly is completely adequate for knowing and applying what God demands of His human creation in relation to Himself and to one another, and this is true for Christians who are still sinners. However, at the same time, if it were not for the promises of the Creed and the supplications provided in the Lord's Prayer, the Decalogue standing by itself is only a voice of condemnation and despair for all who rightly understand that it is not fulfilled without love and the complete willingness of the heart.

The Old Testament continued to preoccupy Luther's attention in the mid-1520s, especially in the light of "radicals" who either considered the Old Testament irrelevant to Christians or who sought to re-implement the formal law code of ancient Israel. In 1523, Luther began lecturing on the book of Deuteronomy to a small gathering made up of Augustinian friars, university colleagues, and even his future pastor Johann Bügenhagen (1485–1558). Luther made transcripts of his own personal lecture notes and edited a complete edition in 1525.[52] Even prior to the outbreak of the antinomian controversy in 1527–1528, Luther already alludes to a certain group of men who want to reject Moses, the Law, and the Old Testament altogether, an extreme conclusion probably drawn from his own emphasis on faith and the New Testament Gospel. Luther instead openly praises the books of the Old Testament as containing rich stories of faith and godliness and wise and useful, though not binding, civil and ceremonial laws.

In the lectures, Luther identifies the inability of the office of Moses by itself to lead to righteousness and the kingdom of salvation, and, in keeping with his understanding that all Scripture points to Christ, that

---

51. *LW* 43 (*Personal Prayer Book*, 1522): 14–24; *WA* 10^2: 388.

52. George Rörer (1492–1557) was an amanuensis of many of Luther's lectures and sermons in Wittenberg. His transcript of the lectures on Deuteronomy 1–7 is extant, while Bugenhagen only provides notes on chapters 1–4. See the introduction by Jaroslav Pelikan and Richard R. Caemmerrer in *LW* 9: ix–x.

Moses' exclusion from the Promised Land of Canaan foreshadows this. The Law only has the power to take people as far as the wilderness of Moab, represented by death. Joshua, however, succeeded Moses and led Israel into the Promised Land, but even Canaan was only a temporal and conditional promise to Israel for obedience under the Mosaic Covenant. The New "Testament," which Luther is careful to distinguish from the Old "Covenant" on account of its temporality and conditionality on the basis of works, was fulfilled by Christ in time but promised long even before the coming of Moses, stretching back before time itself. Thus, Christ does not usher His people into a physical land like Joshua, the temporal enjoyment of which was based on conditional promises, but into a spiritual and eternal inheritance through faith in unconditional promises.[53]

Yet, despite the weakness of the Law on account of sin to lead sinners to eternal salvation, it still remains the proper place for His human creation to look for knowing how God desires to be worshipped and obeyed. Apart from the Word of God, sinful people create their own idolatrous works, such as prayers and fasts, thinking that God is pleased by them: "The people of God should seek wisdom nowhere or know anything except from the Law of its God, where it will find richly and happily how it should conduct itself toward God and man in prosperity and adversity, peace and war. Wisdom gained anywhere else is nothing but stupidity before God."[54] "People of God" comes from the Old Testament reference to Israel and refers more generally to the whole social body of the Church for whom the Decalogue properly defines the created structures of human community under God. As Luther has stated repeatedly, however, only those truly justified by faith among the people of God are able to desire the keeping of God's laws freely from the heart.

As made clear in earlier writings, the First Commandment of the Decalogue is not merely a physical law prohibiting the worship of God in the form of an image, but it is the principal and chief commandment to believe and trust in the One true God above all else with complete faith and integrity. It is the "measure and yardstick of all others, to

---

53. *LW* 9 (*Lectures on Deuteronomy*, 1525): 42–43, 63; *WA* 14: 578–80, 602–3. For the argument that Luther preferred "testament" over "covenant," see Lillback, *Binding of God*, 58–67; Hagan, "The Testament of a Worm," 15–16.

54. *LW* 9 (*Lectures on Deuteronomy*, 1525): 53, 56–57; *WA* 14: 587–88, 590–91.

which they are to yield and give obedience." Moses himself impressed the importance of the First Commandment throughout the book of Deuteronomy, which shows that he himself understood how all the other commandments derive their value from the faith and worship of the one true God.[55]

Luther then speaks of the importance of rightly dividing the Word of God by Law and Gospel. While the Gospel sets the conscience free and at peace with God by eliminating the need for all works and exalting the utter passiveness of faith in the righteousness reckoned in Christ alone, Luther explicitly warns: "see to it that you do not free the flesh through the Gospel, but hold it down and mortify it through the Law and works, just as it is proper for the old man and body of sin to be destroyed." The Gospel rightly preached, understood, and believed does not excuse Christians from moral action in the world or from the responsibility to actively resist the sins of the flesh. On the contrary, the truth of the Gospel creates the right motivation for these in the freedom and sincerity of the heart and excludes all pretense of seeking to earn the favor of God by them. For Luther, teaching Law and Gospel as it pertains to the "inner and outer man" (*interiorem et exteriorem*) is to rightly "part the hoof," an allegorical reference to the dietary laws in Deuteronomy 14. The Gospel is the promise of justification and peace before God in Christ to those who repent and receive the promise with the passiveness of faith, whereas the Law applies to the response of the Christian in obedient action in the world for others: "Therefore let the heart become free through the word of grace, and let the body become a servant through the law of love; then the hoof will be properly parted."[56] This careful balancing of the right preaching of Law and Gospel is essential for avoiding the twin extremes of works-righteousness and moral licentiousness.

Luther also allegorizes the emancipation of household slaves in the Old Covenant "Year of Jubilee" (Deuteronomy 15:16), which symbolizes the sinner being set free from slavery to sin under the Law by the Gospel. While the sinner labors to please the Master under the Law as a slave, he or she finds its demands impossible and harsh. Consequently, hatred toward the Law and the Master swells leading to an increase of sin and judgment. However, a freed slave in ancient times might choose to have

---

55. *LW* 9 (*Lectures on Deuteronomy*, 1525): 68–70, 109; *WA* 14: 608–12, 638.
56. *LW* 9 (*Lectures on Deuteronomy*, 1525): 136; *WA* 14: 650.

his ear pierced with an awl, revealing his intention to freely remain in the service of his beloved master: "the man now free in spirit nevertheless subjects his flesh the more strongly to the Law and by means of the iron and rigid Law forces it to obedience, as Paul says: 'I pummel my body and subdue it' (1 Corinthians 9:27). Thus he remains a slave and a freeman at the same time."[57] While being set totally free from all obligation to the Law with regard to earning the favor of the Master, the Christian remains intentionally subject to that very same Law in grateful obedience to the Master and in opposition to the contrary desires of the flesh.

Luther again contrasts the prophetic ministries of Moses and Christ, and he repeats his insistence that both offices must be preserved throughout time. Although not equal in respect to the outcome of their ministry, the work of the Mosaic Law to humble and the work of the Gospel of Christ to comfort both bear the stamp of divine authority. Both are necessary to bring about salvation, for without death by the Law there can be no new life through the Gospel.[58]

Luther adamantly rejects those who only trouble consciences by adding more and more works, ceremonies, and laws as means for achieving righteousness. This conflicts with the Gospel being the end and fulfillment of the office of Moses. Luther makes another important distinction between the Mosaic ministry of the Law and the commandments of the New Testament directed to the justified Christian. Luther scholars such as Paul Althaus have thus distinguished the "Law" (*Gesetz*) from an evangelical "command" (*Gebot*), and Wilfried Joest prefers to speak of evangelical exhortations and moral implicatives of the Gospel in Luther rather than a "third use of the Law."[59] In the lectures, Luther does differentiate the form of the "commandments" of the New Testament from the form of the "Law" in its Mosaic ministry under the Old Covenant. Yet, even as Althaus admits, for Luther these evangelical exhortations constitute "Law" in accordance with Luther's more general definition.[60] The distinction that Althaus and Joest make, then, is fair to Luther so long as it is clear that he never thought the moral teachings of

---

57. *LW* 9 (*Lectures on Deuteronomy*, 1525): 150; *WA* 14: 659–60.
58. *LW* 9 (*Lectures on Deuteronomy*, 1525): 176–78; *WA* 14: 675–77.
59. Althaus, *Divine Command*, 2, 6–7, 12–21.
Joest, *Gesetz und Freiheit*, 14–16, 195.
60. See Althaus, *Theology of Martin Luther*, 271 (see also n. 23).

Christ and the apostles to be an entirely new ethic different in substance from that of the Ten Commandments as taught by Moses. Luther has already praised the Decalogue in his writings of the early 1520s as the clearest expression of the divine will for the created human community. The proper distinction to be made is in emphasizing the distinct audience, aims, and rhetorical, or pedagogical, form of the preaching of the Law under the Mosaic Covenant compared with the commandments of the New Testament taught by Christ to His disciples. The latter are uniquely given in light of the coming of Christ and His fulfillment of all righteousness for the forgiveness of sins and eternal life, which enables the believer to desire the keeping of them from the heart. The Law in its Mosaic office only compels works by force and, acting as an accuser and a mirror of sin, always precedes faith by driving the conscience to seek refuge in the mercy of God, but here Luther speaks of another type of moral exhortation given specifically in light of the Gospel with its own distinct purpose for the life of the Christian.

Luther explicitly states that the commandments in the New Testament are directed toward the justified Christian, though he specifies that this is obviously not on account of their faith that "hastens of its own accord," but "to kill the remnants of the old man in the flesh, which is not yet justified."[61] Elsewhere in the lectures, Luther speaks again of Law and Gospel in the Christian life with reference to active and passive righteousness: "The spirit and freedom should be within, in the heart, but the Law and the yoke of deeds should be outside, in the body, so that there is bondage without liberty for the flesh, liberty without bondage for the spirit, but not bondage and liberty on both sides."[62] Again, this language is not to be understood dualistically, as if the Gospel establishes an enmity between the soul and body to be overcome in the life of the Christian. In fact, Luther is describing the ideal Christian life by saying that, though through faith in the Gospel the heart is no longer in bondage to the Law for righteousness *coram Deo* and is at peace, a heart of faith nevertheless serves the Law in the body in the doing of good works *coram mundo* on behalf of others in love and in resistance to the opposing desires of the flesh. The commandments of Christ and the apostles, then, uniquely serve the justified Christian not as a cage to restrain a wicked heart lacking the Spirit nor as an accuser of the

61. *LW* 9 (*Lectures on Deuteronomy*, 1525): 178–79; *WA* 14: 677–78.
62. *LW* 9 (*Lectures on Deuteronomy*, 1525): 225; *WA* 14: 705.

conscience of the eternal wrath and judgment of God leading to repentance and faith in His mercy for justification (later identified as the first and second "use of the Law"), but to exhort the justified Christian on the very basis of grace, though on account of sin and the flesh, to active resistance against sinful promptings and desires and to diligent moral action for others in the world. Thus, the dialectic of Law and Gospel has a unique application in the life of the Christian as *"simul justus et peccator,"* which corresponds to complete freedom from the Law and works in the conscience before God through the Gospel and, account of that very Gospel, slavery and duty to the Law and works in resisting sinful desires and in acting morally on behalf of others in the world. Whereas the not justified, unregenerate person is completely "old man" and entirely under the force, dominion, and condemnation of the Law, the Christian with regard to faith in the Gospel is both a "new man" totally free from any obligation to the Law before God yet delighting in His Law and also an "old man" who needs to be mortified daily through the Law and works.

The particular relationship of Old Testament laws to Christian freedom became a practical issue in Wittenberg in the early 1520s. Thomas Müntzer had begun his ministry in Zwickau in 1520 at the recommendation of Luther, and within a year three self-proclaimed prophets from this very town found their way to Wittenberg claiming private revelation and rejecting infant baptism. Beginning in 1522, Luther began to combat the teachings of Müntzer and the Zwickau Prophets, dubbed as "enthusiasts" (*Schwärmer*). By 1523, it was becoming clear to Luther that Müntzer and others were promoting a militant revolution that far exceeded his own zeal for reform, which he interpreted as nothing less than the work of the Devil. In 1524, John Frederick, the future Elector of Saxony in 1532 and son of Duke John, brother to Frederick the Wise and Elector in 1525, consulted with Luther on the specific question of the continuing validity of the Mosaic Law, which was being used by enthusiasts like Müntzer to endorse a violent, apocalyptic purge of idolatry and all idolaters. In July 1524, Müntzer preached before Duke John and John Frederick in Allstedt Castle, the town of his recent ministry activities, declaring his readiness to lead these rulers in the purging of Christendom with the civil use of the sword.[63] Luther did not agree with

---

63. For the background, see Brecht, *Shaping and Defining*, 146–57. See also Lindberg, *European Reformations*, 135–68.

Müntzer's militant approach to implementing reform and believed that the Spirit works perfectly well through the pure preaching of the Word. In fact, Luther perceived that it was precisely for such social revolutionaries as Müntzer that God instituted governments. Thus, Luther allowed for some slowness to the pace of reform and acknowledged a need for patience toward doctrinal pluralism and ignorance.[64] Müntzer's rejection by the Saxon dukes led him, in turn, to support the economic grievances of the peasants in revolting against the established authorities until his capture and death in 1525.

Luther also had to contend with his former Wittenberg colleague Andreas Karlstadt (c.1480–1541) who was hastily introducing liturgical changes in Wittenberg in 1521–22 and even challenging the practice of infant baptism and the doctrine of the Real Presence of Christ in the Eucharist. Luther, in response to a request from church leaders such as Martin Bucer (1491–1551) in Strassbourg, wrote a letter to expose the theological errors of Karlstadt, who had visited Strassbourg after being expelled from Electoral Saxony in 1524.[65] In an earlier sermon preached in Wittenberg in 1522, Karlstadt had called for the immediate abolition of images in churches, and this led to some disorderly removal and destruction by zealous parishioners.[66] In his "Letter to the Princes of Saxony Concerning the Rebellious Spirit" (1524), Luther stresses that ceasing from image worship is really an inward matter of the heart, and though he did not wholly disapprove of the orderly and timely removal of images linked with idolatrous abuses, he interprets Karlstadt's promotion of urgent "iconoclasm" as a wrongful application of Old Testament law and a new form of legalism and works-righteousness. Luther contends in the letter that the Old Testament injunction to smash images was given to Israel in the context of the Mosaic Covenant involving the promise of Canaan, whereas the Christian in the New Testament combats idolatry through the proclamation of the Word.[67] Similarly, in his "Letter to the Christians at Strasbourg" (1524), Luther rejects Karlstadt's preaching as ensnaring consciences by imposing works un-

---

64. Brecht, *Shaping and Defining*, 152.

65. *LW* 40 ("Letter to the Christians at Strassbourg in Opposition to the Fanatic Spirit," 1524): 61; WA 15: 391–97; Brecht, *Shaping and Defining*, 162–63.

66. Brecht, *Shaping and Defining*, 39–40, 162–66.

67. *LW* 40 ("Letter to the Princes of Saxony Concerning the Rebellious Spirit," 1524): 58–59; WA 15: 219–21.

der the guise of righteousness, works which are not even commanded for New Testament Christians anyway: "For we know that no work can make a Christian, and that such external matters as the use of images and keeping of the Sabbath, are, in the New Testament, as optional as all other ceremonies enjoined by the law."[68]

Thus, in the early to middle part of the 1520s, Luther found it necessary to explain how the freedom of the Christian relates to law, government, and the social order. This was especially true during the years of the so-called "Peasants Revolt" (1524–1526), the culmination of a century of increasing economic exploitation of the lower classes by landowning nobility. Though Luther early on sympathized with the oppressive plight of the peasants and even upheld the legitimacy of some of their grievances, especially their desire to appoint their own local pastors, in his *Against the Robbing and Murdering Hordes of Peasants* (1525) princes are encouraged to suppress the revolt as a threat to the social order. Luther was angered that the Word of God, the freedom of the Gospel, and even his own words were being used to call for a social revolution and to justify the use of violence and aggressive militant action in rebellion against the established government. Luther did later criticize the princes' bloodthirsty suppression of the peasant uprising in his subsequent "An Open Letter on the Harsh Book Against the Peasants" (1525), but he continued to defend his earlier statements that aggressive popular insurrection against the government must be repressed for the sake of order no matter what the grievances.[69]

Even before the uprisings, in the spring of 1522 Luther had preached on the obligation to government in a series of sermons on the New Testament book of 1 Peter later printed along with sermons on 2 Peter and Jude in 1523.[70] Luther stresses throughout these sermons the importance of the Old Testament as a foreshadowing of the Gospel. On the other hand, against those who sought to justify iconoclastic violence on the basis of Mosaic laws against idolatry, Luther responds by distinguishing between God's peculiar government of the Jews under the Old Covenant with His present government of Christians. Whereas under

---

68. *LW* 40 ("Letter to the Christians at Strasbourg in Opposition to the Fanatic Spirit," 1524): 67–69; *WA* 15: 395.

69. See the introduction by Robert C. Schultz in *LW* 46: 47–48, 61; Mullett, *Martin Luther*, 159–70.

70. See the introduction by Jaroslav Pelikan in *LW* 30: ix–xi.

the Old Covenant God governed the moral life of the Jews by enforcing many external civil and ceremonial laws, with the coming of Christ He rules over the hearts of Christians by the Spirit through His Word. The particular civil and ceremonial laws of the Old Covenant have all ceased as commandments in Christ, although the natural-moral Law of love was, is, and always will remain in effect for all people regardless of nationality. Nevertheless, nations require civil governments and laws, for Luther acknowledges that not all are true Christians. For while those who live by faith through the Spirit require no civil law to compel them to live upright lives as members of society, those without the Spirit require the threat of the sword for the sake of preserving public peace and the temporal order: "God has instituted government for the sake of unbelievers." Christian believers, however, need no other government than the Word of God. If everyone were a Christian living in the spirit of faith in the Gospel, there would no longer be any need for government, for people would do good deeds without compulsion, restraint, or threat of punishment, serving one another as Christ has served them.[71]

Although Christians are indeed free from all obligation to the Law with regard to righteousness before God, whether ceremonial, civil, or moral laws, true Christians are obedient to the government in so far as its laws serve their interests in loving and respecting others. Jesus was the perfect example of one who was not in Himself subject to any earthly government, but out of love for others freely submitted thereunto in obedience to the Father for the salvation of humanity. As such, true Christians love one another whether any civil law existed or not, since laws exist to protect the welfare of people: "Therefore I do not want to be compelled to be subject to secular princes and lords; but I will be subject to them of my own accord, not because they command me but to render a service to my neighbor."[72] To be Christian is to acknowledge that the conscience is absolutely free of all laws for justification before God through faith in Christ, which Luther believed Karlstadt was endangering by zealously reimposing Old Testament laws against idolatry. At the same time, the Christian along with that freedom is to respect the laws of the civil government for the sake of human welfare and the public good, which Luther believed Müntzer and the peasant

---

71. *LW* 30 (*Sermons on the First Epistle of Peter*, 1522): 19–21; 75–76; *WA* 12: 275–77, 329–31.

72. *LW* 30 (*Sermons on the First Epistle of Peter*, 1522): 77–79; *WA* 12: 331–33.

uprisings in 1524–26 were endangering by revolt and the use of violence in zeal against moral and spiritual corruption. Thus, Luther states in 1525 against the peasants: "for there stands our Master, Christ, and subjects us, along with our bodies and property, to the emperor and the law of this world, when he says, 'Render to Caesar the things that are Caesar's'. . . For baptism does not make me free in body and property, but in soul . . ."[73]

Luther had made this point a few years earlier in the presence of Duke John in the fourth of a series of sermons delivered in October 1522 in response to the suppression of the German New Testament in Ducal Saxony by Duke George. This sermon, probably preached extemporaneously, was later published in the spring of 1523 as *Temporal Authority: To What Extent it Should Be Obeyed*.[74] According to Luther, Christians are citizens of the spiritual kingdom of God by faith and are not subject to the laws of the civil government in the same way as unbelievers who do not possess the Spirit. Instead, being led by the Spirit, Christian believers do even above and beyond what the law requires since the government can only rule over outward actions. In this way, true Christians are obedient to the civil law on account of the fact that they have learned to love their neighbor from the heart: "for this reason it is impossible that the temporal sword should find any work to do among [true] Christians, since they do of their own accord much more than all laws and teachings demand." According to 1 Timothy 1:9, it is the unrighteous who require the civil law and its punishments for the sake of keeping the public peace. A true Christian, however, needs to be told to do good unto others as much as a good tree needs to be commanded to bear good fruit. The context of this statement deals particularly with the compulsion of civil law by the rule of government in particular and cannot imply that the Decalogue or New Testament commandments are without purpose in exhorting the Christian to a life of good works on account of the flesh. In this sermon, Luther all but formally defines what he would later identify as the two-fold "*usus legis*," and he even refers his audience back to the *Wartburg Postil*. Aside from the use of the Law characterized in 1 Timothy 1:9, what Luther later refers to formally as the "civil use" of the Law and the work of God

---

73. *LW* 46 (*Against the Robbing and Murdering Hordes*, 1525): 51; *WA* 18: 358–59.

74. For the background, see the introduction by Walther I. Brandt in *LW* 45: 78–79. See also Brecht, *Shaping and Defining*, 117.

in restraining the wicked for the sake of upholding social order within the human community, Luther identifies in Paul another function of the Law as an accuser of sin and a judge of the conscience under the wrath of God. Luther then interestingly states that Christ does a similar thing, meaning he describes a function of the Law, which is the depiction in His Sermon on the Mount of the life of a Christian.[75] In this sense, the Law has a descriptive role in outlining the true Christian life lived through faith in the Spirit. Yet Luther was not overly confident that any Christian lives so perfectly ruled by the Spirit in the absolute power of faith and he already acknowledged that the New Testament commandments are specifically directed to the justified for the sake of controlling the flesh. Thus, whenever Luther speaks of the Christian not needing to be told to do good works he is thinking in terms of the Christian only with regard to his or her faith, which indeed has no need of ethical instructions, laws, or commandments.

In *Temporal Authority*, Luther also makes the important distinction between the "two governments" (*zwei Regiment*) established by God, one which is "spiritual" ruled by the Holy Spirit in the hearts of true Christians, and one that is "temporal," ruling the outward behavior of the unregenerate to preserve a semblance of social order in the world. Luther reiterates that there would be no need for temporal government if the world were made up of "real Christians," but Luther admits these "are few and far between," warning that the government must not be abolished until the world is filled up with true Christians.[76] While there is such a temporal government, Christians are among those who submit to it, but they do so freely for the sake and welfare of others whom they love through the power of the Gospel. Christian submission to the government includes paying taxes and doing whatever else is necessary in supporting the work of the common good. Though a Christian must never take up the sword in personal vengeance and retribution, he or she supports the cause of the government in punishing criminals for the sake of the protection and welfare of others. In this way, Luther could even encourage Christians to fill vacant positions as "hangmen, constables, judges, or princes" in so far as these vocations

---

75. *LW* 45 (*Temporal Authority: To What Extent it Should Be Obeyed*, 1523): 88–90; *WA* 11: 250.

76. *LW* 45 (*Temporal Authority: To What Extent it Should Be Obeyed*, 1523): 91; *WA* 11: 251–52.

were established to protect the people. In fact, Luther states that "For the sword and authority, as a particular service of God, belong more appropriately to Christians than to any other men on earth."[77] With regard to personal affliction, every Christian in obedience to the Sermon on the Mount must bear suffering as his or her own cross even as Christ tolerated personal injustices without retaliation.[78] In this way, the Old Testament concepts of holy war and capital punishment for criminal offenses are completely agreeable to Christians, not on account of any perpetual binding authority of the Old Covenant office of Moses, but in so far as they serve to protect the life and property of others. In fact, every civil and ceremonial law of the Old Testament would be worth keeping if it could be proven that they indeed serve the welfare of others in accordance with the natural law of love written in creation: "For everyone is under obligation to do what is for his neighbor's good, be it Old Testament or New, Jewish or Gentile . . . For love pervades all and transcends all; it considers only what is necessary and beneficial to others, and does not ask whether it is old or new."[79]

Temporal government, then, has every right and power to make laws that protect human life and property, but it does not possess any authority to prohibit the work of the Gospel or to contradict the Word of God. Luther, of course, has in mind in this published sermon the evangelical-minded Christians living under the repressive Catholic rule of Duke George. On the other hand, it is well known that Luther himself earlier in 1520 had appealed to the German nobility as fellow baptized Christians of the one body of Christ, sharing the same "spiritual estate" with those in the pastoral offices, to contribute through the means of their vocation to the much needed work of reforming the Church: "Inasmuch as the temporal power has become a member of the Christian body it is a spiritual estate, even though its work is physical. Therefore, its work should extend without hindrance to all the members of the whole body to punish and use force whenever guilt deserves

---

77. *LW* 45 (*Temporal Authority: To What Extent it Should Be Obeyed*, 1523): 95, 100; *WA* 11: 254–55, 258.

78. *LW* 45 (*Temporal Authority: To What Extent it Should Be Obeyed*, 1523): 101–3; *WA* 11: 259–60.

79. *LW* 45 (*Temporal Authority: To What Extent it Should Be Obeyed*, 1523): 97–98; *WA* 11: 256.

or necessity demands, without regard to whether the culprit is pope, bishop, or priest."[80]

In the wake of peaking social unrest later in 1524–1525 and with the religious freedoms granted legally to the German estates by the First Diet of Speyer (1526), princes, nobles, and city councils indeed became much more proactively involved in the establishment of religious order in favor of evangelical reforms in their territories and cities. Luther made frequent appeals to the Elector of Saxony in the second half of the 1520s to support the work of reform in the parishes.[81] Yet it was never his intent either in 1520 or in the latter half of the 1520s to capitulate complete spiritual authority over the Church and its faith and doctrine to the State. In his *Address to the Christian Nobility*, it was his desire to breakdown the absolutism of a corrupt ecclesiastical hierarchy by appealing to lay Christians in positions of temporal authority and with regard to the particular privileges and responsibilities they possessed as heads of state. Furthermore, not one of the reforming theses in *To the Christian Nobility of the German Nation* deals explicitly or significantly with the innovative doctrinal insights that Luther had developed by 1520 but rather, more subtly perhaps, with issues involving the interference of the Roman Curia (Church) in the autonomies of the German nation (State). This was a point which resonated quite profoundly with an already burgeoning spirit of nationalism among the German nobility, including the sympathy of imperial knights Ulrich von Hutten (1488–1523) and Franz von Sickingen (1481–1523). The other theses are largely concerned with curtailing religious abuses tied to the surplus of new religious orders, endowments for private Masses on behalf of the dead, and new pilgrimage destinations, of which not even humanist *intelligentsia* would disapprove.[82]

Luther, then, obviously had no trouble in calling upon heads of state to be involved in some capacity with reforming the Church in their realms, but according to *Temporal Authority* whenever earthly governments establish laws commanding Christians to believe or to

80. LW 44 (*To the Christian Nobility of the German Nation Concerning the Reform of the Christian Estate*, 1520): 127–31; WA 6: 408–10. For the common priesthood of the believer and the worth of all vocations before God in the theology of Luther, see also Wingren, *Luther on Vocation*.

81. See Brecht, *Shaping and Defining*, 259–73; Mullett, *Martin Luther*, 169–70; Dixon, *Reformation in Germany*, 155–57.

82. See Mullett, *Martin Luther*, 102, 107–9.

do things contrary to the Word of God or harmful to faith and the Gospel, they misuse their ordained power and must be disobeyed by Christians in allegiance to God, though without any use of force. The Fourth Commandment to honor earthly authority, then, may be broken in honor of the supremacy of the First Commandment to honor God in truth above all else. The temporal government also possesses no rightful power to enforce conversions or to punish dissent with capital punishment, but it can bring civil action against dissenters who nurture social unrest leading potentially toward physical harm against the general population.[83] Luther was of the mindset that magistrates possessed both the authority and the obligation to put down insurrection for the sake of upholding public peace and order, which includes religiously inspired movements of an aggressively or defensively militant nature.[84] However, in the 1530s, Luther does cautiously develop a tolerance for evangelical military resistance against the threat of war from Charles V on the basis of allowances made within imperial law itself for acts of self-defense against imperial tyranny and, ultimately, for the protection of the Gospel and the salvation of souls from the real enemy behind the call of the Emperor to war, the diabolical leadership of the Catholic Church.[85] Furthermore, his promotion in the early 1540s of an aggressive program of civil persecution of the Jewish religion shows the evolution in Luther's understanding of the role of the State in guarding and protecting true Christian religion.[86]

Luther's treatise *Against the Heavenly Prophets in the Matter of Images and Sacraments* (1525) was one of two other important works developing the themes of Law and Gospel in light of the volatile situation of the 1520s, particularly that of the legalism of Karlstadt and other "Schwärmer." In this treatise, Luther describes five core articles of the Christian faith, and the most fundamental are those that set the conscience free. The first article is the preaching of the Law for the revealing of sin. The second article that follows is the offering of

83. *LW* 45 (*Temporal Authority: To What Extent it Should be Obeyed*, 1523): 105, 111–12; *WA* 11: 261–62, 266–67.

84. For example, see his *LW* 40 ("Letter to the Princes of Saxony Concerning the Rebellious Spirit," 1524): 49–59; *WA* 15: 210–21.

85. See Brecht, *Shaping and Defining*, 412, 415–17; Lindberg, *European Reformations*, 241; Mullett, *Martin Luther*, 207–9.

86. On Luther's intolerance toward the Jews in his later years, see Mullett, *Martin Luther*, 241–50.

grace in the Gospel. Beyond this there is the outgrowth of Christian obedience, which Luther defines as the mortification and subjection of the "old man" in the life of the Christian. Regarding the fourth article, good works are to flow freely towards the neighbor in imitation of the kindness of Christ. Luther describes the fifth and final article of the Christian faith as proclaiming the Law for the "crude and unbelieving" who need the discipline of the Law "in the manner in which we control wild animals with chains and pens," which is necessary for the preservation of common peace.[87] In the first and fifth articles, the substance of the later two-fold "*usus legis*" is plainly evident, and the third and fourth articles on mortification of sin and obedience in service to others imply a "third use" for the Law in the life of the Christian.

The fundamental error of Karlstadt that is the backdrop for this particular treatise is his urging of congregations in the 1520s to cease using images and other ceremonial practices associated with the Mass, such as kneeling before the host, elevating it, and calling it a "sacrament." In the opinion of Luther, Karlstadt is making such obedience necessary to being a true Christian. Luther interprets this as dangerously similar to papal teaching and another threat to the freedom of the Gospel. Whereas the papacy establishes its own good works not commanded by God, Karlstadt establishes his own prohibitions not forbidden by God. Both the papacy and Karlstadt are more concerned about adding or subtracting external matters than about the attitude of the heart changed by the Gospel. With regard to the traditional use of liturgical images and other ceremonial practices, Luther considers these to be matters of congregational preference, the use of which is neither inherently detrimental to the chief articles of salvation nor in clear violation to any commandment or prohibition in Scripture. Certainly, Luther recognizes that images can be abused and become objects of idolatry, but he argues that this is fundamentally a problem of the heart that requires the proper education of the Word rather than a problem with the external object in itself. A person is not any more a sinner or any less a Christian when using images in an appropriate way. Thus, as it is not necessary for Christians to keep the commandments invented by the papacy, Luther argues that is it not necessary for Christians to follow the prohibitions imposed by Karlstadt: "Dear friend, do no lightly regard this prohibition of what God has not forbidden, or the violation

---

87. *LW* 40 (*Against the Heavenly Prophets*, 1525): 81–84; *WA* 18: 63–67.

of Christian freedom which Christ purchased for us with his blood, or the burdening of conscience with sins that do not exist."⁸⁸

Luther rejected the use of the Old Covenant Mosaic Law to justify the necessary removal of images. Luther states again that the commandment to destroy idolatrous images was given only to the Jews with regard to the Promised Land in the context of a national covenant. Furthermore, Luther argues that the First Commandment of the Decalogue and its prohibition against idolatry is really aimed at the worship of God in an image and not the making of images for other purposes, even as the Israelites themselves were told to do on occasions. Thus, Luther did not object to looking upon an image of a saint or even a crucifix if done as a remembrance. Nevertheless, he admits that his purpose for writing the treatise is not to urge the use of images, and Luther recognizes the occurrence of abuses, even supporting the timely removal of those images more blatantly idolatrous or associated with pilgrimages. Yet, this is to be done in an orderly manner through appeals by the people to the local magistrates.⁸⁹

Luther challenges Karlstadt to prove on the basis of the New Testament that it is necessary for Gentile Christians to abolish the use of images. If Karlstadt is bent on urging one Old Covenant law upon Christians, so Luther argues, then he must urge the whole Mosaic Law, which also includes the rite of circumcision. The ceremonial, judicial, and moral laws of the Decalogue cannot be divided in so far as they constitute one body of Mosaic legislation. In fact, Luther argues that the prohibition against worshipping images and the commandment concerning the strict keeping of the Saturday Sabbath in the Ten Commandments should actually be considered ceremonial, rather than moral, laws.⁹⁰

Luther refers to the entire Mosaic Law as the "*Sachenspiegel*" of the Jews, whereas the natural-moral core of the Decalogue cuts across all historical, cultural, and national boundaries.⁹¹ The Ten Commandments, then, continue in use precisely because "the natural laws were never so orderly and well written as by Moses." Therefore, with regard to their

---

88. *LW* 40 (*Against the Heavenly Prophets*, 1525): 128–30; 151–52; *WA* 18: 110–13, 141–42. See also Brecht, *Shaping and Defining*, 251–52, 257–58.

89. *LW* 40 (*Against the Heavenly Prophets*, 1525): 87–92; *WA* 18: 69–76.

90. *LW* 40 (*Against the Heavenly Prophets*, 1525): 92–94; *WA* 18: 76–77.

91. *LW* 40 (*Against the Heavenly Prophets*, 1525): 97–98; *WA* 18: 81–82.

precise form as recorded in Exodus 20, the Ten Commandments are not the obligation of the Christian under the terms of the New Testament. This is why Luther could reject the smashing of images and the strict keeping of the Saturday Sabbath on the seventh day as binding laws, which were commanded of the Jews only and not discernable in natural Law. With regard to the Sabbath, however, what is not necessary to keep is the precise form and day for which it was commanded, though Luther does argue that it is reasonable for people to set aside time to cease from labor for physical rest and, more importantly, to sit together under the teaching of the Word of God. However, one day is not any more holy than another, nor is any one day of the week the only lawful day. That Sunday should be maintained for the traditional gathering of public worship is for Luther a matter of historical continuity, common order, and not of binding law or divine commandment.[92] The issue of the Sabbath became a subject of real concern for Luther in the 1530s with the Sabbatarians in Moravia, a Christian sect that began observing the Saturday Sabbath as a result of local Jewish influence.[93]

Luther continued these same themes in a series preached on the book of Exodus from 1524 to 1527. One of these sermons was published independently in 1526 as a pamphlet entitled *How A Christian Should Regard Moses*. The very title of this work suggests its obvious importance for understanding Luther's theology of Law and Gospel, but it must be interpreted in the context of his debate with Karlstadt and others who sought to impose Old Testament Mosaic regulations on Christians.[94]

Luther reasserts that the giving of the Law at Sinai, including the tables of the Decalogue and all the ceremonial and judicial laws connected with it, were demanded only of the Jews. With this in mind, Luther states that "Moses has nothing to do with us. If I were to accept Moses in one commandment, I would have to accept the entire Moses." For Luther the whole Old Covenant legislation given by Moses composes a single body, and is incapable of division into three unrelated parts. To reject one part is to reject them all. Not even the Ten Commandments in the precise form as they were recorded for the Jews were intended for Gentiles. The Decalogue was given as it was to the nation that God

---

92. *LW* 40 (*Against the Heavenly Prophets*, 1525): 97–98; *WA* 18: 81–82.
93. Mullett, *Martin Luther*, 243–44.
94. See the introduction by E. Theodore Bachmann in *LW* 35: 158–59.

delivered from Egypt and with whom He had made a special covenant at Sinai with regard to the inheriting the land of Canaan. It was not Gentiles whom God rescued from Egypt, yet the Gentiles do have the natural Law written on their hearts, which in almost every way agrees with the Ten Commandments. Thus, on the one hand, Luther can say, "not one little period in Moses pertains to us," but at the very same time that "We will regard Moses as a teacher, but we will not regard him as our lawgiver—unless he agrees with both the New Testament and natural law."[95]

The Mosaic legislation was a national law code for the Jews just as the Germans have their own "*Sachenspiegel*." Luther states that the temporal governments of Europe could even learn a lesson or two from the judicial commandments of Moses, but they would do so in their own free choice and not because it was commanded of them under the divine authority of Moses. Moses must only be kept by other nations and times in so far as he agrees with natural Law. With regard to the life of Christians, and in place of the authority of Moses, "We have our own master, Christ, and he has set before us what we are to know, observe, do, and leave undone." Thus, Luther again acknowledges that Christ, while primarily coming to fulfill the Law as a righteous satisfaction for sins, also teaches good works to His disciples, which are nothing more than His interpretation of what the Decalogue really commands and how it is properly fulfilled. Luther speaks as he did in the early 1520s of the Decalogue as the finest expression of natural-moral Law and, in preaching on the Sermon on the Mount later in 1530–1532 in Wittenberg during the absence of Bugenhagen, that "no one, not even Christ Himself can improve upon it."[96] Yet, again, Luther warns that it is imprecise and even dangerous to simply equate the Law as it was given through Moses with the moral teachings of Christ to His disciples.[97] According to Luther's *Bondage of the Will*, published at the end of 1525 and written in reply to Erasmus' essentially moral and practical argument for the power of free-will to desire the good,[98] a significant error of the latter was in failing to distinguish the Mosaic ministry of the Law with its

---

95. *LW* 35 (*How A Christian Should Regard Moses*, 1525): 161–66; *WA* 16: 363–75.

96. *LW* 21 (*The Sermon on the Mount*, 1532): 68–70; *WA* 32: 356. See the introduction by Pelikan in *LW* 21: xx–xxi.

97. *LW* 35 (*How A Christian Should Regard Moses*, 1525): 166–74; *WA* 16: 375–93.

98. See the brief discussion in Mullett, *Martin Luther*, 170–78.

warnings of threats and promises of rewards from the ethical teachings of Jesus in the New Testament. These teachings are not the path of merit before God in imitation of the life of Christ but are spoken with love to His disciples that they might work with gratitude for the grace already promised fully in the Gospel. The former only troubles consciences with the burden of works and so leads to condemnation, whereas the latter exhort on the basis of fellowship with God through faith in the Gospel: "to stir up those already justified and have obtained mercy, so that they may be active in the fruits of the freely given righteousness and of the Spirit, and may exercise love by good works and bravely bear the cross and all other tribulations of the world."[99]

Luther makes this same distinction in his *Lectures on 1 John*, which were delivered from August to November of 1527 to the faculty and students remaining in Wittenberg after an outbreak of the plague.[100] Luther is especially careful to counter abuse of the Gospel and to attack false presumption by stressing good works as the sign and demonstration of real faith. Indeed, Luther even states that "the knowledge of Christ has been handed down to us in order that we may fulfill the commandments of God."[101]

Luther readily acknowledges the need for exhortation to good works in the life of Christians and warns against yielding smugly to the flesh. Luther even explains that to give in to the rule of sin, which is fundamentally to lose a heart of repentance, reveals that "Christ and the [spiritual] birth have been lost," for "if the works of the devil are in a person, Christ cannot be there." He encourages Christians to "retain the seed of the living God," which is the "Word of God," in order that they might be shielded from the complete control of sin and succumb to a carnal presumption of divine mercy.[102] Final acceptance into heavenly glory, at least from a temporal perspective, only follows a life of persevering repentance and faith that results in a life devoted to the mortification of sins and good works. While election to eternal life is the hidden and sovereign work of God in those whom He alone chooses,

---

99. *LW* 33 (*Bondage of the Will*, 1525): 150–51; *WA* 18: 693.

100. The American Edition translates the notes of Jacob Propst first published in 1708 and are preferred to the notes belonging to George Rörer. See the introduction by Jaroslav Pelikan in *LW* 30: ix–xi.

101. *LW* 30 (*Lectures on I John*, 1527): 238; *WA* 20: 641.

102. *LW* 30 (*Lectures on I John*, 1527): 273; *WA* 20: 706–7.

made abundantly clear by Luther in his *Bondage of the Will* (1525),[103] the pastoral responsibility of the preacher of the Word is to diligently warn Christians against hardness of heart and the deceitfulness of sin.

Luther recognizes that all Christians are beset with temptations, but reasserts that a faithful Christian always does "battle against himself." Although all Christians yield to sin at one time or another, the faithful quickly rise up again through repentance and faith to new obedience. While Luther claimed that the Devil would often trouble him about his own salvation so that he would call forth the memory of his baptism as assurance of the favor of God toward him promised by the Gospel, Luther also attacks those who place a false trust in their baptism so that they might sin and be disobedient without repentance. This is presumptuous of the Gospel and a false faith, for "[Christ] appeared in the flesh to take away sins, not to give license to sin." At the same time, acceptance before God and the assurance thereof never rests on the basis of works whatsoever, though these can be reassuring evidence that Christ has indeed made the person righteous through faith in the Gospel. Echoing comments made earlier in *The Freedom of A Christian*, Luther states that good works never make a person Christian, but they are evidence that one has been made a Christian already: "What is the source of this goodness? It does not come from the fruits; it comes from the root. It does not come from sanctification; it comes from regeneration."[104]

As made explicit in a sermon of the early 1520s,[105] Luther again describes good works as self-assurances of faith to the point of even strengthening it: "Faith is established by its practice, its use, and its fruit ... The consciousness of a life well spent is the assurance that we are keeping the faith, for it is through works that we learn that our faith is true." Good works are a reflection to the Christian of the presence of the Holy Spirit within and, by implication, a genuine faith in the Gospel. The good works Luther has in mind are, of course, the various ways in which love is shown to others. For the one who has true faith, the commandment to love one another from the heart is not burdensome,

---

103. See Althaus, *Theology of Martin Luther*, 274–86.

104. *LW* 30 (*Lectures on 1 John*, 1527): 238, 263–64, 269–74; *WA* 20: 641–42, 690–92, 699–708; See also Oberman, *Luther*, 105.

105. For example, see "A Sermon for the Second Sunday after Mary's Ascension. Preached at Wittenberg by Dr. Martin Luther, 1522," *Complete Sermons of Martin Luther*, 2.2: 296–97; *WA* 10^3: 278.

for Christ has loved sinners by bearing the burden and severity of the Law for them, forgives them, and by the Holy Spirit through faith in the Gospel frees them to love others in like manner.[106] Christ removed the severity and judgment of the Law in his obedience to death on the cross, eliminating it as a curse and a burden upon the conscience and allowing for genuine obedience to issue forth as the response of faith to the mercy of God. In his exposition of the fifth petition of the Lord's Prayer in the *Large Catechism* of 1529, Luther even speaks of the ability of Christians to forgive others, though not itself meriting the forgiveness of God, as a special sign sanctified by God to strengthen assurance in the promise of His forgiveness in the Gospel.[107]

The stress in 1 John upon love as the evidence of true faith in the Gospel does not mean, for Luther, that the Christian should be burdened in his or her conscience with a concern for good works: "it is the sum and substance of the Gospel that you should believe and hope." Luther encourages those whose consciences feel the weight of personal unworthiness before God and who are experiencing the harassment of the Devil in the Law to find peace in the promise of the Gospel and not in the enumeration of works. Although genuine faith is distinguished from false presumption by a hatred of sin and a zeal for good works, despair of personal salvation is never calmed by looking at works, but only by faith in the Gospel.[108]

Aside from the Law as an existential burden and means of driving the sinner to the Gospel, the Christian through faith in Christ now delights in that same Law in obedience to the will of God. This point is made by Luther in his *Lectures on Isaiah* (1527–1530) delivered between 1527 and 1530. The lectures were interrupted once by the plague and a second time by the Colloquy at Marburg called by Phillip of Hesse in 1529 to unite the German Lutheran and Swiss Reformed traditions in counteraction to the threat of imperial Catholic resurgence.[109] In the

---

106. *LW* 30 (*Lectures on 1 John*, 1527): 279, 298, 309; *WA* 20: 715–16, 749, 768–71; Althaus, *Theology of Martin Luther*, 245–50, 448–54; See also Beeke, *Quest for Full Assurance*, 23–24.

107. *LC*, Tappert, 433, Kolb and Wengert, 352–53; *BSLK*, 682–85.

108. *LW* 30 (*Lectures on 1 John*, 1527): 279–80, 308–9; *WA* 20: 715–16.

109. The American Edition translates the lecture notes of Anthony Lauterbach (1502–69), which were probably much closer to what Luther actually said in the lecture hall than his own *scholia* published in Wittenberg in 1532 and later in 1534. See the introduction by Jaroslav Pelikan in *LW* 16: ix–xi (Isaiah 1–39), and by Hilton C. Oswald in *LW* 17: ix–x (Isaiah 40–66).

lectures, Luther states again that "the Law is no longer outrageous in its dictates but an agreeable companion. The Law itself indeed is not changed, but we are." True Christian liberty is a freedom of the conscience from the judgment of the Law before God, but not freedom from the Law with regard to a life of moral action: "This is indeed a great knowledge, to know well the use of law, namely, for outward government, not for the conscience. This has been set free by Christ, if only we believed."[110] Similarly, in his *Lectures on 1 Timothy* given in Wittenberg in 1527–1528,[111] Luther states: "To the Christian the Law is most sacred. Because it is divine wisdom it is a very fine and sacred thing. The fact of the matter is this: but the wicked and the pious man have the Law. Both have a very good thing. But they disagree over its use. The former misuse a very sacred thing." The misuse Luther obviously has in mind is "when I assign to the Law more than it can accomplish. Good works are necessary and the Law must be kept, but the Law does not justify."[112] When a Christian, then, hears the commandments of Christ in the New Testament, he or she hears the voice of the Law but without its compulsion and the sting of its condemnation. This agrees with comments found later in his *Lectures on Galatians* (1531–1535), in which Luther clearly states that "there are commandments in the Gospel," which are "expositions of the Law and appendices to the Gospel."[113] Similarly, in preaching on the Sermon on the Mount in the early 1530s, Luther describes that "Christ here deliberately wanted to oppose all false teaching and to open up the true meaning of God's commandments," though Luther admits he does so in a more "friendly way."[114]

Therefore, when scholars such as Althaus and Joest differentiate between "commandments" or "evangelical exhortations" in the New Testament from the "Law" in the Mosaic sense of coercing obedience and revealing sins deserving judgment this can potentially mislead if it is not equally underscored how that the will of God remains essentially

110. *LW* 16 (*Lectures on Isaiah* [1–39], 1527–30): 99; *WA* 31 ^{2}: 69; *LW* 17 (*Lectures on Isaiah* [40–66], 1527–30): 207; *WA* 31 ^{2}: 421–22.

111. The lectures are extant in the transcripts of George Rörer who did not prepare his notes or edit them for publication. See the introduction by Hilton Oswald in *LW* 28: ix–xi.

112. *LW* 28 (*Lectures on 1 Timothy*, 1527–28): 231–32; *WA* 26: 14–15.

113. *LW* 26 (*Lectures on Galatians* [Chapters 1–4], 1535): 150; *WA* 40^1: 260.

114. *LW* 21 (*Sermon on the Mount*, 1532): 3–4, 10, 67–70; *WA* 32: 299–300, 305, 354–57.

one and the same. Lutheran scholar Eugene Klug goes even further in arguing that Althaus and Joest fundamentally succumb to the error of the antinomians in closely associating the commanding of good works with the Gospel rather than the Law. If Luther considers "Law" to be a valid descriptor for Jesus' commandment in the New Testament to love one another, so long as the particular audiences and rhetorical techniques of Moses and Christ are properly distinguished, and if the good works Jesus and the apostles teach are directed specifically to justified Christians, then identifying a "third use of the Law" in this sense is perfectly consistent with his theology. This also agrees with Luther's proper definition of the "Law" as always teaching what is to be done and left undone, whereas the proper ministry of the Gospel is to declare forgiveness and the promise of hope and grace in Jesus Christ, in whom also is given the power through faith to obey the Law from the heart.[115]

At the first Diet of Speyer in 1526, with Emperor Charles V distracted by Turkish aggression from the East and by war with a papal-French alliance in Italy, the enforcement of the Edict of Worms condemning Luther and his growing number of followers was temporarily suspended by Charles' brother and regent, Ferdinand I, pending a future settlement. This gave princes the right *de juro* to govern religion in their own kingdoms (*cuius regio, eius religio*). In 1529, this legal action was rescinded much to the objection of the "Protestants" in the second Diet of Speyer and then again after failing to secure permanent legal recognition from Charles at the Diet of Augsburg in 1530. Nevertheless, between 1526 and 1529 the evangelical movement was able to spread and consolidate with legal sanction in lands ruled by favorable princes, nobles, and city councils.[116] Even before the first Diet of Speyer, visitations of the Electoral Saxon parishes had been commissioned under Duke John and his son John Frederick, including a visit by Luther to Orlamünde in 1524 to counteract Karlstadt's introduction of more radical reforms and the overstepping of his position as acting archdeacon. Other visitations were made by Jacob Strauss to Eisenach and Nicholas Hausmann to Schneeberg in 1525 in order to promote evangelical preaching. Luther initially envisioned these visitations to focus on the administration of the salaries of parish ministers to support their work in educating the people, but it was also apparent that the

---

115. Klug, "The Third Use of the Law," in Preus, *Formula of Concord*, 201–2.
116. Lindberg, *European Reformations*, 234–40; Mullett, *Martin Luther*, 198–209.

parishes needed adequately trained evangelical preachers. In the wake of the first Diet of Speyer and the space it created for the establishment of evangelical reform in Electoral Saxony, "visitors" were appointed as executives to oversee and administrate the transition to an evangelical church order, including Luther's own nomination of Melancthon from the University of Wittenberg. Luther had prepared to write a catechism for the parishes as early as 1525,[117] and by 1529 his *Small Catechism* and *Large* (or *German*) *Catechism* were published to correct the deplorable doctrinal ignorance that was observed during the visitations of 1527–1528.[118]

One particular issue that became apparent during these visitations was the lack of emphasis on the teaching of the Decalogue as a means of urging repentance. This was the substance of the first antinomian controversy that erupted between Melancthon and Agricola in the late 1520s, and though Luther's formal dispute with Agricola actually occurred a decade later, he himself reviewed and published with his own preface Melancthon's *Instructions for the Visitors of Parish Pastors in Electoral Saxony* (1528). The aim of these particular instructions was to compensate for the inadequate theological education of the parish clergy.[119] Since the predominant theme of both the controversy and the instructions was the issue of Law and Gospel, and since Luther had some personal involvement in the revision of the *Visitation Articles* and their publication as the *Instructions for the Visitors*, it seems only appropriate to discuss them in context of Luther's understanding of Law and Gospel at the end of the turbulent 1520s.

Johann Agricola (1494–1566) was an early admirer of Luther and a student at the University of Wittenberg in 1515-16. He was later present as a secretary at Leipzig during Luther's debate with John Eck in 1519, and he was a witness to Luther's burning of the canon law and papal bull of excommunication outside the Wittenberg city walls in 1520. By 1524 he had become an influential teacher, preacher, and catechist in Wittenberg and was praised by Melancthon. The following year he returned to his hometown of Eisleben to pastor the parish of St. Nicolai,

---

117. Brecht, *Shaping and Defining*, 259–63, 273–74; Bornkamm, *Luther in Mid-Career*, 485–91.

118. *SC*, Tappert, 338; Kolb and Wengert, 347–48; *BSLK*, 501.

119. Brecht, *Shaping and Defining the Reformation*, 264–68; Bornkamm, *Luther in Mid-Career*, 497–98.

where he soon became the focal point of a major controversy related to the parish visitations in 1527–28. Ten years later he would return to Wittenberg only to become embroiled with Luther in a series of public theological disputations over Law and Gospel.[120]

The dispute originated with Agricola's objections to Melancthon's original *Visitation Articles*. Melancthon drafted this series of theological articles after a meeting in Torgau in 1527 and the unpublished manuscript found its way to Agricola in Eisleben. These articles were reworked by Luther and Bugenhagen in consultation with the visitors and again after a second conference at Torgau in November of 1527. The final form appeared with Luther's preface as the *Instructions for the Visitors* in March of 1528.[121] The published work certainly reveals a thoughtful treatment of the issues discussed at Torgau in November, but it is not certain to what extent Luther was personally involved in the editing of the final version.[122] Although the work is primarily ascribed to Melancthon, Luther was personally involved in its creation and development, and it was published with his full consent and with his contribution of a preface.

The articles express a concern that the forgiveness of sins is being preached openly in the churches but without urging the need for repentance or "the acknowledgment of sin."[123] Thus, the *Instructions* urge pastors to preach the "whole gospel," which is identified as the complete Word of God including both the preaching of repentance and faith together: "There neither is forgiveness of sins without repentance nor can forgiveness of sins be understood without repentance."[124] The *Instructions* state that "repentance and law belong to the common faith," and that it is necessary to first believe that God "threatens, commands, and frightens" before believing that He is a God who justifies by grace through faith in Christ. The former belongs to the realm of the Law, whereas the latter is the proper work of the Gospel.[125]

---

120. Joachim Rogge, "Innerlutherische Streitigkeiten," 188–89, 194–97; Kjeldgaard-Pederson, *Gesetz, Evangelium, und Busse*, 9–18.

121. See Wengert, *Law and Gospel*, 118; Bornkamm, *Luther in Mid-Career*, 493–97. See also the editorial comments of Conrad Bergendoff in *LW* 40: 265–67.

122. Bornkamm, *Luther in Mid-Career*, 497.

123. *LW* 40 (*Instructions for Visitors*, 1528): 276; *WA* 26: 203.

124. *LW* 40 (*Instructions for Visitors*, 1528): 274–75; *WA* 26: 202.

125. *LW* 40 (*Instructions for Visitors*, 1528): 40: 275; *WA* 26: 202.

The *Instructions* exhort pastors to teach the Ten Commandments, "for all good works are therein comprehended," and to warn of God's temporal punishment for failure to keep the Law. It was the responsibility of the pastors and teachers to encourage "repentance" or "contrition" (*Busse* or *Rew*) by preaching the Law, for true faith "cannot exist without earnest and true contrition and fear of God." On the one hand the despair of Saul and Judas was a failure to go from Law to Gospel, from contrition to faith, but on the other hand, "faith without contrition ... is presumption and carnal security."[126]

For Agricola, the Law was God's plan under the dispensation of the Old Covenant with Israel, but it was replaced with the Gospel because of its inherent inadequacies to bring about true obedience.[127] The *Instructions* agree that the laws of Moses are no longer binding, and that Christians should obey the laws that govern their own lands: "Thus each shall follow his own national law ... So, we are subject to all authority, not only Christian but Gentile." Even the strict keeping of the Saturday Sabbath is not a law for Christians, though what does persist is the need for the organized assembly of believers for the preaching of the Word. At the same time, since the Ten Commandments given under Moses are in perfect agreement with the natural Law and teach what are truly good works, they should be taught regularly "so that people be exhorted to fear God."[128]

For Agricola, the preaching of the Law under the dispensation of the Old Covenant used threats, demands, and warnings of God's wrath, but this only increased Israel's despair, rebellion, and condemnation. Repentance, faith, and love are sufficiently nurtured by the preaching of the sufferings of Christ in the Gospel alone. Repentance, then, comes as a result of faith and the knowledge of the "violation of the Son" (*violatio filii*) rather than the "violation of the Law" (*violatio legis*).[129] It is important to understand that Agricola never taught that Christians can go on sinning without restraint after faith, but, like Luther and Melancthon,

126. LW 40 (*Instructions for Visitors*, 1528): 276–77; 294–96; WA 26: 203–4; 217–19.

127. Rogge, "Innerlutherische Streitigkeiten," 190–92, 196–97; Osslund, "*Imputatio iustitiae Christi*," 76–78, 83; Wengert, *Law and Gospel*, 73, 129.

128. LW 40 (*Instructions for Visitors*, 1528): 279–87, 302–5, 308; WA 26: 206–11, 226–28, 230.

129. Rogge, "Innerlutherische Streitigkeiten," 190–92, 196–97; Osslund, "*Imputatio iustitiae Christi*," 76–78, 83; Wengert, *Law and Gospel*, 73, 129.

expected that good works would issue forth as the fruit of faith in the Gospel. Luther was probably misinformed when he once admonished Agricola for disparaging the importance of works, not aware that Agricola was speaking with reference to justification by faith before God.[130]

Indeed there is much in Agricola's thought that bears a strong resemblance to many of Luther's own opinions, including the inherent incapacity of the Mosaic ministry of the Law to produce the fruits of righteousness. Luther had also described the ministry of the New Covenant, properly speaking, as the preaching of the Gospel. Furthermore, Luther recognized that the narratives of the sufferings of Christ powerfully induce sorrow and contrition in sinners, but that this is alien to their proper work in declaring the forgiveness of sins. Luther was also never willing to go as far as Agricola in jettisoning the Mosaic ministry of the Law altogether from the present age of the Church, which is necessary to restrain the wicked and to draw people to Christ to receive forgiveness. The real difference between the two parties involves whether contrition is properly the work of the Law or the Gospel. For Luther and Melancthon, there is a contrition or sorrow for sin that necessarily precedes faith in the Gospel of forgiveness, and such contrition belongs to the preaching of the Law. For Agricola, true contrition shows that faith is there already and, in fact, is not even possible without such faith in the Gospel.

The *Instructions* published in 1528 reflect the compromise of sorts reached at the November conference at Torgau in 1527. It was accepted that repentance indeed follows faith, but the *Instructions* explicitly identify this faith as the "common faith" in God as a righteous punisher of evil to be distinguished from the faith that justifies in Christ.[131] Luther had earlier asserted that the battle between Melancthon and Agricola was really a "war of words." Wengert proposes that Luther was not minimizing the weight of the issue as one of semantics but was indicating that the burden of theological proof fell heaviest upon Agricola.[132] Over breakfast on the last day of the conference, Agricola commented that Christians were obliged to keep only the precepts of Paul and not the

---

130. Rogge, "Innerlutherische Streitigkeiten," 194.

131. Schurb, "Melancthon," 18; Wengert, *Law and Gospel*, 72, 131–34; *LW* 40 (*Instructions for Visitors*, 1528): 275; *WA* 26: 202.

132. Wengert, *Law and Gospel*, 116–17; Bornkamm, *Luther in Mid-Career*, 494–98.

Old Covenant Decalogue. Melancthon retorted that Paul basically reiterated the Decalogue and that the Law is nothing but the instructions of God to do this and not do that.[133]

It is important to understand that Melancthon's controversy with Agricola was not about whether repentance is to be expected, but whether it derives properly from the preaching of the Law or the preaching of the Gospel. For Agricola, among other issues theological and hermeneutical, the *Visitation Articles* seemed to imply that salvation was conditional upon something else prior to faith in the Gospel, which to him smacked of a return to late the medieval scholastic theology that Luther himself had attacked. For Melancthon and Luther, it was inconceivable that a person could really believe in the Gospel without possessing a sober awareness of his or her condemnation under the terror of the Law of God. Furthermore, to make repentance the property of the Gospel confuses its proper work of promising the hope and comfort of forgiveness with the power of the Law to convict and accuse.

There is some debate whether or not the *Instructions* imply an independent "third use of the Law." Gerhard Ebeling observes hints of a "third use of the Law" this early in Melancthon's career.[134] According to Wengert, however, Melancthon's 1527–1528 *scholia* only explicitly identifies two functions of the Law. A "third use" is not really identified until his 1534 *scholia* on Colossians. However, Wengert does argue that the "third use of the Law" was formulated by Melancthon as a result of the antinomian controversy with Agricola in the 1520s, at the same time that his understanding of justification was developing an emphasis on the forensic imputation of the righteousness of Christ. The third use of the Law was logically formulated, then, as a way of justifying a role for good works in the life of a Christian.[135]

In an extreme response to the late medieval excessive stress on penance, prayers, pilgrimages, and meritorious works, Melancthon had discovered that parish ministers in the 1520s were exalting freedom and grace to the neglect of urging contrition toward the Law of God, which was contributing to moral indifference and complacency within the Saxon parishes. The *Instructions* obviously have in mind the importance of preaching the Law in the Church for the sake of the unregenerate and

---

133. Schurb, "Melancthon," 19; Wengert, *Law and Gospel*, 165.

134. Ebeling, "Triplex Usus Legis," 69.

135. Wengert, *Law and Gospel*, 135, 193–205.

the not justified to coerce them into obedience and to draw them in repentance to justifying faith in Christ. However, the *Instructions* also state that repentance and faith are to continue and increase throughout the Christian life, which implies a continuing function for the preaching of the Law even for the justified Christian on account of the flesh for the renewing of repentance, faith in the forgiveness of God, and devotion to good works and the mortification of sins. The doing of good works is identified in the *Instructions* as the "third element" of the Christian life, and they speak of the mortification of sin and of "holding the carnal nature in check" as the "work of a new life" resulting from "nothing else than true contrition."[136] Thus, contrition and the regular confession of sin in the life of Christians brought about by the preaching of the Law leads to a recharge of faith in the promise of forgiveness in the Gospel of Christ and the struggle against sin for a life devoted to good works. This point, along with Melancthon's retort to Agricola at the conclusion of the Torgau conference that the Decalogue and the apostolic exhortations given to Christians essentially constitute the same will of God, foreshadows his more formal development of a "third use of the Law" in the mid-1530s. In this case, Luther's own involvement in the controversy, the revision of the *Visitation Articles*, and the publication of the *Instructions for the Visitors* is critical with regard to discerning his relationship to the origins of the "third use of the Law."

As he had proposed to do earlier in 1525, Luther published catechisms for the Saxon parishes in 1529. Luther distances himself from Agricola in the catechisms by openly acknowledging the importance of the Decalogue for the Christian Church. Of course, the format and content of the catechisms was not wholly in response to Agricola. Aside from his desire to draft a catechism well before the outbreak of the controversy, Luther's *Personal Prayer Book* (1522) clearly establishes the format of these later catechisms. In 1528, Luther also preached sermons on the Ten Commandments, the Creed, and the Lord's Prayer in Wittenberg during the absence of Bugenhagen. The *German Catechism*, more commonly known as the *Large Catechism*, was started first and intended primarily for pastors and teachers. Luther attached a new preface to the catechism in 1530. His *Small Catechism* was intended for the education of children and for use in the home.[137]

---

136. *LW* 40 (*Instructions for Visitors*, 1528), 277; *WA* 26: 203–4, 218.

137. See background comments in Tappert, 337–38, 357–58.

As in his *Personal Prayer Book*, the Creed does not incidentally follow the Decalogue. The order obviously reflects Luther's understanding that the Law brings about the knowledge of sin so that sinners might seek after the help of the Gospel, in which is found the power to truly keep the Law. Similar to his previous writings of the 1520s, Luther describes obedience to the First Commandment, which relates to belief in the articles of the Creed, as the sum and source of obedience to all the other commandments.[138]

Aside from this, the Law, with the warnings of temporal blessing for obedience and temporal punishment for disobedience, is also useful to restrain the acts of the wicked and unregenerate. In his preface to the *Small Catechism*, he urges local pastors to emphasize particular laws for particular social classes of people. For example, the law against stealing is to be stressed for workers, shopkeepers, farmers, and servants, and the commandment to honor parents is to be stressed for all children, and particularly those who have difficulty submitting to temporal authority of any kind.[139]

Although Luther has acknowledged that temporal sufferings benefit even Christians for the sake of preserving a spirit of humility toward sin and dependence upon the grace of God, this statement about temporal blessings and punishments at first glance seems to be inconsistent with Luther's earlier emphasis on the freedom of the Christian from the coercion of the Law. It is doubtless, however, that Luther has in mind here the majority of the not justified that make up a local parish. As such, they can only be encouraged to obey with the promise of rewards and threats until they are properly converted by faith in the Gospel. In the meantime, their outward obedience to the Law is to the common benefit of all. In this way, the Mosaic preaching of the Law in the Church supports the established government in the maintenance of social order for the protection of the Church and the Gospel. This is why, for Luther, young people particularly need to be instructed properly in the Law since they will be the future leaders of the nation.[140] The connection between the preaching of the Law in the Church as it concerns the wider social context is suggested by Luther when he states: "Although

---

138. McDonough, *Law and the Gospel in Luther*, 93–94.

139. *SC*, Tappert, 340, 342–44; Kolb and Wengert; 350–51, 354; *BSLK*, 504–5, 507–10.

140. Brecht, *Shaping and Defining the Reformation*, 262.

we cannot and should not compel anyone to believe, we should nevertheless insist that the people learn to know how to distinguish right and wrong according to the standards of those among whom they live and make their living. For anyone who desires to reside in a city is bound to know and observe the laws under whose protection he lives, no matter whether he is a believer or, at heart, a scoundrel or knave."[141] Yet the justified Christian can still benefit from the revelation of sin in the Law, which even implies a use for the stern warnings against disobedience to the commandments if they have strayed from the faith to become self-righteous or weak against the temptations of the flesh. The conviction of the Law reminds Christians that they are still unrighteous in themselves, which leads to regular confession of sin, the desire of forgiveness in Christ, followed by a renewed zeal for righteousness.[142] According to the Catholic scholar of Luther, Thomas McDonough, differentiating the use of the Ten Commandments and their accompanying retributive "sanctions" in the life of the justified and the not justified requires a "*split perspective.*"[143]

In the earlier preface, which was based on a 1528 sermon, Luther states that a "catechism" by nature is intended for children and the uneducated.[144] In the 1530 "New preface" (*Neue Vorrede*) to the *German Catechism*, however, and in the hopes of dispelling notions that the catechism is only useful for the simple-minded, Luther admits that even he, as a learned "doctor and a preacher," intentionally devotes time as "a child and pupil" to the daily study and review of the whole catechism." Luther acknowledges that he has not yet himself become a master of the catechism, in the sense of no longer needing to sit under it as a learner.[145] This obviously includes the Decalogue as well, which would imply that Luther clearly perceived his own constant need for the Law in living the Christian life. Luther identifies the whole catechism as a strong weapon against the temptations of the Devil, the tribulations of the world, and the ferocity of the flesh. To ponder over, sing of, and meditate on God's "commandments and words" in the Catechism is "the true holy water,

---

141. *SC*, Tappert, 339; Kolb and Wengert, 348–49; *BSLK*, 504.

142. *LC*, Tappert, 415–20; Kolb and Wengert, 335–40; *BSLK*, 653–62. See also McDonough, *Law and Gospel in Luther*, 87, 101.

143. McDonough, *Law and the Gospel in Luther*, 86–88.

144. *LC*, Tappert, 362; Kolb and Wengert, 383–84; *BSLK*, 553–54.

145. *LC*, Tappert, 358–59; Kolb and Wengert, 379–80; *BSLK*, 545–48.

the sign which routs the devil and puts him to flight." For Luther, the Devil hates few things worse than the steady attention of the Christian to the Word of God, including meditation on the holy commandments of the Decalogue.[146] In the concluding section of the catechism, Luther speaks of the valuable importance of regular confession of sin to others. Although not compulsory, as it was formerly mandated by the Fourth Lateran Council in 1215, Luther expects that a true Christian who feels burdened by sin and the accusations of the Law in the conscience will naturally seek for the reassuring comfort and sanctifying strength of absolution confirmed in a special way by a pastor or a trusted brother or sister in Christ.[147]

Luther speaks with further adulation about the Decalogue in the body of the *German Catechism*, although not the Decalogue in its precise form under the administration of Moses in the Old Covenant. Thus, Luther reiterates that the law concerning the Saturday Sabbath and the particular promise of prosperity in the land of Canaan were only for the Jews, although the underlying principles still apply. In fact, God's warnings of temporal blessings and punishments apply to all of the commandments.[148] It is worthwhile to quote Luther's praise of the Decalogue throughout the Large Catechism:

> This much is certain: anyone who knows the Ten Commandments perfectly knows the entire Scriptures. In all affairs and circumstances he can counsel, help, comfort, judge, and make decisions in both spiritual and temporal matters. He is qualified to sit in judgment upon all doctrines, estates, persons, laws, and everything else in the world ... Here, then, we have the Ten Commandments, a summary of divine teaching on what we are to do to make our whole life pleasing to God. They are the true fountain from which all good works must spring, the true channel through which all good works must flow. Apart from these Ten Commandments no deed, no conduct can be good or pleasing to God, no matter how great or precious it may be in the eyes of the world ... It will be a long time before men produce a doctrine or social order equal to that of the Ten Commandments, for they are beyond human power to fulfill...you will surely find so much to do that you will neither seek nor pay attention to any

---

146. *LC,* Tappert, 359–60; Kolb and Wengert, 379–83; *BSLK,* 549.

147. *LC,* Tappert, 457–61; Kolb and Wengert, 479–80; *BSLK,* 725–33.

148. *LC,* Tappert, 375–77, 383–86, 408–9; Kolb and Wengert, 397–99, 404–7, 429; *BSLK,* 580–86, 594–601, 641–42.

> other works or other kind of holiness ... we are to keep them incessantly before our eyes and constantly in our memory, and practice them in all our works and ways. Everyone is to make them his daily habit in all circumstances, in all his affairs and dealings, as if they were written everywhere he looks, and even wherever he goes or wherever he stands ... From all this it is obvious once again how highly these Ten Commandments are to be exalted and extolled above all orders, commands, and works which are taught and practiced apart from them ... We should pride and value them above all other teachings as the greatest treasure God has given us.[149]

The Creed "properly follows" the Ten Commandments in the order of the catechism, since only a heart fully trusting in the promise of the Gospel can keep the commandments of the Law as God wants them to be kept. Although the Law drives sinners to find refuge in Christ, the Christian in turn knows and accepts cheerfully his or her duty to that Law, not for righteousness or justification, but to use it in mortifying sin and the flesh and to structure life for the good of others. To accomplish all this, the Lord's Prayer provides a model for expressing total reliance upon God for all things.[150]

Beginning with his earliest lectures on the Bible, Luther developed an understanding that righteousness before God is never merited either by natural or supernatural works in obedience to the Law, but that obedience to the Law comes freely from a heart believing in the Gospel of righteousness promised in Jesus Christ alone. To be free from the Law with regard to the conscience before God, understood correctly, is to possess the freedom to keep the Law rightfully with regard to moral action in the world. Luther repeats and develops these themes throughout the reforming crises of the 1520s. Not only does he continue to emphasize justification by faith alone but he also stresses against critics and radicals the rightful importance of the preaching of the Law for the good of Christendom as a whole and of the unique importance of the Law for Christians. Luther praises the Law of the Decalogue interpreted spiritually all throughout the 1520s as the definitive standard of a holy life, and this applies equally to the Christian who is exhorted by Christ and the apostles on the basis of the grace of the Gospel to good works in

---

149. *LC*, Tappert, 361, 407–8, 410–11; Kolb and Wengert, 382, 428–29, 431; *BSLK*, 552, 639–41, 645.

150. *LC*, Tappert, 411; Kolb and Wengert, 431; *BSLK*, 646.

accordance with the Decalogue for the control of the flesh in service to others. Luther begins at the end of the 1520s to develop more explicitly how the preaching of the Law continues to work repentance leading to the renewal and increase of faith and sanctification (defined by Luther as the forgiveness of sins),[151] but Luther stated early on that the Christian life after baptism is a life of repentance, his publication of the *Personal Prayer Book* communicated the importance of the Law in the life of Christian devotion, and he frequently spoke of worldly tribulation and affliction as a cross and an effective remedy against the flesh.

The decade of the 1520s was a significant period in which Luther was confronted with the opportunity to incarnate his theology of Law and Gospel in a variety of circumstances, including his ongoing attempt to convince Catholics of the truthful integrity of his insights and correcting "radicals" who took those insights to extreme, even violent, conclusions. Though the assurance of eternal salvation and the complete favor of God are promised only in the Gospel through faith alone in Jesus Christ, Luther repeatedly affirmed the continuing and indispensable value of teaching the Ten Commandments for the health of the Church and surrounding society. Not only did the preaching of the Law serve in ruling the rebellious spirit of false Christians that filled Saxon towns, villages, and congregations, it also taught them to despair of themselves and their own inability to keep the Law and to believe and hope for justification before God in the promises of the Creed. For those who did believe in the Savior, who were no longer under the curse, condemnation, and coercive hold of the Law, Luther upheld the Law and its interpretation by Christ and the apostles as epitomizing the spiritual life of a faithful Christian. Though the Christian with regard to his or her faith in Christ and through the Spirit needs no such outward instruction, the Law is still necessary on account of the paradoxical reality that the Christian also remains a sinner and has the flesh that must be subdued to the Law. For the Christian, then, the Law functions in preserving repentance and the knowledge of intrinsic sinfulness, thus rekindling faith in the Gospel, which then uses that same Law to kill the promptings of sin and to work in the world for the happiness and welfare of others.

---

151. See *LC*, Tappert, 415–20; Kolb and Wengert, 335–40; *BSLK*, 653–62.

4

Law and Gospel in Luther's Later Years and His Dispute with the Antinomians (1530–1540)

AFTER THE FAILURE TO OBTAIN LEGAL RECOGNITION OF THE AUGSBURG Confession in 1530, the Lutheran territories were put on guard against the threat of an offensive war from Charles V to remake Catholic Christendom. The Protestants began banding together in 1531 to form a defensive military alliance known as the Schmalkaldic League led by Electoral Saxony and Hesse. Yet, in light of new attacks from the East by Turks, Charles again, for the sake of garnering support from the imperial lands, held off on his conquest of the Protestants in the Nuremberg Standstill of 1532. For more than a decade after this, Lutheran reform continued to expand and consolidate, incorporating newer territories and imperial cities into the League.[1] During the relative calm of this decade, Luther continued to lecture, preach, debate, and write, working both to stoke and to confine the fires of reformation.

One of the most important works for understanding Luther's theology of Law and Gospel in the 1530s is his revised lectures on Galatians, delivered from July to November of 1531 and published as a commentary from the transcript notes of George Rörer in 1535.[2] Although not entirely rejecting his earlier lectures published in 1519, Luther looks back upon them as merely the first dawn of his evangelical breakthrough on the Gospel of justification by faith in Christ alone now requiring greater clarity for a new generation. In the new Galatians lectures, Luther describes justification and grace with an even sharper

---

1. Lindberg, *European Reformations*, 239–42.

2. Luther admits elsewhere that the words of the commentary are mostly his, despite the fact that they came from the published notes taken down by his colleagues. See the editorial comments of Jaroslav Pelikan in *LW* 26 (Galatians 1–4): ix–x, and *LW* 27 (Galatians 5–6): 145.

emphasis on the imputation of righteousness in Christ through faith alone.[3] At the same time, Luther revises his earlier emphasis against the righteousness of works in late medieval theology with even greater stress now on the necessity of repentance and obligation to the Law in the light of the antinomian tendencies discovered in the recent parish visitations.

Luther describes the book of Galatians as "his Katie," a term of endearment and an obvious reference to his wife Katherine von Bora whom he married in 1525 as a vivid testimony to his own preaching of freedom from ecclesiastical laws and vows of celibacy in favor of the sanctity of married life. The commentary, much like his first lectures, speaks so profoundly of Christian freedom from the Law, but Luther also speaks positively of the Law and its importance in the life of the Christian. At the very outset of the lectures Luther states profoundly that, "Therefore the highest art and wisdom of Christians is not to know the Law, to ignore works and all active righteousness, just as outside the people of God the highest wisdom is to know and study the Law, works, and active righteousness." However, Luther goes on to explain that such disparagement of the Law has to do with living "before God" (*coram Deo*) as if divine acceptance was attainable by works, which is contrary to the Gospel promise that justification is available through faith alone in Jesus Christ. Furthermore, Luther goes on to state: "works and the performance of the Law must be demanded in this world as though there were no promise or grace. This is because of the stubborn, proud, and hard hearted, before whose eyes nothing must be set except the Law, in order that they may be terrified and humbled. For the Law was given to terrify and kill the stubborn and to exercise the old man."[4] This statement clearly excludes the position of the antinomians. It occurs years before his open dispute with Agricola in 1537, yet it obviously bears the imprint of his involvement in the parish visitation controversies of 1527–1528. For Luther, the issue at hand is a confusion of "two kinds of righteousness" (*duas iustitias*), the "active" (*activam*) righteousness of works with relation to others and the "passive" (*passivam*) righteousness of grace before God through Christ. As stated by Luther much earlier in his biblical lectures on Romans and Galatians and all throughout the 1520s, the Law in its Mosaic ministry needs to

---

3. See Green, *How Melancthon Helped Luther*, 68.
4. *LW* 26 (*Lectures on Galatians* [1–4], 1535): 5–6; *WA* 40^1: 43–44.

be preached for the sake of the wicked and the not justified. In the life of the Christian, the Law and works have a role to play with regard to the flesh. Thus, "as long as we live here, both remain," that is, both Law and Gospel: "that in a Christian the Law must not exceed its limits but should have its dominion only over the flesh, which is subjected to it and remains under it . . . But if it wants to ascend into the conscience and exert its rule there, see to it that you are a good dialectician and that you make the correct distinction."[5]

The proper place of the Gospel is in the conscience before God to assure it of the promises of His complete grace and favor apart from all works, whereas the proper place of the Law is then to rule over the flesh in obedience to God. The distinction must be maintained, for whereas failure to uphold the latter will lead to a license to sin, failure to uphold the former will lead to despair and bondage under the Law in sin: "Therefore whoever knows well how to distinguish the Gospel from the Law should give thanks to God and know that he is a real theologian. I myself do not know how to do this as I should." The distinction between Law and Gospel is compared to that of heaven and earth, light and darkness, or day and night, and yet it would be better "If we could only put an even greater distance between them." Luther describes the proper distinction of Law and Gospel as the "summary of all Christian doctrine . . . There is a time to hear the Law and a time to despise the Law. There is a time to hear the Gospel and a time to know nothing about the Gospel . . . in a matter apart from conscience, when outward duties must be performed, then, whether you are a preacher, a magistrate, a husband, a teacher, a pupil, etc. this is no time to listen to the Gospel. You must listen to the Law and follow your vocation. Thus the Law remains in the valley with the ass, and the Gospel remains with Isaac on the mountain."[6] This echoes the point Luther had made years before in his *A Freedom of A Christian* (1520), wherein he stated that the Christian is paradoxically both a totally freeman before God and yet a slave with regard to his calling and obligation to mortify the flesh in service to others.

Luther reaffirms this proper balancing of Law and Gospel in a series of sermons on the Gospel of John preached on Saturdays from

---

5. *LW* 26 (*Lectures on Galatians* [1–4], 1535), 7–11; *WA* 40¹: 45–50.
6. *LW* 26 (*Lectures on Galatians* [1–4], 1535), 91, 113–17; *WA* 40¹: 168–9, 203–10.

1530–32 in the absence of Bugenhagen.[7] Whereas Luther early on in his career stressed the preaching of the Gospel to counteract a theology of works-righteousness, in these sermons He urges the preaching of the Law to counteract presumption and moral complacency. To keep from creating lazy Christians through the preaching of the Gospel, the Law is urged upon the *alten Adam*: "Refrain from sin! Be pious! Desist from this, and do that!" Yet, at the instant the conscience begins to feel burdened by the accusations of the Law as if the righteousness of justification was by obedience in works, the Law must yield to the promise of the Gospel.[8] In a conversation recorded by Veit Dietrich in 1533, Luther states that such a proper distinction of the Gospel in relationship to the Law is a mighty rebuke against the torments of the Devil who troubles consciences by confusing the Gospel with Law and righteousness with works.[9]

Righteousness before God belongs to Christians through passive trust in the promise of the Gospel, but moral action is the obligation of Christians in their duty to the Law and to the battle against the flesh: "as long as the body is alive, the flesh must be disciplined by laws and vexed by the requirements and punishments of laws, as I have often admonished. But the inner man, who owes nothing to the Law but is free of it, is a living, righteous, and holy person . . ."[10] The Christian with regard to faith is entirely free from the demands and torments of the Law and is fully righteous before God but the "flesh" remains at enmity with the work of the Spirit and must still be controlled by the Law.

---

7. A manuscript was compiled and edited by Johannes Aurifaber (1519–75) on the basis of the work of four scribes recording the sermons. A later commentary was published by Aurifaber in 1565. This commentary checked against the manuscript is the basis of the English translation. See the editorial comments of Jaroslav Pelikan in *LW* 23: ix–xi.

8. *LW* 23 (*Dr. Martin Luther's Exposition of the Sixth, Seventh, and Eighth Chapters of the Gospel of St. John* [6–8], 1530–32): 271–72; *WA* 33: 432.

9. *LW* 54: 105 (*Table Talk*: No. 590, "Devil Upsets Distinction Between Law and Gospel," Summer or Fall, 1533); *WA Tr* 1: 276. Veit Dietrich was an important amanuensis for the lectures and sayings of Luther. He had accompanied Luther to the Marburg Colloquy in 1529 and to the Castle Coburg during the Diet of Augsburg in 1530. He stayed with the Luthers and dined at their table in their home in the former Augustinian Cloister in Wittenberg. See the editorial comments of Theodore Tappert in *LW* 54:5–6.

10. *LW* 26 (*Lectures on Galatians* [1–4], 1535): 164; *WA* 40^1: 279–80.

In a very key passage in the new Galatians lectures, Luther gives his first formal definition of a "double use of the law" (*duplicem esse legis usum*).[11] The first use of the Law is its "civic" (*civilis*) use,[12] which God uses to restrain the wicked and not justified by coercing them into outward obedience by the means of the civil sword and temporal threats and punishments: "This is why God has ordained magistrates, parents, teachers, laws, shackles, and all civic ordinances, so that, if they cannot do anymore they will at least bind the hands of the devil and keep him from raging at will." God uses the Law in this way to maintain public peace and social order so that the wicked do not utterly destroy one another and so that the Gospel can be free to do its work unhindered "by the tumults and seditions of wild men."[13]

The most important and primary use of the Law for Luther, however, is its "theological or spiritual one" (*Theologicus seu Spiritualis*). This use of the Law reveals to unconverted consciences "sin, blindness, misery, wickedness, ignorance, hate and contempt of God, death, hell, judgment, and the well-deserved wrath of God." Instead of the Law having the ability to make people good or acceptable to God, this use breaks down all presumption and self-righteousness and shows people how bad they really are at the core of their being. When confronted with the impossible demands of the Law and the threat of eternal judgment for disobedience, the first reaction is to hate the Law and to hate God, wishing that neither existed. In this way the Law actually increases sins, but with the purpose that God will use such knowledge to convert sinners in their desperation to desire and believe the mercy promised in the Gospel. This use of the Law is the most important for Luther because it is a prelude to justifying faith and the gift of eternal life: "Therefore the Law is a minister and a preparation for grace."[14] These statements again reaffirm Luther's agreement with Melancthon (and vice versa) against Agricola in the *Instructions for the Visitors* (1528).

---

11. Melancthon around this time also begins to use the formulae "*usus legis*" and "*duplex usus*" in his revised commentary on Romans (c. 1532). See Ebeling, "Triplex Usus Legis," 67–69.

12. His early reference is to a "*usus civilus*," but in the 1535 and 1538 editions of the lectures it becomes a "*usus politicus*." See Ebeling, "Triplex Usus Legis," 70.

13. *LW* 26 (*Lectures on Galatians* [1–4], 1535): 308–9; *WA* 40^1: 478–81.

14. *LW* 26 (*Lectures on Galatians* [1–4], 1535), 309–10, 313–15; *WA* 40^1: 481–83, 487–90.

To drive the sinner to Christ for justification is the primary function of the Law for Luther, "so when the Law is being used correctly, it does nothing but reveal sin, work wrath, accuse, terrify, and reduce the minds of men to the point of despair. And that is as far as the Law goes." Influential scholars such as Ragnar Bring argue that statements like this indicate that Luther never conceived, either explicitly or implicitly, of a "third use of the Law" for the Christian life. Rather, the Law continues to function in the life of the Christian in terms of the first and second uses, which are not a "third use."[15] One problem with this interpretation is that the second, or theological, use of the Law always drives the sinner to faith in Christ in the mind of Luther, but Luther also believed that the commandments of the New Testament, which are kindlier interpretations and explanations of the Law, are taught to Christians in the very light of the Gospel promise in order to exhort them who believe to obedience on account of the flesh. Furthermore, it is important to observe that, for Luther, the formal definition of the "second use of the Law" is to terrify, accuse, and condemn the consciences of the not justified of the eternal wrath of God. It is the Mosaic preaching of the Law with threats and warnings that is nullified through faith in Christ,[16] but that does not mean that the Christian has no need to use the Law against the flesh in obedience to God.

According to Luther, however, the Christian does live in a paradox of times, the "time of Law" and the "time of grace." The time of the Law did end in a sense when Christ fulfilled the Law and abolished the Old Covenant, yet it ends "personally and spiritually every day in any Christian, in whom are found the time of Law and the time of grace in constant alternation." The Christian sins, though "not coarse sins like murder, adultery or theft," but "feelings of impatience, grumbling, hatred, and blasphemy against God." Therefore, the Christian remains under the "time of the Law" as it "disciplines, vexes, and saddens me, when it brings me to a knowledge of sin and increases this" [that is, it increases the knowledge of sin]. Ironically, the oscillation between the knowledge of sin and trust in the Gospel is vital to abiding in Christ so that repentance and faith continue and increase throughout the Christian life, being properly synthesized against the extremes of despair and pre-

---

15. See Bring, "Gesetz und Evangelium," 54–55.
16. *LW* 26 (*Lectures on Galatians* [1–4], 1535): 313, 317; *WA* 40¹: 486, 492–93.

sumption.¹⁷ Luther recognizes that the Law will never cease in bringing to mind the knowledge of sin throughout the Christian life and even the condemnation that it deserves, but reassurance of the favor of God promised in the Gospel also never ceases.¹⁸

When Luther speaks of the continuing role of the Law in revealing sins, however, he is not simply equating this with the formal "theological" or "spiritual use," which troubles and terrorizes the consciences of those "who are to be justified" (*iustificandi*). Even Ebeling recognizes the fact that many scholars have overlooked the different mode of the *usus theologicus* in the *pii* compared with the *impii*, although he is not willing on this account to associate this with a "third use." Luther states, however, that those "who are to be justified" are: "disciplined by the theological use of the Law for a time; for it does not last forever, as the civic use does, but it looks forward to the coming of faith, and when Christ comes, it is finished. From this it is abundantly clear that all the passages in which Paul treats the spiritual use of the Law must be understood about those who are to be justified, not about those who have already been justified."¹⁹ Althaus also recognizes that the ongoing theological use of the Law in revealing sins and evoking contrition in the life of the Christian for the renewal of repentance and the battle with sin is to be clearly distinguished from the theological use of the Law to terrorize the consciences of the not yet justified who stand condemned under the Law.²⁰

Much like his earlier Galatians lectures, Luther interprets Paul's description of the Law as a "schoolmaster" in Galatians 3:24–25 as referring to the complete freedom of the Christian from the Law with regard to faith in Christ through the Spirit. Just as the office of the hired tutor was never meant to be permanent, so in a similar manner the office of the Law to rule by compulsion and terrors is finished with the coming of faith in Christ, in whom there is freedom from the slavery, harassment, and tyranny of the Law. However, Luther is quick to acknowledge that the justified do not "take hold of" Christ perfectly and, later on, that

---

17. *LW* 26 (*Lectures on Galatians* [1–4], 1535), 336–38, 340–43; *WA* 40¹: 518–21, 524–27.

18. *LW* 26 (*Lectures on Galatians* [1–4], 1535), 161–62; *WA* 40¹: 274–77.

19. *LW* 26 (*Lectures on Galatians* [1–4], 1535), 343–44; *WA* 40¹: 528; Ebeling, "*Triplex Usus Legis*," 77.

20. Althaus, *Theology of Martin Luther*, 268–73.

"the flesh, the world, and the devil do not permit faith to be perfect." Thus, as long as Christians remain sinners and their faith imperfect, the Law will return to harass and trouble them again and again, yet they must also grasp the Gospel in faith with the assurance "that according to our conscience we are completely free of the Law. Therefore, this custodian must not rule in our conscience, that is, must not menace it with his terrors, threats, and captivity."[21] A healthy understanding of the role of the Law in the Christian life is to allow it to have "dominion over the flesh and the old self; let this be under the Law; let this permit the burden to be laid upon it; let this permit itself to be disciplined and vexed by the Law; let the Law prescribe to this what it should do and accomplish, and how it should deal with other men. But let the Law not pollute the chamber in which Christ alone should take His rest and sleep." Elsewhere, he says that "the Law of the Decalog has no right to accuse and terrify the conscience in which Christ reigns through grace, for Christ has made this right obsolete."[22] As a help to Christians to convince them of this truth, Luther explains in his *Commentary on Psalm 45*, originally part of a larger series of lectures on the Psalms delivered in the early 1530s, that the Mosaic ministry of the Law has even been removed symbolically in the historical event of the fall of Jerusalem in 70 AD: "Not only has the divine worship ceased, but the temple and Jerusalem have been destroyed, and the Jews have been dispersed throughout the entire world—and justly."[23]

The Christian life is for Luther really a growth in the apprehension of Christ and the promise of His grace. For Luther, Christian maturity is always defined in terms of growth in faith. Whereas the Law will never cease in this life to convict Christians of their being still sinners, Christ in the Gospel continually comforts and reassures them of His grace: "Thus the conscience takes hold of Christ more perfectly day by day; and day by day the law of flesh and sin, the fear of death, and whatever other evils the law bring with it are diminishing. For as long as we live

---

21. *LW* 26 (*Lectures on Galatians* [1–4], 1535), 345–51; *WA* 40¹: 528–39.

22. *LW* 26 (*Lectures on Galatians* [1–4], 1535), 391–92, 446–47; *WA* 40¹: 595–96, 670–72.

23. *LW* 12 (*Commentary on Psalm 45*, 1533–34. Translated by E. B. Koenker): 275; *WA* 40²: 577. The notes of George Rörer on Psalm 45 were transcribed and published in the year 1533–34 with some hesitation by Luther who did not edit their final form. The entire series was published by Veit Dietrich in 1546. See the editorial comments of Jaroslav Pelikan in *LW* 12: vii–x.

in a flesh that is not free of sin, so long the Law keeps coming back and performing its function, more in one person and less in another, not to harm but to save. This discipline of the Law is the daily mortification of the flesh, the reason, and our powers, and the renewal of our mind."[24]

Bring rightly argues that Luther describes Christian conversion as a daily and ongoing experience rather than a single past event or moment of existential crisis. He argues that misinterpretations of Luther's theology of Law and Gospel result precisely from the influence of Pietism on modern Protestant evangelicalism in its emphasis on an identifiable conversion experience (*die Bekeherten*) of being "born-again" (*widergeborenen*). In Luther, however, Bring says the emphasis in regeneration and conversion is a daily process continuing throughout the entire life of the Christian. Therefore, the Law continues its old ways because the Christian life is a daily cycle from repentance under the Law to a renewal of faith in the Gospel.[25]

Bring is certainly right to an extent to interpret Luther in this way, but it is important to keep in mind that perseverance through this process describes the experience of the justified. Even weak faith is justifying from the moment of its first inception. Such a young or immature Christian with weaker faith may indeed suffer much more under the vexations of the Law, but the Law has just as much right to condemn him or her as it does a person of much stronger faith. Luther describes the one who has the beginnings of faith and the first fruits of the Spirit in terms of a lump of dough not yet fully leavened. The leaven represents the miniscule, even imperceptible, redeeming presence of Christ in faith, whereas the lump that hides the leaven is characterized by feelings of "greed, sexual desire, anger, pride, the terror of death, sadness, fear, hate, grumbling, and impatience with God." It is impossible for these attributes to be completely eradicated in the Christian life this side of the resurrection, yet they do not result in condemnation even for those who would "fulfill" them in weakness because they do not give full consent to them with indifference. It is with regard to sinful promptings, frequent stumblings, and so that faith might not become presumption through the flesh that: "there is still need for a custodian to discipline and torment the flesh, that powerful jackass, so that by this discipline

---

24. LW 26 (*Lectures on Galatians* [1–4], 1535): 349–50, 354, 360; WA 40¹: 536–38, 542, 553–54.

25. Bring, "Gesetz und Evangelium," 49–50, 114–15.

sins may be diminished and the way prepared for Christ . . . so He comes to us spiritually without interruption and continually smothers and kills these things in us."²⁶ This amounts to an ongoing, even increasing, experience of repentance in the life of the Christian, which results in the increase of faith and the daily mortification of sin. As this relates to the action of the Law in the life of the justified Christian, this appears to be something developed more explicitly by Luther in his theology of the 1530s and probably resulted from his involvement in the recent parish visitation controversies over the doctrine of repentance.

Yet when it comes to the matter of being justified before God, the Law cannot be downgraded enough: "we cannot speak of it in sufficiently vile and odious terms either. For here the conscience should consider and know nothing except Christ alone." When it concerns moral action, however, the Law should be spoken of with the highest regard: "Apart from our conscience we should make a god of it, but in our conscience it is truly a devil . . ."²⁷ As Luther made clear in his earlier *The Freedom of A Christian* (1520), a Christian relates to God entirely on the basis of faith in Christ alone while relating to others through obedience to the Law and good works. All truly good works are directed, not to God to merit His favor in justification, but to others for "the peace of the world, gratitude toward God, and a good example by which others are invited to believe the Gospel."²⁸ For Luther, faith toward God, who has no need of works, and moral action on behalf of others, who have no need of faith, is the very sum of the Christian life.²⁹

Near the middle of 1535 and on into the decade of the 1540s Luther lectured on the book of Genesis. The lectures were interrupted once in July 1535 by an outbreak of the plague in Wittenberg and were resumed at the beginning of 1536. By 1538–1539, Luther had only reached chapter twenty. As was the case with many other published sermons and lectures of Luther, these are not from his pen nor are they even an unedited transcript of his actual lectures. An anachronistic reference to the death of Robert Barnes (d. 1540), the uniform accuracy of classical quotations, and even a positive reference to astrology, reinforces the opinion of some scholars that the theology presented in these lectures

26. LW 26 (*Lectures on Galatians* [1–4], 1535): 350; WA 40¹: 537–38.
27. LW 26 (*Lectures on Galatians* [1–4], 1535): 364–65; WA 40¹: 555–58.
28. LW 26 (*Lectures on Galatians* [1–4], 1535): 373; WA 40¹: 570.
29. LW 27 (*Lectures on Galatians* [5–6], 1535): 30, 49, 51; WA 40²:37–38, 61–65.

may have been adulterated to conform to the concerns of the second generation of Lutheran reformers. Yet, Jaroslav Pelikan argues that the lectures, while clearly edited by Veit Dietrich, are still basically Luther's voice and must be compared with even more reliable works of the later 1530s and not just with his earlier writings.[30]

In these lectures, Luther distinguishes between the giving of the Law before the Fall, after the Fall, and in the context of the New Covenant of faith and grace. To Adam, despite his innocence and righteousness, God gave a Law, "that he might have an outward form of worship by which to show his obedience and gratitude toward God." In a similar sense, even the "guiltless" angels are given commandments and instructions to follow in service to the will of God.[31]

Luther makes a similar point in a contemporaneous sermon series preached on the Gospel of John 14–16 in the spring of 1537. Caspar Cruciger (1504–1548), an in-law to Luther through the marriage of their children, recorded the sermons and edited them as a commentary in 1538–1539. Luther prized them above all his other works.[32] According to the sermons, Luther observes that Christ in the Gospel of John gives commandments to His disciples in the context of fellowship with Him. In this regard, the commandments are quite similar to the commandments given to Adam in the Garden in that they are not given so that the favor of God, already possessed, might be merited, but with regard to showing gratitude through obedience. Christ teaches the disciples as one would speak lovingly to a friend and commands them to love one another as He has loved them. The instruction is not harsh as if burdening the conscience with works and threats of God's wrath without providing any help to obey. The commandment is given precisely in the light of the promise of the grace of God in Jesus Christ. To lack the desire to obey this commandment shows that such a person has not yet accepted the gift of fellowship with God by faith in Christ.[33] This comparison of the Mosaic ministry of the Law with the moral entreat-

---

30. See introductory comments of Jaroslav Pelikan in *LW* 1: ix–xii.

31. *LW* 1 (*Lectures on Genesis* [1–5], 1535): 101, 108–10; *WA* 42: 77, 82–83. See also Wannenwetsch, "Luther's Moral Theology," 124–26.

32. See the editorial comments of Jaroslav Pelikan in *LW* 24: ix–x.

33. *LW* 24 (*Dr. Martin Luther's Exposition of the Fourteenth, Fifteenth, and Sixteenth Chapters of the Gospel of St. John*, 1537): 101–2, 145–46, 252–56; *WA* 45: 552–54, 593–95, 691–95.

ies of Christ given in the context of fellowship with God by His grace is entirely consistent with what Luther has already expressed earlier in the 1520s.

During the years that Luther lectured on the book of Genesis, he also became more outspoken against the antinomianism of Agricola.[34] In the *Table Talk*, from personal notes recorded by Anthony Lauterbach and Jerome Weller, Wittenberg students and frequent visitors in the Luther home, Luther criticizes Agricola for pitting the *violatio legis* against the *violatio filii*, as if the latter was the only true violation. Furthermore, the sufferings of Christ on the cross do inspire contrition or repentance, but in so doing they are acting as Law in the proper sense rather than the Gospel.[35]

Recent scholarship argues that significant divergences between Agricola and Luther over the nature of Law and Gospel appear much earlier than the later 1530s. Kjeldgaard-Pederson argues that differences can be traced as far back as 1524 in Agricola's earliest printed works.[36] Wengert observes that Agricola's works of 1525–1527 lack any acknowledgment of a function of the Law before faith and justification. For Agricola, the preaching of the Law can do nothing but create despair, which led him conclusively to a "*de facto* exclusion of the law before the gospel."[37]

Yet Luther did not enter into personal dispute with Agricola until late in the 1530s. Luther had apparently been ill during much of Melancthon's debate with Agricola at Torgau in 1527 and was content with the compromise. As mentioned in the previous chapter, despite a public reconciliation, Melancthon wrote to Justus Jonas that he and Agricola continued debating over breakfast after the end of the formal debate.[38]

Upon returning to Wittenberg from Eisleben in 1536, Agricola boarded with Luther in his home, even filling in for him as preacher and

---

34. Rogge, "Innerlutherische Streitigkeiten," 191, 192, 196–97.

35. *LW* 54 (*Table Talk*, No. 3554: "A Blast against Agricola's Antinomianism." March 21, 1537): 233; *WA Tr* 3: 405–6. The notes ascribed to Lauterbach and Weller are found in *LW* 54: 201–249, 253. See also the editorial comments of Tappert in *LW* 54: 203, 253.

36. Kjeldgaard-Pederson, *Gesetz, Evangelium, and Busse*, 380.

37. Wengert, *Law and Gospel*, 26–45, 73.

38. Brecht, *Shaping and Defining*, 265; Wengert, *Law and Gospel*, 135.

lecturer while Luther was away at a conference of Protestant allies in Schmalkalden in 1537. Luther had been asked by Elector John Frederick to propose theological articles to be considered by the members of the Schmalcaldic League identifying what concessions it could and could not make were it to send representatives to a council summoned by Pope Paul III in 1536.[39] The articles, though not adopted officially by the League on account of their divisiveness, were published in 1538 with the addition of a preface and were adamant in affirming the importance of preaching the Law for repentance.[40] Ironically, this was the very theological perspective that Agricola had long since come to reject. Other theologians in Wittenberg were not as welcoming of him, and it is possible that their opinions were instrumental in turning Luther against his former friend by the time he returned from Schmalkalden. At this time, a series of anonymous theses denouncing the preaching of the Law also began circulating in Wittenberg. Luther ascribed them to Agricola and published them along with his own refutations and a challenge to public disputation. In September of 1537 Luther preached sermons against Agricola, and the first disputation took place in December, though in Agricola's absence.[41] In a telling comment recorded by Lauterbach and Weller, Luther states: "I've had him at my table, he has laughed with me, and yet he opposes me behind my back ... But to reject the law, without which neither church nor civil authority nor home nor any individual can exist, is to kick the bottom of the barrel. It's time to resist. I can't and won't stand for it!"[42]

A second disputation took place in January of 1538, and this time Agricola publicly agreed to keep private his own opinions on the matter. However, Luther became frustrated when the insincerity of Agricola's compliance soon became apparent. In September of 1538, a third public disputation was held in the hope that Agricola would finally recant, though Agricola again failed to show up.[43] In the context

39. Brecht, *Preservation of the Church*, 178–85.

40. *The Smalcald Articles* (1537), Tappert, 303–4; Kolb & Wengert, 311–13; *BSLK*, 436–37; Brecht, *Preservation of the Church*, 182–84.

41. Rogge, "Innerlutherische Streitigkeiten," 194–95; Brecht, *Preservation of the Church*, 159–66. See also the editorial comments of Martin H. Bertram in *LW* 47: 101–6.

42. *LW* 54 (*Table Talk* no. 3650a: "A Public Disputation on Antinomianism Between November 1 and December 21, 1537."): 248; *WA Tr* 3: 481.

43. Rogge, "Innerlutherische Streitigkeiten," 194–95; Brecht, *Preservation of the*

of this third disputation, Luther explains why he now so adamantly defends the preaching of the Law in light of the fact that the urgency of his earliest writings was weighted significantly towards the preaching of the Gospel:

> True it is that at the early stage of this movement we began strenuously to teach the gospel and made use of these words which the Antinomians now quote. But the circumstances of that time were very different from those of the present day. Then the world was terrorized enough when the pope or the visage of a single priest shook the whole of Olympus, not to mention earth and hell, over all which that man of sin had usurped the power to himself. To the consciences of men so oppressed, terrified, miserable, anxious, and afflicted, there was no need to inculcate the law. The clamant need then was to present the other part of the teaching of Christ in which he commands us to preach the remission of sin in his name, so that those who were already sufficiently terrified might learn not to despair, but to take refuge in the grace and mercy offered in Christ. Now, however, when the times are very dissimilar from those under the pope, our Antinomians—those suave theologians—retain our words, our doctrine, the joyful tidings concerning Christ, and wish to preach this alone, not observing that men are other than they were under that hangman, the pope, and have become secure, forward, wicked violators—yea, Epicureans who neither fear God nor men. Such men they confirm and comfort by their doctrine. In those days we were terrorized so that we trembled even at the fall of a leaf ... But now our softly singing Antinomians, paying no attention to the change of the times, make men secure who are of themselves already so secure that they fall away from grace ... Our view hitherto has been and ought to be this salutary one — if you see the afflicted and contrite, preach grace as much as you can. But not to the secure, the slothful, the harlots, adulterers, and blasphemers.[44]

Church, 159–66. See also the introductory comments of Martin H. Bertram in *LW* 47: 101–6.

44. *LW* 47 (The English translation in the American Edition is taken from James Mackinnon, *Luther and the Reformation* [London, 1930] IV: 171–172): 104–5; *WA* 39^1: 571–74. This text is found in five of the seven manuscripts: Goth. 264, Rig., 243, Helmst. 83, Monac. 940, and Bresl. 45. Luther also makes a similar observation regarding his change in emphasis, though not theology, in *LW* 4 (*Lectures on Genesis* [21–25], 1539–41): 50–51; *WA* 43: 171–72.

In 1539, Luther published *Against the Antinomians*, which was basically a document of recantation prepared at Agricola's request.[45] At the beginning of the pamphlet, Luther rebukes the antinomians' belief that the preaching of the Law should be excluded from the Church. That the temporal government has the power to exercise the civil use of the Law was not denied by Agricola, although it is not certain that the particular statement found in the anonymous theses indicating that the Decalogue belongs in courtrooms and not in churches was his own.[46]

Luther expresses surprise that the antinomians view him as their inspiration, since on more than one occasion he has exposited the use of the Law for the Church: "Furthermore, the commandments are sung in two versions as well as painted, printed, carved, and recited by the children morning, noon, and night." Luther's reference to singing the commandments probably refers to hymns he himself composed in 1524 praising the Ten Commandments, including "These are the Holy Ten Commands" and "Man, Wouldst Thou Live all Blissfully."[47]

Luther concedes to the antinomians that the sufferings of Christ are indeed a profound revelation of God's wrath against sin and that he himself had described it this way. Yet Luther argues that the antinomians confuse the proper functions of Law and Gospel. For Luther, it was bad logic to reason that the sufferings of Christ make the preaching of the Law irrelevant. On the contrary, in *Against the Antinomians*, Luther argues that every part of Scripture is valuable in working repentance and not just the "sweet grace and suffering of Christ." In fact, narrating the sufferings of Christ is simply one way of preaching the Law, albeit in its most powerful way: "For in the Son of God I behold the wrath of God in action, while the law of God shows it to me with words and with lesser deeds." Nevertheless, for Luther, the preaching of the Law explains why Jesus had to die on the cross in the first place. For this reason, the Law should always be preached alongside the Gospel, and it is meaningless to do away with the word "Law" as the antinomians do, since the revelation of sin and God's wrath in whatever form it takes performs the proper work of the Law.[48]

---

45. See the editorial comments of Martin H. Bertram in *LW* 47:107–8.

46. See *LW* 47:107 (n. 2).

47. *LW* 47 (*Against the Antinomians*, 1539, trans. Martin H. Bertram): 108–9; *WA* 50: 470; *LW* 53 (*The Hymns*): 277–81; *WA* 35: 426–29.

48. *LW* 47 (*Against the Antinomians*, 1539): 110–14 (see also n. 10); *WA* 50: 471–73.

Luther continued his tirade against the antinomians in his later lectures on Genesis and named them specifically: "Therefore we justly censure the antinomians, who assert that the threats of the Law have no place in the church."[49] Whereas the Gospel is the cure for a conscience troubled by sin and the fear of God, the "hammer of the Law" is there to crush the indolence of the smug, the hard-hearted, and the wicked. For Luther, to promise the Gospel to those who are smug and unrepentant is only to indulge and give license to their wickedness.[50]

The antinomians were known to have said that the sinner need not feel contrition or an impulse to turn from his or her sin before believing in God's forgiveness.[51] Luther criticizes the antinomians for failing to censure sins by the Law out of their fear that free grace be impugned.[52] Luther states emphatically that "God is no antinomian" and that His Word offers the comforting promise of grace only to those whose consciences are burdened by guilt under the Law. Furthermore, to exclude the preaching of the Law excludes the fear of God from the Church along with all the works of God recorded by the Holy Spirit in the Old Testament meant for all ages, such as His outpouring of wrath upon Sodom and Gomorrah in Genesis 19.[53]

For Luther, the visible Church is "never altogether pure; the greater part is always wicked . . ." Thus, the ministry of the Law must certainly continue in the Church for the sake of false Christians. Nevertheless, even the "true saints themselves, who are righteous through faith in the Son of God, have the sinful flesh, which must be mortified by constant chastening."[54] It is true that Luther's contention with Agricola appears to be over the preaching of the Law in the Church for the sake of the not justified.[55] Indeed, this was the same issue that split Melancthon and Agricola ten years earlier. However, Luther also acknowledges that the harsher preaching of the Law is still useful even for Christians on account of the flesh and for the sake of repentance: "for sins should be

---

49. *LW* 3 (*Lectures on Genesis* [15–20], 1538–39): 281; WA 43: 76.

50. *LW* 3 (*Lectures on Genesis* [15–20], 1538–39), 222–23; WA 43: 33–34.

51. See WA 39¹: 344.

52. *LW* 4 (*Lectures on Genesis* [21–25], 1539–41): 240–41; WA 43: 307–9.

53. Luther refers to Agricola by name ("Grikel"). *LW* 3 (*Lectures on Genesis* [15–20], 1538–39): 243 (and n.5), 336; WA 43: 48–49, 116.

54. *LW* 3 (*Lectures on Genesis* [15–20], 1538–39: 224–25; WA 43: 36.

55. See Schuetze, "On the Third Use of the Law," 208–9.

denounced, and God's wrath should be exhibited for the sake of the unbelievers who are in the church, yes, also for the sake of the believers, lest they yield to sin, which still adheres to them, and to their natural weakness."[56] As mentioned before, this description of the Mosaic ministry of the Law as a service to the Christian seems to be something developed more explicitly in Luther's theology in the 1530s in the light of the visitation controversies. Whereas Luther had always acknowledged that the life of a Christian is one of ongoing repentance, now he makes more explicit how the preaching of the Law in terms more akin to the Mosaic pedagogy relates to the Christian life of repentance. Of course, as mentioned already, Luther assumes there to be a significant difference between the preaching of the Law in this way for the justified and the not justified. The former do not need the preaching of the Law that they might become justified by faith, but nevertheless they still have the flesh and old man that remains powerfully opposed to faith and the Spirit. Therefore the Christian, to keep from becoming presumptuous and lazy, also has need of the preaching of the Law for a life of ongoing repentance and restoration through the Gospel for the battle against sin and the flesh.

In a conversation recorded in the table talk notes of Lauterbach and Weller, Luther comments at length that:

> anybody who abolishes the law in an ecclesiastical context ceases to have a knowledge of sin. The gospel doesn't expose sin except through the law, which is spiritual and which defines sin in opposition to God's will. Away with him who claims that transgressors don't sin against the law but only dishonor the Son of God ... they teach everything confusedly and say things like this, 'Love is the fulfillment of the law, and therefore we have no need of law.' But those wretched fellows neglect the minor premise: that this fulfillment (namely, love) is weak in our flesh, that we must struggle daily against the flesh with the help of the Spirit, and this belongs under the Law.[57]

Not only is the preaching of the Law necessary for the not justified to restrain the wickedness of them who do not have the Spirit and to properly lead them to Christ for forgiveness, it also restores

---

56. *LW* 3 (*Lectures on Genesis* [15–20], 1538-9): 269; *WA* 43: 67–68.

57. *LW* 54 (*Table Talk* No. 3554: "A Blast against Agricola's Antinomianism, March 21, 1537"): 233; *WA Tr* 3: 405.

repentance and the battle against the flesh in the life of the justified Christian. Although Luther can praise the antinomians for preaching that the grace of Christ in the Gospel is given apart from works, he believes they do this at the expense of the necessity of censuring sin and upholding obedience and good works by their neglect to also preach the Law. In his work *On Councils and the Church* (1539), written preemptively to undermine the authority claimed by a future Catholic council (Trent), Luther argues that preaching the Gospel of forgiveness without also preaching the Law is to exclude the need for repentance that leads through faith to obedience. This is like "granting the premise and denying the conclusion." In fact, he goes on to state that: "they may be fine Easter preachers . . . they are very poor Pentecost preachers . . . he [Christ] has purchased redemption from sin and death so that the Holy Spirit might transform us out of the old Adam into new men . . . so that we might have not only forgiveness of, but also cessation from sin . . ."[58] In Luther's opinion, the exclusive preaching of Gospel by the antinomians essentially encouraged the unrepentant to presume upon the mercy of God. The great challenge of pastoral ministry is to appropriately temper the preaching of both Law and Gospel so as to maintain the proper balance between despair under the Law and presumption upon the Gospel.[59]

In the light of their differences over Law and Gospel, Luther succeeded in keeping Agricola from being elected as dean of the arts faculty at the University of Wittenberg and even proposed that he be placed under the ban. Agricola responded by appealing to the university rector and the Electoral Prince to secure a public hearing, which Luther himself countered in his *Against the Eislebener* (1540). Count Albert suggested that Agricola be arrested, whose falling out with the leaders of Saxony motivated him to sneak out of Wittenberg in 1540. He fled to Berlin and later became court preacher to Elector Joachim II of Brandenburg. Agricola eventually submitted a retraction and was allowed the right to reenter Electoral Saxony without the fear of arrest,

---

58. Luther refers here explicitly to "sanctification" ("*Heiligung*") and identifies this as the "new life in Christ" that proceeds from a heart of repentance and faith. *LW* 41 (*On Councils and the Church*, 1539): 113–14; *WA* 50: 599–600.

59. *LW* 3 (*Lectures on Genesis* [15–20], 1538–39): 236–37, 240–41; *WA* 43: 44–48.

though Luther retained doubts about his sincerity and the two were never reconciled.[60]

Luther's theology of Law and Gospel remained quite consistent throughout the twenty years spanning the height of his reforming career. In so far as the New Testament commands taught by Christ to His disciples agree with natural Law and the Law of the Decalogue, Luther always acknowledged an important role for the Law in living the Christian life. This went beyond merely describing the life lived spontaneously by faith in Christ through the power of the Spirit, for the Christian always lives in conflict with sin and the flesh and, on that account, must actually heed written moral prescriptions.

Although a role for the Law in the Christian life was not new to his theology in the 1530s, what is new, or at least now made more explicit, is his emphasis that the revealing of sin by the preaching of the Law with threats and warnings is necessary even for the justified Christian with regard to the life of repentance. As Luther himself claims, this emphasis was a direct response to the reactionary overemphasis on the exclusive preaching of the Gospel witnessed in the parish visitations in the late 1520s.

Another significant development in these later years was Luther's formal definition of the two-fold "*usus legis*" as it relates to the life of the not justified, although this was certainly nothing new to his theology. Luther had always acknowledged that the preaching of the Law in the Church is essential to establishing a functioning society and that it was only after being humbled by the Law that a person can receive the Gospel with true faith.

What place, then, did Luther have in his theology for a so-called "positive" or "third use of the Law"? Although Luther never names such a "third use," his belief that the preaching of the Law in the life of the Christian sustains and renews repentance and faith and that the New Testament commandments, exhorting Christians on account of the flesh to obedience on the basis of the love of God in the Gospel, agree with the will of God in the Ten Commandments is commensurate with Melancthon's more formal definition of the "third use of the Law."

In a set of theses prepared for the doctoral examination of two Wittenberg graduates in 1535, Luther states that the Christian guided

---

60. Brecht, *Preservation of the Church*, 167–68. See also comments of Martin H. Bertram in *LW* 47: 105–6.

by the Spirit in faith and love can create "new decalogues" even as Jesus and the apostles did in applying the law of love to particular situations. While it is tempting to see in these words a rejection of a necessary external norm to guide the practical life of a Christian in good works, Luther immediately tempers this statement by insisting that the anointing of Jesus and the apostles was unique, and that, because "we are inconstant in spirit, it is necessary also on account of inconstant souls, to adhere to certain commands and writings of the apostles, lest the church be torn to pieces."[61] In wanting to avoid the errors of more radical reformers who claimed to be needfully controlled only by the inward rule of the Holy Spirit and faith, Luther emphasizes that the written application of the Law in the New Testament is necessary for guiding Christian behavior.

It is also significant to note that in 1537 Luther praised Melancthon's teachings on the uses of the Law: "Would that we might pay heed to Master Philip! Philip teaches clearly and eloquently about the function of the law. I am inferior to him, although I have also treated this topic clearly in my Galatians."[62] Following this, the Lutheran theologian Martin Chemnitz (1522–1586), in his commentary published posthumously in 1591 on Melancthon's *Loci Communes*, and in the section specifically devoted to the "third use of the Law," has this to say: "Luther in a very learned way sought the foundations of this doctrine in the Epistle to the Galatians, and divided the use of the law into one aspect which was civil and one which was theological. Likewise in Galatians 5 there is one use of the Law in justification and another for those who have been justified. From this Luther constructed the threefold division of the uses of the Law."[63]

It is necessary to acknowledge that Chemnitz's treatment of the uses of the Law is polemical, particularly as it relates to upholding the preaching of the Law against antinomians and with the purpose of demonstrating his alignment with Luther on the matter. Therefore, it is at least possible that Chemnitz's interpretation was skewed by an

---

61. *LW* 34 ("Theses Concerning Faith and Law: The Theses for the Doctoral Examination of Hieronymus Weller and Nikolaus Medler, September 11, 1535"): 113 (Thesis 58); *WA* 39^1: 47. See also Althaus, *Ethics of Martin Luther*, 30–32.

62. *LW* 54 (*Table Talk*, No. 3554: "A Blast Against Agricola's Antinomianism, March 21, 1537"): 233; *WA Tr* 3: 405.

63. Chemnitz, *Loci Theologici*, 439; Chemnitii, *Loci Theologici*, 99.

apologetic and rhetorical agenda. Only a closer look at his actual interpretation of the "third use of the Law" will determine whether or not he captured the theological spirit of the first Martin.

As with Luther, Chemnitz opposes those who justify following their own subjective inclinations by appealing to their freedom through the Holy Spirit and faith. Rather, he states that the "apostles everywhere preach about the new obedience of the regenerate and clearly seek the description of this new obedience in the Decalog." Thus, like Luther, Chemnitz equates the substance of the Decalogue with the commandments of the New Testament. Chemnitz then delineates three separate causes for the "third use of the Law" (*Tertius usus*) in the life of the Christian. First, he states that the Law of the Decalogue prescribes what good works please God. Secondly, the Law continues to reveal the imperfection of the Christian to counteract presumption and to preserve a sense of repenting dependence upon the mercy and grace of God. Though this has to do with the continuing function of the Law to revealing sin in the life of the Christian, Chemnitz, like Luther, also refrains from simply equating this with the formal "second use of the Law" (*Secundus usus Legis*), which he clearly associates with the justification of the unregenerate.[64] Thirdly and lastly, the Law is important on account of the fact that the Christian is not yet fully spiritual, but is paradoxically both "old" and "new man." It is precisely on account of the flesh and the fact that faith, though justifying, is not perfect that the Christian still benefits from compulsion: "For we experience that the new obedience is not so voluntary a thing as a good tree which brings forth its fruit without any command or exhortation."[65] These statements of Chemnitz are essentially the same as those found in the later *Formula of Concord* (1577) and agree with the theology of both Luther and Melancthon. With regard to Luther, however, the preaching of the Law in this regard is made more explicit in his thought in the 1530s.

Luther always praised the Ten Commandments rightly interpreted as the epitome of a truly Christian life. Yet such a Christian life lived independently from union with Christ by faith in the Gospel was inconceivable to Luther, Melancthon, and the *Formula of Concord*. The Law gives no power to do good works from the heart. Truly good works in complete fulfillment of the Law only and ever spring spontaneously

---

64. Chemnitz, *Loci Theologici*, 440; Chemnitii, *Loci Theologici*, 100.
65. Chemnitz, *Loci Theologici*, 440–41; Chemnitii, *Loci Theologici*, 100.

through faith in Christ alone. Yet, on account of the imperfection of faith and the realistic limits of its rule in the life of Christians who are *simul justus et peccator*, the written and preached Law is needed both to summon and to guide the justified in obedience to God.

5

After Lollardy and Humanism

Luther's Writings in England and the Beginnings of "Evangelical" Reformation

THERE ARE SOME SCHOLARS WHO HAVE ARGUED THAT ENGLISH reformers whose careers emerged during the 1520s owe as much, if not more, to late medieval Lollard or humanist influences than to the writings of Martin Luther. Before making an individual assessment of this claim with regard to the life and thought of Tyndale, Frith, and Barnes, it is important to establish the broader context by making some general observations concerning the relationship of Lollardy, Humanism, and Luther's writings to the English Reformation of the 1520s and 30s.

Of course, Luther's works were not the first to inspire a movement calling for the reform of the English Church. Tracing their origins to the influence of the English philosopher John Wyclif (1330-1384), scattered groups of Lollards had begun implementing their own local reforms unofficially since the early fifteenth century, and Italian Renaissance Humanism began to make its impact first on English education and scholarship by the end of that same century. Many of the reforming concerns emerging from these late medieval movements indeed paralleled those of the first generation of English evangelicals living during the reign of Henry VIII. Lollards, Catholic humanists, and evangelicals could all bemoan the presence of superstitious devotion to images and relics among the people, which was the target of reforms under the official Injunctions promulgated by the Henrician court in the second half of the 1530s.[1] In fact, in the light of this continuity it was long believed that Humanism and Lollardy naturally and effectively

---

1. With regard to the specific influence of Erasmian Humanism on official reforming policies, see McConica, *English Humanists and Reformation Politics*.

paved the way for the diffusion of evangelical beliefs imported from the Continent and made for a smoother transition to an established evangelical Reformation during the reign of Edward VI in the late 1540s to early 50s and Elizabeth I in the 1560s.

With regard to Wyclif and the Lollards and to lend historical credibility to the Reformation of the Elizabethan era, John Foxe praised Wyclif as the "mornynge starre" of the English Reformation, and a similar assertion was made earlier by John Bale in 1548.[2] The first and most comprehensive study of Lollardy was published in the early twentieth century and actually adopted a more skeptical attitude with regard to the broader theological impact of Wyclif and the Lollards upon the development of the English Reformation,[3] but studies more positive to the Lollard contribution to Protestant expansion gained popularity after the middle of the twentieth century.[4] Recent research, however, accounting for the weaknesses in Lollard influence by the early sixteenth century, now leans more heavily against this point of view.[5] The influence of Lollardy on evangelical reformers in the early period of English Reformation in the 1520s and 30s is also tenuous from the perspective of both history and theology.

It is important to point out that no new or original Lollard writings were written later than the middle of the fifteenth century,[6] and the first printings of Lollard manuscripts date to the 1530s. The manuscript collection selected by Anne Hudson for her edition of Wycliffite writings dates between 1384 and 1414, and she is certain that none of the writings originates beyond 1425. Although relatively few of the

---

2. Foxe, *A&M* [1570], 523; Hudson, *Premature Reformation*, 60; Aston, "Lollardy and the Reformation," 150, 152.

3. Gairdner, *Lollardy and the Reformation in England*, 1:7–8.

4. Rupp, *Studies in the Making*, 1; Dickens, *Lollards and Protestants in the Diocese of York*; Dickens, *The English Reformation*, 36–37; Dickens, "Lollards and Protestants," in Slavin, *Humanism, Reform, and Reformation*, 106, 109. See also Davis, "Lollardy and the Reformation," 41; Hudson, *Premature Reformation*; Lutton, *Lollardy and Orthodox Religion*.

5. For example, see Rex, *The Lollards*; Haigh, *English Reformations*; Haigh, *English Reformation Revised*; Duffy, *Stripping of the Altars*. For a good overview of the historiography, see Marshall, *Reformation England*, 15–19, 32–35.

6. MacCulloch, "England," in Pettegree, *Early Reformation in Europe*, 175; Hudson, *Premature Reformation*, 451–52; Rex, *The Lollards*, 132; Haigh, *English Reformations*, 52–53.

original manuscripts dating to this period are now extant,[7] evidence in heresy trials does prove that portions of the vernacular translations of the Bible and other pre-existing Lollard manuscripts did continue to circulate rather widely into the sixteenth century.[8] The fact that Lollard manuscripts were even published in the 1530s by evangelical reformers such as William Tyndale is evidence that Lollard writings were accessible well into the sixteenth century.[9]

An apparent lull in official persecution of Lollards that occurs in the historical records between 1430 and 1480 has led some scholars to surmise that a revival of the Lollard heresy occurred in the few generations just prior to, and was reenergized by, contact with the arrival of Luther's works.[10] Foxe does record a number of depositions against heretics in the diocese of London between 1509 and 1527,[11] and episcopal registers in Lichfield and Coventry indicate the suppression of heretical activity in the early 1500s.[12] However, as Richard Rex has wisely observed, this apparent lull could be nothing more than a gap in the historical records themselves. Otherwise, it might indicate a renewal of more intensified efforts to extirpate heresy, especially in the light of foreign heresies being imported. Furthermore, the evidence limits this so-called revival only to those areas already possessing a known stronghold of the heresy, such as Coventry, Bristol, London, and the Chilterns.[13]

Many of the regions with the smoothest turnover to the evangelical Reformation in the late 1540s do have a known history of Lollard strength at the popular level,[14] but, as Rex points out, this is no basis on which to draw a universal conclusion about the relationship of Lollardy

---

7. Hudson, *Selections from English Wycliffite Writings*, 10–11. See also Hudson, *Premature Reformation*, 11–12, 18, 117.

8. Hudson, *Lollards and Their Books*, 10–11, 227–48; Hudson, *Premature Reformation*, 451–53, 470–72, 483–84.

9. Aston, "Lollardy and the Reformation," 162–63.

10. Ibid.; Lutton, *Lollardy and Orthodox Religion*, 157. See also Cooper, "Revival of Lollardy."

11. Foxe, *A & M* [1570], 927–47.

12. Hudson, *Premature Reformation*, 33. See also Thomson, *Later Lollards*, 46–51 (and his appendix, "Major Heresy Prosecutions Recorded 1414–1522," 237–38).

13. Rex, *The Lollards*, 88–89, 112–14; Hudson, *Premature Reformation*, 81, 447–48, 456.

14. MacCulloch, "England," in Pettegree, *Early Reformation in Europe*, 177; Dickens, "Lollards and Protestants," in Slavin, *Humanism, Reform, and Reformation*, 106.

to the English Reformation. He argues that, while some areas with a Lollard presence do indeed show a relatively smooth transition to the evangelical Reformation, some areas devoid of a documented Lollard tradition were also won expediently to the evangelical faith just as others where Lollardy survived were actually centers of great opposition.[15]

Most recently, Richard Lutton suggests that the particular success of Protestantism in the parish of Tenterden in Kent may have resulted from the "broader influence of Lollard heresy upon the types of pieties that may have been susceptible to new doctrines."[16] Yet, regardless of whether Lollard influences affected, or merely overlapped, with late medieval orthodox Catholic pieties in the particular parish of Tenterden in Kent does nothing to explain the origins of such Christocentric pieties throughout the rest of England and elsewhere on the Continent. Furthermore, it is important to point out that the types of pieties Lutton highlights in his study were also evident in places such as Yorkshire that were virtually untouched by Lollardy.[17]

In comparing theological content, it is obviously impossible not to recognize that many of the doctrinal themes of Wyclif and the Lollards are echoed in the evangelical writings of the English reformers in the 1520s and 30s. Besides having a vision for a vernacular Bible, Wyclif criticized the office of the papacy and the temporal power exercised by prelates, he objected to prayers for the dead, the cult of the saints, priestly absolution of sin through mandatory confession and indulgences, misguided devotion to images, relics, pilgrimages, shrines, and the scholastic doctrine of transubstantiation. Yet it is also known that Wyclif maintained belief in purgatory and the doctrine of the Real Presence of Christ in the Eucharist not shared by later English evangelicals.[18]

There are doubts surrounding whether or not Wyclif had any personal role in shepherding the "Lollards" ("mumblers"), a pejorative term loaned from the continent against heretics and highly ambiguous, but he was certainly the major inspiration behind many of the reforming themes that appear in Lollard manuscripts and accounts of heresy

---

15. Rex, *The Lollards*, 119–31.
16. Lutton, *Lollardy and Orthodox Religion*, 202–10.
17. See Duffy's discussion of will preambles in the parish of Otley in *Stripping of the Altars*, 505–19.
18. Rex, *The Lollards*, 25–53; Hudson, *Premature Reformation*, 282–313.

trials.[19] However, for all the agreements shared by Lollards, they lacked universal agreement with each other and even with Wyclif himself, since some went beyond him in adopting a more strictly memorial interpretation of the Eucharist. With regard to images, some Lollards recognized their value if used appropriately, while others promoted a more blatant iconoclasm against idolatry toward the saints. Wyclif's belief in purgatory was also not universally embraced by all Lollards.[20]

Alec Ryrie argues that Lollards were sympathetic to evangelical ideas and became largely integrated into the evangelical reform movement of the 1520s and 30s.[21] Their sympathy was chiefly displayed in the participation of the "Society of Christian Brethren" in the foreign book trade and through the distribution of Tyndale's groundbreaking 1526 New Testament.[22] There is also evidence that Lollards had personal contact with the emerging generation of evangelical reformers. It is well known that, while under house arrest in London, Robert Barnes sold a copy of Tyndale's English New Testament to two Lollards from Essex. The confession of John Tyball before Bishop Tunstall of London in April 1528 gives the famous account of Barnes (here called "Barons") selling the New Testament for *3s. 2d.* in the chamber of his Augustinian house.[23] The early reforming preacher Thomas Bilney also drew crowds of sympathizing Lollards in his criticism of images, pilgrimages, and the cult of saints.[24]

In the minds of the ecclesiastical and secular rulers, the ideas of Luther did seem, in fact, little more than a resuscitation of the earlier indigenous heresy.[25] In fact, in a letter from Bishop of London Cuthbert Tunstall to Thomas More in 1528, licensing him to read and refute

---

19. See the "Book of Conclusions or Reformations" presented to Parliament in 1394 in Foxe, *A&M* [1570], 605–8; Davis, "Lollardy and the Reformation," 39–40; Hudson, *Premature Reformation*, 282–313; Hudson, *Selections from English Wycliffite Writings*, 24–29.

20. Hudson, *Premature Reformation*, 279–89, 303–10.

21. Ryrie, *Gospel and Henry VIII*, 232–34; Ryrie, "Strange Death," 79–82; Rupp, *Studies in the Making*, 1.

22. Dickens, "Lollards and Protestants," in Slavin, *Humanism, Reform, and Reformation*, 109–10; Davis, "Lollardy and the Reformation," 45, 48–49, 52; Rupp, *Studies in the Making*, 6–12, 14; Hudson, *Premature Reformation*, 482–83.

23. *L&P* 4.2: 1859. See also Rex, *The Lollards*, 117–18.

24. Maas, "Thomas Bilney," 8–20.

25. Hudson, *Premature Reformation*, 446.

heretical books, he refers to Luther's heresy as the "foster-daughter of Wycliffe's." Henry VIII similarly referred to Luther's writings as having "kyndeled agayne almost all the embres of those olde errours and heresyes."[26] Such overlapping similarities between Lollard and evangelical beliefs has caused some dispute as to whether a reformer such as Thomas Bilney should be properly classified as Lollard or evangelical.[27]

The emphasis in Bilney's reforming preaching throughout the 1520s against popular devotion to the cult of saints, pilgrimages, and the veneration of images certainly parallels those of the Lollards and even shares some common ground with the reforming criticisms of humanists against a morally vacuous and superstitious devotional ritualism. Bilney was raised in Norfolk and this town was known for Lollardy, but there is no proof that his reforming career was a product of such influence. Bilney later became a prominent member of the circle of scholars that met to discuss Luther's writings in the early 1520s. According to Foxe, it was Bilney who succeeded in converting Robert Barnes, Thomas Arthur, and Hugh Latimer. Bilney's narration of his own conversion to trusting in Christ for salvation from his sins indeed resembles the evangelical experience of Luther. Although his opponents readily associated his teachings with the heresies of Luther, and later of Tyndale, Bilney claimed that his own conversion resulted not from the writings of Luther but from his own reading of the epistles of Paul in Erasmus's *Novum Testamentum* (1519). Perhaps this was then only reinforced and developed through contact with Luther's more developed evangelical theology of justification. In his 1527 trial Bilney did give verbal support to the condemnation of Luther, but he also went on to deny having preached any of the heretical articles attributed to him during that trial. Bilney was later remorseful over his abjuration and resumed his tour of preaching against images and the cult of the saints in 1531 until his martyrdom the same year.[28]

26. Tunstall's letter is quoted in Dickens, "Lollards and Protestants," in Slavin, *Humanism, Reform, and Reformation*, 112; Henry VIII, *Answere Unto A Certaine Letter of Martyn Lther*, sig. A ii ᵛ–A iii ʳ.

27. Marshall, *Reformation England*, 32, 34.

28. Foxe, *A&M* [1570], 1134–35, 1138, 1364; Stackhouse, "Native Roots," 23–26; Maas, "Thomas Bilney," 8–20; Lusardi, "Career of Robert Barnes," in Schuster, Marius, Lusardi, and Schoeck, *Complete Works of Thomas More*, 8.3: 1370; Jacobs, *Lutheran Movement*, 7; Tjernagel, *Henry VIII and the Lutherans*, 39; Marshall, *Reformation England*, 28–29, 32, 34.

Although most of the Lollards probably did eventually become evangelicals, it is important to point out that no leading evangelical clergyman of the Henrician period was of a Lollard background.[29] This is also true of most other leading reforming figures including Tyndale, Frith, and Barnes. Not long before going public in their support of evangelical reform, these three were all active within the elite institutions of the Catholic tradition.[30] However, the assumption that such high profile evangelicals were actually converted from a devout Catholic background has come under some recent scrutiny: "What we do not yet know in any systematic way, aside from the anecdotal self-conscious accounts of the conversion of leading Protestant figures, is whether particular aspects of orthodox culture may have rendered their adherents susceptible to evangelical beliefs . . . that there may already have been changes in orthodox devotion prior to the arrival of outright solafidianism that were lessening the centrality of purgatory and the saints, and reducing some of the more burdensome elements of religious observance."[31] Lutton suggests that such changes were actually inspired by Lollardy, which made an indirect contribution to the acceptance of evangelical beliefs among late medieval Catholics possessing a stronger devotion to the person and work of Christ, but this is not beyond reasonable doubt.

On the other hand, to give the impression that evangelical reformers were ever ignorant of Lollardy would be misleading, since the literature of the older heresy was later revived in the 1530s and 40s "to muster precedent and example."[32] Most historians now agree with John Foxe and John Bale that William Tyndale himself was the editor of Lollard manuscripts in the 1530s. While this does not prove that Tyndale was ever a Lollard or was even influenced by Lollardy early on in his reforming career, since the publication of these manuscripts appears well after his evangelical conversion became public, it does reveal his obvious sympathy for, and identification with, their preceding efforts.[33]

---

29. Ryrie, *Gospel and Henry VIII*, 232–36.

30. Rex, *The Lollards*, 117–19, 133–39; Rex, "New Light," 146.

31. Lutton, *Lollardy and Orthodox Religion*, 208.

32. Ryrie, *Gospel and Henry VIII*, 235–36; Aston, "Lollardy and the Reformation," 152–54, 169.

33. Smeeton, *Lollard Themes*, 256–58; Mozley, *William Tyndale*, 345–46; Hudson, *Premature Reformation*, 493–94.

It is certainly tempting to look for an incipient form of English Protestantism in the fifteenth century. Ian Stackhouse admits that caution is needed here particularly in light of the eventual victory of Protestantism in England.[34] However, although Smeeton and Werrell are more favorable toward the idea that Wyclif and the Lollards taught a doctrine of justification by faith,[35] most scholars argue that neither ultimately challenged fundamental assumptions within medieval soteriology concerning the role of good works in obtaining eternal life, other than with regard to attacking idolatrous devotional practices and a ceremonial or ritual works-righteousness, nor did they ever positively or clearly articulate a clear doctrine of justification by faith in Christ alone so central to the evangelical reformers.[36] The doctrine of justification *sola fide* among English evangelicals was even a distinction recognizable to contemporaries such as Bishop Tunstall.[37] Furthermore, Anne Hudson has shown that, despite the obvious biblicism of Wyclif and the Lollards, their closer continuity with the allegorical tradition of medieval exegesis and interpretation also distances them from Tyndale and other early English evangelical reformers.[38] Besides these differences, it is simply not possible to argue with any substantive evidence that leading early English evangelicals were influenced theologically by contact with the writings of Wyclif and the Lollards.

Lollards never established an organized movement or a coherent denominational structure, and due to its lack of consolidation, suppression from above, the decline in the literary output of new works, and eventual loss of support among the gentry and more educated, contributing to a social isolation largely among families of the rural mercantile classes,[39] the impact of Lollardy was far less significant than formerly thought. A rampant anticlerical spirit at the dawn of the early sixteenth

---

34. Stackhouse, "Native Roots," 20.

35. Werrell, *Theology of William Tyndale*, 19. Smeeton leaves the question more open-ended. See *Lollard Themes*, 127–31.

36. Marshall, *Reformation England*, 33; Rex, *The Lollards*, xii–xiii, 25–53.

37. Stackhouse, "Native Roots," 23; Smeeton, *Lollard Themes*, 127; Hudson, *Premature Reformation*, 500.

38. Hudson, *Premature Reformation*, 271–72.

39. Haigh, *Reformation Revised*, 4–5; Heal, *Reformation in Britain and Ireland*, 111; Hope, "Lollardy," in Lake and Dowling, *Protestantism and the National Church*, 17; Hudson, *Premature Reformation*, 110–17, 134–44, 446–47, 510; Lutton, *Lollardy and Orthodox Religion*, 162–81, 202, 194. See also Marshall, *Reformation England*, 17.

century in England is hard to substantiate historically, leading scholars to conclude that the Protestant reforms implemented during the Edwardian and later Elizabethan periods were enforced upon a largely unsympathetic and devout Catholic populace.[40]

The relationship of Humanism to the evangelical theology of leading English reformers of the 1520s and 30s is also ambiguous. There is no doubt that these reformers received some education in Humanism and were influenced by some of its methodological advancements and reforming concerns. Trueman even states that it was "Humanism which provides the immediate intellectual context in which the English Reformers interpreted and developed the theology of the continental Reformation."[41] Yet it is important to recognize that Renaissance "Humanism" was by no means a uniform movement and, with regard to the reform of late medieval Catholicism, was really interested in cultivating moral virtue through the pragmatic application and eloquent communication of Christian doctrine and practice rather than in completely overturning the cardinal points of Catholic orthodoxy.[42] Thus, although some scholars might argue that there would have been no Reformation without Humanism,[43] "Humanism" is not a universal explanation for either the origins of, or receptiveness to, evangelical theology.

Humanism, or rather the *studia humanitatis*, originated in Renaissance Italy in the fourteenth and fifteenth centuries and began broadly as a movement to reform scholarship and education through direct rhetorical and literary engagement with the ancient classics for the purpose of nurturing practical moral virtue. It did not begin with overt criticism of the Church but scholars trained in Humanism employed its methodological and moralistic emphases more explicitly in criticism of the impracticality of much of medieval scholastic theology and the moral decadence of late medieval Catholic clergy and popular religious

---

40. Haigh, *English Reformations*, 53; Haigh, *English Reformation Revised*, 4–5; Rex, *The Lollards*, 71; Duffy, *Stripping of the Altars*, 2, 6; Hope, "Lollardy," in Lake and Dowling, *Protestantism and the National Church*, 2–6.

41. Trueman, *Luther's Legacy*, 53.

42. McGrath, *Intellectual Origins*, 33–35; Ozment, *Age of Reform*, 304–9.

43. Spitz states that "Without the humanists and without humanism there would not have been a Reformation such as we know from history and from our own experience." See "Humanism and the Protestant Reformation," in Rabil, *Renaissance Humanism*, 3:380–411.

piety.⁴⁴ Humanism in essence imbibed an appreciation for the historical, literary, and rhetorical form of the classical texts of antiquity, including the Scriptures, the Church Fathers, as well as the best of ancient pagan Greek and Latin literature, studied in their original languages using the best available manuscripts. The classical Renaissance phrase coined by humanist scholars, "to the sources" (*ad fontes*), characterized this belief in the reformational value of direct historical engagement with the classics in their most primitive and pristine literary form. To this end it was necessary that scholars be well versed in the languages of Greek and Latin and that the learned have access to the most "critical and authoritative texts" of Scripture, the Fathers, and the acceptable pagan classics.⁴⁵ Thus, Humanism of the late medieval period gave birth to early textual criticism in its search for the best and most accurate texts and translations, including improvements on the Latin Vulgate.⁴⁶

Humanism in England in the early sixteenth century was neither a monolithic nor, as elsewhere, a uniform movement. Humanist scholars differed in their attitudes toward the legitimacy of the speculative, abstract, and dialectical methodology of medieval scholastic theology, the benefits of the vernacular translation of classical texts, and the ancient Christian and pagan writers to be favored. Those influenced by Humanism eventually became split over the acceptance of the new evangelical theology arriving from the Continent in the 1520s, thus forming more distinctively "evangelical" and "conservative," or "Catholic," humanisms. This makes it difficult to establish a universal connection between Humanism and receptiveness to evangelical theology, since many educated humanists rejected the new doctrines and remained orthodox Catholics.⁴⁷ According to Rex, it is clear that Humanism affected religious change on both sides of the divide and, thus, "did not deter-

---

44. D'Amico, "Humanism and Pre-Reformation Theology," in Rabil, *Renaissance Humanism*, 3:349.

45. Dowling, *Humanism*, 1; D'Amico, "Humanism and Pre-Reformation Theology," in Rabil, *Renaissance Humanism*, 3: 356–57.

46. D'Amico, "Humanism and Pre-Reformation Theology," in Rabil, *Renaissance Humanism*, 3: 357–58.

47. Pettegree, "Humanism and the Reformation," in Amos, Pettegree and van Nierop, *Education of a Christian Society*, 9; Rex, "Role of English Humanists," in Amos, Pettegree, and van Nierop, *Education of a Christian Society*, 20–21, 31; MaCulloch, "England," in Pettegree, *Early Reformation in Europe*, 170.

mine or even direct the theological course of the English Reformation."[48] In another essay by Rex, he points out that educated humanists at both Oxford and Cambridge were enlisted as a major force against Luther's heresies.[49] It is clear that many reformers trained in the literary and grammatical methodology of Humanism not only employed its scholarly tools in contrast to the more abstract methods favored by scholastic theologians and to attack clerical immorality and corruption, as well as the moral bankruptcy of medieval ritual and devotional superstition to images and relics, but also to reform more basic theological assumptions about God and salvation through the exposition of Scripture supplemented by recourse to the Church Fathers.[50] Calvin and Zwingli, for example, owe something to their education in Humanism in communicating Christian doctrine and life on the basis of a rhetorical and exegetical engagement with Scripture and the Fathers.[51] Yet, the priority they placed on reforming the very doctrinal and theological assumptions characterizing the mainstream of medieval Catholicism, and this according to a principle of *sola scriptura*, shows them to have moved significantly beyond the original essence and aims of Humanism.[52]

Early on, humanists displayed a common concern for moral reform in the life of the Church, but eventually the influence of the new evangelical theology sharply divided them.[53] By 1521, the year of Luther's imperial condemnation at the Diet of Worms, it was clear that humanists loyal to Catholic orthodoxy needed to distance themselves from the more radical teachings of Luther. In a letter written by Erasmus to Cardinal Wolsey dated May 18, 1518, he denounces rumors of any favorable connection with Luther and reassures Wolsey of his faithfulness to the Pope and to Rome. In his letter to Wolsey, Erasmus states that it has been his preoccupation with writing letters that has kept him from penning a book against Luther thus far, which he eventually did with

---

48. Rex, "Role of English Humanists," in Amos, Pettegree, and van Nierop, *Education of a Christian Society* 39–40.

49. Rex, "English Campaign Against Luther," 87, 89.

50. Dowling, *Humanism*, 1–2; Rex, "Role of English Humanists," in Amos, Pettegree, and van Nierop, *Education of a Christian Society*, 22.

51. Spitz, "Humanism and the Protestant Reformation," in Rabil, *Renaissance Humanism*, 3:380–411.

52. Ozment, *Age of Reform*, 304–5.

53. Dowling, *Humanism*, 38, 40; *L&P*, II.2: 1292, III.1: 551. See also Erasmus's letter to Warham (Aug 23, 1521) in III.2 and to Wolsey (March 1522) in III.1: 897.

his diatribe on free-will in 1524.[54] Catholic humanists were enlisted in the early 1520s as defenders of the Church against heresy and backed off in their own criticisms.[55] When the matter of Henry's divorce (technically, annulment) to Catherine of Aragon came up, the division was furthered even more since influential Catholic humanists like Thomas More (1478–1535) and John Fisher (1469–1535) were unable in good conscience to disavow papal authority, whereas evangelicals supported Henry in his break with Rome in marriage to Anne Boleyn in 1533, herself a sympathetic patron of evangelical ideas.[56]

England's own connection with Humanism originated from itinerant English scholars who visited Italy and Italian humanists who visited England in the 1400s, but there was little humanist scholarship of significance in England before the very end of the fifteenth century.[57] Among the most influential of these English scholars educated in Italy were the so-called "Oxford Reformers": Thomas Linacre, William Grocyn, and John Colet.[58]

The influence of John Colet (1467–1519), in particular, upon the development of Humanism at Oxford is controversial. In the nineteenth century, Frederick Seebohm heralded Colet's university lectures on Paul's epistles delivered in 1496–1499 as foreshadowing later Protestant expository style preaching.[59] The lectures do indeed use a literary hermeneutic with emphasis on the moral application of Scripture, and this contrasts with the more conventional use in university lectures of allegory and scholastic commentary to dispute abstract theological questions. Colet used a similar humanist approach in a sermon later delivered before Convocation in Canterbury in 1512.[60]

---

54. Dowling, *Humanism*, 38–40.

55. Elton, *Reform and Reformation*, 77.

56. Dowling, *Humanism*, 45; Yost, "Reappraisal," 442; Marshall, *Reformation England*, 36–40, 49–50.

57. Dowling, *Humanism*, 7–8.

58. Schoeck, "Humanism in England," in Rabil, *Renaissance Humanism*, 2:7; Tjernagel, *Henry VIII and the Lutherans*, 35.

59. Seebohm, *Oxford Reformers*, 252–55; Gleason, *Colet*, 8; Dickens, *English Reformation*, 66.

60. See Trapp, "Colet," in *ODNB* 12:601–9. The lectures were not published in Colet's lifetime. For a modern English translation of the manuscript lecture notes, see Colet, *Exposition of St. Paul's Epistle to the Romans*.

However, recent scholars have downplayed the novelty of the lectures and circumscribed their impact on the development of Humanism at Oxford. As was the case with Erasmus, Colet also apparently followed Origen in characterizing allegory as one of the four senses of biblical interpretation. Dickens acknowledges that the style of the lectures is undeniably distinct from the common methodology employed in the universities at the time, but he argues that it is not so unlike the preference for the literal sense of Scripture in the hermeneutics of the medieval Parisian commentator Nicholas of Lyra (c. 1270–1340).[61] John Gleason argues that it is also similar to the homiletic tradition of medieval monasticism.[62] Furthermore, though Erasmus acknowledged the popularity of Colet's lectures in personal letters, the methodology used by Colet did not create the shock and consternation that might be expected. Furthermore, according to the foremost scholar on Colet, the Oxford reformer remained theologically orthodox despite the harshness of his criticism of religious abuses in the Church.[63] If Colet made any major contribution to English Humanism in his own time, says Gleason, this probably had less to do with the lectures than with his work in co-establishing and administering the St. Paul's cathedral school in London in 1512. The school was to provide learning in "good literature both laten and greke," which Colet restricted to Christian writers.[64] The influence of Colet on Humanism at Oxford is also questionable since it was Erasmus's *Novum Instrumentum* (1516) that convinced Colet, now in his forties, of the indispensable value of learning Greek, a language he never mastered.[65]

By the early decades of the sixteenth century, it was clear that Oxford and Cambridge had been touched by Humanism. The generous patronage of the Tudor prelates helped contribute to this reality. Lady Margaret Beaufort, for example, demonstrated her support of humanist

---

61. Dickens, *English Reformation*, 64–66.

62. Gleason, *Colet*, 132–36, 141–44.

63. Ibid., 4–5, 117–23; Dickens, *English Reformation*, 65–66; Clebsch, *England's Earliest Protestants*, 169; D'Amico, "Humanism and Pre-Reformation Theology," in Rabil, *Renaissance Humanism*, 3:366.

64. Gleason, *Colet*, 221–34.

65. Ibid., 58–59; Schoeck, "Humanism in England," in Rabil, *Renaissance Humanism*, 2:10–11, 17; Porter, "Introduction," 18–19; Duhamel, "Oxford Lectures of John Colet," 493–99.

learning by co-establishing St. John's College, Cambridge, as did Richard Fox with the founding of Corpus Christi College, Oxford.[66]

St. John's College, established in 1511 and opened for classes in 1516, was co-founded by John Fisher, Bishop of Rochester and Chancellor of Cambridge. The older scholastic curriculum was preserved to such a degree as to avoid confrontation,[67] but emphasis on language studies and grammatical-literary exegesis, rather than on dialectic, logical exercises, and the study of medieval commentaries, contributed to the subtle decline of the older method's dominance.[68]

Humanist scholarship at Cambridge was, then, implemented into the curriculum rather slowly through emphasis upon grammar and language skills and regular readings of classical texts,[69] but it did not immediately replace its medieval educational counterpart, and the reading and study of the medieval scholastic commentaries continued for some time alongside it. In fact, according to Leader, the line demarcating humanists from scholastics was not even quite so clear at Cambridge in 1517.[70] It was not until 1535 that Thomas Cromwell, Vicegerent to Henry VIII, implemented a more comprehensive series of injunctions to abolish the study of canon law in the universities and the "total eradication" of the scholastic theologians from philosophical and doctrinal studies. This, coupled with Henry's break with the papacy, aided the continual consolidation of humanist education in English universities well into the sixteenth and early seventeenth centuries.[71]

The impact of Humanism at Cambridge and Oxford, and all of England for that matter, arguably owes its greatest debt to Erasmus, "the most celebrated European humanist connected with England."[72] Elton argues that it was with Erasmus that Humanism became an actual movement in England.[73] Erasmus had visited Oxford as early as 1499, was present during the lectures of Colet, and later taught the first

66. Schoeck, "Humanism in England," in Rabil, *Renaissance Humanism*, 2: 6–7, 25–26; Tjernagel, *Henry VIII and the Lutherans*, 35.
67. Rex, "Role of English Humanists," 25–26.
68. Leader, *Cambridge*, 308.
69. Ibid., 237.
70. Dowling, *Humanism*, 9; Leader, *Cambridge*, 266–67.
71. Dowling, *Humanism*, 97.
72. Ibid., 141.
73. Elton, *Reform and Reformation*, 13.

official Greek course at Cambridge intermittently between 1511 and 1514. Erasmus, as a student of the *Devotiona Moderna*, was already well known for his description of the virtuous life as the imitation of Christ in his *Handbook of the Militant Christian* (1503), and the final draft of his satirical musings on the moral vacuity of the late medieval Church in the *Praise of Folly* was finished in 1514. While at Cambridge Erasmus also worked on his Greek New Testament. The *Novum Instrumentum*, a Latin translation revised on the basis of the original Greek text, was printed in 1514, but was not published for distribution until 1516 after receiving papal permission.[74] The value of the Greek New Testament to the biblical scholarship of English evangelical reformers is obvious,[75] but the importance of Erasmus was claimed by Catholic humanists as well.[76] As has already been shown, the tools of Humanism could equally be used as a weapon against evangelicals and their theology.

Leading English evangelicals did encounter some humanist influences as young college students and at university in the early sixteenth century, but Catholic theology was still significantly impressed upon them in the scholastic mold. While Humanism did give budding English evangelical clergy, scholars, and theologians tools of literary interpretation, a more direct path to Scripture and the Fathers (Augustine being the most important to them), and a perspective that was as analytical towards texts as it was toward clerical immorality and the moral vacuity of medieval ritual and devotional superstition to images and relics, Luther's works were profoundly influential in shaping their "evangelical" vision to reform English Christian faith and devotion at the root of theological assumption. Thus, it was not enough simply to elevate the virtuous life lived in imitation of Christ as many humanists had done, but it required a whole different outlook on the nature and purpose of human morality on the basis of, what English evangelicals believed was, a more biblical theology of the Gospel in the doctrine of justification before God through faith in Christ alone resulting in truly good works. In fact, it could be argued that the evangelical theology of Luther was the immediate intellectual background in which early English evangelicals interpreted and developed the prior methodological and moral impulses of English Humanism.

74. Bainton, *Erasmus*, 101, 113; Leader, *Cambridge*, 293–94.
75. Rupp, *Studies in the Making*, 17; Dickens, *English Reformation*, 66–67, 71.
76. Rex, "Role of English Humanists," 30.

The influence of Luther and his theology was significant to the story of the English Reformation of the Henrician period, whether it was the serious efforts of the highest offices of government to suppress the importation, distribution, and perceived influence of his writings in the 1520s or, contrariwise, to court the sanction of German Lutheran political support for Henry's break with the papacy in divorcing Catherine and in marriage to Anne Boleyn in the 1530s.

Luther's evangelical writings found their way to England thanks to the trade market established much earlier between England and northern Europe. If it is true that "trade often built the circuits" on which the works of Luther traveled,[77] then, as one historian has observed, the waters that served to defend England in war time were ironically the very channel on which the infection of his religious heresy spread.[78] Antwerp, in particular, was a major importer of English wool, and England was a major importer of books printed by the more highly developed press industry of the Continent: "before and throughout the sixteenth century, the cultural and economic lives of England and the Netherlands were closely and intricately connected."[79] Therefore, it is not all that surprising when laws proscribing a rather lucrative market in the printing and exporting of prohibited books from Antwerp received little cooperation from local authorities.[80] Such books sold at the large Frankfurt book fairs were shipped up the Rhine River, smuggled into London in bales of cloth, and delivered by courageous couriers to interested buyers.[81] Lollards, local merchants, and sympathetic university scholars were those busiest in the trafficking of the works of Luther throughout England in the 1520s. Monasteries such as at Reading and Bury were also important receptacles of his works.[82]

The printing, distributing, and reading of Luther's works really became an international scandal after his preemptory condemnation

---

77. Dickens, *English Reformation*, 69; Pearce, "Luther and the English Reformation," 597; Clebsch, *England's Earliest Protestants*, 33.

78. Avis, "Book Smuggling," 185.

79. Ibid., 180–81; Avis, "England's Use of Antwerp Printers," 234–40.

80. Pettegree, "Humanism and the Reformation," in Pettegree, *Education of a Christian Society*, 2–5, 17.

81. Rupp, *Six Makers*, 16.

82. Rupp, *Studies in the Making*, 11–12; Rupp, *Righteousness of God*, 37.

in the papal bull *Exurge Domine* in May 1520.[83] However, while visiting Rome, the Bishop of Rochester notified Cardinal Wolsey back in England about the bull even before its official release.[84] If it is true, then, that Luther's Latin works were distributed in England as early as 1518,[85] then for almost two years they were imported, distributed, and discussed without legal prosecution.[86]

In 1521, Bishop Cuthbert Tunstall of London urged Cardinal Wolsey in a letter from Worms to prevent Luther's *Babylonian Captivity of the Church* (1520) from penetrating the English border.[87] Wolsey's efforts to forbid the importation of Luther's works were praised by Pope Leo in March of 1521,[88] but Cardinal de Medici suggested that he schedule a more public book-burning ceremony.[89] In a letter dated April of 1521, the Pope also urged Wolsey to burn Luther's works and to forbid them to be read except by those with special permission to refute them. The Pope also notified Wolsey of a summons that had been sent to Luther in Germany to appear in Rome.[90] Wolsey commissioned local bishops to furrow out Luther's works from among the various religious institutions.[91]

Luther's writings were well known at Oxford and Cambridge by 1520. A letter from Archbishop William Warham to Cardinal Wolsey in 1521 speaks of heresy at Oxford with a request that he take serious action against it: "that diverse of that Universitie be infectyd with the heresyes of Luther and of others of that sorte, havyng emong theym a grete nombre of books of the saide perverse doctrine which wer for-

---

83. Pettegree, "Early Reformation in Europe," in Pettegree, *Early Reformation in Europe*, 5.

84. *L&P* 3.2:293.

85. Haigh, *English Reformations*, 57.

86. Meyer, "Henry VIII Burns Luther's Books," 173; D'Alton, "The Suppression of Lutheran Heretics," 253.

87. Rex, "English Campaign Against Luther," 86.

88. *L&P* 3.2:450.

89. Ibid., 455.

90. Ibid., 468. See also Meyer, "Henry VIII Burns Luther's Books," 179–81; Tjernagel, *Henry VIII and the Lutherans*, 5–6.

91. *EM* 1.2:20–25.

boden..."[92] John Dorne was a major marketer of Luther's works, the treatise against the papacy being among the most popular.[93]

Luther's writings also made a noticeable impact upon a circle of intellectuals at Cambridge University, where, according to A. G. Dickens, the "earliest known society of English Lutherans originated." Meetings at the White Horse Inn were the occasion for the discussion of the "new German doctrines" and came to be infamously known as "Little Germany." Many of the future leading evangelical clergymen and supporters of the English Reformation were educated at Cambridge and present at these meetings.[94] Scholars, however, have recently warned against adopting popular characterizations of these meetings as some sort of clandestine "Lutheran club."[95] Indeed the word "Lutheran" is a bit misleading, if not anachronistic, for the early 1520s. Furthermore, though many of its attendees, such as Hugh Latimer, Nicholas Ridley, and John Bale, would go on to become influential evangelical leaders and spokesmen for reform, a regular such as Stephen Gardiner, later Bishop of Winchester, remained an orthodox Catholic. Gardiner had been John Frith's tutor at Cambridge, but would later serve as a chief prosecutor in the trials of both Robert Barnes and John Frith.[96] Attendance at these meetings, then, did not automatically translate into sympathy or support for Luther's evangelical ideas.[97] Nevertheless, as it relates to a movement of reform, Luther was the center of attention at Cambridge in the 1520s.[98]

Although an earlier bonfire of Luther's works had occurred at Cambridge in late 1520, and Erasmus told Oecolampadius in Basle of another possible one he had averted earlier that year,[99] the first official

92. Ellis, *Letters Illustrative of English History*, 1: 239–42; *L&P* 3.2:449.

93. Clebsch, *Earliest Protestants*, 12; Smithen, *Continental Protestantism*, 44.

94. [21]Dickens, *English Reformation*, 66–68.

95. Haigh, *English Reformations*, 58; Tjernagel, *Henry VIII and the Lutherans*, 43–44.

96. Lusardi, "The Career of Robert Barnes," in Schuster, Marius, Lusardi, and Schoeck, *Complete Works of Thomas More*, 8.3: 1370; Wright, *Frith*, 4–5.

97. Foxe, *A & M* [1570]: 1134–35; Jacobs, *Lutheran Movement*, 7; Tjernagel, *Henry VIII and the Lutherans*, 39; Marshall, *Reformation England*, 34.

98. Rex, "Early Impact of Reformation Theology," 42.

99. Dickens, *English Reformation*, 68; Pettegree, "Early Reformation in Europe," in Pettegree, *Early Reformation in Europe*, 1–2; Clebsch, *England's Earliest Protestants*, 12; Meyer, "Henry VIII Burns Luther's Books," 173, 178; *L&P* 3. 2:284.

burning of Luther's books in England took place on May 12, 1521, in the churchyard of St. Paul's Cross in London. It was attended by Cardinal Wolsey, Archbishop William Warham, and other English bishops and papal and imperial emissaries.[100] John Fisher, Bishop of Rochester and Chancellor of Cambridge, preached a public sermon condemning the German friar for his heresy. This was "England's first public assertion of orthodoxy" in reaction to Luther's heresies.[101] All of this took place before the official signing of Luther's condemnation at Worms on May 25, 1521.[102] Later that year, although the extent of his actual contribution is debatable, the invective *Assertio Septum Sacramentorum* was published by Henry VIII and earned him and all future kings of England the title of "*Defensor Fidei*" from the pope.[103] The personal exchanges that followed between the two certainly contributed to the stalemate of the later 1530s and the failure to establish a possible Anglo-German alliance.

Even after 1520-21, those previously involved in the producing, distributing, and purchasing of these books continued their business at the risk of exile or martyrdom.[104] Printers, merchants, and traders endangered their lives by subsidizing the work of English refugees and supervising the smuggling of forbidden works from the Continent. The London merchant Humphrey Monmouth, for example, was later imprisoned in the Tower of London for aiding and abetting Tyndale, and he confessed to boarding Tyndale for half a year and to forwarding him money in Hamburg.[105]

The warning of Bishop Tunstall of London to booksellers and his own personal involvement in supervising the book import later in 1524 was unsuccessful.[106] After 1525, anxieties over the immigration of foreign heresies had by no means been quelled. In fact, a new wave of

---

100. *L&P* 3.1: 485; Rex, "English Campaign against Luther," 95-96.

101. Rex, "English Campaign against Luther," 95-96; Rex, *Theology of John Fisher*, 80. For an English translation of the sermon, see "The sermon ... made agayn the pernicious doctryn of Martin luther [1521]," in Hatt, *English Works of John Fisher*, 77-97.

102. Clebsch, *Earliest Protestants*, 12, 32.

103. *L&P* 3.1:516; Clebsch, *England's Earliest Protestants*, 19-20; Tjernagel, *Henry VIII and the Lutherans*, 11-15; 17-21; Rupp, *Studies in the Making*, 90; Rex, "English Campaign Against Luther," 88-89; Doernberg, *Henry VIII and Luther*, 22, 59.

104. Clebsch, *England's Earliest Protestants*, 261.

105. Foxe, *A & M* [1570]: 1133; *L&P* 4.2:1877, 1883.

106. Reed, "The Regulation of the Book Trade," 265; Clebsch, *England's Earliest Protestants*, 13.

oppression emerged and was centered significantly on the person of William Tyndale. It was being rumored that two Englishmen were preparing a vernacular New Testament to be sent to England from the continent that would infect all of England with Luther's heresies.[107] Bishop Tunstall attempted to put a freeze on the buying and selling of Tyndale's 1526 New Testament,[108] but vast copies had already been circulating throughout the environs of London by the time he ordered the securing of all copies on pain of prosecution.[109] Despite royal proclamations issued by Henry VIII threatening punishment for failure to surrender heretical works and unlicensed English translations of the Bible, the trafficking continued in the years that followed. It is hardly surprising that Dutch and German booksellers and merchants were resistant to the royal decrees.[110]

As Craig D'Alton suggests, this second wave of persecution beginning around 1525 reveals a shift in governmental policy toward more intensified action against native dissenters.[111] Clebsch observes that what was perceived in the early 1520s as a foreign encroachment largely requiring the halting of illegal book trafficking had now become what the hierarchy had attempted to prevent—a growing domestic problem.[112]

Between the years 1525 and 1530, efforts to curb the threat of heresy in general were amplified. The Index of Prohibited Books grew in size significantly after 1526, which by this time now included works by other rising continental reforming leaders such as Ulrich Zwingli, Philipp Melancthon, and Martin Bucer. Luther's writings, however, still dominated the list.[113] Tyndale's *New Testament* and *Prologue to Romans* were the first prohibited writings to be written by a native English evangelical.[114]

107. *L&P* 4. 2: 805; Rupp, *Six Makers*, 13.
108. Haigh, *English Reformations*, 60.
109. Dowling, *Humanism*, 43; Foxe, *A&M* [1570]: 1158–59.
110. Avis, "Book Smuggling," 182, 186; Reed, "Regulation of the Book Trade," 170–71; Meyer, "Henry VIII Burns Luther's Books," 321. For the royal prohibitions, see Hughes and Larkin, *Tudor Royal Proclamations*, 1:181–86; 193–97.
111. D'Alton, "Suppression of Lutheran Heretics in England," 229, 237.
112. Clebsch, *England's Earliest Protestants*, 259–60.
113. Ibid., 260, 262, 269; Foxe, *A&M* [1570]: 1157–58;
114. Clebsch, *Earliest Protestants*, 19; Hume, "English Protestant Books," in Schuster, Marius, Lusardi, and Schoeck, *Complete Works of Thomas More*, 8.3:1065–92.

A second official book burning service took place in 1526 at St. Paul's Cathedral in London. Presided over by Cardinal Wolsey, John Fisher was appointed for a second time to preach the public sermon condemning Luther's heresies.[115] Thomas More had made an unexpected visit earlier that year to the London Steelyard to search for heretical works,[116] and other suspected merchants accompanied the Augustinian friar Robert Barnes in public penance around the bonfire.[117] As mentioned already, the reforming preacher Thomas Bilney was tried in 1527 and later martyred under the banner of Luther's heresy in 1531.[118]

Henry's attitude toward Luther and the evangelicals dramatically changed near the mid-1530s in his courtship of the German theologians and princes in support of his defiance against Charles V and the papacy in divorcing Catherine and in marriage to Anne Boleyn. Luther was hopeful early on for a providential alliance with England but could not give his approval to the divorce, and his optimism was soured over the lack of progress in theological agreement in the second half of the 1530s.[119] Even after the death of Anne Boleyn in 1536, continual efforts were made to establish theological consensus with the Germans until 1539. The evangelical Robert Barnes was a chief player in these negotiations as a royal ambassador to Germany, and evangelicals Thomas Cromwell and Archbishop Thomas Cranmer rose to positions of political favor in the decade that also witnessed the dissolution of the monasteries, the sanctioning of an English Bible for every parish in 1538, and other royal injunctions aimed at deconstructing ritual and devotional superstition to images and relics.[120] Henry VIII, however, refused to adopt the Augsburg Confession as a condition for leadership of the Schmalkaldic League.[121] His passing of the "Act of Six Articles" in 1539, though never so strictly enforced as previously assumed, reaffirmed his

---

115. For an English translation of this sermon, see "A sermon . . . concernynge certayne heretickes [1526]," in Hatt, *English Works of John Fisher*, 145–74.

116. Doernberg, *Henry VIII and Luther*, 12.

117. Clebsch, *England's Earliest Protestants*, 27.

118. Marshall, *Reformation England*, 28–29, 34.

119. Tjernagel, *Henry VIII and the Lutherans*, 148–57.

120. See Duffy, *Stripping of the Altars*, 379–423; Marshall, *Reformation England*, 40–57.

121. Tjernagel, *Henry VIII and the Lutherans*, 148, 157; Rupp, *Studies in the Making*, 91–92, 99–102, 105–18; Doernberg, *Henry VIII and Luther*, 106.

loyalty to Catholic tenets unacceptable to the Lutherans and essentially ended all viable hopes of unity between England and Germany.[122] This hope was severed further with the nullification of Henry's marriage to Anne of Cleves. Although this was followed by a declaration of a general amnesty for all heretics who had been charged prior to July 1, 1540, influential evangelicals like Barnes and Cromwell did not share in this amnesty, which Luther supposed was on account of their opposition to this divorce.[123]

Alec Ryrie argues that it was the king's "suspicion of Lutheranism" as a threat to the social and political stability of nations, as well as his personal dislike and disagreement with Luther, that prevented the lasting impact of Wittenberg on the official course of the English Reformation.[124] Ryrie identifies the year 1540 as essentially the beginning of the end of attempts at diplomacy between England and Germany followed by the more formal "death" of Lutheran influence in England near the end of Henry's reign in 1546.[125] Like Ryrie, MacCulloch sees the influence of Luther waning at this time and supplanted by new relationships with the Reformed Swiss states under Edward VI.[126] The defeat of the Protestant League by Charles V in 1547, Luther's death the year before, theological division among the Lutheran churches over the next few decades, and the growing international influence of the Reformed tradition, also contributed to the weakening of German Lutheran influence on the English Reformation.[127] By the reign of Edward VI, the Swiss Reformed tradition had essentially eclipsed the legacy of the German Lutheran tradition upon developments in English Protestantism, and thus paved

---

122. Doernberg, *Henry VIII and Luther*, 105–8; Tjernagel, *Henry VIII and the Lutherans*, 195, 203, 207–10; 228–38, 248; Ryrie, *Gospel and Henry VIII*, 39; Rupp, *Studies in the Making*, 121–22, 125; The articles include transubstantiation, communion of the Eucharist only under the form of bread, the imposition of priestly celibacy, the lawfulness of vows of chastity, the sanctity of private masses, and mandatory auricular confession to a priest. See Gee and Hardy, *Documents Illustrative of English Church History*, 303–19.

123. Loane, *Pioneers*, 85–86; Lusardi, "The Career of Robert Barnes," in Schuster, Marius, Lusardi, and Schoeck, *Complete Works of Thomas More*, 8.3:1414.

124. Ryrie, "The Strange Death," 66.

125. Ibid., 78, 87.

126. MacCulloch, "England," in Pettegree, *Early Reformation in Europe*, 171–74.

127. Tjernagel, *Henry VIII and the Lutherans*, 253–54.

the way for the emergence of Puritanism.[128] Yet N.S. Tjernagel has argued that the Anglo-Lutheran theological negotiations of the 1530s provided the substance of the later official formularies of Edward VI and Elizabeth I,[129] but the "Lutheran" quality of these later documents is still in dispute.[130]

There never was a "strictly Lutheran movement" in England and neither did England ever really come close to becoming a "Lutheran land."[131] No English evangelical reformer other than Robert Barnes adopted the Lutheran theology of the Real Presence of Christ in the Eucharist, and the breakdown in official dialogue between the two nations and their respective churches at the end of the 1530s only revealed the ultimate intransigence of Henry's loyalty to Catholic doctrine. Yet Luther was a dominant focus of the religious discord characterizing this turbulent period of the early English Reformation, whether it was in attempts to find and destroy his writings and to suppress the perceived growth of their heretical influence in the 1520s or, in a near complete reversal, to court him and his German compatriots for much needed political support in the 1530s.

Much of the research in recent years has intentionally taken the spotlight away from Luther (as well as Zwingli and Calvin) as a defining personality of the broader Reformation to focus on the theological nuances and impact of lesser known reforming figures.[132] There is much to be commended in the very fine and much needed studies that have appeared over the last few decades,[133] but it appears that a reverse discrimination may be in danger of underestimating the defining role that Luther did play on the international scene. In fact, there are still reputable historians who are convinced that the Reformation, if it would have happened, would have looked remarkably different without him.[134] With regard to the English Reformation in particular, including the early Henrician period of the 1520s and 30s, the influence of Luther

---

128. Trueman, *Luther's Legacy*, 56.
129. Tjernagel, *Henry VIII and Luther*, 188–89, 248, 252–54.
130. Marshall, *Reformation England*, 41–42.
131. Hall, "Early Rise and Gradual Decline," in Baker, *Reform and Reformation*, 109; Yost, "Reappraisal," 440.
132. Dixon, *Reformation in Germany*, 20.
133. For example, Steinmetz, *Reformers in the Wings*.
134. Collinson, *Reformation*, 6, 130; Dixon, *Reformation in Germany*, 44.

has been diminished and, in some minor cases, rejected wholesale with regard to the first generation of English evangelicals Tyndale, Frith, and, to a lesser extent, Barnes. Of course, the mere fact that Luther's writings found an eager readership among many learned and influential personalities in the 1520s and became a focus of English politics in the 1520s and 30s does not by itself prove that his ideas were the direct inspiration behind, nor even closely followed by, like-minded English reformers whose careers emerged during this period. That is why it is absolutely necessary to closely assess the life, intellectual development, and theology of each of the leading English evangelical reformers, Tyndale, Frith, and Barnes, on an individual basis and in their own contexts.

6

Law and Gospel in the Theology of William Tyndale

THE LIFE AND THOUGHT OF TYNDALE HAS RECEIVED ACUTE ATTENtion over the last fifty years.[1] The most fruitful area of research has engaged the development of his theology of covenant around the year 1530. Most interpreters assume this to be a radical departure from the Law-Gospel dialectical theology of Martin Luther, but more and more scholars are arguing that Tyndale's thought from the very beginning reveals critical differences with the German reformer on issues of justification and the Christian life. These conclusions deserve careful evaluation, and to do this it is important to begin by unraveling the influences behind Tyndale's earliest writings as an evangelical reformer, which also provides context and perspective for the later development of his theology of covenant in the 1530s.

---

1. The definitive monograph on the theology of William Tyndale has yet to be written. For a recent attempt, see Werrell, *Theology of William Tyndale*. Other works covering select themes in Tyndale's theology include: Trueman, *Luther's Legacy*, 83–120; Smeeton, "The Wycliffite Choice," in Dick and Richardson, *William Tyndale and the Law*, 31–40; Smeeton, *Lollard Themes*; McGiffert, "William Tyndale's Conception of Covenant," 167–84; McGoldrick, *Luther's English Connection*, 70–82, 110–35, 147–78, 190–98; Laughlin, "The Brightness of Moses' Face"; Williams, *William Tyndale*, 122–35; Yost, "Christian Humanism"; Clebsch, *England's Earliest Protestants*, 141–204; Trinterud, "A Reappraisal," 24–45; Knappen, "William Tindale: First English Puritan." On the life of Tyndale, the best and most up-to-date treatment is Daniell, *William Tyndale*; Knappen, "Tyndale," *ODNB* 55:780–87; Daniell, *Bible in English*, 133–59. For other accounts, see also Williams, *William Tyndale*, 1–63; Clebsch, *England's Earliest Protestants*, 137–204; Loane, *Masters*, 55–108; Mozley, *William Tyndale*; Demaus and Lovett, *William Tindale*; Carlisle, "Tyndale," *DNB* 19:1351–58. The earliest accounts are found in: Foxe, *A&M* [1563], 513–20; *A&M* [1570], 1224–29; Foxe, "Here foloweth the historie and discourse of the lyfe of William Tyndall out of the book of Actes and Monumentes Briefly extracted," *Whole Works*.

Though his precise birthplace remains uncertain, John Foxe states in the *Acts and Monuments* that Tyndale was "borne upon the borders of Wales," and historians have confirmed that he was indeed raised in the Severn valley of Gloucestershire, the Vale of Berkeley, probably near the village of Stinchcombe.[2] There is little that is known about Tyndale's youth, and only possible suggestions can be made regarding the potential influences that might have shaped him at this early stage. The most critical to note in the light of the most recent research is Lollardy. Donald Smeeton and Ralph Werrell have provided the most ambitious attempts to link Tyndale theologically to Wyclif and the Lollards.[3] Both work from the Trinterud thesis as it was later developed by P.A. Laughlin and assume that Tyndale from the very beginning had major theological differences with Luther. While not denying that a range of continental influences from Erasmus to Luther had some variable part to play in the development of Tyndale's thought and expression, these writers challenge distorted emphases placed on foreign currents of thought at the expense of a surviving and vibrant native tradition of Lollard dissent.

Smeeton acknowledges that his own argument for Lollard influence on Tyndale's theology is inconclusive and that his conclusions are "tentative." In fact, even the editor of the series reiterates in the preface that Smeeton "is well aware that his own arguments are based on inference and that additional evidence on the main issues of the book would be highly desirable if only it were available."[4] The argument for Lollard influence is based upon the two basic premises that Lollardy on the eve of the Reformation was a socially and culturally significant movement and that semantic and doctrinal similarities suggest likely influence. Both of these premises, however, are highly questionable on historical grounds.

Regarding the first premise, Smeeton's conclusions are based on older research that argued in favor of Lollardy's impact on the English Reformation in the early sixteenth century.[5] However, the consensus of

---

2. For disputes over the location of Tyndale's boyhood home, see Daniell, *Tyndale*, 9–13. See also Moynahan, *God's Bestseller*, 2–3.

3. See also Hudson, *Premature Reformation*, 504–5; Stackhouse, "Native Roots," 19–35.

4. Smeeton, *Lollard Themes*, 11–2, 15.

5. Rupp, *Studies in the Making*, 1; Dickens, *Lollards and Protestants in the Diocese of York*; Dickens, *English Reformation*, 36–37; Dickens, "Lollards and Protestants," in

more recent scholarship now leans heavily against this notion and argues that Lollardy's impact was negligible in comparison to a widespread popular loyalty to Catholicism that persisted well into the Tudor dynasty.[6] With regard to Tyndale, Lollardy is traceable to Gloucestershire, especially the port city of Bristol, but there is no evidence that it was thriving where Tyndale was born and raised.[7] In fact, the evidence actually points to the Vale of Berkeley as a stronghold of mainstream Catholicism.[8] Furthermore, there is no evidence that Tyndale had any contact with Lollards before matriculating at Oxford in 1506: "The social history of Gloucestershire, then, and the analysis (in so far as it can be pursued) of Tyndale's place therein, are hardly such as to establish that Tyndale was exposed to Lollard influences in his upbringing and early development."[9]

Ralph Werrell, however, has recently isolated a statement made by Tyndale indicating he read the vernacular translation of Hugden's *Polychronicon* by John Trevisa as a boy, which happened to be a favorite also of Wyclif and the Lollards.[10] Trevisa was a colleague of Wyclif and Nicholas Hereford at Queen's College Oxford in the fourteenth century, and the preface to the early seventeenth century King James Bible indeed links him to a Wycliffite translation.[11] Whatever the degree of his involvement in the work of Bible translation, or even of the doubtless influence of Wyclif upon him, Trevisa was by no means a complete disciple of Wyclif.[12] Then again, as Anne Hudson has demonstrated,

---

Slavin, *Humanism, Reform, and Reformation*, 106, 109. See also Davis, "Lollardy and the Reformation," 41; Hudson, *Premature Reformation*; Lutton, *Lollardy and Orthodox Religion*.

6. Rex, *Lollards*; Haigh, *English Reformations*; Rex, *English Reformation Revised*; Duffy, *Stripping of the Altars*. For a good overview of the historiography, see Marshall, *Reformation England*, 15–19, 32–35.

7. Thomson, *Later Lollards*, 20–51.

8. Rex, *Lollards*, 69–70, 94–95, 126–27; Rex, "New Light,"145–48. See also Litzenberger, *English Reformation and the Laity*, 28–29.

9. Rex, "New Light," 146, 159.

10. Werrell, *Theology of William Tyndale*, 11, 17–19; Hudson, *Premature Reformation*, 397.

11. Fowler, "John Trevisa and the English Bible," 81–98; Fowler, *The Life and Times of John Trevisa, Medieval Scholar*, 213–34; Hudson, *Premature Reformation*, 395–98; Waldron, "Trevisa," *ODNB* 55:353–54.

12. Fowler, "John Trevisa and the English Bible," 96.

neither were all those generally known as Lollards.[13] However, even if the philology of Tyndale's vernacular translations could be matched to Wyclif and the Lollards through the medium of Trevisa,[14] this does not prove that Tyndale's theological dissent is of a Wycliffite origin.

The second premise based on doctrinal similarities also rests on shaky ground. Certainly, Tyndale and other English evangelicals had much in common with earlier English dissent, and Tyndale showed his own personal sympathies by publishing Lollard treatises later in the 1530s.[15] However, there were also notable differences between Lollards and evangelicals, chief among them being a clear articulation by the latter of the doctrine of justification by faith alone apart from works.[16] Furthermore, the publication of these treatises was years after Tyndale's evangelical leanings had already been made public, and the evidence is strongest that, along with other reformers of his generation, he received his theological training within the boundaries of orthodox Catholicism.[17] The only historically satisfying way to authenticate any direct influence of the Lollards upon the emerging reforming career of Tyndale is to prove that he was thoroughly familiar with Lollard writings and reforming activity around the time he began his public reforming career. Of course, it is then necessary to determine whether or not specific Lollard texts, doctrinal ideas, and theological expressions were incorporated into his own writings. The fact of the matter is that there is simply no way of knowing what, if anything, by Wyclif or the Lollards Tyndale actually read prior to 1530.[18] Rather, the only scholars that it is infallibly certain that Tyndale possessed an early literary admiration for are Erasmus and Martin Luther. As Richard Rex has aptly pointed out, without solid historical proof this argument rests upon the dubious assumption that doctrinal similarity and chronological prece-

13. Hudson, *Premature Reformation*, 279–89, 303–10.

14. Regarding such philological similarities, see Smeeton, *Lollard Themes*, 77–80. See also Werrell, *Theology of Tyndale*, 18–19.

15. The two tracts commonly agreed to have been edited by Tyndale are: *The examinacion of Master William Thorpe* and *The prayer and complaynt of the ploweman*. See also Smeeton, *Lollard Themes*, 256–28; Mozley, *William Tyndale*, 345–46; Hudson, *Premature Reformation*, 493–94.

16. Marshall, *Reformation England*, 33; Rex, *Lollards*, xii–xiii, 25–53.

17. Rex, *Lollards*, 117–19, 133–39; Rex, "New Light," 146; Ryrie, *Gospel and Henry VIII*, 232–36.

18. Rex, "New Light," 160–61.

dence indicates influence, which is to fall prey to the logical fallacy of "after, therefore, because of" (*post hoc ergo propter hoc*).[19] This one-dimensional approach also lies behind the rather brazen assertions of an even more recent work linking Tyndale's reforming criticisms indirectly to Bogomil-Cathar dualism via Wyclif and the English Lollards.[20]

For support of Tyndale's independence from Luther, Werrell cites the comments of Thomas More who considered Tyndale to be ultimately "wors yet in som parte than hys mayster Luther ys hym self."[21] Not only is this comment probably more specifically targeting Tyndale's rejection of the Real Presence of Christ in the Eucharist, but citing the opinion of an incensed critic in the midst of a virulent controversy is hardly a legitimate court of historical appeal. Anne Hudson even states that More cannot even be properly classified as a "theologian."[22] Of course, the point here is not to vainly defend the notion that Tyndale was a disciple of Luther in every regard, yet More himself never identifies differences between Tyndale and Luther with regard to the issues of repentance, faith, justification, and good works.[23] Even if it could be argued that Tyndale is more similar to Lollardy than Luther on some doctrinal points, this itself does not prove beyond historical doubt that he was directly influenced by Lollard writings and activities. A direct theological influence of Lollardy on the writings of Tyndale is simply difficult, if not impossible, to substantiate with any certainty.[24]

To what degree, then, Tyndale had more in common with Wyclif and Lollardy than with Luther, specifically with regard to his understanding of how the Law and Gospel works in justification and the Christian life, obviously needs to be reassessed in the light of these recent arguments. How important this issue is to the overall historiography of the English Reformation itself is noted by Rex: "Tyndale is such a pivotal figure in the history of the English Reformation that, if it

---

19. Rex, *Lollards*, 117; Rex, "New Light," 159–60.

20. Vasilev, *Heresy and the English Reformation*, 81–102.

21. For example, Werrell, "Tyndale's Disagreement," 58–59; More, *Dialogue Concerning Heresies*, in Lawler, Marc'hadour, and Marius, *Complete Works of St. Thomas More*, 6.1:348–50.

22. Hudson, *Premature Reformation*, 504–5.

23. See More, *Dialogue Concerning Heresies*, in Lawler, Marc'hadour, and Marius, *Complete Works of St. Thomas More*, 6.1:376–402.

24. Marshall, *Reformation England*, 34; Rex, *The Lollards*, 117–19.

could be shown that his theology was shaped in significant ways by the pre-existing tradition of Lollardy, then this fact alone would establish the case for the importance of Lollardy to the English Reformation."[25] Indeed, Smeeton, Stackhouse, and Werrell all assume that Tyndale radically differs from Luther on the issue of Law and Gospel, yet not one of these scholars provides any substantial or thoughtful interaction with the writings of the German reformer himself. For example, Rex soundly criticizes Smeeton for his uncritical dependency upon Laughlin apart from a study of Luther's own writings.[26]

The earliest significant influence upon Tyndale's reforming career is undeniably English Humanism. John K. Yost is really the only scholar so far to explore Tyndale's theology in the context of Renaissance Humanism to any significant degree and who argues for its importance more than any other legacy upon his thought. He identifies Tyndale as essentially a "Protestant advocate of humanist reform" and one among the younger generation of "Erasmians" principally concerned with reviving moral Christian piety based on the Sermon on the Mount. As such, Tyndale stands in continuity with the humanist tradition, and, according to Yost, his theology even anticipates the reform policies carried out in 1535–1540 under the administration of the Vicegerent of Spirituals, Thomas Cromwell, and also the later *via media* of the Elizabethan period of the 1560s.[27]

The evidence overwhelmingly weighs in favor of Tyndale's early associations with late medieval Catholic Humanism rather than with Lollardy. It is also common knowledge that Tyndale was ordained to the priesthood sometime before 1520, and Rex has even presented evidence that Tyndale was appointed a chantry priest in Gloucestershire.[28]

It is doubtless that Tyndale encountered Humanism during his studies at Oxford University, and this would be even more true if he visited Cambridge, but Foxe's comment concerning Tyndale's sojourn there is unreliable.[29] It seems likely that Tyndale's own concentration

---

25. Rex, "New Light," 145.

26. Ibid., 160, 166–67.

27. Yost, "William Tyndale and the Renaissance," 168–72; Yost, "Christian Humanism," 3. With regard to the influence of Erasmian humanism on official reform policies, see also McConica, *English Humanists and Reformation Politics*.

28. Rex, "New Light," 148–54.

29. Foxe, *A & M* [1570], 1224; Daniell, *William Tyndale*, 49–54.

on the value of Scripture was, at least initially, a result of his encounter with ideals within Humanism, particularly in the writings of Erasmus. In fact, his mission to produce a vernacular Bible for the common Christian was more likely inspired earliest by Erasmus rather than Lollardy or even Luther. Tyndale's prophetic rebuke against a certain Gloucestershire clergyman that he would see "a boy that driueth the plough to know more of the Scripture then he did" bears stark resemblance to a comment appearing in the *Paraclesis* prefacing Erasmus's *Novum Instrumentum* (1516).[30]

Although Humanism was only beginning to make significant strides in English university curriculum in the late fifteenth and early sixteenth centuries, Oxford had undoubtedly been affected by the new methodology in some measure when Tyndale first matriculated at Magdalen school in 1506 as a grammar student between the ages of 12 and 13. It is important to point out, as Rex does, that the simple fact of Tyndale's attendance at university points to his more orthodox Catholic, as opposed to Lollard, background.[31] It is possible that Tyndale was first introduced to the study of Greek at Oxford, but it does not seem from statements in his own writings that the curriculum had changed all that much by the second decade of the sixteenth century. In his *Practice of Prelates* (1530), Tyndale bemoans that his university education was still profoundly in the scholastic mold, which he claims restricted him from engaging a more direct study of the Scriptures themselves on their own terms.[32] Oxford is the only university that Tyndale indisputably attended. Even Foxe changed his comment in the 1563 edition of the *Acts and Monuments* from "had bene a student of diuinitie at Cambridge" to "made his abode a certaine space" in the 1570 edition.[33] Scholars remain unconvinced even of this revised statement. The important point here is that, according to Tyndale's personal recollections, the methods of scholasticism still dominated the arts faculty at Oxford during his years as a university student. Nevertheless, Foxe does claim that Tyndale meanwhile increased in the knowledge of languages, the arts, and "especially in the knowledge of the Scriptures," even hosting lectures on the

---

30. Foxe, *A&M* [1570], 1225; Richardson, "Tyndale's Quarrel with Erasmus," 53; Daniell, *William Tyndale*, 67.

31. Daniell, *William Tyndale*, 22; Foxe, *A&M* [1570], 1224; Rex, "New Light," 149.

32. Tyndale, *The practyse of prelates*, sig. [E vi^v].

33. Foxe, *A&M* [1563], 514; Foxe, *A&M* [1570], 1224; Rex, "New Light," 148–49.

Bible to other "students and fellows" of Magdalene Hall. Since Tyndale never actually reached the academic level granting him formal authority to lecture on the Bible,[34] this must have been of his own volition and in an unofficial capacity.

The writings of Wyclif had been largely quarantined at Oxford by the early fifteenth century, and this would lend further support to the notion that Tyndale's valuing of Scripture was originally of humanist, rather than Lollard, derivation.[35] Though Erasmus's groundbreaking *Novum Instrumentum* was not published until after Tyndale had taken the M.A. degree in 1515, it is probable that Tyndale was already familiar with Erasmus's *Handbook of the Militant Christian* (1503) and his more recent and enormously popular satire on clerical abuses in *The Praise of Folly* (1514).[36] However, there is no evidence to indicate that Tyndale had made any radical break with the cardinal points of Catholic theology by the time he was awarded the M.A., and it must always be kept in mind that Humanism itself was not inherently opposed to traditional Catholic theology. Humanism was primarily a reform of classical methodology and its chief aim was to inspire and foster morality and virtue. It was not interested in overturning the fundamental teachings of the Catholic Church nor in denying its authority, nor did it even necessarily reject other hermeneutical methods entirely, though it did seek to emphasize the historical, literary, and rhetorical interpretation of Scripture in its original languages. While many English reformers who encountered Humanism as it was beginning to emerge significantly in England in the early sixteenth century did indeed end up reconstructing more basic theological assumptions about salvation and biblical authority, it must also be acknowledged that many humanists, including both Colet and Erasmus, did not perceive the methodological and moral concerns of Humanism to be at all inconsistent with their loyalty to the Catholic Church and its authority or the fundamentals of its theology.[37] The reforming career of Tyndale is certainly one example of how certain elements within the methodology of Humanism might be employed to more radical ends, but it is necessary to consider other sources, such as

---

34. Daniell, *William Tyndale*, 37.
35. Hudson, *Premature Reformation*, 85.
36. Richardson, "Tyndale's Quarrel with Erasmus," 47.
37. Dowling, *Humanism*, 38, 40.

the writings of Luther, in accounting for the origins of his evangelical theology.

After acquiring his M.A., and according to university tradition, Tyndale would have been expected to lecture for at least a year.[38] In the 1570 edition of the *Acts and Monuments*, Foxe mentions that Tyndale next, "spying hys tyme, remoued from thence to the Universitie of Cambridge, where after hee had likewise made his abode a certaine space" became "now further ripened in the knowledge of Gods word."[39] As tempting as it might be to accept this statement on the basis of circumstantial factors, such as the importance of Cambridge to both English Humanism and the early circulation and organized discussion of Luther's writings, most historians today argue that there is simply no evidence other than this one single statement to verify that Tyndale ever visited Cambridge. Tyndale himself never mentions having done so, his name appears nowhere in the university records, and other Cambridge evangelical reformers make no mention of him ever being there around 1520. The first evidence of Tyndale's acquaintanceship with other Cambridge reformers such as George Joye, William Roye, Robert Barnes, and Miles Coverdale occurs only after his flight to Europe in 1524. The one exception is John Frith, whom Tyndale met in London sometime in 1523 or 1524.[40]

Tyndale's early sympathy with Erasmus and Humanism is evident when he returned to Gloucestershire in the early 1520s to become a tutor to the sons of Sir John and Lady Anne Walsh at Little Sodbury Manor. Richard Rex provides strong evidence that Tyndale's gentry patrons were devoted Catholics who regularly dined with local clergy. Foxe mentions that both Erasmus and Luther were the topic of table conversations. On one occasion, Tyndale's objections to the opinions of the local clergy were challenged by Lady Anne. His response, probably presented sometime in 1522, was an English translation of Erasmus's *Enchiridion militis Christiani* (1503).[41] The fact that Tyndale chose this particular work in itself suggests that his reforming sympathies by 1522–23 probably had not extended much beyond that of Erasmian Humanism.

38. Daniell, *William Tyndale*, 22; Mozley, *William Tyndale*, 17.
39. Foxe, *A&M* [1570], 1224.
40. Daniell, *William Tyndale*, 49–50.
41. Ibid., 61–74; Rex, "New Light," 157–59; Foxe, *A&M* [1570], 1225.

The translation of the *Enchiridion* is the first known literary work of Tyndale.⁴² It has been suggested on stylistic grounds that a certain English edition of the *Enchiridion* printed in London by Wynkyn de Worde in 1533 might not be the work of Tyndale nor identical to the original manuscript he presented to the Walshes in the early 1520s. The discussion of its authorship remains unsettled.⁴³ In any case, it is striking how many of the themes of Erasmus's *Enchiridion* relating to the Christian life do recur throughout Tyndale's career. These include a covenantal understanding of baptism, an attack on popular devotional superstition to images and relics in praise of personal discipleship to the life of Christ as presented in the Scriptures, and a disdain for the medieval scholastic method.⁴⁴

After failing to secure patronage for his vernacular New Testament from Bishop Tunstall of London in 1523, Tyndale boarded for about a year in the home of a cloth merchant named Humphrey Monmouth. Monmouth became an important benefactor to Tyndale and, when summoned before Thomas More in 1528 on grounds of abetting heretics, mentions having possession of a copy of the English *Enchiridion* given to him by Tyndale.⁴⁵ Therefore, by as late 1523–1524 Tyndale still appears to esteem Erasmus's "practical book about being Christian in the world."⁴⁶ Although his opinion of Erasmus would change and become more negative,⁴⁷ his indebtedness early on to the legacy of the Dutch humanist cannot be ignored. It is at least clear that Tyndale had more demonstrable sympathies with Humanism than Lollardy during these early years of his intellectual development as a reformer.

Tyndale's skill with the ancient languages is another obvious tribute to the legacy of Humanism, and he shared Erasmus's vision to see

---

42. *A booke called in latyn Enchiridion militis christiani.*

43. See Richardson, "Tyndale's Quarrel," 51; Daniell, *William Tyndale*, 70–72.

44. *Enchiridion*, "truce made bytwene him and god in tyme of baptym . . . And there is none other condicion of peace with hym except that we (as longe as we warre in the fortresse of this body) with deedly hate and with all our myghte sholde fyght agaynst vyces . . . heuen is promysed to hym that fyghteth lustely . . . " sig. A iii-[A v]; "Let thyne eye loke vnto Christ alonely as vnto onely and very felycyte/ so that thou loue nothynge/ meruayle at nothyng/ desyre nothynge but eyther Christe or els for Christe," sig. [G viii ᵛ]–H ii ʳ. See also sig. I i ᵛ -I iii ʳ, L iii ʳ.

45. Daniell, *William Tyndale*, 74.

46. Ibid., 66.

47. Richardson, "Tyndale's Quarrel with Erasmus," 62–65.

the Scriptures in the vernacular and made use of Erasmus's Greek New Testament in his own biblical translations. Yet it would be inaccurate to overemphasize the enduring influence of Erasmus and Humanism upon the evangelical theology of Tyndale after 1524–1525. Although John Yost argues that Tyndale's use of the Church Fathers in his later writings is further evidence of his bonds to the legacy of Humanism, he admits that Tyndale never comes close to matching Erasmus's patristic resourcement. Furthermore, while humanists themselves disagreed concerning which classical pagan authors were appropriate to use, Tyndale's writings post-1524 possessed not a fraction of Erasmus's respect for the ancient pagan poets and rhetoricians. In his later polemics, Tyndale lumps together English humanists such as Thomas More and John Fisher with the scholastic theologians, which shows that a common heritage in the methodologies and reforming concerns of Humanism did not automatically result in theological agreement. A comparison of Tyndale's exegetical method with that of Erasmus also creates some difficulties in aligning the former too closely with the latter.[48]

Erasmus readily accepted the four senses of biblical interpretation as outlined by the third century exegete Origen of Alexandria, whom Erasmus warmly admired in his *Enchiridion,* and he believed that the allegorical meaning is preferable but only when a literal interpretation is unreasonable. Tyndale, on the other hand, inspired in some measure by Luther, openly attacks Origen in his later writings and denies that allegory is a separate sense of Scripture. On account of this, Yost places Tyndale closer to the Humanism of Colet on this issue, although Gleason has argued that even Colet acknowledged the medieval *quadriga* on a theoretical level. Of course, Tyndale recognized the value of allegory as a rhetorical method to illustrate a point stated clearly in another passage of Scripture, but he never classifies allegory as one of four modes of biblical exegesis. In his *Obedience of A Christian Man* (1528) Tyndale asserts that the literal interpretation of the text and its spiritual meaning are the same and that interpreting the Scriptures according to the "letter" does not mean being bound to the earthly sense of the text but to read the Bible as Law without the Gospel. This echoes Luther in his own preference for Augustine rather than Erasmus who obviously favored Origen.[49]

48. Yost, "Christian Humanism," 21–24, 28, 32, 35, 65–74.

49. See his discussion of the "iiii senses of the Scripture" in *The obedie[n]ce of a*

Although Tyndale inherited the rhetorical and literary methodology pioneered by Humanism, and though Erasmus himself considered the study of the Scriptures to be invaluable to fostering Christian morality, the high view of the authority of Scripture Tyndale expresses in his evangelical writings places him much closer to Luther than Erasmus. Erasmus admitted that a doctrine such as Mary's perpetual virginity could not at all be grounded on Scripture, even allegorically interpreted, but he was willing to accept such a matter by faith on the basis of the authority of the Catholic Church.[50] Tyndale also moved closer to Luther than Erasmus in expressing a higher regard for the didactic writings of Paul, arguing that the Gospel is most clearly preached in one epistle of Paul than in any one of the synoptic gospels. Tyndale's Pauline orientation certainly owes more to Luther, and by default Augustine, than to the synoptic orientation in the Humanism of Fisher or Erasmus.[51]

With regard to the moral Law, Yost follows Trinterud by contrasting Tyndale's moral thought with Luther's stark dialectic of Law and Gospel. For Tyndale, the "law of Moses and the law of Christ were not antithetical" and "He lacked the evangelical emphasis upon the antithesis between law and gospel." According to Yost this antithesis was avoided on account of Tyndale's bond to the moralistic concerns of Humanism, and that Tyndale was "a Christian humanist of the younger generation who turned enthusiastically and expectantly to Luther for ecclesiastical reform and religious renewal, but reverted later to a progress of humanist reform." Tyndale's emphasis upon the Law throughout his writings is argued as evidence of the indelible imprint of Humanism upon his thinking. Even with regard to the doctrine of justification, Yost argues that Tyndale emphasizes the obedience of faith to the Law, whereas

---

Christen man, fo. cxxix ʳ–cl. The original bears the name of "Hans Luft of Malborowe," but this was to conceal Martin de Keyser of Antwerp. See Daniell, *William Tyndale*, 156, 224. With regard to Tyndale's hermeneutics, see also Richardson, "Tyndale's Quarrel with Erasmus," 54–55, 57; Barnett, "From the Allegorical to the Literal," and Parker, "Tyndale's Biblical Hermeneutics," in Day, Lund, and O'Donnell, *Word, Church, and State*, 64–73, 87–101. For Luther's discussion of "letter" and "spirit," see *LW* 39 (*Answer to the HyperChristian, Hyperspiritual, and Hyperlearned Book by Goat Emser in Leipzig*, 1521): 182–84, 188; *WA* 7:653–56, 658–59. See also Althaus, *Theology of Martin Luther*, 96–97; Bornkamm, *Luther and the Old Testament*, 87–101. On the relationship of Erasmus to Origen, see the brief discussion in MacCulloch, *Reformation*, 113–14.

50. MacCulloch, *Reformation*, 101.

51. Tyndale, *Obedience*, fo. lxi ʳ; *LW* 35 (*Preface to the Epistle of St. Paul to the Romans*, 1522): 360–62; *WA DB* VI: 8–9, 10–11.

Luther's emphasis is on faith before God: "Tyndale employed Luther's idea of justification by faith alone in furthering the cause of Christian humanism." With regard to his theological anthropology, Yost argues that Tyndale's emphasis on grace enabling the will to perform good works and the moral capacities of the natural intellect places him closer to Erasmus than Luther: "Tyndale agreed with Erasmus concerning the idea of man which was the core of humanist thought. On the other hand, he disagreed with Luther concerning justification by grace alone which was the core of Reformation theology."[52] Luther is caricatured by Yost as if he was only ever concerned with the relationship of the sinner *coram Deo*. Yet like so many other scholars of early English Reformation theology, Yost reveals no real engagement with Luther's own writings. In fact, given the many number of times he asserts there to be a disparity between Tyndale and Luther on the subject of Law and Gospel, it is surprising that the only work by Luther listed in his bibliography is the *Lectures on Romans* (1515–1516).[53]

The point here is certainly not to deny the impression that Humanism made upon the young Tyndale. After all, it was Erasmus's praise of Bishop of London Cuthbert Tunstall that inspired Tyndale to seek his patronage in translating the New Testament into English. Tyndale presented Tunstall with his translation of the Greek oration of Isocrates in order to demonstrate his knowledge of Greek and his skills as a translator.[54] This, along with his earlier decision to translate the *Enchiridion* for Lady Walsh is proof enough of his having some degree of affection for Erasmus early on. However, Yost's classification of Tyndale as essentially a Christian humanist influenced largely by Erasmus, who only for a brief period flirted with Luther's evangelical theology, is a grave overstatement on the basis of the life and career of Tyndale after 1525. Given such crucial differences that do emerge between Tyndale and the principal architect of English Humanism, including a general repulsion for classical pagan literature and the medieval *quadriga*, it seems that labeling him a "Christian humanist" is as much a misleading generalization as scholars say of the badge of "Lutheran."

---

52. Yost, "Christian Humanism," 83–86, 89, 104, 110, 149.

53. Ibid., 486.

54. Tyndale, "W.T. to the Reader," [The *Pentateuch*, 1530]; Daniell, *William Tyndale*, 85–88; Richardson, "Tyndale's Quarrel with Erasmus," 59.

Tyndale was obviously influenced and inspired by certain methodological and reforming considerations within Humanism, including its philological, rhetorical, and literary methods of interpretation and its emphasis on the cultivation of inward Christian character. It is also obvious that he was an early admirer of Erasmus in particular, but this is not enough to justify classifying him over the course of his career as an essentially Christian humanist. Though some might argue that Erasmus himself was even a *"fideist,"*[55] Tyndale's articulation after 1524 of a doctrine of justification by faith alone in Christ apart from all works is a credit to the evangelical influence of Luther not Erasmus. With regard to his theological anthropology, Anne Richardson has shown that Tyndale clearly takes the side of Luther against Erasmus in debates over free-will in the mid-1520s.[56] Erasmus's *Enchiridion* explicitly follows Origen in differentiating between spirit, soul, and body, with sin essentially defined as a breakdown in the rational control of the body and its sensual appetites. Following Socrates, Erasmus identifies the cause of fleshly indulgence as the ignorance of the good, and, like Aristotle, characterizes the achievement of virtue as the result of a process of the disciplined cultivation of moral habits, which Erasmus says is possible with God's help and the example of Christ.[57] Although this work was translated by Tyndale as his first literary work, all of his subsequent writings reveal the influence of Luther's anthropology and his belief in the total depravity and absolute bondage of the *"totus homo"* under the complete compulsion and condemnation of the Law, as well as the active righteousness of the Christian as an *a priori* new state of being established in the heart through faith and the working of the Spirit and not something accumulated through the disciplined increase of moral habits leading to the merit of eternal life.

It is not certain when Tyndale first learned of Luther or became familiar with his writings, but it could not have been any later than 1522 since Luther was a topic of table discussions in the home of Tyndale's noble patrons in Gloucestershire.[58] He could not have been familiar with

---

55. Bainton, "The Problem of Authority," in Olin, Smart, and McNally, *Luther, Erasmus and the Reformation*, 20.

56. Richardson, "Tyndale's Quarrel with Erasmus," 62–65.

57. *Enchiridion*, sig. [C viii ᵛ]–D iiii ᵛ, E i, [E vi ʳ–E viii], F ii ᵛ- F iiii ʳ, [G v ʳ], [L vi ᵛ –L vii ʳ].

58. Foxe, *A&M* [1570], 1225; Daniell, *William Tyndale*, 106; Elton, *Luther in der Neuzeit*, 122–24.

the German reformer any earlier than 1518–1519 when Luther's works began to be exported from Germany and sold in England.[59] Attention to Luther in England multiplied intensely in the years 1520–1521, especially in the environs of London, Oxford, and Cambridge. If Tyndale had contact with Luther's writings by the end of 1520, they would have most likely been accessed in one of these three places. Tyndale was at Oxford from 1506–1516, but Luther was not an international figure at that time. Tyndale was ordained a deacon and then a priest in the diocese of London in 1515,[60] but the next time he appears in London is almost ten years later after fleeing Gloucestershire and seeking patronage from the Bishop of London for his work in translating the New Testament into English. If Tyndale spent time at Cambridge this would have been between the years 1517 and 1520,[61] but there is no corroborative evidence to verify the statement in Foxe. This is further undermined by the fact that Tyndale returned to Gloucestershire as a tutor to the Walshes, a Catholic family of the gentry class, and was appointed as a chantry priest in a chapel in Breadstone in the Vale of Berkeley around 1520. Therefore, at the moment of his return to Gloucestershire in 1520–1521 there was as of yet "no hint of suspicion about his orthodoxy" nor any such links whatsoever to Luther whose charges of heresy by this time had been made official by the Catholic Church in Rome.[62] Although Luther and Erasmus were the topic of table discussions in the home of the Walshes, there is no way to know what the precise content of those discussions was other than that Tyndale showed his superior knowledge of the Scriptures. With regard to Tyndale's now famous words of defiance against the Pope in conversation with a local "Divine," this appears less to have been the influence of Luther than a "certaine Doctour" living in the same region, "an old Channcellour before to a Byshop" and "old familiar acquantance." Furthermore, the immediate context of this invective statement appears to be Tyndale's determination to issue a vernacular Bible, which was initially inspired by the work of Erasmus rather than Luther.[63]

59. Haigh, *English Reformations*, 57.
60. Rex, "New Light on Tyndale," 153.
61. Daniell, *William Tyndale*, 49.
62. Rex, "New Light," 148–54, 157.
63. Foxe, *A&M* [1570], 1225.

Tyndale's desire to work under the patronage of Bishop Tunstall, who was praised by Erasmus for his humanist leanings, is evidence of his much closer associations with Erasmus by the date of 1523, as is his passing of the *Enchiridion* on to Humphrey Monmouth.[64] Perhaps Tyndale's desire for episcopal sanction was nothing more than a desire for physical protection and financial subsidization, but it also might have been because Tyndale had simply not yet moved in the more radical theological direction of Luther. After all, this is now two years after Luther had been formally excommunicated and condemned by the Empire. Tyndale's early activities in London seem unlikely for a person sympathetic to a renegade German monk officially condemned for heresy by the Catholic Church. One scholar has argued that the doctrinal differences between Erasmus and Luther were not even clear before the public controversy over free-will in 1524–1525,[65] but Luther as early as 1516 had already expressed disagreement with Erasmus on the issue of justification and the bondage of the will. Besides, Luther, not Erasmus, was demarcated a heretic in 1521.

It is likely that during Tyndale's brief stay in London in 1523–1524 he became more familiar with and sympathetic to the theological reforms of Luther, whose own German translation of the New Testament had been recently published in September 1522. Knowledge of this event coupled with Tyndale's growing awareness that "there was no place to [translate the New Testament] in all of England" must have been the inspiration behind his decision to join the company of like-minded opportunists across the channel.[66]

Tyndale left England for the Continent in the spring of 1524. Visits to both Hamburg and Wittenberg rest completely on contemporary testimony alone. For the former, Monmouth's confession to the Bishop of London recorded by Foxe in his *Acts and Monuments* is principal evidence. Tyndale's visit to Wittenberg is far more controversial due to the sensitivity surrounding the discussion of Luther's influence, but it, too, is based on the contemporary testimony of Catholic apologists Thomas More and John Cochlaeus (1479–1552). Foxe also records that "At his first departing out of the realme, he tooke hys iourney into the further partes of Germany, as into Saxonie, where he had conference

64. Ibid., 1225; Tyndale, "W.T. To the Reader," [*Pentateuch*, 1530].
65. Knappen, "First English Puritan," 210–11.
66. Foxe, *A&M* [1570], 1226.

with Luther and other learned men in those quarters." J. F. Mozley took Foxe's statement one step further in his classic biography by suggesting that a "*Guillelmus Daltici ex Anglia*," a name appearing in the 1524 matriculation registers of the University of Wittenberg, is none other than Tyndale himself (*Daltici* being close to "*Daltin*," which is a reversal of "*tin-Dal*"). Though this appears to be quite the stretch, Mozley argues that it would not have been necessary for Tyndale to officially matriculate in order to benefit from association with the Wittenberg reformers:

> Wittenberg had an university, and offered all the helps that a scholar might need. There he would find books and libraries; there he could take counsel with Melancthon professor of Greek, Aurogallus professor of Hebrew, Bugenhagen (Pomeranus) rector of the town church, and other learned men. Above all, there was Luther himself, no mean scholar, and one that had lately performed the very task which Tyndale had in his mind . . . it would be strange if he did not desire to meet the great captain, who had braved the might of pope and emperor, and had successfully raised the standard of reform.[67]

There is no other evidence apart from contemporary testimony that Tyndale ever visited Wittenberg, much less met Luther personally. It is interesting to note that Luther never mentions Tyndale in his writings or correspondences, and Tyndale even later objects to More's accusation that he was ever "confederate with Luther." However, Tyndale biographers keenly observe that this statement hardly constitutes a denial of ever having visited Luther or Wittenberg.[68] In any case, Tyndale's sojourn in the German Empire would certainly have been enough to bring him into the fuller orb of Luther's influence than if he had stayed in England. Indeed it is in 1525 and afterwards that an indisputable connection of Tyndale to Luther becomes evident beginning with the printing of the first English translation of the Greek New Testament in the imperial free city of Cologne.

---

67. Demaus and Lovett, *William Tindale*, 116–27; Mozley, *William Tyndale*, 51–57; Daniell, *William Tyndale*, 108; A&M [1570], 1133, 1226–27.

68. Demaus and Lovett, *William Tindale*, 118–19; Mozley, *William Tyndale*, 52; Daniell, *William Tyndale*, 298–300.

Along with Antwerp and Hamburg, Cologne had a developed printing industry and was a city with strategic economic ties to England.[69] Tyndale would later settle in Antwerp prior to his betrayal and arrest, but it was in Cologne that Tyndale would first see his vision for a printed English New Testament come to fruition in the printing house of Peter Quentell. Accompanying him in the work was William Roye, a converted friar from Greenwich who matriculated at the University of Wittenberg in 1525 where he possibly met Tyndale. The printing of the New Testament, however, was interrupted in the middle of Matthew 22 after authorities were tipped off by John Cochlaeus who overheard intoxicated employees of Quentell describe how two Englishmen were printing Luther's New Testament in English to make all of England Lutheran.[70]

The surviving *Cologne Fragment* of 1525 is the first evangelical work by Tyndale as well as the first evangelical work printed in English. The extent of its actual "Lutheranness" is the subject of much debate. Heresy hunters and Catholic apologists such as Thomas More viewed Tyndale as little more than a mimic of Luther and the one principally responsible for spreading Luther's heresy in England in the late 1520s.[71] Even modern scholars only a few generations ago typified Tyndale as an essentially English Luther.[72] At first glance, the *Cologne Fragment* does seem to be largely a translation of Luther's *September Testament* (1522). The prologue, marginal notes, and even the accompanying woodcuts undeniably borrow from Luther's edition. Even Trinterud, whose essay was written to minimize Luther's influence on the theology of Tyndale, recognizes the obvious indebtedness of Tyndale's prologue and marginal notes to Luther. Nevertheless, he goes on to state that Tyndale "used Luther rather than agreed with Luther," and that "About one eighth of Tyndale's prologue consists of a good translation of roughly half of Luther's prologue."[73]

---

69. Daniell, *William Tyndale*, 108. The surviving fragment printed from Cologne by H. Fuchs in 1525 is in the British Library. For a facsimile, see *Beginning of the New Testament Translated by William Tyndale*.

70. Daniell, *William Tyndale*, 108–9.

71. Rex, "New Light," 170.

72. Rupp, *Studies in the Making*, 49.

73. Trinterud, "Reappraisal," 25–26; Werrell mistakenly applies this statement of Trinterud's to Tyndale's prologue to Romans. See Werrell, "Tyndale's Disagreement," 58.

Upon closer inspection, the two texts are indeed not identical. Tyndale's prologue is considerably longer than Luther's own "Preface" (*Vorrhede*) to the New Testament, and Tyndale does not follow Luther's translation of Matthew on every turn, often preferring to translate directly from the Greek while utilizing Luther judiciously along with the revised Latin text of Erasmus.[74] With regard to the marginal notes, biographer David Daniell argues that only a third could be ascribed independently to Tyndale. The other two-thirds include verbatim translations, modifications, and expansions, along with a few reductions and complete omissions.[75] Nevertheless, although the marginal notes are hardly identical to Luther's, the parallels are still very significant. In essence, they are a continuance of the evangelical themes discussed in the prologue, that "rightwesness/ ys fulfilled when we forsake all oure awne rightwesnes/ that god only maye be counted he which is rightwes/ and maketh rightwes/ throw faith."[76]

Although a comprehensive philological analysis and comparison of the biblical translations of Luther and Tyndale would be valuable,[77] the scope of the following discussion focuses primarily on the prologue and the theological themes pertaining to Law and Gospel, repentance, faith, justification, and the Christian life of good works. As Smeeton has pointed out, "The debate about the degree to which Tyndale was influenced by Luther's thought hinges on the interpretation of the Englishman's soteriology."[78] The main point to be explored is whether or not the undeniable semantic and structural differences existing between the two texts belie a fundamental indebtedness to Luther's theology, especially as it pertains to Law and Gospel.[79]

Daniell describes the Cologne prologue as essentially "the first printed Lutheran document in English to reach England." Yet he also

---

74. Daniell, *William Tyndale*, 110–15.

75. Ibid., 117–19.

76. Tyndale, [*New Testament*, 1525], fo. Iiii; See *WA DB* 6:22 (m.g.). This is the German text of the 1522 edition.

77. With regard to general literary and structural observations, see Daniell, *William Tyndale*, 108–33.

78. Smeeton, *Lollard Themes*, 123.

79. The prologue was reprinted separately as the treatise *Pathway to the Holy Scriptures* in 1530/31. The University of Cambridge, Emmanuel College Library, has a copy of the *Pathway* printed in London by Thomas Godfray (1536?). Comparisons with the original prologue of 1525 will be discussed later with other writings of the 1530s.

observes that Tyndale doubles the length of Luther's prologue with new and expanded material, which includes an opening section devoted to defending the vernacular translation of Scripture. Tyndale also omits the stratification of New Testament books that comes at the end of Luther's prologue,[80] especially with regard to doubts about the apostolic canonicity of James. Though Tyndale acknowledges the reasoning for such doubts, he is much more readily accepting of its canonicity than Luther. Some scholars have wanted to interpret this as a possible connection to Lollardy, since the latter were known to have placed a great stake on the book.[81] However, as Rex points out, Tyndale in his career rarely utilizes or quotes from James. In fact, "there are only one or two books of the New Testament—minor Pauline epistles—which Tyndale cites less frequently than James."[82] It is also important to remember that Luther himself praised James for the works that it taught, although he harshly criticized it for failing to explain how these are truly possible.[83] Furthermore, Tyndale's use of James is not so unlike Luther who, despite the more disparaging tone toward James in his *Vorrhede*, actually makes exegetical use of James in other writings, including a sermon dating to the very same year.[84]

In the prologue, Tyndale follows Luther rather closely by prefacing the New Testament with an interpretive grid and according to an evangelical understanding of Law and Gospel. The theology of the prologue bears the stark imprint of Luther here, and it does so either by extracting lines verbatim from Luther or by developing a line of thought that is reminiscent of other early works of Luther.

One important example of a near verbatim translation of Luther's own preface is the passage containing his definition of Law and Gospel. Tyndale's *Cologne Fragment* of 1525 reads: "The olde testament is a boke/ where in is wrytten the law and commaundments of god/ And the dedes

80. Daniell, *William Tyndale*, 119–20.

81. Smeeton, *Lollard Themes*, 156.

82. Rex, "New Light," 169–70.

83. *LW* 35 (*Preface to the Epistles of St. James and St. Jude*, 1546): 395; *WA DB* 7:384–87.

84. For example, see Luther's *Ein sermon von dem unrechten Mammon. Luk. xvi* published in the *Wartburg Postil* (1522). Luther openly uses James 2 to affirm that genuine faith is always accompanied by good works. *WA* 10³:287–88. An English translation of the original preached version appears in Lenker, *The Complete Sermons of Martin Luther*, 2.2:291–301.

of them which beleueth them ore beleue them nott. The new testament is a boke where in are Conteyned the promyses of god/ and the Dedes of them which beleue them Or beleue them nott . . . *Euangelion* (that we cal the gospel) is a greke worde/That signyfyth good/mery/ glad ioyfull tydings/ that maketh a mannes hert glad/ and maketh hym synge/ daunce and leepe for ioye."[85] Luther's own German preface translated by the American Edition (LW) reads: "Just as the Old Testament is a book in which are written God's laws and commandments, together with the history of those who kept and of those who did not keep them, so the New Testament is a book in which are written the gospel and the promises of God, together with those who do not believe them . . . For 'gospel' [*Euangelium*] is a Greek word [German New Testament actually has *deutsch*] and means in Greek a good message, and good tidings, good news, a good report which one sings and tells with gladness."[86] That Tyndale freely copied from Luther's definition is undeniable and the differences are minor and heavily outweighed by the almost identical appearance of the two texts.

Tyndale's prologue continues closely in step with Luther following this definition by describing the Gospel as rightly called a "New Testament," in so far as it was fulfilled in and confirmed by the death of Jesus Christ, even though at the same time it was prophesied long before to Adam and Abraham.[87]

Tyndale stops trailing Luther at the end of his discussion of Old Testament messianic prophecy. Whereas Luther goes on for a few more paragraphs to contrast the ministries of Christ and Moses before concluding with his stratification of New Testament books, Tyndale goes into an extended discussion relating the themes of Law and Gospel to fallen human nature and divine grace respectively. Yet, in his marginal notes on Matthew 16, Tyndale does lament over the fact that prelates of his own day have made the Gospel "biterer then the olde law" and the burden of Christ "hevier than the yooke of Moses," so that "oure

---

85. Tyndale [*The New Testament*, 1525], sig. A ii ᵛ.

86. *LW* 35 (*Preface to the New Testament*, 1546): 358. The American Edition translates the German Bible of 1546 with notes on minor variations from Luther's 1522 German New Testament. In this particular passage, there is text found in the 1522 edition that is not reproduced by Tyndale in the *Cologne Fragment* and is also omitted by Luther in the 1546 edition. See *WA DB* 6:2–3.

87. Tyndale, [*New Testament*, 1525], sig. A iii ʳ; *LW* 35 (*Preface to the New Testament*): 357–58; *WA DB* 6:2–3, 4–5.

condicion and estate ys ten tymes more grievous than was ever the jewes." This hearkens to the contrast Luther strikes between the proper ministries of Christ and Moses in his own prologue, but Tyndale also makes mention in the marginal note that the Pharisaical rituals of the "new goddes" (Catholic clergy) reveal they have "feyned Rede Erasmus annotacions."[88] Tyndale still shows some regard here for the textual insights of Erasmus accompanying his Greek New Testament and with regard to his criticism of the saturation of contemporary Christian piety with rituals and ceremonies, but his underlying theological position by this time has much more obvious affinities with Luther. His description of the Law in the prologue as fundamentally the revelation of natural human depravity and absolute spiritual bondage, "to brynge vs vnto the knowlege of oureselves," is certainly more reflective of Luther's pessimistic outlook on human nature rather than of the anthropology of Erasmus. For Tyndale, like Luther, the Law demands what is impossible, namely the love of a pure heart, and in this way it only brings with it the sentence of judgment and wrath. The Gospel, on the contrary, is the "grace," or "favour," of God in Christ toward repentant sinners and it ministers salvation by its promises: "of lyfe/ of mercy/ of perdon frely by the merites of Christ ... In the gospell when we beleve the promyses/ we receave the spyrite of lyfe/ and are iustified in the bloud of Christ from all things whereof the lawe condemned vs."[89] Although the themes of spiritual bondage and the receiving of the righteousness of justification and the Spirit through faith and the merits of Christ are also found in Augustine whose influence on Tyndale could be attributed to his education in humanist methodology, his strong correlation of faith, both here and elsewhere in the treatise, with the receiving of the Spirit and the favor of God in Christ that justifies from the condemnation of the Law is evidence of the particular evangelical influence of Luther. Although Tyndale's prologue has at this point branched off from Luther's text, the theology of this entire section still very much breathes the influence of his understanding of Law and Gospel.

This section continues with Tyndale's description of the Old Testament containing many promises alongside the Law to comfort troubled consciences, and the New Testament containing Law alongside the preaching of the Gospel to condemn those who do not yet be-

88. Tyndale, [*New Testament*, 1525], fo. xviii ᵛ–fo. xix ʳ.
89. Ibid., sig. A iii ᵛ.

lieve the promises. Tyndale, like Luther, believed that the preaching of the Law and Gospel must always abide together in history, the former to humble the self-righteous and proud and the latter to keep contrite sinners from despair. Even the imperfect works of Christians need to be evaluated in the perfect light of the Law so that God always receives the praise for His mercy and grace. Tyndale's prologue then identifies two sorts of people who are deceived and who do not properly humble themselves before the Law. The first seek to justify themselves by outward works, though inwardly their hearts are far from pure, which is revealed by attitudes of self-righteous superiority over others. Such a person has failed to understand that the Law demands inward purity and that he or she only obeys the Law because of its outward compulsion. Inwardly they would wish the Law to vanish while they disregard the hope of the promises by trusting in their own merits. The second kind of deceived person lives in open sin "with full consent," presuming upon God's promise of forgiveness and pardon while living an immoral life without repentance. For Tyndale, this is not the kind of saving faith that comes from the Spirit of God but is merely "dremynge," an "ymaginacion," and "folisshe opynion." It shows a lack of respect both towards God's Law and the kindness of His promises. The kind of faith that saves is that which follows only after a deep remorse for sin in repentance. This "right fayth" consents that the commandments and the God who established them are just, and even though the Law cannot be fulfilled perfectly by anyone, a "right christen man consenteth to the lawe" by hating what is forbidden and pleading with God for greater strength to do what He commands. Although true faith is not without love and good works, "yet is oure savinge imputed nether to loue nor vnto good werkes, but vnto fayth only." Thus, in the meantime of praying for greater strength to do the will of God more perfectly, the Christian confides in the promises of God in the blood of Christ for pardon resulting in continual gratitude and praise unto His mercy.[90] All of these ideas and themes, though perhaps not always the same wording or phraseology, can be readily found in Luther's evangelical writings of the 1520s.

At this point in Tyndale's prologue a subheading is introduced: "Here shall ye see compendiously and plainly set out the order and practise of everythynge afore rehearsed." Based on the opinion that the theology and tone of this later section do not quite sing "in Tyndale's

---

90. Tyndale, [*New Testament*, 1525], sig. A iii ᵛ– B ii ʳ.

voice," Daniell proposes that the last five pages might actually belong to William Roye.[91] Even if this was true, and Daniell does make some thought-provoking observations, it is hard to imagine that Tyndale would allow the second half of the completed prologue to be published if it were containing any questionable material.

Under this subheading, Tyndale also describes natural men as "heyres of the vengeaunce of god by byrth." Just as poison is inside a serpent before it ever strikes, so the heart of a person is evil before he or she even does one single outward deed. Using a biblical metaphor, Tyndale asserts that the quality of a person's works, like the fruit of a tree, are determined by the quality of the person inwardly, whether good or bad. Likewise, "so doo nott oure evyll deds make vs evyll: but because that of nature we are evell/therfore we bothe thynke and doo evyll . . ." Though Smeeton has shown that the analogy of the tree and its fruit was common even among the Lollards,[92] it also appears frequently in the more contemporary works of Luther. Furthermore, Tyndale's use of the analogy is closer to Luther because it occurs in the context of a more clearly articulated doctrine of justification before God in Christ through faith alone apart from works and not merely in describing faith as the source of love and good works.

Tyndale goes on to describe the preaching of the Gospel and the power of the Holy Spirit to open the hearts of the elect to trust in the mercy of God, which in turn results in righteous desires to fulfill the Law. Those reborn of the Spirit are never satisfied with imperfection. A righteous sorrow remains in them and they depend upon the atonement of Christ for the pardon of all their deficiencies. Until more strength is given, God takes pleasure in the heart that longs after His will. Tyndale makes it clear, though, that it is by faith alone that men are saved and "only in belevynge the promyses." Love and good deeds, even those virtues described in the Beatitudes, are the fruit of being pardoned by "fayth onlye," and they "certyfyeth us in oure hertes that we are goddes sonnes/ that the holy gost is in us." In and of themselves, love and good deeds are never the basis of pardon, and there is no deed done in this life that is untainted by sin, including that of Christians. Even great apostles like Peter and Paul perpetually "syghed after" the fullness

---

91. Daniell, *William Tyndale*, 131–33.
92. Smeeton, *Lollard Themes*, 136.

of moral righteousness.⁹³ Again, all these themes reflect Luther's evangelical theology of the Christian as *simul justus et peccator*. As for good deeds acting as self-assurances of true faith, this is also made explicit in Luther's early writings.⁹⁴

Carl Trueman argues that Tyndale does not explicitly develop his doctrine of the atonement in terms of the objective removal of moral guilt or the satisfying of the wrath of God, but rather interprets and emphasizes the work of Christ more as impacting the regeneration of the moral will. Trueman acknowledges that Tyndale openly speaks about God's wrath and vengeance against sin and even about the blood of Christ as making satisfaction, but that he never speaks explicitly of Christ as propitiating God's wrath nor that satisfaction is made directly to God for sin: "he fails to emphasize the guilt of man before God, he consequently places little emphasis upon the God-ward aspects of Christ's work. As a result, his theology of atonement is extremely vague . . . salvation is concerned more with man's ability than with his guilt before God."⁹⁵

Although Tyndale may not have developed his theology of the atonement quite to the satisfaction of a systematic theology, it is quite clear from the prologue that he, like Luther, perceived the human will to be in bondage to the Devil and to sin until the conscience becomes free of the knowledge of guilt under the righteous condemnation of the Law and of the fear of the deserved wrath of God through faith in the justifying, atoning, and pardoning work of Jesus Christ on the cross. Althaus provides a useful critique of Gustaf Aulén's *Christus Victor* and its strict association of Luther with the "classical" theory of atonement, arguing convincingly that Luther interpreted the classical emphasis on the victory of God over evil powers precisely in terms of the Godward satisfaction of justice made in Christ.⁹⁶ Tyndale's own statements concerning the necessity of contrition or repentance under the Law to drive

---

93. Tyndale [*New Testament*, 1525], sig. A iiii–B iii ʳ; "a mannes dedes declare what he is within but make him nether good ner bad," sig. [B iiii ᵛ]. See also m.g. for Matthew chapters 5 and 12, [*New Testament*], fo. v ʳ, xiiii ʳ.

94. "A Sermon for the Second Sunday after Mary's Ascension. Preached at Wittenberg by Dr. Martin Luther, 1522," *Complete Sermons*, 2.2:296–97; WA 10³:278. See also See LW 30 (*Sermons on the Second Epistle of St. Peter*, 1523): 158–59; WA 14:23.

95. Trueman, *Luther's Legacy*, 84, 87–89, 99.

96. Althaus, *Theology of Martin Luther*, 218–23. Tyndale does say that Christ "peased the wrath of God." See [*New Testament*, 1525], sig. A iii ᵛ – [A iiii ʳ], sig. B ʳ – Bii ʳ.

the sinner to Christ and the love and good works that flow liberally from faith in Christ cannot even be understood or appreciated apart from his awareness of the profound moral guilt of all before God atoned only in and through the righteousness of Christ.

Tyndale describes in the prologue how the Law acts upon the conscience to bring about repentance and that this always must precede the pardon offered by the Gospel so that the promise of salvation in Christ from a terrifying future is received genuinely as "good tydings." It is by the preaching of the Law that sinners first become aware of how captive they are to the Devil and how, like him, they are inwardly enemies of God and His will. The preaching of the Gospel of forgiveness softens the contrite heart of the elect and, by the restoration of the rule of the Holy Spirit, they are liberated from bondage to Satan. In this way the Law binds and the Gospel looses. They act together as two "salves" to cure the disease of sin, the Law acting as the diagnosis and the Gospel as the medicine.[97]

According to Tyndale's prologue, the truly repentant Christian will desire to be completely cured of all unrighteousness and not just of guilt, just as a sick man wants to be made completely whole and well again. The Christian, then, wants to fulfill the Law more and more because it is the good will of God. Though Christ is first and foremost the Redeemer whose redemptive accomplishments belong to them that believe, He is also an example to follow in doing good works out of love for the sake of others. Christ obeyed the Father not to gain a heavenly favor he already possessed, but considered "nothinge but oure welth . . . Bond servaunts werke for hyre/ Children for love. For there father with all he hath/ is thers alreddy." Contrary to Werrell's opinion that Tyndale, unlike Luther, stresses that "man's salvation is primarily for the glory of God" and not the benefits of man, this is one instance where Tyndale indeed describes salvation in terms of the benefits God gives to humanity.[98] Though Tyndale acknowledges that rewards are promised for holy living in Scripture, rewards can never be the objective of a truly good and Christian work, which is always selfless by nature. Rewards are indeed promised, but not as merits or earnings. Rather, they follow

---

97. Tyndale [*New Testament*, 1525], sig. [B iiii ʳ].
98. Ibid., sig. B iii; Werrell, "Disagreement with Luther," 61–62.

the obedient life that springs of its own accord from faith without any thought of reward.[99]

Although Tyndale's prologue expands much beyond Luther's shorter prologue, there is nothing here to warrant the claim of any major theological disagreement. In fact, Tyndale seems to copy heavily from other early sources of Luther besides his *Vorrhede*, most notably *The Freedom of A Christian* (1520). Scholars exaggerate Tyndale's independence from Luther on the basis that he expands or develops a line of reasoning beyond what is visibly found in the text of Luther's own preface. Yet they have not adequately considered whether or not Tyndale is appropriating other early writings of Luther. For example, though Luther does not go into as long a discussion of human nature and depravity in his own preface, Tyndale's description of the natural will in bondage to sin certainly resembles Luther's own position formulated by 1518 well before his differences with Erasmus were made more public on this issue in 1524–1525.

A fair number of scholars have adopted Trinterud's thesis by distancing Tyndale from Luther at this early stage, placing his approbation of the moral Law in closer proximity to Humanism and the Reformed tradition. Accordingly, Luther's supposedly rigid polarization of Law and Gospel is not even adopted by Tyndale here in 1525. According to Trinterud, Luther spoke of the love of God and neighbor as the fruit of justifying faith, whereas Tyndale also stressed love for the very commandments of the Law themselves.[100]

On the contrary, Tyndale does polarize Law and Gospel in precisely the same manner as Luther. First, he does this by starkly contrasting the very "nature of the lawe and the nature of the evangelion." The preaching of the Law always goes before to bind consciences so that the Gospel might follow after and liberate: "When a preacher preacheth the Lawe/he byndeth all consciences/ and when he preacheth the Gospell/ he lowseth them agayne." Tyndale agrees with Luther that the preaching

---

99. See also Tyndale's marginal glosses for Matthew 6, [*New Testament*, 1525], fo. vi ᵛ- vii ʳ.

100. Trinterud, "Reappraisal," 26–27; See also Greenman, "William Tyndale," in Greenman and Larsen, *Reading Romans Through the Centuries,* 125; Mayote, "William Tyndale's Contribution"; Laughlin, "Brightness of Moses' Face"; Trueman, *Luther's Legacy,* 101–2; Trueman, "Theology of the English Reformers," in Bagchi and Steinmetz, *Cambridge Companion to Reformation Theology,* 163–65.

of Law and Gospel, defined according to their proper senses, have their own distinctive ministries in the human heart.[101]

Paul Laughlin argues that Tyndale obviously employs Luther's language of "Law and Gospel," but that he had already at this point developed a "quasi-covenantal configuration" that resembles the emerging "covenantal" theology of the Swiss and Rhineland reformers. Therefore, Tyndale's later formal emphasis on the "covenant" in the 1530s merely represents a shift in his homiletic "schemata" and not in his fundamental theological understanding. Yet Laughlin can even admit that Luther at times referred to the Law more positively as a guide for Christian behavior, though he argues this is de-emphasized when compared with the centrality it receives in Tyndale's thought.[102] Smeeton at least acknowledges that greater emphasis does not necessarily betray fundamental theological disagreement.[103]

Laughlin also argues that "Gospel" in Luther usually refers to "proclamation," whereas for Tyndale it refers to "the promises." He also asserts that Luther conceives of the object of faith in terms of the promises in Christ, whereas for Tyndale the object of faith is in both the promises and Christ as if each has an "independent soteriological function." Trueman also argues that Tyndale's reference to "faith in the promises" removes God's mercy from its Christological context. However, on the very next page Trueman himself observes that Tyndale uses "promises" to refer to "the work of Christ, the benefits of which are appropriated by the believer through faith in them."[104]

First of all, that Luther could speak of "promises" interchangeably with "Gospel" has been effortlessly demonstrated by Rex with regard to Luther's *Freedom of A Christian* (1520).[105] Secondly, Luther does not simply reduce "Gospel" to "proclamation." Indeed, in the *Vorrhede* he does literally translate the bare Greek word "*Euangelion*" as "good message," "good tidings," "good news," and "a good report," but Tyndale does

---

101. Tyndale, [*New Testament*, 1525], sig. [B iiii ʳ].

102. Laughlin, "Brightness of Moses' Face," 5–8, 128–31, 141–43, 151.

103. See *Lollard Themes*, 139. See also Thompson, "The Two Regiments," in Baker, *Reform and Reformation*, 32.

104. Laughlin, "Brightness of Moses' Face," 148–50; Smeeton, *Lollard Themes*, 148–50; Trueman, *Luther's Legacy*, 88–89.

105. Rex, "New Light," 165. See also *LW* 44 (*Judgment . . . on Monastic Vows*, 1522): 256–57; *WA* 8:580–81.

just as much in his own prologue to the *Cologne Fragment*. Furthermore, Luther immediately proceeds from this definition to elaborate the meaning of "*Euangelion*" in its biblical context, which tells of: "a true David who strove with sin, death, and the devil, and overcame them, and thereby rescued all those who were captive in sin, afflicted with death, and overpowered by the devil. Without any merit of their own he made them righteous, gave them life, and saved them, so that they were given peace and brought back to God."[106]

Tyndale wholeheartedly agrees with Luther that "In the olde testament are many promyses/whych are nothinge els but the evangelion or gospell," and his definition of "Gospel," as was shown earlier, is taken almost verbatim from Luther's own preface. It is true that Tyndale does not translate that portion of the text where Luther elaborates on the contrast between the ministries of Moses and Christ, but he does allude to this a few times and openly connects the preaching of the Law with the proper office of Moses and the preaching of grace in the Gospel with Christ. This challenges Smeeton's assertion that Tyndale shared the Lollards' definition of the "Gospel" as a moral rule or "promises" that explain "God's requirements."[107] On the other hand, even Luther could speak of the "Gospel" in terms of the broader ministry of Christ and that good works are among the benefits promised within the Gospel, although its proper work is the promise of forgiveness to contrite sinners. With regard to the relationship between the promises and Christ in Tyndale's thought, he describes Jesus in the prologue as: "oure redemer/ delyverer/ reconciler / mediator/ intercesser/ advocat/ atturney/ soliciter/ oure hoope/ comforte/ shelde/ proteccien/ defender/ strength/ helth/ satisfactien/ and salvacion ... And god (as greate as he is) is myne with all that he hath/ threw Christ and his purchasynge."[108] This makes it hard to accept Laughlin's suggestion that Tyndale could conceive of the salvific promises of God independent of their very fulfillment in and through the person and work of Christ.

With regard to the contrast made between Tyndale and Luther on the subject of Law and Gospel even at this early date, the scholarly consensus also seems to have overlooked and underestimated the significance of those passages and writings in which Luther speaks with open praise and adulation about God's Law, particularly the Ten

106. LW 35 (*Preface to the New Testament*, 1546): 358; WA DB 6:4–5.
107. Smeeton, *Lollard Themes*, 150.
108. Tyndale, [*New Testament*, 1525], sig. B iii ʳ.

Commandments, such as in his *A Treatise on Good Works* (1520), *Personal Prayer Book* (1522), and in his *Preface to the Old Testament* (1523) and *Lectures on Deuteronomy* (1525).[109] It is not so unlike Luther to speak of the Christian as loving, delighting, or even consenting to the Law as scholars assume, although the particular phrase "consent to the Law" does appear more predominant in the writings of Tyndale. Yet in his earlier Romans lectures, Luther explicitly speaks of the Christian life as a life of repentance from sin and that the conscience is made pure and "delights in the Law of God" through faith,[110] and in his *Lectures on Galatians* (1519) Luther describes how the Christian at the final resurrection "consents entirely to the Law."[111] In the *Treatise on Good Works* (1520), faith fulfills the Law because love and good works spring forth naturally from faith,[112] and in *The Freedom of a Christian* (1520) the soul that genuinely trusts in God's promise of mercy will undoubtedly "consent to His will."[113]

There are some modern scholars who argue that Luther, in the name of Christian liberty, resists ever identifying the new obedience of faith and the Spirit with any written Law.[114] Though Luther does argue that the Law written on the heart by the Spirit through faith is superior to the written Law, this is because the written Law cannot supply the power to fulfill its demands as the Spirit can do from within by changing the heart.[115] Similarly, though Luther believes that some situations justify the breaking of a law out of devotion to God or love for others, this does not mean that he perceived the Decalogue to be an inadequate guide for Christian moral behavior. On the contrary, he extolled the Ten Commandments rightly understood and interpreted. Yet, Luther recognized that loyalty to God in the First Commandment trumps loyalty to

---

109. *LW* 44 (*Treatise on Good Works*, 1520): 34–35; *WA* 6:213; *LW* 43 (*Personal Prayer Book*, 1522):14–24; *WA* 10²:388; *LW* 35 (*Preface to the Old Testament*, 1545): 235–38; *WA DB* 8:12–15; *LW* 9 (*Lectures on Deuteronomy*, 1525): 53, 56–57; *WA* 14:587–88, 590–91.

110. *LW* 25 (*Lectures on Romans*, 1515–16): 334, 340; *WA* 56:345–46, 350.

111. *LW* 27 (*Lectures on Galatians*, 1519): 363; *WA* 2:586

112. *LW* 44 (*Treatise on Good Works*, 1520): 22–23, 26, 30–31, 63, 108–9; *WA* 6:204–5, 236, 270–73.

113. *LW* 31 (*Freedom of A Christian*, 1520): 348–52, 365; *WA* 7:54, 64–65.

114. For example, Haikola, *Usus Legis*, 145–50; Joest, *Gesetz und Freiheit*, 195; Pesch, "Gesetz und Evangelium," 328–29.

115. *LW* 25 (*scholia* on Romans, 1515–16): 187; *WA* 56:203.

family and government in the Fourth Commandment if they are ever in conflict. Furthermore, the Ten Commandments are rightly interpreted and applied in service to the law of love. Thus, Tyndale translates Luther's gloss on the apostles' breaking of the ceremonial law of the Sabbath in Matthew 12 as constituting an example of how "the very commaundments of god binde not where love and neade requyre."[116]

Tyndale's statements that "fayth only" justifies and that salvation is "imputed" to "fayth only" apart from the love and works that follow faith show the particular influence of Luther's evangelical theology, and he shares with Luther the idea that God justifies a person on the basis of faith alone because faith justifies God and the truth of His promises in obedience to the First Commandment.[117] Tyndale also compares the righteous desires produced by faith in Christ to a sick man who desires to be made whole and healthy, while through the blood of Christ the weakness that remains with the Christian as a sinner until the resurrection is not imputed for condemnation. The non-imputation of sin in the life of the regenerate is Augustinian but a sanative and proleptic element is also found in Luther's theology of justification and the Christian as *simul justus et peccator*.[118]

Tyndale's description of the offering of Christ first as a gift and then as an example follows Luther's early writings[119] as does his use of the analogy of the tree and its fruit to illustrate that justification is by faith alone without works but that faith naturally produces good works,[120] which are motivated by selfless concern for others and not for rewards or for the favor of God promised freely in the blood of Christ.[121]

Although Luther's *Vorrhede* was a significant influence on the *Cologne Fragment*, Tyndale's prologue does admittedly display an

---

116. Tyndale, [*New Testament*, 1525], fo. xiii ʳ; *WA DB* 6:56.

117. Tyndale, [*New Testament*, 1525], sig. [A iiii ᵛ]–B i ᵛ; *LW* 31 (*Freedom of A Christian*, 1520): 361; *WA* 7:61–62. See also *LW* 44 (*Treatise on Good Works*, 1520): 22–23, 26, 30–31, 63, 108–9; *WA* 6:204–5, 236, 270–73.

118. See *LW* 25 (*Lectures on Romans*, 1515–16): 260, 329–36, 350; *WA* 56:272, 341–47, 350; *LW* 31 (*Freedom of A Christian*, 1520): 358–59; *WA* 7:59–60; Althaus, *Theology of Martin Luther*, 234–41; See also Leininger, "How Lutheran Was William Tyndale," 59–62.

119. *LW* 35 (*A Brief Instruction on What to Look for and Expect in the Gospels*, 1521): 120; *WA* 10¹ᵃ : 12.

120. *LW* 31 (*The Freedom of a Christian*, 1520): 361; *WA* 7:61.

121. *LW* 31 (*The Freedom of a Christian*, 1520), 365–66, 369; *WA* 7:64–66.

obvious sense of independence, both structurally and rhetorically. Tyndale's prologue is anything but a mere replica of Luther's own preface. Nevertheless, the claim of his independence from Luther has been recently stressed too far when this is bound entirely to a direct comparison of the *Cologne Fragment* with Luther's *Vorrhede*. The influence of Luther's other early evangelical writings, with which Tyndale was assuredly familiar by 1525, must be considered as well. Daniell at least considers this a possibility with regard to the last portion of the prologue.[122] A look at the wider corpus of Luther's thought ranging from the years 1515–25 challenges preconceived notions about significant discrepancies existing at this early date between the two reformers. The principal influence of Luther upon Tyndale's early theology of Law and Gospel cannot be so easily dismissed.

After fleeing authorities in Cologne, Tyndale and Roye found their way to the city of Worms where Tyndale's dream of a complete New Testament translated from the Greek and printed in English was finally achieved in 1526. As Daniell states: "Here was suddenly the complete New Testament, all twenty-seven books, the four Gospels, the Acts, the twenty-one Epistles and Revelation, in very portable form, clearly printed. Here was the original Greek, in English."[123] Before the end of the year, Bishop Tunstall intensified his efforts in London to prohibit the buying and selling of Tyndale's New Testament, along with other proscribed evangelical works streaming in from the continent.[124] Such works listed by Foxe include Luther's *Babylonian Captivity of the Church*, *Lectures on Galatians*, *The Freedom of the Christian*, and a work by Zwingli on Anabaptism. It is interesting to note that, although the list visibly grew by 1529 to include works of Zwingli, Bucer, Oecolampadius, and Melancthon, Luther's works still dominated the list.[125] With regard to Tyndale's New Testament, Foxe recounts how Bishop Tunstall struck up a deal with an English merchant in Antwerp named Augustine Packington to buy up all printed copies in order to have them burned,

---

122. Daniell, *William Tyndale*, 131–33.

123. Ibid., 134. This edition of the New Testament was without a prologue and marginal glosses, and only contained a short "To the reder" at the end, which itself probably evolved into the *Prologue to the Epistle of St. Paul to the Romans* printed in the same year. See Trinterud, "Reappraisal," 27.

124. Haigh, *English Reformations*, 60.

125. Foxe, *A&M* [1570]: 1157–58.

not knowing all the while that Packington was taking the revenue to Tyndale who then used it to subsidize later revised editions.[126]

Also printed in Worms in 1526 was Tyndale's *A compendious introduccion/ prologue or preface un to the pistle off Paul to the Romayns*. This is Tyndale's second major evangelical work, even though, again, a sizeable portion of it is a translation of Luther's own German prologue of 1522. Yet, following Trinterud's essay, many scholars have argued that Tyndale used Luther liberally without following him on several important theological points, one of which is his understanding of Law and Gospel.[127]

A cursory glance of Tyndale's prologue reveals that he indeed used Luther's prologue and translated a good portion of it. It is also obvious, however, that Tyndale by no means merely duplicated Luther's German prologue, but interpolated his own comments, phrases, and passages for purposes of elaboration or expansion. Furthermore, a substantial portion of text at the end of Tyndale's prologue has no direct parallel in Luther's prologue. Nevertheless, the German prologue is clearly the principal inspiration and structural model behind Tyndale's own text.

Some scholars have moved beyond mere structural comparison and have attempted to demonstrate that a closer analysis even of the very opening sentences reveals that Tyndale is doctrinally distant from Luther in 1526. For example, Werrell notes that only Tyndale adds "a lyght and a waye unto all the scriptures" to emphasize the central importance of the book of Romans. Werrell, somewhat ironically, uses this very same statement to argue that Tyndale possessed a greater respect for the whole canon of Scripture compared with the hierarchy that Luther gave to the books of the Bible.[128] On the contrary, what is important to recognize here is that Tyndale shows no hesitation in borrowing from Luther's exalted admiration for the book of Romans as the "principal and most excellent part off the newe testament." Furthermore, Tyndale is translating directly from Luther in describing the book as a "bryghte

---

126. Ibid., 1158–59.

127. Trinterud, "Reappraisal," 27–31; Laughlin, "Brightness of Moses' Face," 161–62; Greenman, "William Tyndale," in Greenman and Larsen, *Reading Romans through the Centuries*, 121–36.

128. Werrell, "Tyndale's Disagreement," 59; See also Greenman, "William Tyndale," in Greenman and Larsen, *Reading Romans through the Centuries*, 128.

lyghte and sufficient to geve lyghte un to all the Scripture,"[129] a statement that is nearly identical to the one isolated above by Werrell.

Many other contrasts made by scholars have been exaggerated and, in some cases, contrived. For example, it is argued that Tyndale is more concerned with the glory of God in salvation than Luther,[130] that he lays a far greater stress on the work of the Holy Spirit,[131] and that he speaks of justification more as being made righteous whereas Luther emphasizes it as the declaration or forensic imputation of righteousness.[132]

As far as basic content and structure are concerned, Tyndale closely follows Luther's prologue by defining law, grace, faith, righteousness, flesh, spirit, and he similarly provides chapter summaries of the book of Romans. Luther and Tyndale both interpret "Law" in Romans as referring to the will of God, which is unlike human laws whose conditions are satisfied by mere outward conformity ("works of the law"). To "fulfill the lawe" of God is to do it cheerfully with loving obedience from the very depths of the heart. This is impossible without the Spirit of God empowering a person through faith in Christ. If people were honest, they would actually wish the burden of the Law away so that they might satisfy their own lusts without consequence. Though not a verbatim translation, Tyndale's definition of "Law" as requiring the "grounde off the hert and love from the botome there of" echoes Luther who himself says: "God judges according to what is in the depths of the heart. For this reason, his law too makes its demands on the inmost heart; it cannot be satisfied with works, but rather punishes as hypocrisy and lies the works not done from the bottom of the heart."[133]

Contrary to the claim of many scholars that Luther somehow diminishes the personal role of the Holy Spirit in the conversion of the

---

129. Tyndale, *Romayns* [1526], sig. a ii ʳ; *LW* 35 (*Preface to the Epistle of St. Paul to the Romans*, 1546): 365; WA DB 7:2–3.

130. Werrell, "Tyndale's Disagreement," 61–62.

131. Ibid., 62–63; Werrell, *Theology of William Tyndale*, 16, 119; Smeeton, *Lollard Themes*, 140–44; Laughlin, "Brightness of Moses' Face," 161; Greenman, "William Tyndale," in Greenman and Larsen, *Reading Romans through the Centuries*, 131; Trinterud, "Reappraisal," 30–31; McGrath, *Iustitia Dei*, 286. Trueman argues this point in the context of his discussion of the *Cologne Fragment*. See *Luther's Legacy*, 89.

132. Werrell, "Tyndale's Disagreement," 63; Werrell, *Theology of William Tyndale*, 16; McGrath, *Iustitia Dei*, 286.

133. Tyndale, *Romayns* [1526], sig. a ii v; *LW* 35 (*Preface to the Epistle of St. Paul to the Romans*, 1546): 366; WA DB 7:2–5.

heart, Luther clearly states that: "such a heart is given only by God's Spirit, who fashions a man after the law, so that he acquires a desire for the law in his heart, doing nothing henceforth out of fear and compulsion but out of a willing heart." Elsewhere, he states clearly that: "This pleasure and love for the law is put into the heart by the Holy Spirit ... But the Holy Spirit is not given except in, with, and by faith in Jesus Christ..."[134] Trinterud makes too much of a statement made by Tyndale that works "only" cannot fulfill the Law, as if Tyndale was saying that the love of the heart is necessary, which he argues is out of step with Luther's insistence on faith alone as fulfilling the Law. According to Trinterud, this is characteristic of Tyndale's more Augustinian emphasis on love as the fulfillment of the Law.[135] However, Tyndale in this statement is simply refuting the assumption that God's righteous Law is satisfied by compulsory behavior and outward conformity, which is Luther's point as well. Thus, Tyndale is actually in agreement with Luther that fulfilling the Law means doing what it says from the heart without compulsion or for self-seeking purposes, "even as though there were no lawe at all."[136] This love, however, Tyndale and Luther agree, springs only and spontaneously from faith in Christ.

On the basis of Tyndale's use of phrases like "inward affection and delectation" for the Law, one scholar argues that Tyndale lays a much stronger emphasis on the "inwardness of the law" than Luther.[137] However, this difference is really nothing more than one of literary style. Luther's thoughts are often expressed more tersely, whereas Tyndale tends to be a bit more loquacious. Yet, it should not be concluded on this basis that they are in fundamental disagreement regarding the love that only exists where faith and the Holy Spirit are present. Luther's prologue has: "So it happens that faith alone makes a person righteous and fulfils the law. For out of the merit of Christ it brings forth the Spirit. And the Spirit makes the heart glad and free, as the law requires that it shall

---

134. Tyndale, *Romayns* [1526], sig. a iii–a iiii r ; LW 35 (Preface to the Epistle of St. Paul to the Romans, 1546): 366–67; WA DB 7:4–7.

135. Trinterud, "Reappraisal," 28.

136. Tyndale, *Romayns* [1526], sig. a iiii ᵛ; *LW* 35 (*Preface to the Epistle of St. Paul to the Romans,* 1546): 367–68; WA DB 7:6–7.

137. See Greenman, "William Tyndale," in Greenman and Larsen, *Reading Romans through the Centuries,* 129.

be. Thus good works emerge from faith itself."[138] Tyndale's own prologue reads: "fayth only iustifyeth/maketh rightewes/and fulfylleth the lawe/for it bringeth the Sprite thorowe Christes deservynges/the Sprite bringeth lust/looseth the hert/maketh hym fre/ setteth hym at lyberte/ and geveth hym strengthe to worke the dedes of the lawe with love/ even as the lawe requireth/ then at the last out off the same fayth so workinge in the herth/ springe all good workes by there awne acorde."[139] Tyndale merely expands upon what Luther himself has simply stated more concisely, but there is nothing to indicate any substantial difference of theological opinion. In fact, it seems that Tyndale has merely refashioned Luther's thought using his own wordy style. For example, Luther simply has "make the heart glad and free," whereas Tyndale has "bringeth lust/ looseth the hert/maketh hym free/ setteth hym at lyberte." This use of such obvious repetition or verbosity might communicate a conscious emphasis placed on the idea but could also merely reflect a difference in rhetorical style. It certainly does not betray any fundamental theological disagreement incongruity.

Tyndale follows Luther's prologue by defining "sin" as essentially unbelief, even as all truly good works spring from a heart of faith. "Grace" is defined as the merciful favor of God and the offering of Christ and the Spirit with all His gifts. Christians who wrestle with the lusts of the flesh stand under this grace on account of their faith in Christ and the "begynninge off the Sprite" until sin is fully mortified at death.[140] "Faith" is described as a gift of God, and Tyndale is just as adamant as Luther in rejecting the notion that the doctrine of justification by faith alone encourages lawlessness. On the contrary, justifying faith is freely active in doing good works out of gratitude to the love of God. Faith "maketh vs all togedyr newe in the hert/ mynd/ will/ lust/ and in all oure affeccions and powers of the soule . . ." Faith brings with it the Holy Spirit through whom the believer freely and cheerfully serves others without the need

---

138. *LW* 35 (*Preface to the Epistle of St. Paul to the Romans*, 1546): 368; *WA DB* 7:6–7.

139. Tyndale, *Romayns* [1526], sig. a v ʳ.

140. Tyndale, *Romayns* [1526], sig. a v ʳ–[a vi ʳ]. Luther has: "Because the flesh is not yet slain, we are still sinners. But because we believe in Christ and have a beginning of the Spirit, God is so favorable and gracious to us that he will not count the sin against us or judge us because of it. Rather he deals with us according to our faith in Christ, until sin is slain." *LW* 35 (*Preface to the Epistle of St. Paul to the Romans*, 1546): 369–70; *WA DB* 7:8–9.

for outward compulsion. Tyndale uses Luther's analogy of good being inseparable from faith as heat is from fire.[141]

Werrell argues that Tyndale's emphasis on the role of the Holy Spirit, rather than faith, in conversion sets him apart from Luther,[142] but Luther clearly states that the new heart of cheerful obedience "is the work which the Holy Spirit performs in faith."[143] A disparity between the two is falsely contrived on the basis of the obvious fact that the two parallel quotes are not identical. A reading of the wider context, however, reveals that Tyndale is not departing from Luther here. A few isolated statements of Luther where the "Holy Spirit" is not specifically mentioned should be interpreted in the light of others where, as Rex has aptly demonstrated, the essential work of the Holy Spirit with regard to faith, good works, and divine illumination is explicitly stated.[144] Tyndale himself could equally say, as Luther did, that faith "bringeth the Sprite,"[145] and, on the other hand, his expression that "faith is a thing wrought by the Holy Ghost in us," adapted from Luther's "Faith . . . is a divine work in us," does not warrant the polarization that scholars like Werrell have contrived between the two.[146]

With regard to the doctrine of justification by faith, Luther and Tyndale both agree that faith in Christ brings new life, affections, and desires through the working of the Spirit and is the seed of all active righteousness. Nevertheless, many scholars such as McGrath and Trueman argue that Tyndale defines "justification" and "justified" more in the Augustinian sense of being "made righteous," or a change of nature and will, rather than being "declared righteous," or a change of status, as in the theology of Luther. Trueman places Tyndale closer to Augustine on the supposition that Tyndale placed greater emphasis on the moral implications of justification rather than on the objective, Godward satisfaction of guilt. Jeffrey Leininger argues that Tyndale at

---

141. Tyndale, *Romayns* [1526], sig. [a vi ʳ–a vii ᵛ]; LW 35 (*Preface to the Epistle of St. Paul to the Romans*, 1546): 370–71; WA DB 7:8–11.

142. Werrell, "Tyndale's Disagreement," 63.

143. LW 35 (*Preface to the Epistle of St. Paul to the Romans*, 1546): 370–71; WA DB 7:8–11.

144. See Rex, "New Light," 166–68.

145. Tyndale, *Romayns* [1526], sig. a iiii ᵛ, vi ᵛ, b iii.

146. The latter two quotations are cited in Werrell, "Tyndale's Disagreement," 62–63.

the very least is under the influence of the "early Luther" in 1515–1519 and the "Luther in transition" during the 1520s whose theology of justification as the forensic imputation of righteousness in Christ only became more explicitly defined and developed in the 1530s. However, even Trueman goes on to acknowledge that Tyndale speaks of justification, union with Christ, and righteousness in language that falls just shy of an explicit theology of imputation while admitting that there is a proleptic element in Luther's own understanding of justification by faith. Trueman eventually admits that the difference between Tyndale and Luther is one more of emphasis rather than of real substance.[147] If this is the case, then it should not be stressed too far as if to give the misleading impression that Tyndale differed with Luther profoundly on the nature of justification in the 1520s, and McGrath even acknowledges that Tyndale's works of the early 1530s convey the "basic features" of imputed righteousness.[148] Few scholars have considered that the Augustinian elements in Tyndale's theology are derived from Luther himself and that these elements should be interpreted synthetically with regard to the influence of Luther's particular theological presuppositions and emphases.

Following Luther's prologue, Tyndale does not restrict the meaning of "flesshe" in the book of Romans to physical unchastity, but likewise defines it as the corruption of the entire person in "soule/ body/ wytte/ wyll/ reason." Like Luther, Tyndale describes actual sin as the product of the root of all sin in unbelief, which corrupts every work that does not spring from grace no matter how "good/ holy/ and spiritual they seme to be." On the contrary, truly "spiritual" works spring from faith, which even sanctifies "grose" tasks like fishing and cleaning shoes. A person who is reborn and lives by the Spirit is rightly called "spirituall," as are the good works that issue freely from his or her faith.[149]

---

147. Trueman, *Luther's Legacy*, 92–94. See also Leininger, "How Luther Was William Tyndale," 61–63, 71. For Luther's other use of "justified" in the sense of being "made righteous" or "healed" from sin and his proleptic theology of justification, see Althaus, *Theology of Martin Luther*, 224–42.

148. McGrath, *Iustitia Dei*, 286 (n.6).

149. Tyndale, *Romayns* [1526], sig. [a vii ᵛ–a viii]; *LW* 35 (*Preface to the Epistle of St. Paul to the Romans*, 1546): 372; *WA DB* 7:2. For Luther on the goodness of even the most ordinary activities done in faith, see *LW* 44 (*Treatise on Good Works*, 1520): 23, 30–31; *WA* 6:209–11.

Tyndale follows Luther's lead by providing a summary of each chapter in Romans and agrees with Luther that the order of the book provides a model for ministers to preach the Law followed by the Gospel. This is to foster a sense of humility and contrition among the people for their sin so that they can properly "desyre helpe," acknowledging that their compulsory obedience, or "workes of the lawe," will not justify them in the sight of God: "that the lawe was geven to vtter ande to declare synne only."[150] It is only by faith in Christ that a sinner is "made ryghtewes,"[151] and this righteousness is "deserved . . . for vs" in Christ. Werrell needlessly contrasts "merits for us" (*verdienet*) in Luther's text with Tyndale's "deserved soche rightewesnes for vs." Tyndale agrees with Luther that a Christian is made righteous in a certain sense through justifying faith in Christ and the redeeming power of the Holy Spirit, but that the righteousness of favor with God and the forgiveness of sins is promised in Christ through faith alone. It is "Christes" righteousness that justifies the sinner and Tyndale adds that "faith ys imputed for ryghtwesnes."[152] This is on account of the union of faith with Christ's atoning righteousness in the Gospel and not in the sense that faith is a human work regarded by God as meritorious of His justifying grace.

Tyndale does not translate Luther's chapter summaries verbatim but exercises a significant degree of rhetorical and literary independence. For instance, he adds a substantial amount of running commentary on the bondage of human nature under the Law and on the promise of grace and the indwelling of the Holy Spirit. Yet, even in this, Tyndale echoes Luther by emphasizing the preaching of the Law before the Gospel, and that the Law "causeth wrath" for all who are neither found in Christ nor possess the gift of His Holy Spirit.[153]

Like Luther, Tyndale defines a vital work of faith after justification as the "batayl of the Sprit agenst the flesshe." The flesh lusts against the desires of the Spirit so long as a person lives in his or her mortal body. Nevertheless, God does not condemn the Christian for remaining sin on

---

150. Tyndale, *Romayns* [1526], sig. [a viii ᵛ]–b ʳ; *LW* 35 (*Preface to the Epistle of St. Paul to the Romans*, 1546): 372–73; *WA DB* 7:14–15.

151. The American Edition translates Luther's "*rechtfertig*," as "justifies."

152. Tyndale, *Romayns* [1526], sig. b i ᵛ–b ii ʳ; *LW* 35 (*Preface to the Epistle of St. Paul to the Romans*, 1546): 373; *WA DB* 7:14–15; Werrell, "Tyndale's Disagreement," 62.

153. Tyndale, *Romayns* [1526], sig. b ii ʳ–[b iiii ᵛ]; *LW* 35 (*Preface to the Epistle of St. Paul to the Romans*, 1546): 373–74; *WA DB* 7:14–17.

account of the presence of faith and the Holy Spirit that "fighte agenste it." Tyndale, basically translating Luther, states that to do battle against the flesh and its lusts is to "fulfil oure baptim," or to live out what is signified by the sacrament.[154] This understanding of baptism was not unique to either Luther or Tyndale, and Erasmus in his *Enchiridion* speaks of the Christian life as a living out of the sacrament. To view salvation in terms of a covenant, and particularly in the context of the sacrament of baptism, was a familiar concept by the time of the Reformation, including that of late medieval Catholicism.[155]

Most scholars have come to acknowledge that by the early 1530s, and reaching its zenith in the revised *New Testament* (1534), Tyndale develops an understanding of salvation expressed in terms of a conditional covenant wherein God promises eternal life only to them that keep His laws.[156] Some interpret this as the likely influence of the theology of the Swiss and Rhineland reformers, who shared Tyndale's education in Humanism and an affection for the Law that is supposedly absent from Luther. The "covenant" obviously plays a significant role in the writings of these reformers.[157] More recently, Werrell argues that Lollardy is behind Tyndale's understanding and appropriation of the covenant theme.[158]

It is important at this point to establish that it is not so much Tyndale's supposed affection for the Law that anticipates and foreshadows his more maturely developed theology of covenant as it is his understanding of the Christian life as the living out of baptism. In fact, Tyndale's theology of covenant is grounded in his interpretation and theology of baptism.

In the discussion above, Tyndale does appear to give salvation a certain conditional quality, in that God promises to withhold condemnation if and where faith is present and struggling in the Spirit against sins. While scholars such as Rex argue that Luther's theology of baptism

154. Tyndale, *Romayns* [1526], sig. [b iiii ʳ]; *LW* 35 (*Preface to the Epistle of St. Paul to the Romans*, 1546): 375; *WA DB* 7:18–19. See also *LW* 35 (*The Holy and Blessed Sacrament of Baptism*, 1519): 29–43; *WA* 2:727–37; Althaus, *Theology of Martin Luther*, 353–59.

155. Rex, "New Light," 163–64.

156. See also McGiffert, "William Tyndale's Conception of Covenant," 167–84.

157. Trinterud, "Reappraisal," 33–34, 39; Trinterud, "Origins of Puritanism," 45.

158. Smeeton, *Lollard Themes*, 150–53; Werrell, *Theology of William Tyndale*, 45–62.

"is very much a one-way street," Tyndale here is translating directly from Luther.[159] In his own prologue, Luther encourages Christians with the assurance of God's favor despite sinful impulses: "we are still God's children, however hard sin may be raging within us, so long as we follow the spirit and resist sin to slay it." Tyndale's own translation reads: "we ar never the lesse the sonnes of god and also beloved/ though that sinne rage never so moche in vs/ so longe as we followe the Sprite/ and fyghte agenste synne to kyll and mortify it."[160] Luther had articulated the same idea years before in his treatise on *The Holy Blessed Sacrament of Baptism* (1519).

This is certainly not to suggest that Tyndale's later emphasis on "covenant" as an interpretive scheme was taken over from Luther. However, at this point, Tyndale's understanding of the conditionality of salvation as it pertains to living out the sacrament of baptism through faith is arguably the legacy of Luther. It is certainly possible that Luther's own theology of baptism is among the foundational influences upon Tyndale's more mature theology of covenant.

Tyndale continues to roughly follow Luther's prologue by explaining the true nature of Christian liberty, which is defined as freedom from the burden of condemnation under the Law. Rather, whereas the Law extorts obedience from the unwilling, the Gospel makes people free and willing to serve God with pleasure and without the need for compulsion. For Tyndale, the Holy Spirit "maketh vs love the lawe," so that the Law is no longer at enmity with those who live by faith through the power of the Holy Spirit. Luther himself, in the corresponding passage, expresses it this way: "Grace . . . makes the law dear to us . . . sin is no longer present, and the law is no longer against us but one with us."[161] The difference of language used here should not be exaggerated, and it does certainly reveal that Luther spoke with equal candor about the newfound affection for the Law produced in the Christian through the Gospel. Earlier in the prologue, Luther speaks explicitly of "pleasure and love for the Law."[162] Yet, at the same time, the phrase "love the Law"

---

159. Rex, "New Light," 163.

160. Tyndale, *Romayns* [1526], sig. [b vii r]; *LW* 35 (*Preface to the Epistle of St. Paul to the Romans*, 1546): 377; WA DB 7:22–23.

161. Tyndale, *Romayns* [1526], sig. b iiii v; *LW* 35 (*Preface to the Epistle of St. Paul to the Romans*, 1546): 375; WA DB 7:18–19.

162. *LW* 35 (*Preface to the Epistle of St. Paul to the Romans*, 1546): 366–67; WA DB 7:4–7.

need not be interpreted only as love toward the written Law itself, but that the inward desires of the Christian correspond spontaneously to the written Law. Indeed, both Luther and Tyndale define the obedience that comes from faith as occurring without the compulsion of the Law, "ye though there were no lawe."[163]

Both Luther and Tyndale acknowledge a new affection for the Law that comes through the Holy Spirit by faith, yet Tyndale, like Luther, argues that the "beste" and proper way to think about the purpose of the Law is its work in revealing sin and the condemnation deserved by it.[164] Only after a person becomes conscious of sin by the Law can he or she properly believe in Christ for salvation and begin to follow the will of God by doing battle with the flesh, which is the "ryghte werke of fayth."[165]

Tyndale mostly follows Luther's prologue to the end and largely translates his comments on the duties of all people to obey the government, although true Christians ruled by the Spirit (in Luther "the good") have no need of any such government to coerce them to respect the lives and property of others. Luther only in passing defines love as the sum of the Christian ethic, but Tyndale adds that "spirituall love" needs moral pressure just as much as a loving mother needs to be told to care for her one and only son. Finally, Tyndale imitates Luther by urging readers to become diligent students of the book of Romans, which is the "lyghte and the effecte of the olde testamente."[166]

An additional nine pages in Tyndale's prologue include a treatise on the *Pater Noster*, "to fill vpp the leefe with all." Scholars have identified this as an adaptation from the summary appearing at the end of Luther's own widely circulated tract on the Lord's Prayer published in Wittenberg in 1519. This fact was overlooked by Werrell who argues that Luther's Christocentric theology caused him to devalue the

---

163. Tyndale, *Romayns* [1526], sig. b iiii v; *LW* 35 (*Preface to the Epistle of St. Paul to the Romans*, 1546): 366–67, 376; *WA DB* 7:4, 6, 18, 20. See also *LW* 44 (*Treatise on Good Works*, 1520): 26; *WA* 6:207.

164. Tyndale, *Romayns* [1526], sig. [b v ᵛ]; *LW* 35 (*Preface to the Epistle of St. Paul to the Romans*, 1546): 377; *WA DB* 7:20.

165. Tyndale, *Romayns* [1526], sig. [b vii ʳ]; *LW* 35 (*Preface to the Epistle of St. Paul to the Romans*, 1546): 378; *WA DB* 7:22, 24.

166. Tyndale, *Romayns* [1526], sig. [b viii ʳ]–c; *LW* 35 (*Preface to the Epistle of St. Paul to the Romans*, 1546): 378–80; *WA DB* 7:24, 26.

"Fatherhood" of God.[167] Tyndale's introduction reviews the themes of Law and Gospel and, like Luther, he describes the Lord's Prayer in terms of a plea for the mercy of forgiveness and a request for the help to do what is impossible to be done by human strength alone.[168] The introduction gives the undeniable impression of Luther's influence in both content and tone, especially with regard to the absolute helplessness and guilt of human nature before the Law: "Marke this well and take it for a sure conclusion/ when God commaundeth us in the law to doo any thinge/ he commaundeth not therefore/ that we are able to do yt, but to bryng us unto the knowledge of ourselves/ that we might se what we are and in what miserable state we are in ... The office of the law is only to vtter sinne and to declare in what miserable damnacion and captivity we are in ...The law then bringeth a man unto the knowledge of him selfe, and compelleth him to morne/ to complayne/ to sorowe/ to confesse and knowledge hys sinne and miserie/ and to seke helpe."[169]

Scholars are certainly right to point out that Tyndale's prologue is more than a mere translation of Luther's prologue, for he exercises a substantial amount of rhetorical and literary independence. However, in many cases where Tyndale does expand quantitatively beyond Luther's text, whether in his comments on human nature or with regard to the work of the Devil, this does not reveal any significant theological divergences from Luther but actually suggests the imprint of other works of Luther dating to the early 1520s. Furthermore, even if the Holy Spirit is named more numerously in Tyndale's prologue, a point that is open to gross misrepresentations, such a comparison seems unfair when the two prologues are so varied in length. It does not appear in the final analysis that, other than the obvious rhetorical and literary variables, Tyndale has "left Wittenberg" behind in his prologue to the book of Romans.

After the publication of his 1526 *New Testament* and *Prologue to Romayns*, Tyndale resurfaced in the city of Antwerp in 1528 where he

---

167. Daniell, *William Tyndale*, 150; Trinterud, "Reappraisal," 31; *LW* 42 (*An Exposition of the Lord's Prayer for Simple Laymen*, 1519): 78–80; *WA* 2:128–30; Werrell, "Tyndale's Disagreement," 60–61. With regard to Luther's appraisal of the Fatherhood of God, see *LW* 42 (*Exposition of the Lord's Prayer*, 1519): 22–23; *WA* 2:83; *LW* 43 (*Personal Prayer Book*, 1522): 29; *WA* 102:395–96.

168. *LW* 43 (*Personal Prayer Book*, 1522): 3–40; *WA* $10^2$375–406. The prayer book was adapted from Luther's earlier *A Short Form of the Ten Commandments, the Creed, and the Lord's Prayer* (1520). See *WA* 7:204–29.

169. Tyndale, *Romayns* [1526], sig. c ii ʳ–c iii.

published two of his most infamous theological treatises: *That fayth the mother of all good workes . . .*[170] and *The Obedience of a Christian Man*. It is not known exactly when Tyndale arrived in Antwerp, but the city with strategic ties commercially to England would be his headquarters for the next several years until his arrest in 1535 followed by imprisonment in the Vilvorde castle.[171]

Scholars readily acknowledge that Tyndale's *Parable of the Wicked Mammon* is loosely based on a published revision of a sermon originally preached by Luther in Wittenberg in 1522. The two texts of the sermon by Luther are mostly similar, but Daniell exaggerates in stating that they are "identical."[172] The text for Luther's sermon is the parable of Jesus in Luke 16:1–13. In the parable, a rich man rebukes his steward for the poor management of his estate. In the impending loss of his employment, the steward becomes an illicit creditor to his master's debtors. By dishonestly reducing their outstanding debts he wins their friendship and secures his future. Jesus refers to the steward rightly as "dishonest," but his cunning methods used in this fraudulent transaction become an illustration of the importance of winning future friends and witnesses in heaven through acts of kindness and charity while on earth.

Luther claims that this text has been inappropriately used in the past to support a doctrine of salvation by works. Thus, his intention is to prove that the parable is only rightly interpreted under the assumption that faith alone justifies before good works.[173] Luther's sermon went

---

170. *That fayth the mother of all good workes* [1528] is hereafter referred to by its more common name *Parable of the Wicked Mammon*. The original bears the name of "Hans Luft of Malborowe," but this was to conceal Martin de Keyser of Antwerp. See Daniell, *Tyndale*, 156, 224.

171. Daniell, *William Tyndale*, 155; Avis, "Book Smuggling," 180–81, 185; Avis, "England's Use of Antwerp Printers," 234–40; Pettegree, "Humanism and the Reformation in Britain and the Netherlands," in Amos, Pettegree, and Nierop, *Education of a Christian Society*, 2–5, 17; Rupp, *Six Makers*, 16; Rupp, *Studies in the Making*, 11–12

172. Daniell, *William Tyndale*, 160–61; Trinterud, "Reappraisal," 31. The original preached version of the sermon is found in WA 10³:273–82 and the reworked text used by Tyndale follows it on 283–92. For an English translation of the original sermon, see "A Sermon for the Second Sunday after Mary's Ascension. Preached at Wittenberg by Dr. Martin Luther, 1522," *Complete Sermons*, 2.2:291–301.

173. This refers to the original 1522 sermon translated in *Complete Sermons*, 2.2:295; WA 10³:276–77. In the reworked text, Luther states at the very beginning that his message agrees with what he had formerly stated in his "Postillen" (or *Wartburg Postil*) and in *"meinen buchlin von Christlicher freiheit und gutten wercken"* (*The Freedom of A Christian*). See WA 10³:283.

through five editions in 1522, one edition in 1523, and it was printed in Wittenberg, Augsburg, Basle, and Erfurt. For Tyndale to use a sermon so widely known and circulated as the basis for his own exposition may indeed show him to be, as Daniell aptly observes, "firmly in the Lutheran mainstream." Vasilev's claim that Tyndale's choice of the parable is likely rooted in Bogomil-Cathar dualist philosophy is simply without any basis whatsoever. However, Daniell does note that Tyndale's longer treatise is hardly an exact copy of Luther's much shorter printed sermon, and he argues that Tyndale's elaborate use of illustrations from human experience linked with scriptural references is more of an evidence of his debt to Erasmus as a rhetorician.[174] This may be true, but literary embellishment cannot be equated with theological divergence. As was the case with Tyndale's *Cologne Fragment* (1525) and the *Prologue to Romayns* (1526), a brief look at the *Wicked Mammon* confirms Tyndale's continued indebtedness, not only to the immediate sermon in question, but to Luther's broader evangelical thinking as a whole.

After a four page introduction "to the reader," in which he strongly distances himself from former translating associate William Roye,[175] Tyndale builds on the main themes of his previous writings, namely the bondage of the natural will under the condemnation of the Law,[176] the necessity of contrition or repentance under the Law (including Christians who sin "throughe fragylytie"),[177] that faith alone "iustyfyeth and setteth us at peace with God,"[178] and that good works in accordance with the Law do not merit heaven or eternal life but are the evidence of the life of the Spirit and of faith in Christ.[179] In fact, this last statement is the whole point of Jesus' parable according to both Tyndale and Luther. The exhortation of Christ to make "frends of the unrighteous mammon" is rightly interpreted as the exercise of faith in kindness and service to others, which gathers up witnesses for the Day of Judgment who will

---

174. Daniell, *William Tyndale*, 161–62; Vasilev, *Heresy and the English Reformation*, 83.

175. For a fuller discussion of the fallout between Tyndale and Roye, see Daniell, *Tyndale*, 142–45, 157–58.

176. Tyndale, *Parable of the Wicked Mammon* [1528], fo. ii, fo. v ᵛ–vi ʳ.

177. Ibid., fo. vi, viii ʳ.

178. Ibid., fo. ii, fo. vii ᵛ–viii ʳ; WA 10³:283–84.

179. Tyndale, *Parable of the Wicked Mammon* [1528], fo. iv ᵛ, xiii ʳ, lix, lxii ᵛ–lxiii ʳ. Luther similarly exegetes James 2 to argue that faith not followed with works is dead, false, and not salvific. See WA 10³:285, 287–88.

be able to "testyfye and witnesse of thy good workes" and, by implication, of true faith in Christ.[180] Although heaven is not a reward earned for contracted labor, it naturally follows upon the doing of good deeds without any thought of personal gain, just as hell awaits those who give full consent to evil even though they do not do evil acts to earn eternal punishment. True believers only need to be put in "remembraunce" of those things that should be done to mortify the flesh and to serve the welfare of others.[181]

Both Laughlin and Trinterud argue that the theology of Tyndale's *Wicked Mammon* transcends Luther's sermon by more strongly emphasizing the role of the Holy Spirit in the doing of good works, by teaching that such good works are a means of assurance to Christians that their faith is true, and by stressing the positive relationship of the Christian to the Law. Contrary to the opinion of Clebsch, who dates the shifting of Tyndale toward an emphasis on good works nearer to 1530, Laughlin argues that "Tyndale already had traveled a long distance from Wittenberg" by the time he published the *Wicked Mammon*.[182] Once again, however, the differences between Tyndale and Luther have been exaggerated and, in some cases, even contrived. Trinterud's essay quotes lengthy passages from Tyndale with only brief interpretive comments interspersed here and there with regard to differences from Luther. He assumes for the most part that the reader will pick up the differences for him or herself since he provides only a rather superficial analysis of the *Wicked Mammon* and other works of Tyndale, and his abrupt references to Luther do not reveal any substantial familiarity with the wider corpus of Luther's writings.

Luther obviously assumes that the Holy Spirit is crucial to the conversion and moral life of the Christian, and Luther openly speaks of good works as being the "fruit of the Spirit." Furthermore, Luther equally acknowledges that good works that come from the heart are a testi-

---

180. Tyndale, *Parable of the Wicked Mammon* [1528], fo. xxiii ^{v}–xxix ^{r}; also xxxix ^{v}–xl ^{v}; Luther, *Complete Sermons*, 2.2:300; WA 10^3:281–82. See also LW 31 (*Freedom of A Christian*, 1520): 357–58; WA 7:59–60.

181. Tyndale and Luther also forthrightly reject any notion that the making of "frends" (*freunde*) in Luke 16 refers to the devotional veneration of saints already in heaven. Tyndale, *Parable of the Wicked Mammon* [1528], fo. xiiii ^{r}–xviii ^{v}, xxi ^{v}, lv ^{v}, lvi ^{r}; WA 10^3:284–85, 289–90.

182. Laughlin, "Brightness of Moses' Face," 167–69, 174. Trinterud, "Reappraisal," 31–33.

mony not only to others but also to oneself regarding the genuineness of professed faith: "if you can give from the heart you may be assured that you believe."[183] Tyndale's remark in the *Wicked Mammon* that "mi forgeving certifieth my sprite that God shall forgeve me" sounds similar to something Erasmus said in the *Enchiridion* but must be interpreted in the context of Tyndale's other statements including "For as a man fealeth god to hym selfe/ so is he to hys neyghboure."[184] In other words, Tyndale is operating in consistency with the assumptions of Luther's evangelical theology that the ability to forgive others is an active reflection of the presence of justifying faith allowing that Christian to have an even bolder confidence in presuming upon the continual mercy of God. Tyndale can speak of forgiveness in terms that very much sound like conditions for salvation, foreshadowing his later theology of covenant, but this conditionality has to do with works being the evidence of justifying faith and a boost to assurance. Luther makes a similar point about the ability to forgive and the assurance of salvation in his exposition of the Lord's Prayer in the *Large Catechism* (1529).[185] Trueman identifies good works as the "primary means of assurance" in Tyndale's *Wicked Mammon*. It is questionable how "primary" they really are, but works as providing some means of assurance is also the point Luther is making in his own sermon. Trueman also argues that Tyndale makes no effort to harmonize this works-based assurance with the priority of faith before works, even though Tyndale explicitly defines good works as always proceeding freely in love following repentance and faith.[186]

The phrase "consent to the Law" that appeared in the *Cologne Fragment*[187] now resurfaces in the *Wicked Mammon* as "the consent

---

183. "A Sermon for the Second Sunday after Mary's Ascension. Preached at Wittenberg by Dr. Martin Luther, 1522," *Complete Sermons*, 2.2:296–97; *WA* 10³:278. See also *LW* 30 (*Lectures on I John*, 1527): 298, 309; *WA* 20:749, 768–71.

184. Tyndale, *Parable of the Wicked Mammon* [1528], fo. xxiv ᵛ–xxv ʳ; "as moche as thou shalt remyt vnto thy brother which is in thy dette/ so moche shall god forgyve vnto the." *Enchiridion*, sig. [P vii ᵛ–P viii ʳ], sig. [S v ᵛ].

185. *LC*, Tappert, 432–3; Kolb & Wengert, 352–54; *BSLK*, 682–85. See also Althaus, *Theology of Martin Luther*, 245–50.

186. Trueman, *Luther's Legacy*, 94–96; Tyndale, *Parable of the Wicked Mammon* [1528], fo. xxii ᵛ–xxiii ʳ, fo. xxv ᵛ–xxvii , xxviii ᵛ, xxxi, xxxiii ʳ,xxxviii ᵛ, xxxiv ᵛ–xxxv ʳ, xl, xlv ᵛ, lii ᵛ, lx, lxii ᵛ–lxiii ʳ; *LW* 35 (*Preface to the Epistle of St. Paul to the Romans*): 377; *WA DB* 7:22–23. See also *LW* 31 (*Freedom of A Christian*, 1520): 358–59; *WA* 7:59–60.

187. Tyndale, [*New Testament*, 1525], sig. [A iiii ʳ].

of the hert vnto the law." Although even the repentance or contrition preceding justifying faith constitutes a certain "consent" to the Law of God for Tyndale,[188] a point that Laughlin overlooks,[189] it seems that this phrase most often refers in Tyndale's writings to the "lust to the Law" following and produced through justifying faith. According to Tyndale's *Wicked Mammon*, the lawful works that please God in gratitude to His grace are found in Scripture, and misguided zeal usurps what God in His Word has clearly commanded should be done or left undone. Luther also directed people to the Word of God for moral instruction in good works, whether the natural-moral Law of the Decalogue or its softer counterpart in the kind entreaties of Christ and the apostles.[190] Like Luther, Tyndale sees no real qualitative difference before God between preaching the Word and washing "thy masters dyshes" with the understanding that these are done with thanksgiving and in a spirit of faith and not as a means to merit favor with God.[191]

Tyndale identifies "consent to the Law" as the evidence of the working of the Spirit within and "the seale and marke" of election, but this is consistent with Luther's own theology of Law and Gospel and his understanding that repentance and devotion to good works are evidences of justifying faith and election to grace.[192] Luther never explicitly says that the "consent of the hert unto the lawe/ ys unite and peace betwene God and man," although he does state on numerous occasions that God does not condemn the sins of the Christian who fights

---

188. Tyndale, *Parable of the Wicked Mammon* [1528], fo. vi ᵛ, lvii ᵛ. See also 'A prologe to the fourth boke/ called Numeri' in Tyndale, [*Pentatuech*, 1530], sig. [A v ᵛ]–[A vi ᵛ].

189. Laughlin, "Brightness of Moses' Face," 179.

190. Tyndale, *Parable of the Wicked Mammon* [1528], fo. xlv ʳ, xlvi ʳ; *LC*, Tappert, 407; Kolb and Wengert, 428; *BSLK*, 639; *LW* 35 (*How Christians Should Regard Moses*, 1525): 166; *WA* 16:375; *LW* 44 (*Treatise on Good Works*, 1520): 34–35; *WA* 6:213; *LW* 43 (*Personal Prayer Book*, 1522):14–24; *WA* 10²:388; *LW* 35 (*Preface to the Old Testament*, 1523):237–38; *WA DB* 8:12–15; *LW* 9 (*Lectures on Deuteronomy*, 1525): 53, 56–57; *WA* 14:587–88, 590–91.

191. Tyndale, *Parable of the Wicked Mammon* [1528], fo. xlii v–xliv r; *LW* 44 (*To The Christian Nobility of the German Nation Concerning the Reform of the Christian Estate*, 1520): 129–30; *WA* 6:408–9; See also Wingren, *Luther on Vocation*.

192. See *LW* 30 (*Sermons on the Second Epistle of St. Peter*, 1523): 158–59; *WA* 14:23. For a criticism of the contrast Trueman and others establish between Luther and Tyndale on the subject of predestination, see Leininger, "How Lutheran was Tyndale," 58–59.

through faith in the Spirit against the flesh. This statement of Tyndale also needs to be interpreted in the light of others where "consent to the Law" is not enough to be "at one with God." In this latter case, "consent to the Law" refers to sorrowful contrition and a despairing repentance that is not enough to justify if it is without faith and hope in the Gospel, and Tyndale clearly states that "fayth therfore setteth the at one wyth God."[193] Therefore, it is faith that establishes unity and peace with God but such faith is not without repentance and a consent to His Law that gives living evidence to the reality of this spiritual communion.[194]

It seems a bit overstated to say, as Daniell does, that the *Wicked Mammon* is mostly "Tyndalian,"[195] unless this refers to its literary structure, which does reflect a great degree of Tyndale's individuality and personal interaction with Scripture. Tyndale indeed expands well beyond Luther's own sermon by expositing a far greater number of New Testament passages, although it is important to point out that Luther's text was a printed sermon and not a formal theological treatise. Yet it is clear that Luther's sermon is the significant influence behind Tyndale's treatise. If not, why translate any portion of it at all? Therefore, even by the publication of the *Wicked Mammon*, Tyndale's fundamental theological perspective with regard to Law and Gospel still bears the strong imprint of the direct evangelical legacy of Luther.

Tyndale's *Obedience of the Christian Man* was published five months after the *Wicked Mammon* and from the same press in Antwerp. It was written by Tyndale chiefly as a response to Thomas More's criticism that the evangelical reformers are the scourge of monarchies stirring up civil unrest and rebellion throughout Europe.[196] The response of

---

193. Tyndale, *Parable of the Wicked Mammon* [1528], fo. xxxv ᵛ, lvii ᵛ; *LW* 35 (*The Holy and Blessed Sacrament of Baptism*, 1519) *WA* 2:728, 731–33; *LW* 35 (*Preface to the Epistle of St. Paul to the Romans*, 1546): 377–78; *WA DB* 7:22–25; *LW* 26 (*Lectures on Galatians* [1–4], 1535): 350; *WA* 40¹:537–38. See also *LW* 30 (*Lectures on I John*, 1527): 238, 263–64, 269–74; *WA* 20:641–42, 690–92, 699–708.

194. This is also how a later statement in his exposition of 1 John (1531) should be interpreted: "Love is the instrument wherewith faith maketh us God's sons, and fashioneth us like the image of God, and certifieth us that we so are." Quoted from Leininger, "How Lutheran was William Tyndale," 69. See also Trueman, *Luther's Legacy*, 100. Contrary to both Trueman and Leininger, Tyndale is not saying that love makes a person God's son by status but by imitation. Thus, love "certifieth," but is not the cause of, our adoption as God's sons.

195. Daniell, *William Tyndale*, 167.

196. Ibid, 223–24. For Daniell's more detailed overview of the entire structure of

the *Obedience* yields little that is truly novel, for Luther had addressed the same challenge years before during the peak of social unrest in the so-called "Peasant's Revolt" in 1524–1525.[197]

Although the *Obedience* is not based structurally on any one specific work of Luther, Tyndale re-emphasizes themes that are consonant with the wider corpus of Luther's evangelical writings, such as the bemoaning of the introduction of Aristotelian ethics into Christian theology, his affirmation of the preaching of the Law as a necessary revelation of the bondage of the will leading to repentance ("the lawe doeth but vtter synne only and helpeth not"), the division of biblical revelation according to "law" and "promyses,"[198] the importance of teaching the Law to urge outward submission to authorities for "long liffe upon the erth" and "worldly prosperite," a rejection of rebellion against temporal authority,[199] and a recognition of the value of adversity for discipline, the testing of faith, and to inspire the "Christen man" weak in the flesh to mortify sins.[200] Like Luther, Tyndale also distinguishes between types of law-keepers, those who keep the Law outwardly for fear of temporal punishment or for the "pleasure/ profit and promocion that foloweth" and those who keep the Law in their heart by the Spirit without the need for compulsion or other such incentives.[201]

Still following Luther, Tyndale understands "repentaunce," otherwise known as contrition, to be a "mornyinge and sorow" for sin under

---

Tyndale's *Obedience*, see 232–34, 387–90.

197. *LW* 30 (*Sermons on I Peter*, 1522): 19–21; 75–79; *WA* 12:275–77, 329–33; *LW* 46 (*Against the Robbing and Murdering Hordes of Peasants*, 1525), 51; *WA* 18:358–59; *LW* 45 (*Temporal Authority: To What Extent It Should Be Obeyed*, 1522–23): 88–91, 95, 100; *WA* 11:250–52, 254–55, 258; *LW* 40 ('Letter to the Princes of Saxony Concerning the Rebellious Spirit,' 1524): 49–59; *WA* 15:210–21.

198. Tyndale, *Obedience* [1528], fo. xvii ʳ–xviii ʳ, fo. xix ᵛ('William Tyndale otherwise called William Hychins unto the Reader'), xlii ᵛ–xliii ʳ, cviii ʳ , cxxxi ᵛ–cxxxii ʳ, cxxxiii ᵛ–cxxxiii ʳ.

199. Ibid., fo. xxii ᵛ–xxiii ʳ ('Prologe'), fo. xxv ʳ–xxxiiii ʳ. See also Rex, "The Crisis of Obedience," 866–67.

200. Tyndale, *Obedience* [1528], fo. xxxiii v–xxx iiii r, xliii v–xlviii r, fo. cx; "nothing else is so good for the mortifying of the flesh as the cross and suffering." *LW* 35 (*Preface to the Epistle of St. Paul to the Romans*, 1546): 377; *WA DB* 7:22–23.

201. Tyndale, *Obedience* [1528], fo. xxxiiii ʳ–xxxvi ʳ, xxxvi ᵛ, xlii ʳ; "The Sprite of Christ hath written the lively lawe of love in their hertes which driveth them to worke of their awne accorde frely and willingly/ for the greate loves sake only which they se in Christe/ and therefore nede they no law to compell them." See fo. cxxiiii, fo. cxxxiii ᵛ, cxxxiiii ᵛ.

the Law. One kind of repentance comes in the form of eternal despair before faith and prepares the heart to receive the promises of forgiveness in Christ. Yet, another kind lasts throughout the Christian life as a godly mourning for the weakness of sin that remains until death. Like Luther, Tyndale rejects the Catholic sacrament of penance on the grounds that inward repentance and faith are wholly adequate for reconciliation with God for all sins committed after baptism. There is no need for any other satisfaction to be made. Nevertheless, Tyndale does assume that an offending sinner who is truly sorry for his or her sins will not fail to seek public reconciliation with the offended. Furthermore, the power of the "keys" is not the authority of the episcopal office to pardon sins in the sacrament of penance but is simply the preaching of the Gospel.[202]

In the *Obedience*, Tyndale defends Luther's theology of justification by faith alone against John Fisher, the Bishop of Rochester and Chancellor of Cambridge, who argued against Luther that faith justifies only after becoming "formed by love" (*caritate formata*).[203] Tyndale responds by arguing that God cannot be loved as Father until there is first assurance of His love as Father. Therefore, justification, defined as the forgiveness of sins and the favor of God, is received through faith alone in Christ though love proceeds by nature from this faith: "Yf thou beleve Gods promises in Christ and love his commaundmentes then arte thou saffe. Yf thou love the commaundmente then arte thou sure that thy fayth is unfayned and that Gods Sprite is in the."[204] This faith is obviously not the kind of historical faith that Satan and his demons have who acknowledge that Jesus was crucified but who cannot believe that the benefits of that death are for themselves. Thus, historical faith alone does not and cannot produce the love of God. It is with this understanding that Tyndale can say that the satisfaction made by Christ for the debt of sin proclaimed in the sacrament of baptism is only for them who repent, believe, and submit to the commandments of God.

---

202. Ibid., fo. xciiii ᵛ–xcv, xcvi ᵛ, xcviii ᵛ– xc ʳ, clx; *LW* 32 (*Defense and Explanation of All the Articles*, 1521): 74–76; *WA* 7:420–22.

203. Hatt, *English Works of John Fisher*, 48. See also Fisher, "A sermon... concernynge certayne heretickes [1526]," in Hatt, *English Works*, 145–74; Clebsch, *England's Earliest Protestants*, 12, 32; Rex, "English Campaign against Luther," 95–96; Marc'hadour, "Tyndale and Fisher's 1521 Sermon against Luther," in Day, Lund, and O'Donnell, *Word, Church, and State*, 145–61.

204. Tyndale refers the reader to his *Wicked Mammon*. See *Obedience* [1528], fo. lxv ᵛ–lxvi.

This does not mean that Tyndale believes in salvation by faith and love and good works, but it is to insist that the kind of faith in Christ that justifies is preceded by repentance under the Law and is followed by the evidence of a willful submission to that Law in love.[205] Truly good works pleasing to God in honor of His commandments must be totally free and cannot have anything to do with seeking to earn the favor of God, which He promises liberally to faith in Christ alone, but they are done with love for the sake of others, the taming of the flesh, and with thanksgiving to God. All of these presuppose justifying faith in Christ. This is also to reject fasts, veneration of images, pilgrimages, and any other works of "ydolatry" and "imagination" perceived as works of merit before God.[206]

There is nothing in Tyndale's *Obedience* to suggest any conflict with the Law-Gospel theology of Luther. In fact, it bears the strong imprint of his evangelical influence. Tyndale clearly follows Luther in logically prioritizing repentance under the Law, faith alone in Christ for forgiveness and favor with God (the apex of Christian conversion), and the resulting love and submission to God's commandments. Tyndale says at one point that "whosoever doeth knowledge his sinnes receaveth forgevenes," but this does not mean that contrition itself justifies. Both Luther and Tyndale recognize there to be such a "consent to the Law" that is without faith and hope in the Gospel and thus without the ability to truly love God and His Law from the heart, which only creates a damning bondage to despair.[207] The point here is that the Gospel promise of forgiveness in Christ to be received through faith is meant for those who are repentant under the Law, and faith in Christ is most likely implied here. Furthermore, Tyndale's comment is a paraphrase

---

205. Ibid., fo. lxvi ᵛ–lxvii, fo. lxx, lxxxix ᵛ–xc ʳ; "The assurance that we are sonnes/ beloved and heyres with Christe and have Gods Sprite in us/ is the consent of oure hertes unto the law of God. Which law is all perfeccion and the marke where at all we oughte to shote . . . For he that loveth not the law and hateth his synne and hath not professed in his herte to fyghte agenst it and morneth not to God to take it awaye and to purge him of it/ the same hath no parte with Christe." See fo. cxxvii ᵛ–cxxviii ʳ, fo. cxxxiii ᵛ, cxxxviʳ.

206. Ibid., fo. cix ᵛ–cx, cxvi ʳ, cxx ᵛ, fo. clxix ᵛ–cl ʳ.

207. Tyndale, *Obedience* [1528], fo. xcvi ᵛ; *Parable of the Wicked Mammon* [1528], fo. lvii ᵛ; *LW* 25 (*scholia* on Romans, 1515–16): 240–41, 251–54, 340; *WA* 56:253–55, 254, 265–66, 350.

of 1 John 1:9, a passage of Scripture that arguably refers to the ongoing intercessory work of Christ on behalf of repentant Christians.

There is one statement in the *Obedience* that does pose some difficulty, however. Tyndale asserts that: "as sone as the herte lusteth to doo the law/ then are we righteous before God and oure synnes forgeven."[208] This statement admittedly appears to make love and earnestness to obedience, rather than faith in Christ alone, the formal basis for the remission of sins and righteousness before God. This interpretation is very unlikely, however, when considering other contemporaneous and unambiguous statements made by Tyndale that justification, understood as the forgiveness of sins and favor of God, is by faith in Christ alone, as well as his recent and explicit rebuttal to Bishop John Fisher's theology of justification by "*fides caritate formata.*" Even earlier within this very same treatise Tyndale states clearly that such love for God and His commandments cannot exist without prior assurance and faith in the forgiveness and favor of God and is actually the evidence of justification, true faith, and the possession of the Holy Spirit. Neither Luther nor Tyndale ever equate true faith with mere historical knowledge of Jesus' death and resurrection, but with a personal and filial trust in the promise of God's love in Christ. The kind of love for the Law Tyndale has in mind here, then, can only be generated by the assurance of faith in the forgiveness promised in Christ alone. Therefore, Tyndale must be emphasizing how intimately related faith and love are in time by saying that love for the Law occurs at the very same moment, though not as the formal basis, of the forgiveness of sins received through faith in Christ alone. In any case, this statement cannot be allowed to stand by itself but must be interpreted with respect to Tyndale's thought more generally. Nevertheless, it does seem that Tyndale, increasingly by the end of the 1520s, is beginning to favor a certain way of expressing and emphasizing the new life that is expected to flow from an evangelical theology of justification by faith alone. In this sense, then, Laughlin is correct to argue that Tyndale never changes his theology but only his mode of expression when he begins to emphasize the covenant in the 1530s. However, the assumption behind his premise, that Tyndale's appraisal of the Law is un-Lutheran all along, is inaccurate. Trinterud's opinion that the *Obedience* "neither demonstrates nor refutes the 'Lutheranism' of Tyndale" might be true in so far as the treatise neither translates nor

---

208. Tyndale, *Obedience* [1528], fo. cxxxiii ᵛ.

is derived from any one specific work of Luther.[209] Yet this widely influential English work on the "political effects of Scripture"[210] still largely bears the influence of Luther's theology of Law and Gospel.

Tyndale's thought does begin to take a noticeable turn in the 1530s from his earlier writings, and this has to do with his development of an emphasis on a theology of covenant, which eventually becomes his key hermeneutical principle. Although Tyndale could not have derived this rhetorical motif of "covenant" from Luther, the concept of covenant is readily found in Luther's theology of baptism. Thus, scholars have been all too quick to assume that Tyndale's theology of covenant shows a significant theological divergence from the influence of Luther.

Trinterud and Clebsch really pioneered the study of Tyndale's turn to "covenant" in the 1960s. Although Clebsch identifies a much starker shift occurring in Tyndale's theology away from an earlier emphasis on faith alone in the doctrine of justification, both scholars argue that Tyndale develops a covenantal moralism that foreshadows the piety of English Puritanism.[211] A decade or so later, Paul Laughlin agreed with Trinterud's thesis that Tyndale's theology remained largely consistent throughout his career and added that Tyndale only significantly shifts from a "Law-Gospel" to a more Reformed "Covenant" scheme as befitting his stress on the need for good works in the life of the Christian.[212] Only in the last few decades have scholars begun to explore whether this theme of "covenant" in Tyndale's later thought is derived from the influence of other sources other than the Swiss and Rhineland reformers. Smeeton, and more recently Werrell, have attempted to locate Tyndale's theology of covenant within the native English Wycliffite-Lollard tradition.[213]

209. Trinterud, "Reappraisal," 33.

210. Daniell, *William Tyndale*, 242–47.

211. Trinterud, "Origins of Puritanism," 37–57; Trinterud, "Reappraisal," 24; Clebsch, *England's Earliest Protestants*, 167, 174, 197. See also Moeller, "Beginnings of Puritan Covenant Theology," 46–67; Greaves, "Origins and Early Development," 26–27; Williams, *William Tyndale*, 129–34; Knox, *Doctrine of Faith*, 19–21; Knappen, "First English Puritan," 201–15. For criticism of the contractual interpretation of covenant in Tyndale's thought, see McGiffert, "William Tyndale's Conception of Covenant," 167–84. See also Trueman, *Luther's Legacy*, 112–17.

212. Laughlin, "The Brightness of Moses' Face."

213. Smeeton, *Lollard Themes*, 150–57; Werrell, *Theology of William Tyndale*, 44–63, 84–85. On a side note, in his attempt to argue that Tyndale's theology of covenant was

It is important to acknowledge outright that, besides the *"pactum"* theology of the scholastic *via moderna*, viewing salvation in terms of a covenant was part of the common parlance of late medieval baptismal spirituality. It has already been demonstrated that Erasmus himself speaks of baptism in terms of a covenant binding people to God in moral obligation.[214] Smeeton has shown that the idea was not foreign to the Lollards.[215] Luther also readily spoke of the baptismal covenant,[216] and Anabaptist reformers in the 1520s used "covenant" language to describe the oath taken by adults at baptism. However, the covenant concept does seem to have flowered most among the leading Swiss and south German Protestants who, in turn, influenced English Puritanism.[217]

As early as 1522, Zwingli, Oecolampadius, and Bullinger each spoke in some manner of the continuity between the two testamental periods straddling the cross, and around the time of Tyndale's arrival at Antwerp in the late 1520s the works of Zwingli and Oecolampadius were being published and proscribed throughout the Low Countries.[218] Yet Luther in the early 1520s, while acknowledging the temporality of the Mosaic Covenant made with Israel, also recognized a substantial unity to the canon of Scripture. In terms of the preaching of the Gospel, for example, the former age dimly proclaimed the Christ who was to come whereas the latter more plainly proclaimed the Christ who had come.[219] It was in response to Anabaptists such as Balthasar Hubmaier

---

familial rather than contractual, Werrell erroneously claims that McGiffert lumps Tyndale with the latter perspective, when in fact his essay was written to prove the exact opposite. See McGiffert, "Tyndale's Conception of Covenant," 184.

214. See Tyndale's translation of Erasmus's *Enchiridion*, sig. A iii ʳ. See also Rex, "New Light," 163–65.

215. Smeeton, *Lollard Themes*, 151–54.

216. *LW* 35 (*The Holy and Blessed Sacrament of Baptism*, 1519): 33–37; *WA* 2:728, 731–33; *LW* 35 (*Preface to the Epistle of St. Paul to the Romans*, 1546): 375; *WA DB* 7:18–19.

217. For an overview of the origins of covenant theology in Reformed Protestantism, see Baker, *Heinrich Bullinger and the Covenant*, 1– 25; Lillback, *Binding of God*, 81–109; Bierma, *German Calvinism*, 31–62.

218. Lillback, *Binding of God*, 83–88; Baker, *Heinrich Bullinger and the Covenant*, 3–5; Duke, *Reformation and Revolt*, 31.

219. *LW* 35 (*Preface to the Old Testament*, 1545): 235–238; *WA DB* 8:12–15; *LW* 9 (*Lectures on Deuteronomy*, 1525): 42–43, 63; *WA* 14:578–80, 602–3. See also Baker, *Heinrich Bullinger and the Covenant*, 181–83; Hagan, "Testament of A Worm," 12–13, 16; Althaus, *Theology of Martin Luther*, 86–102.

in 1525 that Zwingli began to develop a much fuller articulation of the covenantal continuity of Scripture, particularly in the context of legitimizing infant baptism as the replacement of the Jewish covenantal sign of circumcision. Although Bullinger apparently preceded Zwingli in explicitly identifying the origins of a covenant of grace in Genesis 3:15,[220] both agreed that the Abrahamic covenant is the definitive form of the eternal covenant of grace in the Old Testament and stressed the conditionality of participation in the promises of God's mercy by a responsive submission to God's Law. Luther never spoke of a "covenant of grace" *per se*, but he equally recognized that the promise made to Adam and Eve and to Abraham was essentially the preaching of the Gospel.[221]

The point of the following discussion is not to determine whether Tyndale's own theology of covenant was the result of the inheritance of Erasmus, Lollardy, the Swiss Reformed tradition, Luther, or his own reflections on the Old Testament - any one of which is difficult to substantiate definitively.[222] Yet, acknowledging that Tyndale's adoption of a rhetorical emphasis on covenant as an interpretive scheme did not come from Luther, previous scholars have not considered the extent to which Luther's own theology of baptism contributed to Tyndale's more developed formulation of a theology of covenant. If so, then Tyndale's theology of covenant may not be so opposed to Luther's theology of Law and Gospel as is commonly thought.

According to a rather incredible story told by Foxe, occurring sometime between 1528 and 1530, Tyndale suffered a shipwreck while traveling to Hamburg and lost all of his translation work on the Old Testament then to date. Upon arrival, as Foxe continues, he was assisted by Miles Coverdale in completing the *Pentateuch*, published in Antwerp in 1530 from the presses of Martin de Keyser under the pseudonym of "Hans Luft of Marburg."[223] David Daniell rightly acknowledges the significance of this publication for the history of the English Bible: "the first translation—not just the first printed, but the first translations-

---

220. Baker, *Heinrich Bullinger and the Covenant*, 1–4; Lillback, *Binding of God*, 81–83, 89–95; Bierma, *German Calvinism in the Confessional Age*, 31–35; *LW* 35 (*Preface to the New Testament*, 1522): 357–60; WA DB 6:2–7.

221. Baker, *Heinrich Bullinger and the Covenant*, 6;Lillback, *Binding of God*, 95–96; Bierma, *German Calvinism in a Confessional Age*, 34–35, 37.

222. Trueman, *Luther's Legacy*, 117–18; Clebsch, *England's Earliest Protestants*, 199.

223. Foxe, *A&M* [1570], 1227; Daniell first defends the historicity of Foxe's story in *Tyndale*, 198–200, but is rather skeptical in his more recent *Bible in English*, 178.

from Hebrew into English. Not only was the Hebrew language only known in England in 1529 and 1530 by, at the most, a tiny handful of scholars in Oxford and Cambridge, and quite possibly by none.[224]

Even before the appearance of Tyndale's *Pentateuch*, excerpts from his other writings show how comfortable he was in working with the Old Testament. It was probably after arriving on the Continent, and most likely in Germany, that Tyndale achieved proficiency in the Hebrew language. England by the 1520s was still comparatively behind in the knowledge of the Semitic languages.[225]

The linguistic aids that Tyndale may have had at his disposal were Reuchlin's Hebrew grammar and dictionary, the Complutensian Polyglot Bible printed by the University of Alcala in Spain before Erasmus's *Novum Instrumentum* (1516), Zwingli's recently published biblical commentaries, a French translation of the Old Testament, a Hebrew Bible, and an updated Latin text by the Italian Sanctes Pagninus. Though it is not entirely certain that Tyndale used all of these sources, few if any scholars would deny that Tyndale's "biggest help" was Luther's own German translation of 1523, which was the first-ever vernacular translation of the Hebrew Old Testament.[226] Aside from the prologues, the influence of Luther's German text of the Old Testament upon Tyndale's English translation is plain to scholars, although it has also been demonstrated that Tyndale exercised substantial independence from Luther by translating more directly from the Hebrew into English.[227]

The main concern here, however, is far less with the methods of Tyndale's translation of the Old Testament than with the theological themes he discusses in the prologues to each of the books of the Pentateuch.[228] In his prologue to the book of Genesis, Tyndale identifies the core message of Scripture according to the juxtaposition of Law and Gospel (or promises): "Seke therfore in the Scripture as thou readest

---

224. Daniell, *William Tyndale*, 283–91.

225. Ibid., 291–96.

226. Trinterud, "Reappraisal," 33; Hammond, "William Tyndale's Pentateuch," 354–56; Hammond, "Tyndale's Knowledge of the Hebrew," in Day, Lund, and O'Donnell, *Word, Church, and State*, 26–28; Daniell, *William Tyndale*, 293–97.

227. Daniell, *William Tyndale*, 306–12; Hammond, "William Tyndale's Pentateuch," 363–85.

228. Each book of Tyndale's *Pentateuch* has its own title page and prologue and there are dissimilarities in type setting. It appears, therefore, that the five parts were originally printed as separate units. See also Trinterud, "Reappraisal," 33.

it first the law/ what god commaundeth us to doo/ And secondarylye the promyses/ which god promyseth us ageyne/ namely in Christe Jesu oure lorde." The narrative portions of Genesis serve as examples both of God's faithfulness to those who trust in Him even in the midst of adversity and His discipline upon those who reject His laws. McGiffert mistakenly identifies this particular statement and its parallel in the earlier *Wicked Mammon* as foreshadowing Tyndale's more developed theology of covenant.[229] Laughlin and Smeeton also make much of Tyndale's increasing use of the word "promises," contrasted with Luther's usual definition of the "Gospel" as "proclamation," and argue that the former word choice narrows the dialectical gap between Gospel and Law, faith and obedience, promise and ethical obligation.[230] However, this assumption is challenged by the fact that Luther could also use "Gospel" and "promises" interchangeably,[231] and he spoke of the Gospel in the context of baptism with regard to the obligation of the baptized to believe with a heart of repentance and to struggle daily against sin.

At one point Tyndale objects to outward deeds as having the power to justify and make holy, but stresses rather "the inward Spirite receaved by fayth and the consent of the harte unto the law of god." The story of Cain and Abel in Genesis 4 illustrates that there may appear little outward difference between the works of the righteous and the unrighteous, but God sees the heart converted by His Spirit and approves those works that spring freely from it: "the deade is good because of the man / and not the man good because of his deade."[232] Tyndale's understanding of the priority of inward faith working through love in outward deeds continues to bear the influence of Luther's evangelical theology. The fact that he adds "consent of the hart unto the law of god" to "fayth" in the context of the receiving of the Spirit, however, does pose somewhat of an interpretive quandary. Tyndale might be interpreted as saying that the Holy Spirit is received by faith in Christ and love

229. Tyndale, "A prologe shewinge the use of the Scripture," [The *Pentateuch*, 1530]; McGiffert,"Tyndale's Conception of Covenant," 169. Luther similarly speaks of the stories of the Bible as examples of unbelief and faith. See *LW* 35 (*Preface to the Old Testament*, 1545): 237–38; *WA DB* 8:12–15.

230. Laughlin, "Brightness of Moses' Face," 147–50, 175; Smeeton, *Lollard Themes*, 148–49.

231. *LW* 44 (*Judgment . . . on Monastic Vows*, 1522): 256–57; *WA* 8:580–81. See also Rex,"New Light," 165.

232. Tyndale,"A prologe shewinge the use of the Scripture," [*The Pentateuch*, 1530].

toward the Law of God that comes from faith. One way of reading this text could understandably give this impression. Another way, however, is to read the phrase "and the consent of the hart" as referring back to "made them holy" and not the "Spirite receaved by fayth." This latter reading certainly fits better with Tyndale's understanding that it is the receiving of the Spirit through faith in Christ that converts the heart to love the Law of God in the first place. Yet, this still does not explain why Tyndale would say that the Spirit received by faith and consent to the Law of God justifies and makes one holy, unless Tyndale in this context is defining "justify" as "made righteous" and stressing that justifying faith submits to God's Law from the heart in the Spirit. Yet, if "consent of the harte unto the Law of God" merely refers to the repentance that precedes and accompanies justifying faith then all these difficulties are avoided, though Tyndale's choice of word order is misleading in this regard. In any case, this one statement must be interpreted in the light of the whole of Tyndale's thinking during this period.

The word "covenant" does not appear in Tyndale's prologue to the book of Genesis, in the textual glosses, or even in the main body of the translation itself. In Genesis 9, Luther uses "*bunds*" or "*bund*,"[233] and Tyndale uses "bond," "testamente," and "appoynment" interchangeably. In Genesis 17 Tyndale also uses "testamente" and "bonde."[234] However, Tyndale's definition of "Testament" is "an appoyntement made betwene god and man/ and goddes promyses," which does resemble his later definition of covenant, and it is important to note that he explicitly connects the "Testament" to the sacrament of baptism: "which is come in the roume thereof [i.e., circumcision] now signifieth on the one syde/ how that all that repent and beleve are washed in Christes bloud: And on the other syde/ how that the same must quench and droune the lustes of the flesh/ to folow the steppes of Christ."[235]

It has already been shown that Zwingli and Bullinger were not the only ones, nor even the first ones, to view baptism in terms of the making of a covenant with certain expectations, so it is not self-evident that Tyndale borrowed this particular idea from the Swiss Reformed tradition. Even Tyndale's brief reference to baptism as taking "the roume" of circumcision does not reveal any necessary departure from Luther,

---

233. *WA DB* 8:58–59.
234. Tyndale, [*The Pentateuch*, 1530], fo. xi ʳ–xii ʳ, xx ʳ–xxi ʳ.
235. Tyndale, "A table expoundinge certeyne wordes," [*The Pentatuech*, 1530].

who himself states in 1520 that "a sacrament of the Old Law and one of the New" are the same in the sense that faith alone in the promises that are given with these signs justifies. Luther even on another occasion defends the practice of infant baptism on the basis of the Old Testament circumcision of male children.[236]

In his prologue to the book of Exodus, Tyndale states that the stories of the Old Testament teach the universal principle that God's favor rests upon people who believe and obey, or whose faith produces obedience, whereas eventual destruction awaits all those who "through unbelief" resist His laws in disobedience. Though capable of differentiation, Tyndale does not conceive of faith and works as being separable. Rather, the Law becomes a "lyvely thing in the herte" through the Holy Spirit, "so that a man bringeth forth good workes of his awne acord without compulsion of the lawe ... All good workes and all giftes of grace springe out of him naturallye and by their awne accorde."[237] Tyndale still shows he is indebted to Luther's evangelical theology in describing the main purpose of the Law as to "vtter synne onlye and to make it appere" so that through faith in the mercy of God people would keep His commandments from the heart. Tyndale emphasizes the powerlessness of the Law to enliven the heart for the true keeping of the commandments, which comes about only through the remedy of the promise of the New Testament. This "testamente" reaches back to the very beginning of time, so that all sinners throughout history have been justified by faith in the promises of God. The "Old Testament" by contrast was a particular covenant established by God with Moses and the people of Israel. This testament pertained to the promise of the land, physical protection, and material wealth conditioned by outward obedience to laws and ceremonies. It dealt only with temporal prosperity and not with eternal favor. The substance of this "testament" with its temporal

---

236. *LW* 35 (*The Babylonian Captivity of the Church*, 1520): 64–67; *WA* 6:532–33. See also *LW* 40 (*Concerning Rebaptism*, 1528): 243–45; *WA* 26:158. The treatise was written by Luther in December 1527—January 1528 in response to the enquiry of two pastors concerning the growing Anabaptist movement. See *LW* 40:225–28.

237. "For as longe as my soule fealeth what love god hath shewed me in christe, I can not but love god agayne and his will and commaundmentes and of love worke them, nor can they seme hard unto me ..." "A prologe into the seconde boke of Moses called Exodus," [*The Pentateuch*, 1530].

blessings and cursings applies equally to the keeping or breaking of the laws that rule any established nation of the world.[238]

It is common knowledge that Luther saw Christ veiled in the pages of the Old Testament books. He also agreed that justification before God has always been by faith alone in the promises of God, such as in the case of Abraham, and he similarly viewed the Mosaic Covenant and its laws as a temporal ordinance established by God with the Jewish nation in particular. Thus, although the continuity of the covenant throughout Scripture becomes the keystone hermeneutic of the Reformed tradition and also later of Tyndale, each of the themes above agree completely with Luther and were arguably inspired by his own reading of the Old Testament. These parallels between Luther and Tyndale have been overlooked by scholars such as Trinterud.[239]

In his prologue to the book of Leviticus, Tyndale echoes Luther by interpreting the ceremonial laws of the Mosaic Covenant as God's way of keeping Israel from establishing false forms of worship. In a marginal gloss on Leviticus 10, Tyndale uses the story of Nadab and Abihu to illustrate the danger of zeal apart from the Word of God, "so doeth this ensample teach that we maye do no moare than is commaunded." The ceremonial laws also serve as typological figures of the life and intercessory ministry of Christ.[240] Tyndale's interpretation of the efficacy of the old and new symbols seems very similar to Luther, in that both understand that it is faith alone in the promise given with the symbols that justifies. In this sense, Tyndale could say that water baptism instituted by Christ saves just as much as animal sacrifices instituted under Moses.[241] Tyndale makes another connection between circumcision and baptism in this prologue, stating that both sacraments were instituted by God to set apart His people from the world, to serve as a visible confirmation

---

238. Tyndale, "A Prologe in to the seconde boke" [*The Pentateuch*, 1530]. See also his marginal gloss for Exodus 20, fo. xxxv ʳ.

239. On the temporality of the Mosaic Covenant, see *LW* 9 (*Lectures on Deuteronomy*, 1525): 63; *WA* 14:602–3. On the faith of Abraham, see LW 35 (*Prologue to the Epistle of St. Paul to the Romans*, 1546): 373–74; *WA DB* 7:14–17; Trinterud, "Reappraisal," 33–35.

240. Tyndale, "A Prologe in to the thirde boke of Moses, called Leviticus," [*The Pentateuch*, 1530], sig. [A i ᵛ]–A ii ʳ; fo. xvi ʳ; *LW* 35 (*Preface to the Old Testament*, 1545): 239, 247–48; *WA DB* 8:16–17, 28–31.

241. Tyndale, "A Prologe in to the third boke," [*The Pentateuch*, 1530], sig. [A iii] ; *LW* 36 (*The Babylonian Captivity of the Church*, 1520): 65–67; *WA* 6:532–33.

of His favor, and to signify the practical mortification of sin in the life of the Christian. In his *Babylonian Captivity of the Church* (1520), Luther likewise paralleled circumcision with baptism to illustrate that faith alone in the promise behind the sacrament justifies and that the fulfillment of the meaning of the sign is personal consecration to God.[242]

Tyndale's description of the message of the book of Numbers is also similar to Luther's, although his prologue is much lengthier. For both, the importance of the book is the numerous examples it provides of human failure to keep the Law apart from God's grace. The moral failures of the people reveal that the power to fulfill the Law and to avoid succumbing to temptations comes only by grace through faith in the promises of God. For Luther, the book of Numbers is "a notable example of how vacuous it is to make people righteous with laws; rather, as St. Paul says, laws cause only sin and wrath." In fact, for Tyndale as well as for Luther, the major point of the giving of the Law was, ironically, to show people that they utterly lack the strength to do what was commanded.[243]

In the context of his interpretation of vows in his prologue to Numbers, Tyndale rejects the notion that sacrificial offerings, whether of money, goods, or chastity, justify the heart before God. The only proper vow is the one associated with baptism, which is to respond to the mercy of God by walking in His commandments for the sake of others and to mortify the lusts of the flesh. Commitment to a life of voluntary poverty and chastity matters to God only when it serves these purposes. Yet the office of the Law is absolutely essential to the making of a true Christian and the revealing of the complete powerlessness of the sinner to be justified through his or her works, for unless the heart is moved by the Law to repent it has "no part with Christ. For yf thou repent not of thy synne/ so it is impossible that thou shuldst beleue that Christ had delyuered the from the daunger therof." Without faith in Christ, the heart cannot then be prompted to truly delight in the Law

---

242. Tyndale, "A Prologe in to the third boke," [*The Pentateuch*, 1530], sig.[A vii ʳ]; *LW* 36 (*The Babylonian Captivity of the Church, 1520*): 65–66; *WA* 6:532–33. For Luther on baptism, see also *LW* 35 (*The Holy and Blessed Sacrament of Baptism*, 1519): 29–31; *WA* 2:727–29.

243. Tyndale, "A prologe to the fourth boke of Moses /called Numeri," [*The Pentateuch*, 1530], sig. [A i v]–A ii r; *LW* 35 (*Preface to the Old Testament*, 1545): 238, 242; *WA DB* 8:14–15, 20–21. This text in the 1523 and 1545 edition are identical except perhaps with minor variations in spelling.

of God, and to lack such delight reveals the absence of faith and the Spirit. The office of the Law to illicit repentance for the sake of leading the sinner to Christ in faith was of critical importance to both Luther and Tyndale.[244]

Tyndale prizes the book of Deuteronomy above all others in the Pentateuch for it clearly teaches faith and its dynamic relationship to love: "deducinge the loue to God oute of faith, and the loue of a mans neyghboure out of the loue of God." In comparison, Luther similarly extols Deuteronomy for teaching faith and love, "for all God's laws come to that," and for providing the "most ample and excellent explanation of the Decalog" and the best instruction on how to fulfill the Ten Commandments in "spirit and body." Hammond erroneously interprets Luther's many negative comments on the Old Testament as referring to the Hebrew canon as a whole rather than more specifically to the "Mosaic Covenant." His inability to distinguish these two, as well as the Mosaic Law from the natural-moral Law, causes him to overlook the likelihood that Tyndale is extracting from Luther here.[245]

Also echoing Luther, Tyndale interprets the First Commandment as the "fountayne off all commaundmentes," for to obey this commandment is to believe in God with a thankful heart. Through this love for God, people are strengthened to love one another from the heart, and "loue only is the fulfillinge of the commandmentes."[246] Tyndale acknowledges that the blessings and cursings spoken to Israel under the Mosaic Covenant are made fundamentally "with all nacions," but with respect to "the life to come thou must haue the rightuousnesse of faith." In a similar way, Luther interprets the promise of temporal prosperity

---

244. Tyndale, "A prologe to the fourth boke," [*The Pentateuch*, 1530], sig. [A v v]-[A vi v]; *LW* 35 (*Preface to the Old Testament*, 1545): 242; *WA DB* 8:20-21; *LW* 31 (*Freedom of A Christian*, 1520): 358-9, 365-6, 369; *WA* 7:59-60, 64-66. For Luther on vows, see *LW* 44 (*The Judgment of Martin Luther On Monastic Vows*, 1522): 264-66; *WA* 8:585-86.

245. Tyndale, "A Prologe in to the fifte boke of Moses, called Deuteronomye," [*The Pentateuch*, 1530], sig. [A i ᵛ]; *LW* 35 (*Preface to the Old Testament*, 1545): 237-238; *WA DB* 8:12- 15; *LW* 9 (*Lectures on Deuteronomy*, 1525): 6, 14; *WA* 14:498-99, 544-45; Hammond "Law and Love in Deuteronomy," in Dick and Richardson, *William Tyndale and the Law*, 51-52.

246. Tyndale, "A Prologe in to the fifte boke," [*The Pentateuch*, 1530], sig. [A ii ᵛ]. See also Tyndale's gloss on Deuteronomy 19, fo. xxxiiii ᵛ; *LW* 9 (*Lectures on Deuteronomy*, 1525): 68-70, 109; *WA* 14:608-12, 638.

in the Fourth Commandment as applying to people of every nation who obey the rule of God's Law administered by parents and princes.[247]

According to Clebsch, Tyndale's *Pentateuch* reveals the beginnings of a shift from a previously dominant emphasis on faith alone in the doctrine of justification toward a new emphasis on the moral Law and good works after justification. Whereas Luther, as portrayed by Clebsch, treated the Law of the Old Testament only in terms of the ministry of Moses to issue death and judgment, Tyndale is able by 1530 to value the moral Law of the Pentateuch as a guide to Christian moral living.[248] Clebsch's misreading of Luther is easily demonstrated by Luther's praise of the Ten Commandments in his catechetisms and other writings and his perception that the moral teachings of Christ in the gospels are the natural-moral Law of the Decalogue taught lovingly to His disciples in the context of grace. For Luther, the real difference between the preaching of works by Moses and Christ has less to do with actual content or substance than with form and tone and with respect to distinct dispensations of salvation history.[249]

Scholars such as Trinterud and Laughlin are right to point out that Tyndale's earliest writings already emphasize "consent to the Law" and good works as concomitant with justification by faith alone.[250] Thus, they are right to stress the fundamental consistency of Tyndale's theology on this point. Nevertheless, Clebsch is also partly right in the stress he places on a shift occurring in Tyndale's writings in the 1530s. Tyndale does indeed later relegate faith in many passages that speak of God's mercy to a more implicit role with an even greater stress on the conditionality of the salvation promises in the expectation of repentance and the response of faith in good works and obedience to the Law. Yet this

247. Tyndale, "A Prologe in to the fifte boke," [*The Pentateuch*, 1530], sig. [A iiii ʳ]. See also his gloss on Deuteronomy 6, fo.xiiiiᵛ. It is important to note here that Tyndale does not follow Luther's numbering of the Decalogue and identifies the prohibition against the worship of graven images as the second commandment. Therefore, the commandment to honor father and mother is actually number five for Tyndale. Compare Luther's *Large Catechism* with Tyndale's discussion in the *Practice of Prelates*. See *LC*, Tappert, 383–386; Kolb and Wengert, 404–7; *BSLK*, 594–601; Tyndale, *Practice of Prelates* [1530], sig. I ʳ.

248. Clebsch, *England's Earliest Protestants*, 154–59, 165–66.

249. *LW* 35 (*Preface to the Old Testament*, 1545): 235–37, 241–46; *WA DB* 8:12–13, 24–25, 26–27.

250. Tyndale, [*New Testament*, 1525], sig. [A iiii ᵛ]. See also his *Obedience* [1528], fo. cxxvii ᵛ–cxxviii ʳ; also fo. cxxxiii ᵛ, cxxxvi ʳ.

does not mean, contrary to Laughlin, that Tyndale no longer has use for the Law-Gospel theology of Luther,[251] which is amply evident in his description of the chief work of the Law as the revelation of human sin and damnation that leads toward the comfort and life-changing power of the Gospel.

In the same year that his *Pentateuch* appeared, Tyndale published three other works, one of which was a reprinting of a fifteenth century Lollard tract entitled *The Examination of Master William Thorpe*.[252] More well-known is his *The Practice of Prelates* and *A Pathway unto Holy Scripture*, the latter being a slightly revised and expanded edition of his prologue to the 1525 New Testament (*Cologne Fragment*).

With regard to the *Examination*, its late date of publication makes it an unlikely source of Tyndale's theology, although Tyndale obviously valued it as a support to his cause of reform. The tract is an autobiographical account of a local priest named William Thorpe who stood trial before the Archbishop of Canterbury, Thomas Arundel, in 1407. Many of Thorpe's protests foreshadow Tyndale's own frustrations with English clergy. Charges brought against Thorpe while preaching in the town of Shrewsbury include his opposition to transubstantiation, the worship of images, pilgrimages, priestly tithes, and oath swearing all on the basis of the Word of God. Thorpe also opposes the proud and covetous prelates who persecute those of the "true faith of holy chirche," or the faithful Christians who loyally adhere to the commandments of God in His Word and the example of Christ.[253] Thorpe also rejects the necessity of the sacrament of penance on the grounds that God forgives the truly contrite heart without the mediation of an earthly priesthood. Though priests are useful for counsel, Thorpe interprets the "keys" of binding and loosing as the preaching of judgment upon the wicked

---

251. Laughlin, "Brightness of Moses' Face," 181–83.

252. Smeeton, *Lollard Themes*, 256–58; Mozley, *William Tyndale*, 345–46; Hudson, *Premature Reformation*, 493–94.

253. Thorpe, *Examination* [1530], sig. Ci ʳ–Cii. On a side note, Thorpe denies ever speaking out against transubstantiation in Shrewsbury, but argues that Scripture neither grants nor denies the scholastic interpretation of "substance" and "accidents." With regard to images, Thorpe admits to rejecting only those made by "mannes hande," but that the created things of God, especially mankind, are "worshipfull in theire kynde and to the ende that god made them for." Thorpe also denies ever rejecting all pilgrimages by reinterpreting obedience to the "biddinges of god" as the only "trew pilgremis trauelyng toward the blisse of heuen." See sig. D ʳ–E ʳ.

and mercy unto the repentant who sorrow and turn from their sin.[254] Thorpe's emphasis on diligence to the revealed commandments of God resonated with Tyndale.[255] However, Thorpe does not articulate a clearly defined doctrine of justification by faith in Christ alone, and his main concern is to encourage the faithful in the midst of persecution and to contrast the godly who suffer with their wicked persecutors. Tyndale's personal interest in the tract is in its exhortation to the faithful in protesting against unbiblical practices and ritualistic devotion in honor of obedience to the commandments of God and His Word.

Tyndale's *The Practice of Prelates* was written in response to King Henry VIII's impending divorce from Catherine of Aragon, which Tyndale opposed while criticizing the greedy interference and political maneuverings of popes and prelates throughout history, chiefly including Cardinal Wolsey.[256] Tyndale directs the King to the Law of God and urges him as a baptized, professing Christian to bring the question "unto the light of goddes lawe and let us submitte oure causes unto the iugement thereof and be content to have oure appetites [i.e., for answers] slayne therbye/ that we lust no farther then goddes ordinaunce geveth us libertye." He also encourages the King not to let the fear of human opinion, including that of Emperor Charles V, dictate his course of action. Instead the king should trust that God will "kepe them that kepe his lawes. Yf we care to kepe his lawes/ he wyll care for the kepinge of us/ for the truth of his promises."[257] Taken out of context, this statement would seem to communicate the idea that salvation is a "bipartite agreement" or contract stipulated by human obedience to the Law.[258] Yet it is not even self-evident that Tyndale has the promises of eternal salvation in mind in this context. Rather, he is speaking with regard to the temporal welfare and rule of the King, and Tyndale has already made mention in another writing of the fact that even outward submission to the Law of God brings with it the reward of temporal blessing and prosperity.[259]

---

254. Ibid., sig. [F v ᵛ–F vi].

255. Ibid., sig. B. See also "The beleue of the Lorde Cobham" and "The endenture of the Lorde Cobham," sig. [H v ʳ, H vi ᵛ]. John Old Castell was knight and lord of Cobham and was tried and executed for heresy in London in 1413 by Archbishop Arundel.

256. Daniell, *William Tyndale*, 201–5.

257. Tyndale, *Practice of Prelates* [1530], sig. [H vii], sig. [I vii ᵛ].

258. Clebsch, *England's Earliest Protestants*, 161.

259. Tyndale, "A Prologe in to the fifte boke," [*The Pentateuch*, 1530], sig. [A iiii ʳ]. See also his gloss on Deuteronomy 6, fo.xiiiiᵛ.

Tyndale refers to Leviticus 18:16 and Deuteronomy 25:5–7 to defend his opinion about the divorce and in doing so provides important insight regarding his hermeneutical approach to the Mosaic Law. Although Luther and Tyndale came to different conclusions about the divorce, their interpretation of how to apply the Mosaic Law is remarkably similar. Like Luther, Tyndale distinguishes between the ceremonial, civil, and moral laws of Moses. The ceremonial laws were signs pertaining to God's past dealings with the people of Israel, all of which have been surmounted by the sacrifice of Christ. The civil laws of Moses pertained only to the Jews and were a means of protection for the people. In this way, Luther and Tyndale both describe Moses as a "lawegever" (Luther has "*gesetz geber*"), but only for the Jews. However, the moral Law of the Decalogue summarized in the commandment to love God and neighbor is the very "lawe of nature" demanded of every person regardless of nationality. It is a law that even predated Moses and the Sinai Covenant, and would have remained in place regardless of whether or not it had ever been formally codified in writing. For Luther and Tyndale, to have faith and love toward God, which is the keeping of the First Commandment, results in the cheerful keeping of all the other laws pertaining to the neighbor. Trueman even states that, while Tyndale's rhetoric of loving the Law is, in his opinion, uncharacteristic of Luther, "his actual concept of Christian ethics is fundamentally identical with that of Luther."[260] Neither Luther nor Tyndale strictly equate the moral Law with the Decalogue, since both identify the law of the Sabbath as a ceremony abrogated by the New Covenant, which made all such ceremonies free matters. Nevertheless, the spirit of the law in surrender to the authority of the teaching and preaching of the Word of God is expected of every professing Christian. Lastly, both Luther and Tyndale regard the promise of a long life given with the commandment to honor parents (commandment number four for Luther, but five for Tyndale) as basically the temporal promise of a long prosperous life for respectful children and law-abiding citizens.[261]

---

260. Trueman, *Luther's Legacy*, 107. For Tyndale's response to the divorce question, see *Practice of Prelates* [1530], sig. [H viii], sig. I ii, sig. [I iiii ᵛ–v]. For Luther's discussion of the natural-moral Law, see *LW* 35 (*Preface to the Old Testament*, 1545): 241–46; *WA DB* 8:24–27. On Moses as lawgiver for the Jews, *LW* 35 (*How A Christian Should Regard Moses*, 1525): 161–66; *WA* 16:363–75. On the relationship of the First Commandment to the others see *LW* 31 (*Freedom of A Christian*, 1520): 352–53; *WA* 7:56.

261. Tyndale, *Practice of Prelates* [1530], sig. I; *LW* 40 ("Letter to the Christians at Strassbourg in Opposition to the Fanatic Spirit," 1524): 67–69; *WA* 15:395. See also *LW*

Tyndale published *A Pathway unto Holy Scripture* in 1530–1531, which was a minor revision of his 1525 New Testament prologue.[262] Clebsch states that this treatise is, "without exaggeration," the "magna carta of English Puritanism."[263] However, the text bears only slight differences when compared with its predecessor. The following excerpts exemplify some of the more noteworthy additions as it relates to the subject of Law and Gospel (revised material is noted in italics):

> to gyue unto all that *repente and* beleue ... iustified in the bloud of Christ from all things where of the lawe condemned us. *And we receyue loue unto the lawe and power to fulfyl it/ and grow ther in dayly* ... the lawe requyreth love from the bottome of the hert/ *and that loue onely is the fulfyllynge of the lawe* ... obedient to the iustice or rightwesnes that commeth of god / *whiche is the forgyuenes of sine in christes blode unto all that repent and beleue* ...Whatsoever we doo/ thynke/ or ymmagon/ is abominable in the syght of god. *For we can referre nothynge unto the honor of god: neither is his law or wyl written in our membres or in our herts/ neither is there any more power in us to folow the wyl of god/ than in a stone to ascende upwarde of his owne selfe* ... It is not possyble for a naturall man to consent to the law/that hit shuld be good/ rightewes/ or that god shuld be which maketh the lawe *in asmoch as it is contrary unto his nature and dampneth him/ and all that he can do/ and neither sheweth him where to fetch helpe/ nor precheth any mercy/ but onely setteth man at varyance with god* ... do I well/nott for hevens sake/*which is yet the reward of well doyinge*: but because I am heyre of heven by grace and Christes purchasyinge.[264]

---

30 (*Sermons on 1 Peter*, 1522): 19–21; 75–76; WA 12:275–77, 329–31;LW 40 (*Against the Heavenly Prophets in the Matter of Images and Sacraments*, 1525): 92–94, 97–98; WA 18:76–77, 81–82); LW 35 (*How A Christian Should Regard Moses*, 1525): 161–66; WA 16:363–75; *LC*, Tappert, 375–77, 383–86, 408–9; Kolb and Wengert, 397–99, 404–7, 429; *BSLK*, 580–86, 594–601, 641–42.

262. The earliest extant copies of the *Pathway* are dated tentatively to the year 1536 published in London by Thomas Godfrey, one available at the Folger Shakespeare Library in Washington, D.C., and the other at Emmanuel College Library, Cambridge University. Tyndale refers to the *Pathway* in the preface to his exposition of First John published in 1531. Trinterud misleadingly identifies the *Pathway* as an expansion of Tyndale's "1526" prologue to the New Testament, although this edition had no prologue. Trinterud, "Reappraisal," 35, 44 (see also n. 44).

263. Clebsch, *England's Earliest Protestants*, 167.

264. Tyndale, [*New Testament*, 1525] sig. A iii, [A iiii ʳ],B ᵛ,B ii ᵛ, [B iiii ᵛ]; Tyndale, *Pathway* [1536?], [A iiii ʳ], [A vi ʳ], [A vii ᵛ], [B iiii ᵛ]. [B vi ᵛ], [B vii ᵛ], [C v ʳ].

These and other minor additions that Tyndale makes in the *Pathway* do not reveal any new theological insights and are all consistent with his theology as expressed in the earlier *Cologne Fragment* and other writings of the 1520s. Furthermore, rather than putting new stress on the positive relationship of the Christian to the Law, at least two of these additions reemphasize the absolute powerlessness of fallen human nature before the demands of the Law. The additions should be seen as points of clarification rather than revisions *per se*, and, except for the few opening paragraphs of Tyndale's introduction that express his desire to translate the New Testament, no omissions or alterations of the original text have been made.

The most original portion of the *Pathway* is the several folios of completely new material that begins immediately where the original prologue ends. This section begins with a conventional reiteration of the evangelical value of good works, which do not justify a heart before God but are evidences of the life of the Holy Spirit within, are useful to "tame the flesshe" so as not to "choke" out the Word of God and "quence the giftes or workig of the Spirite," and meet the needs of the neighbor resulting in thanks and praise to God.[265]

Next, Tyndale exposits the Decalogue, although much of this material reiterates comments found in his other earlier writings. Although Tyndale numbers the commandments differently than Luther, it is important to note here that Tyndale does not develop the prohibition of worshipping images. Tyndale then expounds on other themes he has elucidated in the past, which have to do with the depraved human condition, the opposition of the natural heart to the Law of God, and the only hope of salvation through repentance and faith in the blood of Christ. Tyndale identifies this as the "inward baptim of our soules." The outward act of baptism "signifieth that we repent and professe to fyght agaynst synne and lustes/ and to kyll them euery day more and more/ with the helpe of god and oure dilygence in folowynge the doctrine of Christ and the ledyinge of his Spirite . . ." To believe in the promise accompanying the act of baptism is to believe that sin is forgiven and the condemnation of the Law removed on account of Christ, and that even the weakness that remains "after we haue gyuen our consente unto the law and yelded ourselfe to be scolers therof" is forgiven by God's grace: "And thus/ repentaunce and faith begynne at our baptyme and

---

265. Tyndale, *Pathway* [1536?], [C vi ʳ]–[C vii ʳ].

first professynge the lawes of god/ and contynue unto our lyues ende/ and growe as we growe in the Spirite." Such diligence to keep God's commandments must not be thought of as meritorious, however, in the sense that these works are deserving of God's favor. Rather, any such moral goodness in Christians is itself the "gyft of grace." The responsibility of the baptized is to have faith in God and the promise of His mercy in Christ while being earnest and diligent to keep His commandments for the reasons already specified above. For His part, God will be faithful to His promises and will bring to perfection what is impossible for human strength alone.[266] Though Tyndale does not specifically use the word "covenant" in the *Pathway*, the notion that he articulates of the respective responsibilities of both God and the baptized comes close to his later formal development of a theology of covenant. This explains Clebsch's identification of the work as proto-Puritan, yet it is important to stress again here how these statements emerge in the context of Tyndale's covenantal theology of baptism, which is not at all novel to him nor is it distinct from the theology of Luther.

Clebsch exaggerates the significance of the *Pathway* as a turning-point in the development of Tyndale's thought. In fact, Trinterud only mentions the work in passing.[267] According to Trueman, although Tyndale does begin to place an even greater emphasis on good works in the Christian life after 1530, this is "fundamentally consistent with his earlier writings."[268] Yet it is hard not to notice a growing tendency on the part of Tyndale around this time to recast his theology of justification and the Christian life of good works using rhetoric that implies a bipartite covenant. Nevertheless, Tyndale continues to contrast the Law over against the Gospel with regard to their proper functions, and the resiliency of Luther's influence is evident in his theological assumption

---

266. Tyndale, *Pathway* [1536?], D ii ᵛ–[D iiii ʳ]. Appended to this edition of the *Pathway* printed by Thomas Godfrey in London are two tracts. The first is "A letter sent unto a certayn frende/ to enstruct him in the understandynge of the Scripture/ translated out of French into Englysshe," and the second is "Of gouernours/ as Judges/ baylyfes/ and other lyke/ An informacion after the gospell." Neither of these appear to be Tyndale originals, and whether or not he is even responsible for their publication along with the *Pathway* is not known. I am not aware of any other scholar who even considers these texts. Furthermore, they do not appear in the 1573 edition of Foxe and Daye's *Whole Works*.

267. Trinterud, "A Reappraisal," 35.

268. Trueman, *Luther's Legacy*, 101–2, 105.

that justification through faith in Christ alone follows repentance under the Law and results in the new obedience of the Christian life.

In 1531, Tyndale published an anticlerical Lollard tract entitled *The Prayer and Complaynt of the Ploweman unto Christ*,[269] a translation of the book of Jonah accompanied by a prologue, a reply to Thomas More's *Dialogue Concerning Heresies* (1529), and an exposition of 1 John. Although the anonymous writer of the *Ploweman* does occasionally refer to the importance of belief and love toward God, as well as repentance, keeping the commandments, and love of the neighbor, its main point is to rebuke the corruption of prelates on the basis of the Sermon on the Mount. Since it does not explore the doctrine of justification by faith and its relationship to the moral obedience of the Christian as any matter of primary concern, it does little to illuminate Tyndale's own opinions on this subject other than his identification of the Sermon on the Mount as a model for Christian piety.

With regard to the translation of the book of Jonah,[270] Trinterud observes that it bears "no connection with any Luther item on Jonah."[271] This is true, although Trinterud is cautious to credit too much to Luther's influence even when Tyndale has made obvious use of his works. Although the argument for indebtedness to Luther would be more strongly supported on the basis of a direct use of his translation and preface to the book, the prologue does reveal the continuing influence of Luther upon Tyndale's theology of Law and Gospel: "Scripture conteyneth . iii. thinges in it. first the law to condemne all flesh: secondaryly the Gospell / that is to saye/ promises of mercie for all that repent and knowledge their sinnes at the preachinge of the law and consent in their hertes that the law is good/ and submitte themselues to be scolers to lern to kepe the lawe and to lerne to beleue the mercie that is promised them: and thirdly the stories and liues of those scolers both what chaunces fortuned them/ and also by what meanes their scolemaster

---

269. Anonymous, *The prayer and complaynt of the ploweman* [1531].

270. *The prophete Ionas* [1531]. For a facsimile see *The Prophete Jonas . . . with an introduction by Francis Fray*. Thomas More refers to this work in his *Confutation of Tyndale's Answer* (1532), which suggests the likely date of 1531. Though the preface was printed numerous times, the translation of Jonah itself was only rediscovered in 1861 bound with three Lollard treatises, one which was *The Prayer and Complaynt of the Ploweman*. See Daniell, *William Tyndale*, 206–7.

271. Trinterud, "Reappraisal," 35.

taught them and made them perfect/ and how he tried the true from the false."[272]

Contrary to Laughlin, Tyndale still obviously uses the word "Gospel."[273] He also continues to summarize the message of the Scriptures according to a theology of Law and Gospel, although instead of simply stating that the Gospel is the "promises of mercie" in Christ he goes on in detail to explain that those promises apply to those with hearts of repentance and intentions of being obedient to the Law of God. Yet this should not be construed as diminishing the distinctive and proper functions of Law and Gospel, as Tyndale will continue to make clear elsewhere, nor is Tyndale saying that repentance and a heart for obedience to the Law actually merit divine mercy. Although repentance is necessary, it is insufficient by itself. It is only faith in Christ that justifies and enables Christians to truly devote themselves in love to the Law. Tyndale did believe that sincere devotion to the Law of God can, in turn, bolster faith in divine mercy on account of it being a sign of true faith and the working of the Spirit. Luther said essentially the same thing with regard to the exercise of faith in good works and that only the sins of those who struggle with faith in the Spirit against the flesh are under the grace of forgiveness and without condemnation.[274] Furthermore, with regard to the necessity of repentance, Luther also believed that the message of the Gospel is intended as a comfort only for the truly contrite, not the unrepentant and self-righteous, and genuine repentance includes not only a desire for forgiveness but also for the strength and power to keep the holy commandments. This is the very reason the Creed follows the Ten Commandments in the order of his catechism.[275]

It is also not evident that Tyndale has shifted toward a more legalistic and moralistic appraisal of the Law as Clebsch argues.[276] Tyndale

---

272. Tyndale, "W.T. unto the Christen reader," *The prophete Ionas* [1531], sig. A ii. See also sig. A iiii ᵛ–A v, sig. C–C ii ʳ; *LW* 35 (*Preface to the Old Testament*, 1545): 237–38; *WA DB* 8:12–15.

273. Laughlin's statement that by 1530 the word "promises" had basically replaced "Gospel" is misleading on this point. Laughlin, "Brightness of Moses' Face," 75, 181–83. For Tyndale's continued use of "Gospel" in reference to the salvific work of Christ, see also Tyndale, *Newe Testament* [1534], sig. [*vii ᵛ].

274. Althaus, *Theology of Martin Luther*, 234–41, 245–50, 448–54.

275. *LC*, Tappert, 411; Kolb and Wengert, 431; *BSLK*, 646.

276. Clebsch, *England's Earliest Protestants*, 165–66, 174–75.

continues to stress that the Law is "all together spirituall," and that it condemns unless "it be written in his herte and untill he kepe it naturally without compulsion and all other respecte saue only pure love to God and his neyboure." Thus, as Tyndale has made abundantly clear before, the Law is never fulfilled by mere outward deeds, which are sin if without perfect love, and the true fulfilling of the Law comes only from a "a fast fayth in christes bloud coupled with our profession and submytttinge ourselues to lerne to doo better." Tyndale clearly states that the forgiveness of sins, as in the story of Jonah, has always been by "faith only without respecte of all workes," though such faith is the kind that naturally coinheres with repentance going beforehand and a sincere heart of love in devotion to the Law going after and, indeed, coming out of that very repenting faith. Yet neither repentance nor a heart for the Law, though necessary in their own way, are in themselves the grounds for receiving and believing in the forgiveness of sins, but "that the promises be geuen un to a repentynge soule that thursteth and longeth after them/ of the pure and fatherly mercie of god thorow oure faith onely with oute al deseruinge of oure dedes or merites of oure werkes/ but for Christes sake alone and for the merites and deseruinges of his werkes/ deth and passions..."[277]

Baptism is a sign that is given only once at birth, but the promise it signifies is good until death, and Tyndale believes that the forgiveness of sins through the blood of Christ is available to anyone who repents and believes, for "we can doo no werkes unto God/ but receave only of his mercie with oure repentynge fayth."[278] Therefore, at the very same time that Tyndale can speak of God's promises as possessing a certain conditionality with regard to the expectation of repentance and a heart of love in obedience to God's Law, he is still obviously of the conviction that justification and reconciliation with God is through faith in Christ alone. This more explicit stress on the conditionality of God's promises is simply his new way in the 1530s of emphasizing how justifying faith in Christ cannot possibly exist in truth without a preceding repentance under the Law and a submission to the Law of God that proceeds natu-

---

277. Tyndale, *The prophete Ionas* [1531], sig. A ii ͮ, Aiii ͮ–A iiii, C. "For in thyne hert is the worde of the law/ and in thyne hert is the worde of fayth in the promises of mercie in Jesus Christe. So that yf thou confesse with a repentynge hert and knowlege and surely beleue that Jesus is lorde ouer all synne/ thou are saffe," sig. C iii–C iiii ͬ.

278. Tyndale, *The prophete Ionas* [1531], sig. C iiii.

rally in love from that very same repenting faith. Although Tyndale's words could be misinterpreted in a works-righteousness and legalistic way, interpreting them in the light of his theological assumptions and in the broader context of other statements and writings shows that he is still under the influence of Luther's theology of Law and Gospel.

In 1531, Tyndale published his reply to Thomas More's *Dialogue Concerning Heresies* (1529).[279] More's treatise implicates Tyndale as the major cause of the infiltration of Luther's heresies into England.[280] More was probably an important contributor to Henry VIII's *Assertio septem sacramentorum* (1521), which was a defense of Catholic sacramental theology and a virulent rebuttal to Luther's own *Babylonian Captivity of the Church* (1520). More's main motivation in joining the attacks on Luther under the direction of Cardinal Wolsey was Luther's scathing reply to Henry VIII in 1522. Within one year, More published his own personal tirade against Luther in his *Responsio ad Lutherum* (1523). By 1529, and at the behest of Bishop Tunstall of London, More changed his approach and began combating heresy using the vernacular. The ensuing product was his *Dialogue*, in which More now specifically targets Tyndale as guilty of perpetuating the spread of Luther's heresies.[281]

In the *Dialogue*, More identifies Tyndale's major link with Luther to be his publication of the English New Testament: "For Tyndall (whose books be nothing else in effect but the worst heresies picked out of Luther's works and Luther's worst words translated by Tyndall and put forth in Tyndall's own name . . ."[282] Yet, as scholars have observed, other comments of More portray Tyndale as even a worse heretic than Luther. Unfortunately, these comments have been used to justify the notion that Tyndale disagrees with Luther on critical matters of Law and Gospel. In response to these claims, it must be remembered that More's highly charged polemical tirade is hardly an objective appeal for interpreting differences between Tyndale and Luther. Even so, More never lists matters pertaining to faith, justification, the Law, or good works as among those differences. Werrell, who makes the most of More's com-

---

279. Tyndale, *An answere vnto Sir Thomas Mores dialoge made by Vvillyam Tindale* [1531].

280. More, *A dyaloge of syr Thomas More knyghte* [1529].

281. See discussion in Daniell, *Tyndale*, 250–69.

282. Clebsch, *England's Earliest Protestants*, 146; More, quoted in Daniell, *Tyndale*, 267–68.

ment, can only identify purgatory, the mass, confession, and patristic authority as areas of supposed difference marked by More.[283] In fact, if scholars are right that Tyndale stressed the importance of the Law and good works more than Luther from the very beginning, then Luther, rather than Tyndale, would be the greater heretic.

Trinterud observes that Tyndale's *Answer to More* is not dependent for its structure or content on any one work of Luther, and he virtually ignores this text in his analysis. Though Tyndale makes a statement in this work denying that he had ever been "confederatt with Luther," most scholars do not accept this as being an absolute repudiation of any associations with Luther whatsoever. The fact that Tyndale ignored a prime opportunity to show explicitly how he differed with Luther and did no such thing is certainly noteworthy in itself.[284] In fact, Tyndale's *Answer to More* is a response to an unabashedly anti-Luther document in which he himself is explicitly linked to the German reformer. This means that Tyndale's work is, in many significant ways, a defense of Luther against the attacks of More.

It is true that the *Answer to More* is not based on any single work of Luther, but the recurring themes connecting repentance under the Law (in the manner of the preaching of John the Baptist),[285] justification by "fayth only" (a "felynge faith"), and a sincere obedience to God's Law under the rule of love reveal the lasting influence of Luther's theology of Law and Gospel upon Tyndale's developing thought: "And yf I beleved the gospell/what God hath done for me in Christe/ I should suerly loue hym agayne and of loue prepare my selfe unto hys commanundementes." Tyndale defends his purposeful translation of "*metanoia*" and "*metanoite*" as "repentaunce" rather than "penance" because of its associations with the idea that sinners can make satisfaction to God for their sins by acts of penance.[286] Even though all Christians remain as

---

283. More, *Dialogue Concerning Heresies*, in Lawler, Marc'hadour, and Marius, *Complete Works of St. Thomas More*, 6.1:348–50, 376–402; Werrell, "Tyndale's Disagreement," 58.

284. Tyndale, *An answere vnto Sir Thomas Mores dialoge* [1531], fo. xcii ^{r}; Trinterud, "A Reappraisal," 35. See also Daniell, *William Tyndale*, 299.

285. Tyndale, *An answere vnto Sir Thomas Mores dialoge* [1531], fo. i ^{v}; also fo. xx ^{r}, fo. xxvi ^{v}. On the necessity of repentance, see also fo. lxvi, lxxxiii ^{v}, lxxxviii ^{v}–lxxxix ^{r}, C iv ^{v}, Cvi ^{v}– Cvii, Cxxi ^{r}– Cxxii ^{r};*LW* 29 (*Lectures on Hebrews*, 1517-8):193–94; *WA* 57^3:192–93; *LW* 35 (*Preface to the Old Testament*, 1545): 241–46; *WA DB* 8:24–27.

286. Tyndale, *An answere vnto Sir Thomas Mores dialoge* [1531], fo. i ^{v}- iii ^{r} ("Wyllyam

"synners" in the imperfection of their deeds and the frailty of their flesh, even falling as heinously as King David, they are at the same time "no synners" on account of their repenting reliance upon God's promises of mercy. Those that do end up yielding in weakness to temptation, doing outwardly what they are enticed to do by the flesh, the Spirit of God in the elect calls them back successfully to be reconciled through a renewal of repentance, faith, and a "new batayle" against sin.[287] According to Tyndale, such persons are the true Church, although Tyndale does later admit that "church" in the Scriptures sometimes refers to the "common rascall of all that beleue," who are without the Spirit, whose faith is mere profession, and who either ignore the Law altogether or heed it only superficially.[288]

Tyndale is surprisingly positive toward the use of images in his *Answer to More*, more so than in the *Obedience*, and this is important to note in the light of the opinion that Tyndale's theology was beginning to maneuver in favor of the Swiss Reformed tradition by the 1530s. In actuality, his balanced approach to images as theoretically useful for reflecting on the work of Christ and the piety of the saints seems much more akin to Erasmus, Luther, and even some Lollards, rather than to most theologians within the Swiss Reformed tradition. Although he supports the timely removal of images, this is not because he views them as inherently idolatrous. Rather, an image "is good and not euel untill it be abused." Tyndale even allows for the act of kneeling before an image, but acknowledges abuses when such kneeling is considered necessary for salvation, as a protection against evil and harmful spirits, or as a means to temporal prosperity. Tyndale even has a somewhat nuanced opinion of pilgrimages, and interprets their value in terms of a journey to hear the Word of God in a place remote from common domestic distractions. The abuse associated with pilgrimages has to do with thinking that God honors devotion to Him only in sacred places, whereas for Tyndale the significance of a pilgrimage is the longing for an environment that stimulates godly meditation, faith toward God, and love toward others: "his pleasure is onlye in the hertes of them that loue

---

Tindale To the reader"), fo. v ʳ, xii ʳ, xxix ᵛ–xxxiii ᵛ, lxxxix ʳ, Ci ᵛ–Ciii ᵛ, Cvii ᵛ, Cxii ʳ, Cxix, Cxxi ʳ–Cxxxii ʳ.

287. Ibid., fo. xvi ᵛ–xvii ʳ, fo. xx ᵛ–xxi ʳ; fo. lxx.
288. Ibid., fo. lxix ᵛ–lxx ʳ.

his commaundementes."²⁸⁹ In all these cases, Tyndale's more moderate position towards images and pilgrimages (not to mention the Sabbath) is more reminiscent of the tone of Erasmus or Luther.

Tyndale does indeed stress the importance of good works and love toward the Law in his *Answer to More*, but he is also unapologetic about his position on the doctrine of justification *sola fide*. Therefore, it is not that Tyndale now considers good works or obedience to the Law as being any more theoretically essential to the Christian life than he did in his previous writings, but he does develop, stress, and explain that point even more fully than before. Although he still does not yet use the explicit concept of "covenant," his stress on the necessity of repentance and a heart of love and obedience to the Law in connection with justifying faith anticipates this in some manner. Tyndale at one point does specifically describe God's promises of mercy as being offered only to them who repent of past wrongdoing with the intention to turn from that sin. This agrees with Luther that true justifying faith that partakes of the mercy of God promised in the Gospel cannot coexist with a lust to continue in sin without remorse. This kind of faith is without sorrowful repentance toward the Law of God and is both a false faith and a wicked presumption upon the precious gift of God's grace as if desiring that God give His divine o.k. to the unbridled satisfaction of sinful lusts.

Among the works of Tyndale listed acrimoniously by More in the *Confutation of Tyndale's Answer* (1532) is his exposition on the epistle of First John published in 1531.²⁹⁰ Trinterud forthrightly states that it proves Tyndale was "not a Lutheran," highlighting both Tyndale's covenantal understanding of baptism and his laudatory praise for the Law in the life of the Christian. With regard to the former, Trinterud does admit that "Luther could on occasion use the figure, for it was age-old," although he asserts that the "figure, or *motif*, was fast becoming the badge of a non-Lutheran."²⁹¹ Trinterud quotes at length from the "Prologge" to 1 John concerning Tyndale's description of the profession of baptism, what Tyndale describes as the "key and lyght of the Scripture." Tyndale's explanation in effect unfolds Luther's own covenantal understanding of baptism and his theology of Law and Gospel. The Law, summarized

---

289. Ibid., fo. xxxv ᵛ–xliiii ʳ, xlvi ᵛ–xlvii ʳ, xlix ᵛ, lix ᵛ, Cx–Cxi ʳ, Cxiv.

290. Daniell, *William Tyndale*, 206–7; Tyndale, *The exposition of the fyrst epistle of seynt Jhon* [1531].

291. See "Reappraisal," 36.

as love toward God and neighbor, can only be fulfilled through love, but love cannot exist except in those who have repented and believed the "promises of mercie." Tyndale then goes on, as Trinterud quotes, to describe the loving and dutiful submission to the Law that characterizes the profession of baptism "wrytten in thyne herte."[292] This sort of submission to the Law is neither works-righteousness nor ethical legalism for it is the righteousness of faith that leads to love and this love is the true keeping of the Law. In fact, any law that goes against faith and love is free to be broken, as Luther himself often stated, "For loue is lorde ouer al lawes."[293]

That Tyndale stresses the ethical responsibility of the Christian in his exposition of 1 John is hardly surprising since this is a major point stressed in the New Testament book itself, and the fact that Tyndale chose to exposit 1 John is not unique. Luther himself preferred 1 John's discussion of good works to that of the book of James because the former more explicitly exhorts on the basis of God's love in the Gospel. In his own series of lectures on 1 John in the late 1520s, Luther clearly identifies one value of good works to be the personal assurance it provides of a faith that justifies.[294] Luther's lectures were not actually published until centuries later, so it cannot be argued that Tyndale knew of them or was directly influenced by them. Nevertheless, this is not the first time that Luther has identified good works as a means of personal assurance, and Tyndale's comments are certainly consistent with the theological implications concerning justifying faith and good works that Luther develops in his own lectures.

Tyndale reasserts in the lectures that the nature of the Law is to "utter synne" and that repentance under the Law necessarily precedes, on account of it creating the opportunity for, justifying faith. Even Christians who succumb in weakness to temptation through negligence of spiritual duties (the "life of penaunce"), if they but heed the discipline of God and renew the profession of their baptism through "repentynge faithe," are forgiven through the blood of Christ. Tyndale does state that God's mercy promised in baptism is conditional upon the fact that "we will submit oure selues vnto his doctryne and lerne to kepe his lawes." Yet it is not as if divine forgiveness is merited by repentance or

292. Tyndale, *seynt Jhon* [1531], sig. A ii, A iii ᵛ.
293. Ibid., sig. E v.
294. *LW* 35 (*Preface to the Three Epistles of St. John*, 1546), ix-xi, 393; *WA DB* 7:327.

submission to the Law though these "condicyons" are associated with the nature of the faith that alone justifies: "So whether light or darknes be in the hert/ it wyll apere in the walkinge . . . that it is not possible for hym that knoweth the trueth and consentyth thereto to contynewe in synne." Though more frequently associated with the sacrament of baptism, Tyndale also speaks of the sacrament of the Lord's Supper in a covenantal-like manner, as a confirming of the "testament made betwen God and us of the forgiueness of synnes in Christes bloude/ for oure repentaunce and faith."[295]

According to his exposition of 1 John, the one "born of God" cannot sin without remorse. The sin of the true Christian is distinguishable from the sin of the false Christian because it is impossible for the former to sin of purpose "without grudge of conscience," or so as to fall beyond a quick return to God through repentance and faith.[296] For Tyndale, the "elect" are known only by God and, though sinning grievously, will never finally fall beyond a return to repentance, faith, and the consent of their hearts to God's Law.[297] In another work, however, Tyndale does state that through slothfulness it is possible that the Spirit can be lost "agayne" as well as the "rightwesnesse of fayth." This indicates that Tyndale believed a person could in some sense have the Spirit and even be in righteous standing before God by faith, but, if not among the elect, will ultimately lack perseverance and become lost.[298]

Tyndale also explains in the lectures that Christ and the Christian "make a chaunge." Christ takes on the sin of the sinner and the Christian receives "mercie" in Christ and "giftes of grace," becoming "gloriouse with the ornamentes of his riches." This statement is significant in the light of the fact that Tyndale is often distinguished from Luther on the nature of justification.[299] The concept alludes to 2 Corinthians 5:21 and was also paraphrased in the writings of Augustine,[300] but it is difficult

---

295. Tyndale, *seynt Jhon* [1531], sig. A ii ᵛ -Aiii ᵛ, sig. [A viii ᵛ]–B, B iii ʳ, B iiii ᵛ–B v ʳ, B viii ᵛ–C ʳ, C ii ʳ, C iii, E ii ʳ, E iii ᵛ, [G vii], H iii ʳ, H iiii ᵛ, [H vi ᵛ].

296. Ibid., sig. [E vii ʳ].

297. For comments by Tyndale on the effectual working of God in the hearts of the elect, see Tyndale, *seynt Jhon* [1531], sig. [C vii], [D viii ʳ], E ii ʳ.

298. Tyndale, *An exposicion vppon the v. vi. vii. chapters of Mathew* [1533], fo. lxxxi ᵛ.

299. Werrell, *Theology of William Tyndale*, 16; McGrath, *Iustitia Dei*, 286; Trueman, *Luther's Legacy*, 92–94.

300. See McGrath, *Iustitia Dei*, 29; Kelly, *Early Christian Doctrines*, 393.

not to recognize in the light of Tyndale's particular emphasis on faith alone an echoing of Luther's own depiction of the "great exchange," or the intimate union with Christ and His righteousness through faith that occurs in justification.[301]

For Tyndale as well as Luther, an important message of 1 John is that the keeping of the commandment to love one another "certifieth us that we be in the state of grace." Luther says the same in his own lectures to the effect that it "is through works that we learn that our faith is true."[302] Contrary to Clebsch, Tyndale has not forgotten the central importance of justification before God *sola fide*,[303] although he does stress the effectual side of justifying faith as "the mother of all love" and the root of the true keeping of the Law from the heart in the life of the Christian. Thus, the one who is capable of showing mercy to others is also the one who at the same time possesses genuine personal trust in the mercy of God in Christ. In turn, he or she will have an even clearer conscience, an even bolder faith, and an even stronger confidence in the benevolence and mercy of God, much like obedient children have greater boldness in the presence of their earthly fathers.[304] Luther states in his own lectures: "Faith is established by its practice, its use, and its fruit. For after one has devoted oneself to a life of idleness, it is difficult to raise the heart up to God. Faith alone raises us up. Hence faith must be put into practice, in order that we may be freed from an evil conscience."[305] Similarly, in a sermon on 2 Peter in the early 1520s, Luther says that: "[faith] is so constituted that through application and practice it becomes stronger and stronger until it is sure of the call and election and cannot be wanting ... If your faith is well exercised and applied, you will finally gain assurance."[306]

---

301. Tyndale, *seynt Jhon* [1531], sig. [C viii]; LW 31 (*The Freedom of A Christian*, 1520); 348–52; WA 7:52–55. See also McGrath, *Iustitia Dei*, 199–200.

302. Tyndale, *seynt Jhon* [1531], sig. D ^{v}–D ii ^{r}, E [vi], [E viii ^{r}]- F ^{r}, F ii ^{r}, [F vi ^{r}], [F vii ^{v}]; LW 30 (*Lectures on 1 John*, 1527): 279; WA 20:716.

303. Clebsch, *England's Earliest Protestants*, 171.

304. Tyndale, *seynt Jhon* [1531], sig. D iii ^{v}–D iiii ^{r}, E iii ^{v}- E iiii ^{r}, F ^{r}–F ii ^{v}, [F viii ^{r}], G.

305. LW 30 (*Lectures on 1 John*, 1527): 279; WA 20:715.

306. LW 30 (*Sermons on the Second Epistle of St. Peter*, 1523): 158–59; WA 14:23. See also Althaus, *Theology of Martin Luther*, 448–54.

There is nothing in Tyndale's exposition of 1 John to suggest any real differences with Luther's theology of Law and Gospel, and both reformers expressed in their lectures an accolade for the Law and the obligation expected of every professing Christian to keep it diligently. The Law for Luther as well as Tyndale is summarized in Jesus' commandment to love one another. Furthermore, although the baptismal covenant never becomes a theological, rhetorical, or hermeneutical *motif* for Luther, Tyndale is not at all against Luther in describing the sacrament and its promise in terms of a covenant. The unfolding of this covenant *motif* in justification and the Christian life itself still reflects the foundational influence of Luther's understanding of Law and Gospel upon Tyndale's theological assumptions. Thus, it is not self-evident that Tyndale is consciously moving away from Luther theologically, although the extent to which the covenantal rhetoric takes precedence in his thought indeed suggests the possible influence of the emerging Reformed tradition.

In 1533, Tyndale published an exposition on Jesus' Sermon on the Mount in Matthew 5–7. Luther had delivered a series of sermons on this text between the years 1530 and 1532 in the absence of Johann Bugenhagen. Trinterud openly acknowledges that Tyndale's "literary dependence" upon Luther's sermons is "undeniable." George Joye had even accused Tyndale of taking too much personal credit for his exposition. Trinterud recognizes Tyndale's description of the power of the Law in the conviction of sin and in driving the sinner to Christ as the influence of Luther. However, Trinterud also argues that the looming presence of Tyndale's "conditional-covenant" theology, along with statements allowing for a more positive role for the Law in the Christian life, reveal he "had learned more from Basel than from Wittenberg."[307]

Like Luther, Tyndale does not view the Sermon on the Mount as a new Law nor is Christ a new Lawgiver. Rather, the truth of the Ten Commandments is unveiled by Christ in its most spiritual sense as it relates to the demands placed upon the human heart. Thus, "the lawe in hir right understandinge is the keye, or at the least waye the first and principall keye to open the dore of the Scripture. And the lawe is the very waye that bringeth unto the dore Christ . . . the dore, the waye, and the grounde or foundacyon of all the Scripture." This resonates

---

307. Trinterud, "Reappraisal," 37–39; Brecht, *Shaping and Defining*, 433; Rupp, *Studies in the Making*, 50. For the text of Luther's sermons, see *WA* 32:299–544.

with Luther's own way of approaching the Scriptures through Law and Gospel with Christ at the center. Tyndale understands that the express purpose of the Law is to drive the sinner wounded in conscience toward Christ, who alone can do for people what the Law by itself could not do through Moses in only bringing death and judgment.[308]

Tyndale does go beyond Luther in so far as he lays even greater stress on the conditional nature of God's promises in terms of the "couenaunt." Though the statements in the "Prologe vnto the reader" echo what Tyndale has already said in discussing the sacrament of baptism as a covenant, they expand, develop, and emphasize more than anywhere else thus far in his writings his knowledge of the certain conditional quality of God's promises:

> All the good promyses which are made vs thorow out all the scripture for Christes sake, for his loue, his passion or sufferinge, his bloude shedinge or deathe all are made vs on this condicion and couenaunt on oure partye, that we henceforthe loue the lawe of God, to walke therin and to do it and fassion oure lyues therafter. In so moche that who soeuer hath not the lawe of God written in his harte, that he loue it, haue his lust in it, and recorde therin night and daye, vnderstondinge it as God hath gyuen it, and as Christ and the Apostles expounde it: The same hath no parte in the promises, or can haue anye true fayth in the bloude of Christ: Because there is no promise made him, but to them onlye that promise to kepe the lawe . . . Euen so, none of vs can be receaued to grace but vpon a condicion to kepe the lawe, neyther yet continue anie lenger in grace then that purpose lasteth.[309]

As explicit as this passage is in stressing the need for a heart toward good works and submission to the Law in love as certain conditions for partaking in the promises of mercy in Christ, this does not mean that forgiveness actually follows upon, or on the basis of, such love toward the Law. Tyndale is still operating under the theological assumption that to have the love that truly keeps the Law is to have true justifying faith in the sacrifice of Christ and not a false presumption. Nevertheless, this kind of faith also emerges only from a heart of sincere repentance toward the Law. The grace of forgiveness, then, that

---

308. Tyndale, "Prologe," *exposicion vppon the v. vi. vii. chapters of Mathew* [1533], fo. ii ᵛ–iii ᵛ, xi ᵛ, xxxi ᵛ, xxxiiᵛ, xxxvii.

309. Ibid., fo. iiii ᵛ–v ʳ.

is promised in Christ and to be received through faith alone is only for the truly repentant who intend to keep the Law and, in response to the receiving of God's mercy in true faith, will strive with love in the doing of good works and in battle against sin. This striving gives evidence of justifying faith and reassures Christians that they are indeed partakers of the mercy promised in Christ through faith alone.

Tyndale illustrates this by describing a wise king who refuses to pardon any unrepentant criminal who has no intent whatsoever on moral amendment if pardoned. The pardon is always enacted before the Law is actually kept in deeds, yet it is "on that condycyon that thou endevoure thyselfe to synne no moare, is the promyse of forgyuenes made unto the." Thus, the pardon is not received after the keeping of the Law in outward deeds, although it is conditioned on the "purpose" of the heart to "endevoure thyselfe" and to "henceforthe" keep the Law after being pardoned. This condition, however, is easily met through what Tyndale has already referred to before as a "repentyng faith" in Christ that justifies. In order to remain underneath the protection of that pardon, a certain moral perseverance is required, but this does not mean for Tyndale that moral exertion and good works themselves are what justify, but that moral discipline guards the heart. According to Tyndale, without persistent and diligent dependence upon God in prayer, serving others through the giving of alms, and mortifying the indulgences of the flesh by fasting, the Christian is vulnerable to being overcome by the lure and power of sin. Yet God by His "couenaunt" has promised to forgive all who fall into temptation "if they will turne agayne" and so long as they do not yield to the rule of sin to the degree that they become indifferent to it lacking a heart of repentance. The distinction Tyndale makes between sins committed "vnder grace" in repentance and sins committed "under the lawe and vnder the damnacion of the lawe" without repentance agrees wholeheartedly with Luther's theology and his own description of the terms of the eternal covenant made in the promise of baptism.[310]

To battle against sin, for Tyndale as well as Luther, is a certain condition of the promise of grace made in the baptismal covenant in the sense that earnestness to obey the will of God reflects a heart truly justified through repenting faith in Christ. True faith in the mercy of

---

310. Ibid., fo. v, fo. vii ʳ, viii ʳ–ix ʳ, fo. xxxii ᵛ–xxxiii ʳ, lxvi ʳ, lxvii ʳ, lxxii ᵛ–lxxiii ʳ, lxxvii ᵛ, lxxxi ᵛ–lxxxiiii ʳ.

Christ produces thankfulness to God and love for the Law, which is the "profession and religion of a Christen man" and the "inward baptime of the hart." While faith, hope, and love are inseparable from one another, and though each has its own proper "office," Tyndale is explicit that faith alone justifies. Thus, Tyndale makes a distinction between affirming salvation by "fayth onlye" and salvation by a "fayth that is alone," or without works that follow.[311]

According to Tyndale, when Jesus in the Sermon on the Mount promises blessings to the merciful, to the peacemakers, and to the faithful in persecution, this refers to people who are already justified and have been converted to God by a repenting faith. Thus, the Beatitudes are not conditions for receiving forgiveness, justification, and eternal life in the sense that forgiveness follows upon obedience to them so much as they are conditions for marking that one has been forgiven, is a child of God already, and is justified with the promise of eternal life. In the case of the promise of heaven and its rewards for patient suffering and well-doing, this is not as if heaven is a wage deserved or merited by works. Rather, God's promise to bless those works in this life and the life to come is entirely a gift of His mercy, and He would be righteous to command unquestioned obedience even without the promise of a good future. Yet, as Tyndale asserts, God gave these promises and mercifully bound Himself to them to add a comforting incentive to Christians to be "more wyllynge to do that is oure dutie." One such duty includes forgiveness and mercy owed to an offender, and anyone who presumes to be forgiven of God for his or her own personal offenses by default enters into "couenaunt" with Him to forgive others in like manner as He commands. Yet such righteous action does not merit the forgiveness of God but naturally proceeds from a heart that is forgiven and righteous through a justifying faith in Christ. The righteousness for reconciliation with God is always alien and "cometh of God altogether," although thereafter the person is divided from "one man, all flesh," into "two." The Christian is made righteous in so far as he or she has the beginnings of love through the Spirit, but unrighteous in so far as that love always remains "unperfecte." The weaknesses and imperfections that remain are forgiven and covered under the mercy of justification in Christ.[312]

311. Ibid., fo. ix, x ʳ–xi ᵛ, fo. xxxi ᵛ, cviii ᵛ–cx ᵛ, cxiiii.

312. Tyndale, *exposicion vppon the v. vi. vii. chapters of Mathew* [1533], fo. xviii ᵛ–xxv ʳ, lviii ᵛ, lxiv ᵛ, lxv ᵛ, lxxiii, lxxv ᵛ–lxxviii ᵛ, xciiii ʳ, xcv, cxv ʳ. At one point, Tyndale reasserts

The idea that the Christian has the beginnings of the Spirit while his or her remaining sin is forgiven or not imputed is found in Augustine as well as Luther, but Tyndale's emphasis on Christ as the righteousness of the sinner before God in justification reflects more of the influence of the latter. Furthermore, Luther himself was not entirely opposed to speaking of the consolation of heavenly rewards (even "merits") in the context of greater glory, not eternal life itself, promised in heaven to faithfulness in suffering.[313]

That Tyndale understands the extrinsic righteousness of Christ to be imputed in justification is clear from his statement that "Christ is the fullfillynge of the lawe for us" and that "his fulfillynge is imputed to us." This "fullfillynge" probably implies the entire righteousness of Christ's life, but it certainly refers to the culmination of His death as a worthy atonement for sin. In any case, Tyndale states that this "fullfillynge" is just as necessary for the first reconciliation with God as it is for each time a Christian falls "afterwarde." It is even essential to sanctify "oure best workes all our liffe lange."[314] The reliance of the Christian by faith on the atoning righteousness of Christ imputed in justification that covers a person and all his or her works throughout life shows the continual influence of Luther on Tyndale's developing theology. Although Tyndale does often stress the effective side of faith, his strong emphasis on justification as the objective removal of guilt (in Christ) is also reflected in his repeated use of the courtroom analogy and the king's pardoning of the repentant criminal.

Tyndale describes the office of the preacher as the preaching of the Ten Commandments ("the law naturall"), warning people that disobedience merits both temporal discipline and "everlastinge payne in hell," while "everlastinge life" is promised to them who submit themselves to keep the Law in love from the heart "thorow fayth in Christ."[315] The keep-

---

his typical *ordo salutis*, though working backward according to its inverse order. See fo. lxxvii.

313. Althaus, *Theology of Martin Luther*, 453–54, and n. 50. Luther, quoting from Augustine that God crowns His own gifts, states that all true Christians receive the forgiveness of sins for eternal life through faith alone in Christ but that God gives good works and their glory to some more than others. See *LW* 54 (*Table Talk*, No. 4331:"Are We Rewarded in View of Our Works?" Between January 15 and 21, 1539. Recorded by Anthony Lauterbach): 327; *WA Tr* 4:226–27.

314. Tyndale, *exposicion vppon the v. vi. vii. chapters of Mathew* [1533], fo. ciiii, cxiiii ʳ.

315. Ibid., fo. xliii ᵛ - xlv ʳ.

ing of the Law spiritually from the heart has the greater advantage of being followed by eternal blessings, though only those who have already been justified by faith in Christ can truly keep the Law and partake of these promised blessings. This echoes Tyndale's earlier statements made in his *Parable of the Wicked Mammon*, which borrowed from Luther's own sermon. For both reformers, heaven is not a reward earned by the deeds themselves, which are never perfect, but the promise of heaven is given to a justifying faith in Christ confirmed through good deeds.

Other areas where the influence of Luther is witnessed in Tyndale's exposition is in his differentiation between the "kyngedome of heaven which is the regiment of the Gospel" and the "kyngedome of this worlde which is the temporall regiment," in his interpretation of Jesus' prohibition of personal retribution and popular insurrection, in his understanding that all baptized persons are a "double person and under both regimentes," and in his allowance for Christian participation in just war.[316]

Tyndale's exposition of the Sermon on the Mount does not reveal that he is consciously moving away from the influence of Luther in his basic theological assumptions concerning Law and Gospel. However, the "covenaunt" *motif* and his continued stress on the conditionality of the promises does receive more explicit and prevalent emphasis in Tyndale's writings of the 1530s than that found in Luther. Tyndale is certainly putting a certain weight on the need for repentance and good works by his intentional use of the rhetoric of covenant conditionality, yet this does not mean that Tyndale thought these were any more necessary than Luther did. Tyndale does often make faith in Christ more implicit in his later writings, but this is not in abandonment of his underlying assumption that to fulfill the terms of the covenant means that justifying faith in Christ by its very nature is preceded by a heart of genuine repentance under the Law of God and followed by submission to that same Law in love and gratitude to God for His mercy. Tyndale's understanding of the conditionality of the promises was something he had already asserted earlier in the context of speaking about the sacrament of baptism as a covenant. Though his adoption of a covenantal theology of baptism was itself not necessarily the influence of the Swiss or South

---

316. Ibid., fo. li ʳ–lviii ᵛ. For Luther on the two kingdoms, see *LW* 45 (*Temporal Authority: To What Extent it Should Be Obeyed*, 1523): 95, 97–98, 100–103; *WA* 11:254–56, 258–60.

German Reformed tradition, his elevation of covenant to such a place of rhetorical and hermeneutical prominence in the 1530s suggests this. Yet, though certainly debatable, Werrell recently argues that even this is not self-evident, and he argues that Tyndale's more Trinitarian, federal theology of covenant and its familial application in the life of the elect sets him significantly apart from a more contractual and jurisprudent framework in the theology of the continental reformers.[317]

Scholars have not appreciated the extent to which Luther often spoke of baptism in terms of an evangelical theology of covenant and this at the same time that his own theology of Law and Gospel was maturing. Furthermore, Tyndale's understanding of how the covenant works and unfolds in the life of the Christian shows the Law-Gospel influence of Luther. Entering into the covenant of mercy and remaining under the covenant is conditioned by the intentionality of the heart to keep the Law, which is to say that genuine repentance under the Law is necessary as a prelude to the faith in Christ that really justifies and that this is demonstrated through love and a willing submission to God's Law in response to the kindness of God's mercy. As Luther himself explained, this intentionality is guarded in the faithful by dutiful meditation upon the Law of God's Word accompanied by dependence upon God for mercy and help in prayer, resistance to the flesh through fasting, and the discipline occasioned by suffering and affliction.

Tyndale published a revised translation of the book of Genesis in 1534.[318] Whereas his previous *Pentateuch* of 1530 translated *b'rith* as "bond," in the revised edition of 1534 this explicitly becomes the "couenaunte." Similarly, "couenaunte" replaces all but one reference to "appoyntmente" in 17: 9. Tyndale also adds a new gloss to Genesis 3:14, identifying the promise of the coming of Messiah, the seed of Eve who would save all who believe and hate the "deuels workes," as a "couenaunt."[319] These textual revisions show Tyndale's increasing preference for the use of "covenant" as a way of stressing the conditional nature of God's promises of mercy according to a repenting faith that flows into love, good works, and obedience to God's Law.

317. Werrell, *Theology of William Tyndale*, 12, 46–47, 62–63.
318. *The firste boke of Moses called Genesis newly correctyd* [1534].
319. Tyndale, *firste boke of Moses* [1534], fo. iiii, xi ʳ–xii ᵛ, xxi ʳ–xxii ʳ. See also Mombert, *William Tyndale's Five Books of Moses, Called the Pentateuch*.

In the prologue to Genesis, Tyndale explicitly states that Christians are to "Seke therfore in the Scripture as thou readest it, chefely and aboue all, the conuenauntes made betwene god and vs." Tyndale obviously does not refer to Law and Gospel explicitly here, but he does go on to define the covenant in terms of a theology of Law and Gospel, the "lawe and commaundementes which God commaundeth vs to do" and the "mercie promysed vnto all them that submite themselues vnto the lawe." The latter obviously emphasizes the conditionality of the promises of mercy in the repentance that accompanies and precedes justifying faith and the expected response of that faith in obedience: Tyndale further states that: "all the promyses thorow out the hole scripture do include a couenaunt. That is: god byndeth himselfe to fulfil that mercie vnto the, onlye if thou wilt endeuoure thyselfe to kepe his lawes: so that no man hath his parte in the mercie of god, saue he onlye that loueth his lawe and consenteth that it is righteous and good, and fayne would do it, and euer mourneth because he now and then breaketh it thorow infirmite, or dothe it not so perfectly as his harte wolde."[320]

The fact that Tyndale here speaks of partaking of the mercy of God without even explicitly referring to faith in Christ lends some credibility to Clebsch's point that the emphasis on faith alone in the doctrine of justification is often stressed less explicitly in Tyndale's writings of the 1530s. Yet other scholars are right to argue that underneath this change in rhetoric and what is an even greater emphasis than before on repentance and good works there is yet a fundamental theological consistency that understands obedience to the Law as necessarily flowing from a repenting faith in Christ that justifies. When interpreted in the light of his theological assumptions and other contemporary passages where Tyndale continues to explicitly affirm that justification before God is by faith alone in Christ apart from all works, passages that stress the covenant conditionality of the promise of mercy in repentance, a heart of obedience to the Law, and a life of good works are implying and assuming the faith in Christ that alone justifies.

As he had promised back in 1526, Tyndale published a revised *Newe Testament* in 1534, now with a prologue for each book with the exception of Acts and Revelation.[321] Laughlin describes the *Newe*

320. Tyndale, *first boke of Moses* [1534], sig. A ii ᵛ–A iii ʳ.
321. Tyndale, *The Newe Testament dylygently corrected and compared with the Greke* [1534]. STC 2826 is the authentic revised New Testament belonging to Tyndale. A New

Testament as containing the pinnacle of Tyndale's "new and sophisticated moralism and legalism." Though even he admits that Tyndale's contractual theology of covenant does not reveal a complete break with elements of Luther's Law-Gospel scheme, Laughlin follows Trinterud in assuming that Tyndale had always reinterpreted this scheme by laying greater stress than Luther did on the ethical implications of the Gospel. Laughlin argues that Tyndale probably borrowed this covenant scheme from the Swiss or South German theologians as a preferable way to express his more positive view of the Law and the necessity of good works in the life of the Christian. Laughlin does not consider Erasmus or Lollardy as rival sources for Tyndale's covenantal thought, and he does not appreciate the fact that Luther also spoke of a conditionality connected with God's promise of grace in baptism. He does leave open the possibility, however, that Tyndale's theology of covenant was a product of his own study and exegesis of the Old Testament.[322]

Clebsch argues that Tyndale still uses Luther literarily in the 1530s but not theologically. Yet, at the conclusion of his discussion, Clebsch still identifies Luther as the single most significant influence on his theology.[323] Trinterud perceives that the biblical scheme of covenant "had been taking form in Tyndale's earlier writings," although it "reached its fullest development in the apparatus of this 1534 New Testament."[324] Daniell, who acknowledges Tyndale's early debt to Luther more positively, also argues that Tyndale had clearly drifted away from the German reformer by 1534: "these 1534 prologues can show Tyndale markedly less Lutheran, and moving more to something of his own, something English."[325]

Testament was also printed earlier in 1534 in Antwerp "By me wyddowe of Christoffel [Ruremond] of Endhoue[n]" (STC 2825), but this was a fourth pirated edition of Tyndale's earlier 1526 New Testament and the work of George Joye. One major correction Joye makes on numerous occasions is the replacement of Tyndale's reference to the "resurreccion" with "the lyfe after this lyfe." Not only did he do this in Tyndale's name without his permission, but Tyndale caught wind that Joye essentially denied the bodily resurrection of the last days, instead believing that the resurrection takes place at the departure of the soul from the body at death. See Tyndale's quarrel with Joye in "Willyam Tindale/ yet once more to the Christen reader," *The Newe Testament* [1534], sig. **.iiii.ʳ-[**.vii.ᵛ]. See also the discussion in Daniell, *William Tyndale*, 322–26.

322. Laughlin, "Brightness of Moses' Face," 184–89, 192, 207–8, 213, 232, 245.
323. Clebsch, *England's Earliest Protestants*, 195–96, 206.
324. Trinterud, "Reappraisal," 40.
325. Daniell, *William Tyndale*, 320, 327.

Tyndale opens the prologue to his *Newe Testament* by stating that: "Here thou hast (moost deare reader) the new Testament or covenaunt made wyth vs of God in Christes bloude." Tyndale uses the word "Testament" interchangeably with "covenaunt" and that this is established upon the death of Christ. In his *Babylonian Captivity of the Church* (1520), Luther also speaks of the death of Christ as setting in motion the promise of the "New Testament," which he translates from the Greek word "*diatheke*" in Luke 22:20 and 1 Corinthians 11:25. The reason for Luther's choice of "Testament" is largely due to its associations with the death of the testator and thus more appropriate to use in the context of honoring Christ's sacrifice in the Lord's Supper. However, Luther acknowledges that the Old Testament frequently made use of the word "compact, covenant, and testament of the Lord" and consistently translates the Hebrew *b'rith* as "Covenant" (*Bund*). Luther does emphasize how these ancient promises were really a foreshadowing that "God would one day die" in Christ, but it is inaccurate to simply refer to his use of "testament" in support of the notion that Luther repudiated any idea of conditionality tied to the Gospel promises. Of course, Luther rejected the late medieval scholastic concept of covenant defined as a congruous merit of mercy and the infusion of justifying righteousness in those who are contrite apart from prevenient grace (*facere quod in se est*), but he spoke openly of the covenant conditionality of God's promises with regard to repentance and the obedience that comes from faith in struggle against sin in his *A Treatise on the Holy Sacrament of Baptism* (1519). Furthermore, it is interesting to note that in Tyndale's revised *Newe Testament*, he also chooses to translate "*diatheke*" as "testament."[326] Like Luther, he makes an important distinction in his revised New Testament between the eternal "new testament" (Tyndale also adds "couenanunt") seldom spoken of before the first century and the "olde testament" or "temporall couenaunt made betwene God and the carnall children of Abraham/Isaac and Jacob other wise called Israel/ upon the dedes and the obseruynge of a temporall lawe." Like Luther, Tyndale perceives that the Mosaic Law was essentially a national covenant with

---

326. Tyndale, *Newe Testament* [1534], sig. [*.i.ᵛ] ('W.T. To the Reader'), fo. Cxv (Luke 22:20), cclii ʳ (1 Cor. 11:25); LW 36 (*Babylonian Captivity of the Church*, 1520): 38; WA 6:513–14. See also Hagan, "Testament of a Worm," 12–18.

the Jews promising certain temporal privileges for outward obedience to the Law.[327]

In the prologue to the *Newe Testament*, Tyndale does again refer to the "profession of oure baptyme or covenaunts made betwene God and vs" as the "ryght way, ye and the onlye way to understande the scripture vnto oure salvacion." This basically reiterates what Tyndale stated earlier in his exposition of 1 John.[328] Tyndale's identification of the covenant as an all-encompassing biblical hermeneutic does not come from Luther, yet Luther also interpreted the promise in the sacrament of baptism in terms of a covenant, and the practical outworking of the premise of covenant as it relates to the justification of the sinner and new obedience of the Christian is essentially Luther's theology of Law and Gospel.

Tyndale defines the one covenant made between God and all people past, present, and future as His promise to "be mercifull vnto us/ yf we wilbe mercifull one to another: so that the man which sheweth mercie vnto his neyboure/ may be bolde to trust in God for mercie at all nedes ... For God hath promysed mercie onlye to the mercifull." Tyndale further states that:

> The generall couenaunt wherin all others are comprehended and included/ is this. If we meke ourselves to god/ to kepe all his lawes/ after the ensample of Christ: then God hath bounde himselfe vnto vs to kepe and make good all the mercies promysed in Christ/ thorow out all the Scripture ... Wherfore I have ever noted the covenauntes in the mergentes/ and also the promises [that is, in the 1534 *Newe Testament*]. Moreover where thou findest a promyse and no covenaunt expressed therewith/ there must thou vnderstonde a covenaunt. For all the promyses of the mercie and grace of Christ hath purchased for vs/ are made vpon the condicion that we kepe the lawe.[329]

It would be tempting to interpret these statements as Tyndale having completely abandoned the doctrine of justification by faith alone for a doctrine of salvation by works, or that he had at least adopted what

---

327. Tyndale, *Newe Testament* [1534], sig. [*.vii.ᵛ]–[*.viii.ʳ].

328. Ibid., sig. *.ii.ᵛ.

329. Ibid., sig. *.ii.ᵛ–*.iii.ʳ With regard to his identification of "covenaunt" or "covenaunts" in the margins, see especially Tyndale's marginal notes on the blessings promised in the Sermon on the Mount and the promise of forgiveness spoken of in the Lord's Prayer. See fo. v, x ᵛ, lxxxv, lxiiii ʳ.

Laughlin calls works-righteousness "once removed."[330] Yet Tyndale is operating under the theological assumption, as elsewhere, that those who genuinely come to Christ to be justified by faith alone come in repentance with every intention "to kepe the commaundementes," and, though still imperfect, the love and obedience to the Law that their faith produces gives them an even greater confidence in praying for His daily mercy.[331] Not that good works merit the favor of God, but kindness and mercy reflect a heart of repentance and the faith in Christ that alone justifies. Luther also spoke of assurance of God's mercy as dependent in a certain conditional sense upon the ability of Christians to show mercy and forgiveness to others in his exposition of the Lord's Prayer in the *Large Catechism* (1529).[332]

Whereas Tyndale defined repentance earlier more explicitly as sorrowful contrition, he defines "repentaunce" in the 1534 New Testament as the "conuersion or turnynge" of the heart to God and His will. These definitions are not necessarily different in substance, and Tyndale continues to maintain that, if "unfayned," this repentance is characterized by a genuine confession and contrition under the Law followed by faith in Christ for mercy and forgiveness and the amending of all offenses made against others with love from the heart.[333]

According to the prologue of Tyndale's *Newe Testament*, a person who lacks the desire to turn from sin and to follow the Law of God has no right to claim the mercy promised in Christ, for a faith that is without repentance is false and a blasphemous presumption upon the kindness of God's mercy as if His grace condoned the practice of sin. Like Luther, Tyndale states that Christ and the apostles could not improve upon the moral Law of Moses, but they emphasized its internal demands upon the heart. Since love is the fulfillment of the commandments and conversion is ultimately a turning from self to God and to others, the ability to show mercy is for Tyndale the principal self-assurance distinguishing

---

330. Laughlin, "Brightness of Moses' Face," 218.

331. Tyndale, *Newe Testament* [1534], sig. *.iii.^{r}-*.iiii.^{r}; "that none shalbe partaker of the mercie/ saye he that will fyght agynst the fleshe/ to kepe the lawe," sig. [*.vi.^{r}]. On the point of intentionality in Tyndale's thought, see also Laughlin, "Brightness of Moses' Face," 237–38; Trueman, *Luther's Legacy*, 114.

332. *LC*, Tappert, 432–33; Kolb & Wengert, 352–54; *BSLK*, 682–85; See also Althaus, *Theology of Martin Luther*, 245–50.

333. Tyndale, *Newe Testament* [1534], sig. [*.viii.^{v}]–**.i.^{r}

true faith in Christ from a carnal presumption.³³⁴ Thus, reconciliation to God by His mercy through faith always follows genuine repentance and it is a reasonable condition and expectation that such a repentant Christian will henceforth strive to obey God's Law in love as a response to His mercy: "The gospell is glad tydynges of mercie and grace and that oure corrupt nature shalbe healed agayne for Christes sake and for the merites of his deseruinge onlye: yet on the condicion that we will turne to God/to lerne to kepe his lawes . . ."³³⁵

Tyndale does state that "oure awne dedes thorow workynge of the spirite of God/ helpe vs to contynew in the fauoure and grace/ into which Christ hath brought vs/ and that we can no lenger contynew in fauoure and grace than oure herte are to kepe the lawe."³³⁶ This does not mean, however, that a Christian keeps favor with God by the performance of mere outward deeds or that the intention of those deeds should be to earn the keeping of His favor. Tyndale has mentioned before that devotion to good works is useful in guarding the heart from yielding to the complete consent and control of sin to the loss of repentance, and he makes clear that such devotion is the working of the Spirit and that it is actually the perseverance of the "herte" to keep the Law that reflects a continued position of favor with God established through faith in Christ.

Other prologues and marginal glosses in Tyndale's *Newe Testament* of 1534 recapitulate the theme of covenant conditionality:

> Though fayth iustifie from synne and though Christ deserued the rewarde promysed yet is the promyse made on the condicion that we embrace Christes doctrine and confesse him with worde and dede...we are iustified to do good workes, and in them to walke to the saluacion promysed . . . The couenaunt of mercie in Christ is made onlye to them that wyll worke . . . The promyses of mercye in Christes bloude/ are made vs on that condicion that we kepe the lawe and loue one another as Christ loued vs . . . As ye be saued from synne thorow faith so worke accordynge to the couenaunt vntyll ye come to the salvacion of glory. For yf ye cease workige/ the spirite quencheth agayne/ and ye cease to be partakers of the promes . . . All the mercie

---

334. Ibid., sig. *.iii.ʳ. See alsosig. [*.vi.ᵛ]–[*.vii.].

335. Ibid., sig. [*vii ᵛ].

336. Ibid., sig. [*.vi.ᵛ]. See also Tyndale's marginal glosses for John 14 and 15, fo. clxvi ʳ, clxvii ʳ.

that is set forth in the two vpper chapters [i.e., Colossians 1–2]/ is promysed to them onlye that will folowe Christ and lyue as herafter foloweth ... Here [i.e., 1 Peter 1] Peter (as other true apostles do) fyrst setteth forth the treasure of mercye which god hath bounde himselfe to geue vs for Christes sake and then oure dutie what we are bounde to do agayne yf we will be partakers of the mercie ... the promes of Christ is made us upon that condicion/ that we henceforth worke the wyll of God and not of the flessche ... therby to be sure that they have the true fayth/ as a man knoweth the goodnes of a tree by his frute ... He that hath soche workes maye be sure that he is electe and that he hath the true faith ... and kepeth vs in the myddle waye/ that we beleue in Christ to be saued by his workes onlye/ and then to knowe that it is oure dutie for that kindnes/ to prepare ourselues to do the commaundment of god ... here ye se that Christ and synne cannot dwell together for Christes spirite fyghteth agaynst synne ... By loue we knowe that we are in the truthe and haue quyet consciences to god warde ... but how ofte soeuer he synne let him begynne agayne and fyght a freshe/ and no doute he shall at the last ouercome/ and in the meantyme yet be under mercie for Christes sake because his harte worketh and wolde fayne be lowsed from under the bondage of synne ... here foloweth oure dutye/ if we will be partakers of the mercye before rehersed ... For God promised them onlie forgeuenes of their synnes which turne to god/ to kepe his lawes ... And to the mercifull hath God bounde himselfe to show mercie ... God hath promysed all mercie to the mercifull onlye ... For godes promise partayneth to the mercifull onlye ... For God hath promised no mercie: but to him that wyll do his godlye will.[337]

337. M.g. on Romans 10, *Newe Testament*, fo. ccxxxi ʳ; M.g. on Galatians 6, *Newe Testament*, fo. cclxxvii ᵛ; M. g. on Ephesians 2, *Newe Testament*, fo. cclxxx ʳ; M.g. on Philippians 2, *Newe Testament*, fo. cclxxxvii ʳ; M.g. on Colossians 2, *Newe Testament*, fo. ccxciii; M.g. on 1 Peter 1, *Newe Testament*, fo. cccxv ᵛ; "A Prologe to the Seconde epistle of S. Peter," fo. cccxx ᵛ, and m.g. on 2 Peter 1, fo. ccxxi ᵛ. Luther has "Therefore he exhorts them to test themselves by good works and become sure of their faith, just as one knows trees by their fruits." *LW* 35 (*Preface to the Second Epistle of St. Peter*, 1546): 391; *WA DB* 7:314–15; Tyndale, "A Prologe upon the thre epistles of S. John," fo. cccxxiv ᵛ –ccxxv ʳ; m.g. on 1 John 2, fo. ccvii ʳ; m.g. on 1 John 3, fo. cccvii ᵛ. Luther similarly has: "It keeps us in the true middle way, that we become righteous and free from sin through faith; and then, when we are righteous, that we practice good works and love for God's sake, freely and without seeking anything else." *LW* 35 (*Preface to the Three Epistles of St. John*, 1546): 393; *WA DB* 7:326–27; Tyndale, "The Prologe to the Epistle of S. Paul to the Hebrewes," *Newe Testament*, fo.cccxxxii ᵛ–cccxxxiii ʳ; m.g. on Hebrews 3, fo. cccxlii ʳ. See also fo. cccxlvi ᵛ; Tyndale, "The Prolge upon the pistles of S. James and Judas," *Newe Testament*, fo. cccxlviii ʳ. See also m.g. on James 2, fo. cccl, fo. ccclii ʳ.

However, in the light of the emphasis that previous scholars place on Tyndale's explicit stress on the covenant conditionality of God's promises in repentance and obedience to the Law in the 1530s, it is particularly illuminating to observe that his prologue to the book of Romans in the revised *Newe Testament* of 1534 remains largely unchanged from its earlier counterpart. This of course challenges the perception that the substance of Tyndale's theological assumptions has really changed all that much between 1526 and 1534. Except for a few sentence expansions,[338] changes made in grammar and spelling, an additional section on sin as the fruit of unbelief in violation of the First Commandment,[339] and some rearranging of the order of the content,[340] the most original contribution in the *Newe Testament* of 1534 is actually three new folios of additional commentary on the doctrine of justification by faith alone: "The summe and hole cause of the wrytinge of this epistle/ is/ to proue that a man is iustifieth by fayth onlye . . . And by iustifyinge/ understonde none other thinge then to be reconciled to God and to be restored unto his fauoure/ and to haue thy synnes forgeuen the." Tyndale defines justification here, as he has before, as the forgiveness of sins and the favor of God through faith only. In fact, Tyndale says quite clearly that without the knowledge of Paul's teaching on justification by faith alone in Romans, "not only this epistle and all that Paul wryteth/ but also the hole Scripture" would be "locked up."[341] Thus, for all the emphasis Tyndale places on covenant conditionality in the 1530s, he still views the book of Romans and its teaching on justification by faith in Christ alone, much like Luther, as the theological capstone of the Scriptures.

---

338. For example, the *Newe Testament* of 1534 adds "though he appeare outward full of good workes" to "nether can kepe it [the Law]" in the 1526 edition. See "A Prologe to the Epistle of Paule to the Romayns," *Newe Testament* [1534], fo. cciii ʳ.

339. The interpolated text begins with "And John viii. he sayth" and ends with "is unbelefe the grounde and rote of all euell and all euell workes." See "Paule to the Romayns," *Newe Testament* [1534], fo. ccvi.

340. Ibid., fo. ccxiii ʳ.

341. Ibid., fo. ccxviiiᵛ- ix ʳ (see also m.g.). In the *Newe Testament* of 1535, Tyndale introduces an extended section on faith bringing "the Sprite." See *The Newe Testament yet once agayne corrected by Willyam Tindale*, fo. clxxv ᵛ. See also *The Byble which is all the holy Scripture . . . by Thomas Matthew* [1537], lxᵛ. See also Daniell, *William Tyndale*, 333–38.

Although Tyndale does refer twice in this new section to the "couenauntes of mercie,"³⁴² it is rather intriguing that, instead of taking the opportunity to thoroughly revise his Romans prologue according to his new theological *motif* of covenant, he actually appends more material defining and defending the evangelical doctrine of justification by faith alone as the key to the whole Scripture. In fact, whereas in the prologue to the *Newe Testament* Tyndale stresses that divine mercy is conditioned upon repentance and submission toward the Law of God and that no one can lay claim to the promises who lacks a heart of mercy toward others, he here emphasizes that works cannot quiet the conscience but only faith in the work of Christ: "For the promyse of mercie is made the for Christes workes sake/ and not for thyne awne workes sake ... I cannot once begynne to loue the lawe/ except I be fyrst sure by fayth that God loueth me and forgeueth me."³⁴³

Similarly, a marginal gloss on Romans 2 states that "Dedes are an outeward righteousnes before the worlde and testifie what a man is withinne: But iustifie not the hert before god: ner certifye the conscience that the foresynnes are forgeuen."³⁴⁴ What appear to be two conflicting points of view can be harmonized by interpreting Tyndale's prologue statements as stressing the necessary signs that must accompany any profession of justifying faith in Christ to distinguish this from a false presumption and to gird up personal assurance, whereas his statements in the prologue to Romans stress that the person and work of Christ are the sole object, ground, and assurance of justifying faith itself.

Furthermore, despite the obvious increase in emphasis on the covenant conditionality of the promises in the 1530s, Tyndale is still able to contrast the dialectical ministries of Law and Gospel in his marginal glosses on Romans: "The lawe iustifieth not before god/ but vttereth synne onlye ... the law encreaseth synne and maketh oure nature more gredie to do euell ...³⁴⁵Similarly in his prologue and marginal glosses on the book of Galatians, he states: "the lawe is cause of more synne and

---

342. Tyndale, "Paule to the Romayns," *Newe Testament* [1534], fo. ccvi.
343. Ibid., fo. ccxix.
344. Ibid., fo. ccxxii ᵛ.
345. See marginal glosses on Romans 3 and 5, *Newe Testament* [1534], fo. ccxxiii ʳ, ccxxv ᵛ.

bringeth the cursse of god vpon us ... The lawe vttereth my synne and dampnacion ... the lawe curseth: but fayth blesseth."[346]

Tyndale encourages the reader to follow the order of Paul's familiar logic, in which contrition under the Law drives the sinner to faith in Christ and is then followed by a heart of diligence against sin: "that Christ made not this atonement that thou shuldest anger God agayne: nether dyed he for thy sinnes/ that thous shuldest lyue still in them ..." Tyndale even states importantly that his own emphasis on the necessity of repentance, submission to God's Law, and a life devoted to obedience in love and good works as covenant conditions for partaking of God's promises of mercy in no way undermines his persistent conviction that justification is by faith in Christ alone. For Tyndale, it is simply to be expected that repentance under the Law coupled with a true profession of faith and claim upon God's mercy will result in love and devotion to the will of God in the Law, and Tyndale explicitly acknowledges that being overcome by slothfulness and ingratitude will eventually result in the loss of "this fauoure and mercie agayne."[347] Interpreting salvation in terms of a conditional covenant, then, is for Tyndale simply to stress how true faith in Christ is concomitant with repentance and manifests itself in a changed heart and a life devoted to the Law and good works. Justification is indeed by faith in Christ alone, but not just any kind of faith. True justifying faith in Christ is defined in relationship to repentance, which creates the necessary conditions for the emergence of such faith, and also to the love and good works inherent to this faith that flow out of it as a natural response to the receiving of grace.

With the exception of the book of Hebrews, a cursory glance of the remaining prologues in the New Testament of 1534 reveals a basic literary and structural dependence of Tyndale upon Luther. Tyndale continues in many of the prologues and marginal glosses to reiterate the moral obligation of the Christian in terms of the covenant conditionality of the promises:

> Though fayth iustifie from synne and though Christ deserued the rewarde promysed yet is the promyse made on the condicion that we embrace Christes doctrine and confesse him with

---

346. Tyndale, "The Prologe upon the epistle of S. Paul to the Galathyans," *Newe Testament* [1534], fo. cclxxii[r]. See also marginal glosses on Galatians 2 and 3, fo. cclxxiiii [r] –cclxxv [r].

347. Tyndale, "Paul to the Romayns," *Newe Testament* [1534], fo. ccxx [r].

worde and dede...we are iustified to do good workes, and in them to walke to the saluacion promysed ... The couenaunt of mercie in Christ is made onlye to them that wyll worke ... The promyses of mercye in Christes bloude/ are made vs on that condicion that we kepe the lawe and loue one another as Christ loued vs ... As ye be saued from synne thorow faith so worke accordynge to the couenaunt vntyll ye come to the salvacion of glory. For yf ye cease workige/ the spirite quencheth agayne/ and ye cease to be partakers of the promes ... All the mercie that is set forth in the two vpper chapters [i.e., Colossians 1–2]/ is promysed to them onlye that will folowe Christ and lyue as herafter foloweth ... Here [i.e., 1 Peter 1] Peter (as other true apostles do) fyrst setteth forth the treasure of mercye which god hath bounde himselfe to geue vs for Christes sake and then oure dutie what we are bounde to do agayne yf we will be partakers of the mercie ... the promes of Christ is made us upon that condicion/ that we henceforth worke the wyll of God and not of the flessche ... therby to be sure that they have the true fayth/ as a man knoweth the goodnes of a tree by his frute ... He that hath soche workes maye be sure that he is electe and that he hath the true faith ... and kepeth vs in the myddle waye/ that we beleue in Christ to be saued by his workes onlye/ and then to knowe that it is oure dutie for that kindnes/ to prepare ourselues to do the commaundment of god ... here ye se that Christ and synne cannot dwell together for Christes spirite fyghteth agaynst synne ... By loue we knowe that we are in the truthe and haue quyet consciences to god warde ... but how ofte soeuer he synne let him begynne agayne and fyght a freshe/ and no doute he shall at the last ouercome/ and in the meantyme yet be under mercie for Christes sake because his harte worketh and wolde fayne be lowsed from under the bondage of synne ... here foloweth oure dutye/ if we will be partakers of the mercye before rehersed ... For God promised them onlie forgeuenes of their synnes which turne to god/ to kepe his lawes ... And to the mercifull hath God bounde himselfe to show mercie ... God hath promysed all mercie to the mercifull onlye ... For godes promise partayneth to the mercifull onlye ... For God hath promised no mercie: but to him that wyll do his godlye will.[348]

348. M.g. on Romans 10, *Newe Testament*, fo. ccxxxi ʳ; M.g. on Galatians 6, *Newe Testament*, fo. cclxxvii ᵛ; M. g. on Ephesians 2, *Newe Testament*, fo. cclxxx ʳ; M.g. on Philippians 2, *Newe Testament*, fo. cclxxxvii ʳ; M.g. on Colossians 2, *Newe Testament*, fo. ccxciii; M.g. on 1 Peter 1, *Newe Testament*, fo. cccxv ᵛ; "A Prologe to the Seconde epistle of S. Peter," fo. cccxx ᵛ, and m.g. on 2 Peter 1, fo. ccxxi ᵛ. Luther has "Therefore he exhorts them to test themselves by good works and become sure of their faith, just as one

It is this repeated rhetorical emphasis on the covenant conditionality of the divine promises of mercy that really sets Tyndale apart from Luther. Yet Luther could be just as adamant that justifying faith cannot be without repentance and good works, that the Law is the positive form of Christian obedience, that love and truly good works are the result of justification and a living faith, and even that God's promises of justification in baptism come with a certain covenant conditionality in the sense that justifying faith in Christ is never without repentance, a heart for obedience to the Law of God, devotion to love and good works, and a struggle with sin in the Spirit. Tyndale is still under the evangelical influence of Luther's theology of Law and Gospel in his assumption that good works in keeping with the spirit of the Law are those done from the love of a heart converted through repenting faith in Christ, and that "fayth which hath no good dedes folowinge/ is a false fayth and non of that fayth iustifieth or receaueth forgeuenes of synnes."[349]

Shortly after Tyndale was arrested in May of 1535, discovery was made in Antwerp of a copy of the widely circulated last will and testament of the Gloucestershire gentleman William Tracy bound with an exposition written by John Frith and another one by Tyndale in Frith's handwriting. The will itself was dated October, 1530, and was condemned as heretical in March of 1531. Tracy's body was ordered to be exhumed by the authorities and this actually took place later in October 1532. Both expositions by Tyndale and Frith were completed in their final form sometime after this date, although they probably were not published until after Tyndale's death in October 1536.[350]

---

knows trees by their fruits." *LW* 35 (*Preface to the Second Epistle of St. Peter*, 1546): 391; *WA DB* 7:314–15; Tyndale, "A Prologe upon the thre epistles of S. John," fo. cccxxiv ᵛ –ccxxv ʳ;m.g. on 1 John 2, fo. ccvii ʳ; m.g. on 1 John 3, fo. cccvii ᵛ. Luther similarly has: "It keeps us in the true middle way, that we become righteous and free from sin through faith; and then, when we are righteous, that we practice good works and love for God's sake, freely and without seeking anything else." *LW* 35 (*Preface to the Three Epistles of St. John*, 1546): 393; *WA DB* 7:326–27; Tyndale, "The Prologe to the Epistle of S. Paul to the Hebrewes," *Newe Testament*, fo.cccxxxii ᵛ–cccxxxiii ʳ; m.g. on Hebrews 3, fo. cccxlii ʳ. See also fo. cccxlvi ᵛ; Tyndale, "The Prolge upon the pistles of S. James and Judas," *Newe Testament*, fo. cccxlviii ʳ. See also m.g. on James 2, fo. cccl, fo. ccclii ʳ.

349. Tyndale, "The Prolge upon the pistles of S. James and Judas," *Newe Testament* [1534], fo. cccxlviii ʳ.

350. *The testament of master Wylliam Tracie esquier, expounded both by Willism Tindall and Iho[n] Frith* [1535]; Day, "Tyndale and Frith," in Day, Lund, and O'Donnell, *Word, Church, and State*, 162–82; Mozley, *William Tyndale*, 189–90, 240–41; Daniell, *William Tyndale*, 222.

Apart from a treatise on the sacraments,[351] this is the last theological work by Tyndale to be published before his execution. In the will, William Tracy expresses his desire to entrust his soul to the merits of Christ alone and breaks with the religious custom of his day by refusing to donate his temporal goods to the Church for the sake of easing his suffering through purgatory. The will clearly expresses a doctrine of justification by faith alone: "that a good worke maketh not a good man/ but a good man maketh a good woorke/ for faith makethe the man booth good and rightwyse/ for a rightwyse man lyueth by faith …."[352] Tyndale expresses open admiration for Tracy as a man of learning and even comments that he was the greatest Augustine scholar in all of England in the 1520s.[353]

Tyndale uses Tracy's will as a basis for expounding the doctrine of justification by faith alone, that "thy live faith is sufficient to iustification with oute addynge to of any more helpe."[354] At the same time, true justifying faith by its very nature cannot coexist with a callous consent to continue in sin and there is a certain covenant conditionality connected with the promises. The faith that justifies is:

> in the promes made apon the apoyntment betwene god and us/ that we shulde kepe his lawe to the uttermost of our power/ that is he that beleueth in Christ for the remission of synne/ and is baptized to do the wyll of Christ/ and to kepe his lawe/ of loue/ and to mortifie the fleshe/ that man shalbe saued … for God neuer made promes but apon an appoyntment or couenaunt under which who so euer wyll not come can be no partaker of the promes. True faith in Christ/ geueth power to loue the lawe of god … Hast thou no power to loue the lawe so hast thou no faith in Christes bloude.[355]

Tyndale stresses in this passage the explicit conditionality of God's promises in obedience to the Law with love from the heart but under the assumption that justification by faith alone follows after a genuine

---

351. *A brief declaration of the sacraments* [1548]. Most scholars agree that an earlier treatise, *Supper of the Lord* (1533), was written by George Joye. In both cases, the Real Presence is rejected. See Trinterud, "Reappraisal," 41; Lund, "Tyndale and Frith on the Eucharist," in Day, Lund, and O'Donnell, *Word, Church, and State*, 187.

352. Tracy, *testament of master Wylliam Tracie* [1535], sig. A ii ᵛ.

353. Day, "Tyndale and Frith," 167–68.

354. Tyndale, *testament of master William Tracie* [1535], sig. [A v ʳ].

355. Ibid., sig. [A vi ʳ].

repentance under the Law and leads naturally by way of response into a life that is devoted in love and gratitude to the will of God. Tyndale explicitly and adamantly rejects the implication that the covenant conditionality of God's promises assigns works a role in justification. In fact, a Christian is forgiven before ever having the chance to do any outward deeds. Even if a Christian should fall into some grievous sin, Tyndale states that reconciliation with God is only and always on the basis of a repenting faith in Christ. It is not works that deserve justification and reconciliation with God, but rather vice versa. Tyndale again uses the analogy of a king and the pardoning of a criminal to illustrate that only those who show genuine sorrow for their crimes and desire to correct their ways will receive the pardoning of the king who knows they will receive it with faith and gratitude and will henceforth endeavor to abstain from the very vice that brought down their guilt and otherwise deserved punishment. To remain in the good favor of the king is then conditioned upon the respecting of his pardon through a constant diligence to uphold his laws.[356] With regard to justification and the Christian life, a heart for obeying the Law of God and a perseverance to strive in the keeping of it is reflective of a repentant faith in the merciful pardon promised in Christ.

According to the records of Latomus of Louvain, one of the Catholic theologians commissioned to Vilvorde for the prosecution, Tyndale continued to defend the doctrine of justification by faith alone during his incarceration. These last writings, however, are lost and were never published except what can be inferred from Latomus' replies.[357]

At the end of his influential essay, Trinterud concludes by stating that Tyndale "was a 'Lutheran' only in the contemporary loose sense of the word," and that it is more accurate to describe him as an Erasmian humanist-turned-evangelical in the tradition of other Swiss and Rhineland reformers. Even while acknowledging that Tyndale was "influenced by Luther" (literally), Trinterud argues that he did not follow Luther's "developing thought."[358] Werrell similarly states that "Tyndale could never have been a follower of Luther," and that he even changed the German reformer's doctrine "into his own."[359]

356. Ibid., sig. [A vi ʳ]–[A vii ʳ].
357. Daniell, *William Tyndale*, 374–81; Mozley, *William Tyndale*, 329–39.
358. Trinterud, "A Reappraisal," 41–42.
359. Werrell, *Theology of William Tyndale*, 172.

It is certain that Tyndale was always confident enough to exercise a certain degree of literary independence from Luther, including those works he obviously translated. The degree to which Tyndale repeatedly emphasizes the covenant conditionality of the Gospel promises in the 1530s does reveal a more significant rhetorical, though not theological, departure from Luther. His underlying theological assumptions concerning justification and the Christian life never really changed and these assumptions were shaped significantly by the influence of Luther's evangelical theology of Law and Gospel. Indeed, many of the themes in Tyndale's theology reflect Augustinian elements, such as spiritual bondage apart from grace, the effectual side of justifying faith in love and good works through the Spirit, and the non-imputation of sin in the life of the justified Christian, but this could be said of Luther's theology as well. Furthermore, these themes are interpreted by Tyndale through an emphasis on justification and grace as the favor of God and remission of sins through faith alone in Christ and His atoning righteousness.

As Laughlin argues, a theology of covenant increasingly became Tyndale's preferred way to stress the need for, or rather expectation of, repentance and a heart of obedience to the Law of God and a life of good works concomitant with truly justifying faith in Christ. However, Tyndale never abandoned Luther's theology of Law and Gospel according to their proper ministries and he always associated the former with the commands, instruction, and conviction driving sinners to seek the mercy, forgiveness, help, and power promised in the latter. In fact, Tyndale continues to appropriate the themes of Law and Gospel in his description of justification and the Christian life as it plays out under the terms of the covenant.[360]

Although Luther obviously never stressed the covenant conditionality of the promises with such frequent prominence as Tyndale does in the 1530s, previous scholars have not appreciated the extent to which Luther does in fact often speak this way, especially in context of the sacrament of baptism viewed as a covenant. It is interesting to note that Luther's own description of baptism as a covenant occurs at the very same time of the maturing of his theology of Law and Gospel. Luther did not develop or emphasize the notion of covenant conditionality throughout his writings to quite the extent that Tyndale does, though he does continue to speak of baptism as an eternal covenant later in

---

360. See also Trueman, *Luther's Legacy*, 113.

the 1520s and 30s,[361] but he must not have perceived there to be any inherent theological conflict between baptism viewed as an evangelical covenant and his theology of Law and Gospel. The same could also be said of Tyndale.

Yet even if Tyndale stresses the effectual side of justifying faith in love and good works more than Luther, many scholars have often exaggerated Luther's dialectical theology of Law and Gospel to such a degree that they underrate the extent to which he also speaks positively about the Law in the context of Christian obedience and even of love and devotion to good works as contributing to a fuller assurance of the grace of God. This misperception has understandably caused many to polarize Luther and Tyndale on the subject of Law and Gospel. It also has led to the undervaluing of the reality that Tyndale, even in the 1530s, continues to speak with as many negative overtones as Luther about the Law when describing the moral and spiritual bondage of the sinner under condemnation before God apart from justifying faith in Christ.

A direct literary indebtedness to Luther's writings may be more evident in Tyndale's early career, but even into the 1530s the influence of Luther's theology of Law and Gospel is still readily evident in his understanding that repentance under the preaching of the Law is the necessary antecedent to a genuine faith in Christ alone for the promise of justification, or the remission of sins and imputation of righteousness in Christ, which together result in the power of a new life lived in the Spirit devoted to keeping the Law and the doing of good works in struggle against the flesh with love and gratitude from the heart.

---

361. Kolb and Arand, *Genius of Luther's Theology*, 192–93.

7

Law and Gospel in the Theology of John Frith

THE IMPORTANCE OF JOHN FRITH TO THE HISTORY OF THE EARLY ENGlish Reformation in the 1520s has often been overshadowed by more high profile figures like William Tyndale, Robert Barnes, Hugh Latimer, and Thomas Bilney. There is actually very little secondary scholarship on either the life or theology of Frith in comparison to Tyndale or Barnes.[1] This is interesting to note in the light of Foxe's own high praise of Frith in his *Acts and Monuments*: "there hath bene none a great tyme which seemed vnto me more greueous, then the lamentable death and cruell handlyng of Ihon Fryth, so learned and excellent a yong man: who had so profited in all kinde of learning and knowledge, that skarsly there was his equal amongest al his companions, and besides withall had suche a godlines of life ioyned with his doctrine, that it was hard to iudge in whether of them hee was more commendable, bring greatly prayse worthy in them both."[2] Similarly, C. S. Lewis, although describing Frith as looming "larger as a man than as an author," stated that he was "not contemptible even in the second capacity."[3]

---

1. On the life of John Frith, see Daniell, "Frith," *ODNB* 21:42–43. The most recent monograph by B. Raynor adapts material from the unpublished manuscript of the late Frank Clark who was working on a second expanded account of Frith before he died in 1994. See Raynor, *John Frith, Scholar and Martyr*, 17. See also Clark, *John Frith: Kentish Martyr*. The most authoritative treatment is still Wright, *Work of John Frith*, 1–80. Other accounts include: Marcus Loane, *Pioneers*, 1–46; Clebsch, *England's Earliest Protestants*, 78–136; Fulop, "John Frith (1503–1533)"; Bickley, "Frith," *DNB* 7:718–20; Foxe, *A&M* [1570], 1173–80; "The Storie, life, and Martirdome of Iohn Frith ..." in Foxe, *Whole Works*. For more in-depth treatment of his theology, see Hard, "The Origin and Development of John Frith's Doctrinal Adiaphora"; Wright, *Work of John Frith*, 21–80; Trueman, *Luther's Legacy*, 121–55; Clebsch, *England's Earliest Protestants*, 78–136; Knox, *Doctrine of Faith*, 43–55.

2. Foxe, *A&M* [1570], 1173.

3. Lewis, *English Literature in the Sixteenth Century*, 196.

John Frith was born at Westerham in Kent in 1503. In the most recent biography, Raynor suggests the possibility of 1506 on the basis of a comment made by John Bale that Frith (d. 1533) was "not twenty-seven years old the year he was executed." Furthermore, Raynor observes that, if Frith was born in 1503, he would have been older than was typical for entering college. However, the evidence Raynor provides is inconclusive, and he acknowledges that the date of 1503 has been generally accepted by scholars and is based on a comment by Frith's own parents recorded in Foxe's *Whole Works* that he was martyred at the age of thirty.[4]

More important than the date is the location of his birth and upbringing. The consensus among scholars is that Kent was a known stronghold of Lollardy in the early sixteenth century.[5] However, there is simply no historical evidence to link the Frith family to Lollard sympathies. It was Humanism, rather than Lollardy, which made the earliest visible intellectual impression upon the young Frith.

Early on in his childhood, the Frith family moved to Sevenoaks where his father became employed as an innkeeper. Wright suggests that Frith was first introduced to humanist educational reforms, and possibly even to the study of Greek, when he was sent to Eton College at the age of seventeen.[6] What is doubtless, however, is that Frith encountered the new scholarship when he transferred first to Queen's and then later King's College, Cambridge University, where he obtained his BA in 1525.[7]

Humanism had taken root at Cambridge by the early sixteenth century in the co-founding of St. John's College by Lady Margaret Beaufort, mother of Henry VII, and the Bishop of Rochester and University Chancellor, John Fisher. However, the scholastic curriculum was also still in place.[8] It was also at Cambridge that the famous humanist Erasmus taught Greek between the years 1511 and 1514 at the request of Bishop Fisher and began work on his monumentally influential Greek

---

4. Raynor, *Scholar and Martyr*, 33, 37; DNB 7:718; ODNB 21:42–43.

5. Marshall, *Reformation England*, 32; Dickens, "Lollards and Protestants," in *Slavin, Humanism, Reform, and Reformation*, 106. See also Richard Lutton's recent study of Tenterden in *Lollardy and Orthodox Religion*.

6. DNB 7:718; ODNB 21:42–3; Wright, *Work of John Frith*, 3.

7. ODNB 21:42.

8. Schoeck, "Humanism in England," in Rabil, *Renaissance Humanism*, 2:6–7, 25–26; Rex, *Theology of John Fisher*, 17–22; Leader, *Cambridge*, 237, 266–67, 308.

and revised Latin text of the New Testament (*Novum Instrumentum*) published in Basle in 1516. Erasmus spoke fondly of Cambridge at least as a suitable environment for his Greek scholarship.⁹

Foxe describes Frith as being a diligent scholar of both Latin and Greek. In the *Acts and Monuments* of 1570, Foxe mentions this in the context of Frith's Cambridge period, but in his edition of *Whole Works* it follows after his transfer to Oxford in 1525.¹⁰ The reason for this discrepancy is uncertain, but it seems likely that Frith would have flourished in Greek studies first at Cambridge. In any case, his scholarly aptitude was recognized by Cardinal Wolsey who chose Frith to join other junior canons of his newly established Oxford college (later Christ Church). This might suggest that Frith at this time was still an orthodox Catholic influenced by humanist sympathies, but it is possible that Frith's more radical theological loyalties were undetected by Wolsey. Foxe mentions that the men chosen were not just from Cambridge and that the list was much longer than what he recorded. This certainly makes it possible for individuals and their deeper doctrinal convictions to sneak below Wolsey's radar.¹¹

Although Foxe states in his earlier *Acts and Monuments* (1563) that Frith met Tyndale while in attendance at Mary Hall, Oxford, he later records that it was during his years at Cambridge. Foxe also claims that it was through Tyndale that Frith "first receyued into his hart the seede of the gospell and syncere godlines."¹² J. F. Mozley and Marcus Loane argue that this meeting most likely took place at Cambridge in the early 1520s, although Foxe himself is not actually explicit about the precise location, and Tyndale's presence at Cambridge at this time is not accepted by most recent scholars. Both Mozley and Loane are right to discredit the account given in *Whole Works*, which indicates that Frith first became acquainted with Tyndale in London after his release from imprisonment. This would mean that they met in London sometime in 1528, which is impossible since Tyndale had left for the continent

9. Halkin, *Erasmus*, 30–40; Bainton, *Erasmus of Christendom*, 101, 113, 133; Leader, *Cambridge*, 293–94; Rex, *Theology of John Fisher*, 51; Marc'hadour, "William Tyndale entre Erasmus et Luther," 185. My thanks to Suzanne Bernal for translating this article.

10. Foxe, *A&M* [1570]: 1173–74; "The Storie, life, and Martirdome of Iohn Frith." *Whole Works*.

11. Foxe, *A&M* [1570]: 1174.

12. Ibid., 1173–74. See also Day, "Tyndale and Frith," in Day, Lund, and O'Donnell, *Word, Church, and State*, 164 (n. 4).

four years earlier.[13] Yet it is also doubtful that Tyndale met Frith at Cambridge in 1520–21. It is more likely that the two met sometime in 1523 or 1524 near the completion of Frith's B.A. and before he was transferred to Oxford by Wolsey. Furthermore, Raynor only considers the possibility that Tyndale visited Frith at Cambridge, but this meeting probably took place in London where Tyndale was residing prior to his departure for the Continent in the spring of 1524. It is also in London that Tyndale first conferred with Frith about translating the Bible.[14] Thus, Foxe's *Whole Works* is probably correct in identifying London as the location of their initial acquaintance,[15] but the chronology in *Acts & Monuments* is more consistent with what is known about Tyndale's own whereabouts in the mid-1520s.

Sometime after transferring to Oxford, Frith and others were accused of "conferryng together vpon the abuses of Religion being at that time crept into the Church," and "were therefore accused of heresie vnto the Cardinall, and cast into a prison . . . where their saltfishe was layde." Foxe's account in *Whole Works* more specifically identifies the suspected heresy to be sympathy with "Martyn Luthers doctrine."[16] The simple fact that Frith was imprisoned does not necessarily prove that he was beyond the bounds of mainstream orthodox Catholic theology at this time. According to Foxe, it was not until after the men were imprisoned that they were even formally examined.[17] Neither does all criticism toward religious "abuses" indicate the necessary stamp of Luther's influence, and it must be kept in mind that the name of Luther overshadowed nearly every heresy hunt of the 1520s.

Yet there are good reasons to believe that Frith had indeed moved well beyond a mere Erasmian critique of religious abuses after 1525. It is certainly reasonable to conclude that Frith was well acquainted with the name of Luther before he ever arrived at Oxford, and Foxe does claim that he was evangelically "converted" through acquaintance with William Tyndale before this. Wolsey certainly had good reason to be cautious of heretical activity at his newly established Oxford college. He

13. Mozley, *William Tyndale*, 20 (and n. *); Loane, *Pioneers*, 4.

14. Wright, *Work of John Frith*, 4; Foxe *A&M* [1570]: 1226; *DNB* 7:719; Raynor, *John Frith, Scholar and Martyr*, 39.

15. See also *DNB* 7:718.

16. Foxe, *A&M* [1570], 1174; Foxe, "Martyrdome of Iohn Frith," *Whole Works*.

17. Foxe erroneously lists "Tindall" among the accused. *A&M* [1570]: 1133.

and Bishop Tunstall's earlier efforts to stop the trafficking of evangelical works into England proved ultimately unsuccessful and now a new wave of trouble was emerging with the publication of Tyndale's English New Testament in 1525-26.[18]

Foxe indicates that the investigation of Frith and his companions at Oxford included a search for prohibited "bookes" in their bedrooms.[19] Among these "bookes" were likely the works of Luther and perhaps other continental reformers, but even more significant was Tyndale's recently printed English New Testament of 1526, a work which Frith himself appears to have been involved with in its earliest stages in London in 1524. Although the statement made by Foxe that Tyndale "consydering in his mynde, and partely also conferring with Ioh. Frith ..." chronologically follows Tyndale's departure for Germany in the narrative, this conferral could not really have occurred at this time since Frith remained in England until 1528. Although Trueman is probably right in asserting that Frith did participate with Tyndale in the later translation of the Pentateuch and the book of Jonah in the later 1520s, the context of Foxe's narrative is referring to the translation of the New Testament and to Tyndale's initial flight to Germany. Furthermore, the section that follows is actually a parenthesis describing the whole development of Tyndale's vision for the work of Bible translation, after which the story picks up again with his departure from England. Therefore, this conferral mentioned only in passing by Foxe probably refers to Frith and Tyndale's early acquaintanceship in London in 1523 or 1524.[20]

Tyndale's English New Testament and other proscribed books were being sold in London and Oxford by a parish priest named Thomas Garrett, and it was knowledge of this fact that aroused suspicion and eventually brought charges against Frith and the other men who were imprisoned.[21] Frith, therefore, was linked to an underground evangelical reform movement that was being fueled by forbidden works, including one by an English exile, imported from the Continent.

---

18. Reed, "Regulation of the Book Trade," 265; Clebsch, *England's Earliest Protestants*, 13; *L&P* 4.2:805; Rupp, *Six Makers*, 13; Haigh, *English Reformations*, 60.

19. Foxe, *A&M* [1570], 1174.

20. Foxe *A&M* [1570]: 1226, *DNB* 7:719; Trueman, *Luther's Legacy*, 15; *ODNB* 21:42.

21. Foxe, *A&M* [1570], 1366-70; Loane, *Pioneers*, 5-6.

After the prisoners became infected and a few died from the stench and diet of the saltfish, Wolsey released Frith and the other survivors "vpon the condition, not to passe aboue ten myles of Oxford."[22] Hearing of the heresy trials of Oxford colleagues Thomas Garret and Anthony Dalaber, however, compelled Frith in 1528 to flee "across the sea" to join Tyndale in Flanders. Foxe provides no other details concerning Frith's sojourn other than that this initial visit lasted a little more than two years.[23] Except for a brief return to England during Lent in 1531, Frith resumed his exile on the Continent until the summer of 1532. Throughout his exile, Frith was in attendance at the colloquy of Marburg (1529), was married in Holland, and authored his first three works expressing an evangelical theology.[24]

One of those three works that Frith composed during his exile was a translation from Latin into English of the Scotsman Patrick Hamilton's *Divers Fruitful Gatherings of Scripture* and dubbed by Frith as "Patrick's Places" (1531): "For it entreateth exactelye of certeyne comen places/ which knowne/ ye haue the pith of all divinite."[25] The story of Patrick Hamilton is important in itself for understanding Frith's connection to Luther and the influence of his theology of Law and Gospel.

Hamilton (1504?–1528) was born of Scottish nobility, was made a titular abbot in 1517, and studied at the University of Paris where he received his MA in 1520. Hamilton probably learned of Luther while at Paris since his works were receiving significant attention at the Sorbonne by 1519. However, it is impossible to know precisely what impact Luther had on Hamilton at this time, and his reforming sympathies may not have extended much beyond Humanism. Hamilton moved to the University of Louvain in 1520–22, and then returned to Scotland as a new faculty member at the University of St. Andrews in 1523. His reforming criticisms, however, made him an enemy of Archbishop James Beaton, and he fled first briefly to Wittenberg and then soon after to the recently established University of Marburg in Hesse in 1527. One of

---

22. Foxe, *A&M* [1570], 1174.

23. Ibid.; *ODNB* 21:42; Foxe, "Martirdome of Iohn Frith," *Whole Works*; Loane, *Pioneers*, 8.

24. *ODNB* 21:42; Raynor, *John Frith, Scholar and Martyr*, 97; Clark, *John Frith: Kentish Martyr*, 11–12; Wright, *Work of John Frith*, 8–9.

25. Frith, [*Paitrikes places*] [1531?]. Though probably translated in 1529, the work was not published until later. Clark, *John Frith: Kentish Martyr*, 8.

Hamilton's teachers was a former Franciscan, now Luther-sympathizer, named Francis Lambert, who had just been appointed to the faculty at Melancthon's recommendation. While in Marburg, Hamilton composed the *Fruitful Gatherings*, a series of biblical theses expounding the doctrine of justification by faith in Christ alone under the rubric of Law and Gospel. Hamilton returned to Scotland after just six months and was tried and executed for heresy in 1528. John Knox later considered Hamilton's martyrdom to be the starting point of the Scottish Reformation, and he published Frith's *Patrick's Places* in his *History of the Reformation in Scotland* (1559-71).[26] Frith never had the opportunity to meet Hamilton, who returned to Scotland before Frith arrived on the Continent, though Loane suggests that Tyndale met him during a brief hiatus in Marburg in 1527.[27] Yet Frith's decision to publish *Patrick's Places* shows not only his admiration for Hamilton as a reformer and martyr but also his adoption of an evangelical theology of Law and Gospel influenced by Luther.

Patrick's Places is organized by pithy theological propositions and Scripture quotations that follow an intentional progression from Law to Gospel and from faith to hope, love, and good works. The central theme underlying the entire work is justification by faith in Christ alone apart from, but resulting in, good works. Hamilton begins the work with a discussion of the Law, which he identifies with the commandments and prohibitions of God encapsulated in the Ten Commandments and interpreted by the law of love. The Law is then characterized by Hamilton as something impossible for any natural person to do without first having faith and grace: "He that hath the fayth/ loveth god/ and he that loveth god kepeth all his commaundementes: ergo he that hath the faith kepeth all the commaundementes of god." Thus, the Law by itself only makes a person aware of his or her weakness and guilt without providing any remedy or solution. That remedy is found in the Gospel, which Hamilton defines as the "good tydyngs" that in Christ all the requirements of the Law have been satisfied and He is "oure rightwysenes ... oure satisfaccyon ... oure redemptyon ... oure goodnes." Hamilton effectively establishes the dialectical relationship of Law to Gospel with

---

26. See Torrance, "Hamilton," *ODNB* 24:884-886; Daniell, 217-18; McGoldrick, "Patrick Hamilton," 81-88; McGoldrick, *Luther's Scottish Connection*, 35-54; Ryrie, *origins of the Scottish Reformation*, 31-32.

27. Loane, *Pioneers*, 7-8.

an evangelical theology of justification by faith alone through a series of propositional dialogues: "The lawe sayeth/paye thy dette. The gospell sayeth Christ hath payed it . . . The lawe sayeth thou art a synner/ despayre and thou shalt be dammed. The gospell saieth/ thy sinnes are forgeuen the be of good comforte thou shalt be saued."

The work then proceeds to exalt the priority of faith and all that springs from it as pleasing to God: "He that hath the faith is iust and good / and a good tre bereth good frute: ergo all that is done in fayth pleaseth god." The work clearly upholds the doctrine of justification by faith in Christ alone apart from works and that "faith onlye maketh a man good and rightwise . . . faith onlye saueth vs." At the same time, hope and "cherite" are inherent to justifying faith, with hope pertaining to the promises made to faith and love pertaining to the welfare of others for their own sake with no thought of reward. According to Hamilton, works possess neither the ability to condemn nor to justify. Rather, condemnation comes by unbelief, and justification comes by faith in Christ alone, although works flow naturally from a heart of true justifying faith: "A man is good ere he do good workes/ and evell ere he doo evel workes/ for the tre is good ere it bere good frute and evel ere it bere evel frute."[28]

This short work breathes the inspiration of Luther and the influence of his evangelical theology of Law and Gospel. It might also be argued that Hamilton's emphasis on the preaching of the Law as the revelation of human culpability and weakness apart from grace so that faith in Christ only justifies or makes a person righteous reflects the influence of Augustine as a legacy of Humanism. However, it should not be assumed that Luther's own way of speaking about justification was wholly dissimilar to Augustine, though with some important qualifications.[29] Furthermore, the particular Law-Gospel organization of Hamilton's *Fruitful Gatherings*, the emphasis in his understanding of the Gospel and his theology of justification on the remission of sins in the righteousness of Christ through faith alone, and his time spent in Wittenberg and Marburg all point strongly toward the influ-

28. Frith, [*Paitrikes places*] [1531?].

29. McGrath, *Iustitia Dei*, 204–5; *LW* 54 (*Table Talk*, No. 347:"Augustine at First Devoured and Then Put Aside," Summer or Fall, 1532): 49; *WA Tr* 1:140; See also *LW* 54 (*Table Talk*, No. 85:"About Augustine and Justification," Early November, 1531), 10; *WA Tr* 1:32. *LW* 54 (*Table Talk*, No. 4567:"The Church Fathers and Biblical Interpretation," May 7, 1539; recorded by Anthony Lauterbach): 352; *WA Tr* 4:380–81.

ence of Luther. It is uncertain to what degree Hamilton had adopted Luther's theology before fleeing Scotland, although this was assumed by Archbishop Beaton to be the case, but Hamilton most assuredly knew of Luther's evangelical theology and of Tyndale's English New Testament prior to his departure for the Continent in 1527.[30] It may be that his time at Wittenberg and Marburg only confirmed his evangelical sympathies developed earlier between 1523 and 1527.

According to Foxe, Frith had already been converted through the influence of Tyndale, so it is questionable what amount of direct impact Hamilton's work had upon the shaping of his evangelical theology. Nevertheless, his decision to translate it obviously shows that he valued its author and his theological message, a message that reflects the evangelical priorities Luther had outlined by 1520. Of course, as Clebsch argues, the fact that Frith translated the work does not necessarily mean he agreed with Hamilton on every particular,[31] but this point is impossible to prove.

In 1529 Frith published a three-part work under the pseudonym of "Richarde Brightwell," the core of which was a translation of Luther's own antipapal exposition of the eighth chapter of Daniel (*Ad librum eximii Magistri Nostri Magistri Ambrosii Catharini, defensoris Silvestri Prieratis acerrimi, responsio, 1521*).[32] In the prefatory *A Pistle to the Christian reader*, the influence of Luther is evident in Frith's description of the possessive character of saving faith, that it "is not therefore sufficient to beleve that he is a sauiour and redemer," since even the Devil and his demons have such belief, "but that he is a sauiour and redemer vnto the..."[33] Like Luther and also Tyndale, Frith asserts in the *A Pistle* that repentance is necessary "in the order of thy iustification," although this does not mean that enumerating sins itself justifies. Rather, the

---

30. Loane, *Pioneers*, 7; McGoldrick, *Luther's Scottish Connection*, 33–34; Ryrie, *origins of the Scottish Reformation*, 29–30.

31. Clebsch, *England's Earliest Protestants*, 82.

32. *A pistle to the Christen reader* [1529]. More recently, the actual publisher has been identified as Martin de Keyser in Antwerp. See *ODNB* 21:42; Daniell, 218. Frith probably used Luther's Latin text, which can be found in WA 7:705–78. Wright states that Frith translates the portion of the text found on 722–72, 778. See *Work of John Frith*, 9, 35. The *DNB* and Loane only identify the text as a translation from an unknown German manuscript or book. *DNB* 7:720; Loane, *Pioneers*, 10.

33. *A pistle to the Christen reader* [1529], fo. ii ᵛ–fo. iii ʳ; Trueman, *Luther's Legacy*, 124; McGrath, *Iustitia Dei*, 200.

faith in Christ that alone justifies must by its very definition follow a humble acknowledgment of guilt and weakness before the Law of God that seeks such grace. Frith quotes directly from Augustine whose claim of helplessness before the demands of the Law had aroused the ire of Pelagius in the fourth century. The preaching of the Law does not imply that the works it commands are possible for people to accomplish on their own strength, but instead reveals the need for the help of the grace of God. The self-consciousness of moral weakness accompanied by an acknowledgment of the righteousness of the will of God in the Law is not meant to bind a sinner indefinitely to despair. The answer is in the Gospel, which is the promise that Christ has made atonement to God for sins and is "wisdome/rightewesnes/holynes/ and redemption/ fulfillinge the lawe for us."[34]

Trueman argues that while Frith and Tyndale are in complete agreement concerning the relationship between faith and good works, although Tyndale develops a much more explicit emphasis on this in terms of covenant conditionality, Frith has a much more objective (theocentric) view of the atonement. Guilt and propitiation are at the center of Frith's doctrine of atonement rather than the liberation of the will as in Tyndale.[35] Trueman is right that Tyndale does not speak explicitly or as often about the "propitiation of the wrath of God" as Frith does, but the contrast he establishes seems unwarranted and misleading. It is obvious that Tyndale assumes along with Frith that an important work of Christ on the cross was the objective removal of moral guilt. Tyndale spoke openly about being "hated of god" for the poison of sin and for the vengeance deserved for human guilt. Though he did stress the liberation of the will that results from faith in the work of Christ, he also clearly describes the blood of Christ as pardoning, atoning, and making satisfaction for sins condemned under the Law. In fact, he states openly that by His work on the cross Christ "peased the wrath of God."[36] According to Tyndale, it is the objective work of Christ that makes it even possible to speak about the subjective conversion of the sinner, and he assumed along with Luther that the bondage of the moral will to

---

34. *A pistle to the Christen reader* [1529], fo. iii–iiii.
35. Trueman, *Luther's Legacy*, 154–55.
36. Tyndale, [*New Testament*, 1525], sig. A iii ᵛ–[A iiii ʳ], sig. B ʳ–Bii ʳ.

sin results precisely from the estrangement of the conscience from God and from the assurance of His absolute favor.[37]

The *A pistle to the Christen reader* then proceeds by arranging Scripture quotations and paraphrases into a progressive narrative expounding the biblical themes of spiritual bondage, the Law, flesh and spirit, faith and the Gospel, the obligation of the Christian to resist the "old man of synne," and good works as the fruits of genuine faith. With regard to his interpretation of "flesh" and "sprete," Frith's anthropology reflects the particular influence of Luther in that "flesh" refers to "all things that we do/ thinke or speake/ yee our hole body soule reason/ with the cheffe and hyghest powers of them/ yf they be not led and gowerned with the Sprete of God" and "sprete" as "every outward and inward worke that a man havinge faith and cherite (which are the frutes and gyftes of the Sprete) doth worke seakinge spirituall thinges."[38]

The whole arrangement of the *A pistle* shows the influence of Luther's dialectic of Law and Gospel on the evangelical theology of Frith as was the case in *Patrick's Places*. Most of the text is simply extracted from Scripture with little or no personal exposition added by Frith, and it serves as a backdrop for his principal point that false prophets and Antichrists are identified by the ungodly behavior and lifestyle that is out of step with their profession of faith: "And perfect fayth hath with him sure hope and cherite and of these foloweth the fulfillinge of the commaundmentes necessarylye/ Even as the light foloweth the fyre." Frith blames the ignorance of the laity on the purposeful withholding of the truth by the leaders of the Church who oppress the people by religious fasts and penances. The persecution of those who try to give the light of truth to the people shows that those in power are indeed the offspring of Ishmael, the persecutor of Isaac and the symbol of all who oppress God's chosen. On account of this, Frith identifies such religious oppressors as Antichrists.[39]

Frith's quoting from Augustine in the *A pistle* reflects certain methodological legacies inherited from Humanism and does show his theological agreement with the ancient bishop at least concerning the powerlessness of the Law to make sinners righteous in the sight of

---

37. See *LW* 35 (*A Treatise on the New Testament, that is, the Holy Mass*, 1520):79; *WA* 6:353.

38. *A pistle to the Christen reader* [1529], fo. iiii–vii ʳ.

39. Ibid., fo. viii ᵛ–fo. ix.

God. However, his use of Augustine must not be stressed too far as if to diminish the particular influence of Luther's evangelical theology of Law and Gospel, and it must be remembered that the *A pistle* prefaces a translation of a work authored by Luther himself.

The *Revelation of Antichrist* is largely a translation of Luther's own exposition published in 1521. The chief charge brought against the unholy rule of the pope and his successors in both treatises is the suppression of the doctrine of justification by faith in Christ alone. Through a preaching of works-righteousness (especially ceremonial and ritualistic righteousness), and under the deceptive front of power and prestige, the ecclesiastical rulers spite the truth concerning faith, "which alone doth truly iustifye and make holye." New Testament passages, especially the epistles of Paul, are used to demonstrate that such attacks on the Gospel had been prophesied long ago by the apostles.[40] Not only popes are arraigned, but all those who are in his service, including bishops, cardinals, and priests. Even Thomas Aquinas is referred to acrimoniously as the theologian chiefly responsible for introducing the works-righteousness of Aristotle's ethical philosophy into the medieval university.[41]

The influence of Luther is apparent in objections to making Christ into a new Moses, as if Christ also compels externally without providing any spiritual assistance to accomplish good works. Instead, Christ purchased people so that He might live and reign within them and in all their works through faith.[42] Frith largely translates Luther's expanded discussion on the topic of the liberty of the Christian in rebuke of the papacy and the compulsory works it enforces upon people. Christ not only takes away the condemnation deserved by sin, but also the very occasion for sin prompted by the compulsion of the Law, which only arouses rebellion and forces the doing of works reluctantly without a free and willing heart. These are not good works at all but are sin. A righteous and true Christian needs no such compulsion, but does good works even as if there were no commandment. In the New Testament, Christ and the apostles are ministers of the Spirit, or Gospel, and not the letter, or Law.[43] On at least one occasion in another work, Frith does explicitly use "letter" and "Spirit" to differentiate a literal (physical) from

---

40. Frith, *Revelation of Antichrist* [1529], fo. x–xv ʳ, fo. xiiii ᵛ–xix ʳ; *WA* 7:722–28.
41. Frith, *Revelation of Antichrist* [1529], fo. xxxv ᵛ, lxxxiii ʳ; *WA* 7:736–39.
42. Frith, *Revelation of Antichrist* [1529], fo. xix ʳ.
43. Ibid., fo. lxii ᵛ–lxiv ᵛ.

an allegorical (figurative or spiritual) interpretation of Scripture. The most notable example of this is Jesus' command to "eat his body and drink his blood" in John 6. Frith quotes Augustine, though also in agreement with Luther, and interprets this not as a reference to the sacrament of the Eucharist but as figurative of abiding in Christ through faith.[44] Nevertheless, the hermeneutical association of "letter" and "Spirit" with "Law" and "Gospel" is more typical of Frith's writings. Although Augustine also spoke in this way and influenced Luther to a certain degree, Frith's contrast of compulsory obedience under the force of the Law versus the freedom of the Christian for true obedience through justifying faith in the *Revelation of Antichrist* is carried directly over from Luther's own treatise.

Although the proper ministry of Christ and the apostles was the preaching of the Gospel, Frith's treatise also acknowledges that the gospels teach good works, but they do not do this harshly or with the same force of compulsion as under Moses. Rather, Christ and the apostles exhort gently concerning what to do and leave undone: "So he hath not delivered vs from the lawe/ but from the power and violence of the lawe/ which is the very true losinge/ gevinge all men libertye at their awne perill to do other good or evill." True Christian freedom is not freedom from obedience to the Law, but freedom from the obedience compelled by the fear of punishment. In Christ fear is removed and replaced by the freedom of a willingness to obey. The temporal government, however, is still necessary for the compulsion of outward obedience and for the punishment of evil, but they serve those who are not yet of His kingdom, "untyll they are made spirituall/ and then frely and with a glade harte serve god." The popes, then, corrupt the faith by creating new opportunities for sin by binding consciences to so many laws, traditions, and ceremonies, and by deceiving the people into thinking they are righteous in obeying them. In this way they have put consciences in bondage all over again after Christ came to set them free. For Luther and Frith, this is nothing less than the work of the Antichrist.[45]

Frith appends his own brief statement encouraging the Christian reader to charity, patience, and to fighting the antichrists in the Church with good living rather than with violence. Though Wright is correct to

---

44. See *A boke made by Iohn Frith prisoner in the tower of London answeringe vnto M mores lettur* [1533], sig. C.3., [C.7.ᵛ]–[C.8.].

45. Frith, *Revelation of Antichrist* [1529], fo. lxii ᵛ–lxiv ᵛ; WA 7:759–60.

point out that Luther's treatise rages on to the end of the work without a similar word of explicit restraint or caution, the German reformer likewise in the 1520s argued that such corruption in the leadership is not justification for militant insurrection, even when that corruption could be interpreted with such apocalyptic invective.[46]

Following the *Revelation of Antichrist*, Frith attached the *Antithesis, wherin are compared to geder Christes actes and oure holye father the Popes*. This is an adaptation and considerable expansion of an anonymously published tract probably belonging to Philipp Melancthon entitled *Passional Christi und Antichristi* (1521), which included a series of illustrative woodcuts designed by Lucas Cranach. Whereas Melancthon's *Passional* contained only thirteen theses, Frith's *Antithesis* expands the number to seventy-eight, and only eleven from the *Passional* are paralleled in the *Antithesis*.[47]

The series of theses vividly contrast the humble lifestyle of Jesus and his teachings on faith and love over against the material opulence, power obsession, and legalistic tyranny of the Pope and his bishops. A few theses in particular speak more directly to the subject of Law and Gospel and the priority of faith before good works.

Frith contrasts the teaching of the "lawe" by Christ and Moses with the "Pope and his Bisshopes" and "their awne traditions." Although Frith could differentiate between the law of Christ and the whole Law of Moses, this does not mean that Christ's moral teachings are anything new in substance from the Law of the Decalogue. Rather, his point here is to contrast the divine origin of the Mosaic laws and the teachings of Christ with the man-made accretions of the medieval Catholic Church. Furthermore, Christ not only practiced what he preached, but He "confirmed it with his awne death." In fact, as a later thesis testifies, Christ satisfied both the "old law and the new/ and all rightewesnes." Another thesis states that "Christes lawe is fulfilled thorow charite." The clergy, however, have utterly ignored "christes" law so as to erect their own to "maynten their fatte belyes."[48]

---

46. Frith, *Revelation of Antichrist* [1529], lxxxvii ᵛ; Wright, *Work of John Frith*, 36–37; *LW* 45 (*Temporal Authority: To What Extent it Should Be Obeyed*, 1523): 105, 111–12; *WA* 11:261–62, 266–67; *LW* 40 ("Letter to the Princes of Saxony Concerning the Rebellious Spirit," 1524): 49–59; *WA* 15:210–21.

47. Wright, *Work of John Frith*, 35, 37.

48. Frith, *Antithesis* [1529], fo. xci ᵛ–xcii ʳ (theses xxiii-xxiiii), xciii ʳ (thesis xxvxi), xcvi (thesis lv), xcviii ʳ (thesis lxiiii).

Frith sounds like Tyndale when stating that "Christ promisseth forgyvnes of synnes. And the kingdome of heven vnto them that repent and will amend their lyves." As often the case with Tyndale in the 1530s, faith in Christ alone is not explicitly mentioned here in connection with the forgiveness of sins, but it is assumed by Frith as much as it was by Tyndale. The stress in this particular statement is on the concomitance of a true justifying faith in Christ with a heart of repentance.[49]

In another thesis Frith uses the tree and fruit analogy used before by Luther and Tyndale to illustrate the priority of faith before all good works, which are the outward testimony of inward faith. Nevertheless, Frith cautions that human judgment in discerning inward justification by outward works is not infallible. Only God is able to see true faith in Christ before that faith, working through love, is demonstrated in deeds before the watching eyes of the world: "although we can not know the tre is good/ but by his frute (for we can iudge nothinge but by his outward operation) yet god seyth the quickenes in the rote/ which in the tyme that god hath apoynted him/ shall bringe forth his frute. And approveth the tre to be good/ although he seme dead vnto vs. The tre is faith which is the mother of all good workes/ which ever worketh by charite when he seyth occasyon."[50] Thus, Frith shares Luther's evangelical theology that true justifying faith in Christ produces love and good deeds and that God, and only God, knows infallibly that such faith ("the tre") is good and right for justification before any outward actions ("frute") are observable to others.

Frith returned to England for a brief period during Lent in 1531, and this is somewhat surprising since Thomas More had succeeded Cardinal Wolsey as Chancellor to King Henry VIII. Despite the intensity of Wolsey's campaign to suppress heresy, it is said that he "lacked the persecutor's temperament."[51] It was under Thomas More, who was given license in 1528 from Bishop Tunstall to refute heretical works in the vernacular,[52] that focus shifted with intensified urgency to the burning of heretics more than their writings.[53] Thomas Bilney, who had

49. Ibid., fo. xcv ʳ (theses xlvi–xlvii), xciiii ʳ (thesis xxxix).

50. Ibid., xcix ᵛ–xciiʳ (thesis lxxi).

51. Elton, *Reform and Reformation*, 96, 127; Tjernagel, *Henry VIII and the Lutherans*, 28.

52. *L&P* 4.2:1788.

53. Haigh, *English Reformations*, 67; D'Alton, "The Suppression of Lutheran Heretics," 241, 244, 253.

been persuaded to abjure for his earlier offense, resumed his reforming activities and was martyred at the stake in August of 1531. Others, such as Richard Bayfield and John Lambert, experienced a similar fate.[54] The list of prohibited books had grown considerably by 1530, and now more works were appearing by English exiles.[55] The King had been mustering support in the latter half of the 1520s for a divorce from Catherine of Aragon, and though Henry had earlier praised Tyndale's fealty to higher authority in *Obedience of A Christian Man* (1528), he now had to contend with Tyndale's objection to the divorce in his *Practice of Prelates* (1530).[56] Thus, on the one hand, things had become worse, not better, for English evangelicals by 1531. On the other hand, Stephen Vaughn had been commissioned by the English court to seek out and persuade both Tyndale and Frith to return to England under royal protection, albeit unsuccessfully.[57] Indeed, the situation for protagonists of evangelical reform would shift in their favor by the mid-1530s, beginning with More's resignation as Chancellor in 1532, the appointment of Cranmer as Archbishop of Canterbury in 1532, the crowning of Anne as Queen in 1533, the elevation of Thomas Cromwell to the role of Vicegerent of Spirituals in 1535, and parliamentary negotiations with German Protestants that peaked between the years 1536 and 1538.[58]

Foxe narrates the arrest of Frith at Reading, and this most likely took place during his brief return to England in 1531,[59] though some scholars have dated it to his final return to England in July of 1532 (Daniell's article in the *ODNB* incorrectly identifies 1531 as the year of his final return). Raynor at least leaves open the possibility that the arrest took place in 1532.[60]

---

54. Marshall, *Reformation England*, 28; Raynor, *John Frith, Scholar and Martyr*, 86.

55. Hume, "English Protestant Books Printed Abroad," in Schuster, Marius, Lusardi, and Schoeck, *Complete Works of Thomas More*, 8.3:1065–92.

56. Marshall, *Reformation England*, 36–39.

57. Wright, *Work of John Frith*, 13; Raynor, *John Frith, Scholar and Martyr*, 92–97.

58. Tjernagel, *Henry VIII and the Lutherans*, 26, 73, 77–79; Marshall, *Reformation England*, 40–47.

59. Raynor, *John Frith, Scholar and Martyr*, 87–89; Wright, *Work of John Frith*, 12–13.

60. *ODNB* 21:42; *DNB* 7:719; Loane, *Pioneers*, 16; Raynor, *John Frith, Scholar and Martyr*, 82, 118–19.

Foxe records that Frith "came over for exhibition of the Prior of Readyng (as is thought) and had the Prior ouer with hym."⁶¹ In Foxe's *Whole Works*, the Prior of Reading Abbey is described among Frith's "frendes," and scholars have indeed identified this Prior as one who had for some time been actively involved in the underground evangelical reform movement.⁶² Reading was a monastery known early on as a receptacle of Luther's works.⁶³ While at Reading, Frith was arrested as a "vacabound" and "set in the stockes." He was eventually released due to the intervention of the local schoolmaster, Leonard Cox, a very learned man who developed a scholarly admiration for Frith. Again, Foxe leaves out the details but seems to imply that Frith then fled persecution and returned to the Continent before his final return to England and arrest in London in 1532. Many scholars have overlooked Foxe's claim that after Frith was released from the stocks, Thomas More, identified as still "Chancellour of England" (until May 1532) "persecuted hym both by lande *and sea*" (my italics).⁶⁴

After this first brief return to England, Frith reappeared in Antwerp and published his *A disputacio[n] of purgatorye*.⁶⁵ He was also probably involved in seeing Tyndale's *Answer to More* (1531) through the press.⁶⁶ As Wright suggests, the *Disputation of Purgatory* moves Frith more into "the realm of original theological writing." It demonstrates his abilities as a skilled theologian as well as his confidence as a polemicist. It certainly is the first ever extensive biblical and theological argument against the doctrine of purgatory published by an English evangelical. However, the assertion that this work reflects originality can be potentially misleading. While it must be acknowledged that, unlike his earlier works, the *Disputation of Purgatory* is neither a translation nor direct adaptation of any single writing belonging to another reformer, its evangelical theology reflects the influence of Luther.

---

61. Foxe, *A&M* [1570], 1174.

62. "Martirdome of Iohn Frith," *Whole Works*; Raynor, *John Frith, Scholar and Martyr*, 87–88; Wright, *Work of John Frith*, 12; Clark, *John Frith: Kentish Martyr*, 9.

63. Rupp, *Studies in the Making*, 11–12; Rupp, *Righteousness of God*, 37.

64. Foxe, *A&M* [1570], 1174.

65. *A disputacio[n] of purgatorye made by Ioh[a]n Frith*, [1531?].

66. Wright, *Work of John Frith*, 10–11; Raynor, *John Frith, Scholar and Martyr*, 94; Loane, *Pioneers*, 11–12; Clebsch, *England's Earliest Protestants*, 95.

As far as his rejection of the doctrine of purgatory itself is concerned, the influence of Luther cannot be dismissed, although Zwingli also objected to the existence of purgatory in the *67 Articles* (1523).[67] In the *Ninety-Five Theses* (1517) the existence of purgatory was simply assumed by Luther despite the abuses surrounding the sale of indulgences.[68] Even by 1521, Luther still retained a personal belief in it though admitting he was unable to prove it by Scripture or reason. For this cause, he left the matter open to individual conscience. However, by this time Luther was also arguing that certain passages of Scripture had been incorrectly interpreted as referring to purgatory when they actually spoke about the suffering of the saints on earth. He also objected to grounding belief in purgatory on a statement about praying for the dead in the intertestamental apocryphal book 1 Maccabees, the canonicity of which he rejected.[69] Although Trueman pushes Luther's objection to the doctrine of purgatory all the way back to 1530, by 1522 and thereafter, Luther, still of the opinion that purgatory is not an article of faith provable by Scripture, had now come to openly deny that it was even a particular place. Instead, he stressed the taste of hell that the just experience in this life as the true purgatory and suggested that all souls after death, with few exceptions, lie in a bodiless sleep until the final resurrection and Day of Judgment.[70] Frith echoes both Luther and Tyndale in expressing some agnosticism concerning the experience of dead saints on the basis of the silence of Scripture, and he simply affirms as they did that justified souls are "resting in peace" in God's keeping and will be reunited with their resurrected bodies in full glory at the Last Judgment.[71]

67. Stephens, *Theology of Huldrych Zwingli*, 118.

68. *LW* 31 (Theses 17–19, *Ninety Five Theses*, 1517): 26–27; *WA* 1:234. See also *LW* 31 (Theses 17–19, *Explanations of the Ninety-Five Theses*, 1518): 125– 45; *WA* 1:559–67.

69. *LW* 32 ("The Thirty-Seventh Article," *Defense and Explanation of All the Articles*, 1521): 95; *WA* 7:450, 452.

70. Trueman, *Luther's Legacy*, 130; *LW* 48 ("To Nicholas von Amsdorf. Warburg, January 13, 1522"): 360–62; *WA Br* 2:422–23; *LW* 52 ("The Gospel for the Festival of the Epiphany, Matthew 2[:1–12]," 1522): 180; *WA* 101a: 588–89. For Luther on "soul sleep," see also Althaus, *Theology of Martin Luther*, 414–17.

71. Frith, *A disputacio[n] of purgatorye* [1531], i 2. See also Frith's personal commentary on *The testament of William Tracy* [1535], sig. C ; Wright, *Work of John Frith*, 45 (and n. 6); Day, "Tyndale and Frith," in Day, Lund, and O'Donnell, *Word, Church, and State*, 176–81. For Tyndale on the state of dead believers before the resurrection of the last days, see his *exposition of 1 John* [1531], E iii ʳ. See also the comments he makes

Frith's own objections to the existence of purgatory on the basis of the lack of exegetical support reflects the influence of Luther, but even more significant to his case is the doctrine of justification by faith in Christ alone, which Frith concludes does away with any need for purgatory. Luther's own increasing objections to the existence of purgatory in the early 1520s seem to be made more on the grounds of its lacking exegetical support in Scripture rather than by emphasizing the doctrine of justification by faith in Christ alone, although he later recounts how the preaching of the Gospel naturally swept away belief in purgatory and all the ritual piety associated with it.[72] Whether or not Frith's application of the doctrine of justification by faith in Christ alone in objection to the existence of purgatory was itself influenced by Luther, his understanding of justification and his evangelical theology of Law and Gospel is very much the legacy of the German reformer.

The *Disputation on Purgatory* is split up into three books, each dealing with a different Catholic opponent and his unique contribution to defending the doctrine of purgatory. The first book is a response to the printer and brother-in-law of Thomas More, John Rastell, and his use of natural reason in *A New Book of Purgatory* (1530). The second book is predominantly a response to the exegetical arguments of Thomas More in *The Supplication of Souls* (1529). Rastell and More's own treatises were both inspired by recent objections to purgatory made by Simon Fish in his *The Supplication of Beggars* (1528). Fish is mentioned by name in Frith's prologue. His attack on the doctrine of purgatory, however, was not so much on theological or exegetical grounds but on the basis that the doctrine of purgatory is a front for the greed of the ecclesiastical magisterium: "that the pope were a mercilesse tyraunte whych (as he sayeth humsilfe) maye delyuer them from thence and wyll not excepte he haue monye." The criticisms Fish made against the claims of papal power over souls in purgatory are reminiscent of Luther in his *Ninety-Five Theses*, wherein Luther acknowledges the justifiable complaints of the laity regarding the selling of indulgences.[73] Frith's third book cri-

---

in context of a disagreement he and Frith both had with George Joye who identified the "resurrection" with the separation of soul and body at death. Joye had even altered Tyndale's translation of "resurrection" in John chapter five to "verie lyfe." See "Willyam Tindale/ yet once more to the christen Reader," *Newe Testament* [1534], sig. **.v.^r-[**.vi.^v].

72. See *LW* 26 (*Lectures on Galatians*, 1535): 221; *WA* 40¹:353.

73. Frith, "A prologe," *A disputacio[n] of purgatorye* [1531?] sig. [a 7 ^r], sig. [g 8]; *LW* 31 (Thesis 82, *Ninety Five Theses*, 1517), 32; *WA* 1:237; Loane, *Pioneers*, 12.

tiques the patristic resourcement and biblical exegesis of John Fisher, Bishop of Rochester, in his *Assertionis Lutheranae Confutationem* (1523). Fisher had denounced Luther in two public sermons preached at St. Paul's in London (1521 and 1526), and his *Confutatio* was written in refutation of Luther's *Assertio Omnium Articulorum* (1520), a work of self-defense against the papal bull *Exurge Domine*.[74] In the case of both Rastell and Fisher, Frith argues somewhat on their terms but makes his ultimate and definitive appeal to the authority of Scripture: "Suffer therfore all thinges, whatsoeuer they be/ to be tryed and examined by the Scripture."[75]

Rastell's book is a dialogue between a Muslim Turk named Gingemin and a Christian named Comingo, the former proving to the latter by the use of natural reason the existence of God, the immortality of the soul, and the doctrine of purgatory. Frith does not even deal with the first two doctrines and encapsulates his objection to the third by arguing that "it is hoellye iniuryous vnto the bloude of Chryst and the destruccyon of all chrysten fayth" to believe in purgatory.[76] The only "purgatoryes" necessary are, first, the cleansing of the heart through faith in Christ who made full atonement for sin and appeesed the wrath of the Father: "This faith purefyth the harte and geueth us a will and gladdnes to do what so euer oure most mercifull father commaundeth us." The second is the experience of adversity and tribulation. This is necessary even for the elect because of the weakness in "oure membres," "that we can not eschewe sinne as oure harte wolde and as oure will desyreth," and so "that we maye remembre his lawe and mortefye the olde Adam and fleshlye lust which els wolde waxe so rebellious that it wolde subdue vs/ raigne in vs and holde vs thraulde under sinne." These purgatories will cease to be necessary after death, "when deeth hath subdued oure coruptible bodye/ and oure flesh committed to rest in the erth ..."[77] Even though Christians are still sinners in the imperfection of their faith and love, and though the rebelliousness of the flesh wages war against the obedience of the Spirit, yet they are fully righteous in

---

74. Wright, *Work of John Frith*, 39 (and n. 3); Rex, *Theology of John Fisher*, 80–81.

75. Frith, *A disputacio[n] of purgatorye* [1531?], sig. a 3 ᵛ ("Johan Frith unto the Christen Reader"), sig. [a 8ᵛ], c 3 ʳ, h 3 ᵛ–h 4 ʳ.

76. Ibid., sig. [a 7 ᵛ–a 8 ʳ] ("A prologe. Wherbye a man maye the better perceaue the occasyon and hole cause of thys boke"), [b 8 ᵛ]–c ʳ.

77. Ibid., sig. a 5 ("unto the Christen Reader"), b 3 ʳ, b 5.

Christ and His atonement so that sin is neither "imputed nor rekened" to them.⁷⁸ The idea that Christians have the beginnings of the Spirit and love while their remaining sins and imperfections are not imputed to them is certainly Augustinian in form but is not so unlike Luther's own doctrine of *"simul justus et peccator"* and the proleptic element in his theology of justification. The particular influence of Luther's evangelical theology is found in Frith's emphasis on Christ and His atonement as the extrinsic righteousness that justifies the sinner in acceptance before God. Frith's stress on suffering and affliction as a necessary "medicyne" for aiding the Christian in the mortification of the sinful flesh until the redemption of the body also echoes statements made by Luther.⁷⁹

Frith objects to the idea that a loss of the fear of purgatory would encourage people to sin, when in fact to abstain only because of fear is itself already sin and is to live under the Law: "For we ought not to abstayne from euel because of the punishment that foloweth the cryme but onlye for the loue that we have vnto god with out any respect either of saluacyon or of damnacyon." Whereas human laws are satisfied by outward observance, God "requireth a thing to be done with a wel willinge harte/ and euen for pure loue." A heart that obeys begrudgingly resists both the Law and the God who made it.⁸⁰ This reflects the influence of Luther's own thoughts on the power of the Law, Christian liberty, and the nature of truly good works.

Frith describes God dealing with Christians on the basis that He "clothe[s] vs with a nother mannes iustice [that is Christes]." Christ's obedience even unto death belongs to the sinner through faith and is counted as if it were his or her own obedience and death.⁸¹ Scholars have argued that Frith never expresses an understanding of justification

---

78. Ibid., sig. a 2 ᵛ ("unto the Christen Reader"), b 3 ᵛ–b 4 ʳ; See also Frith, *An other boke against Rastel* [1537?], sig. [B.viii. ᵛ]–C.i. This work was written in 1532 while Frith was in prison as a rejoinder to the criticisms made by Rastell against his 1531 treatise on purgatory. It was not published until or after 1537 with a short preface describing the death of Frith and the conversion of Rastell. See Wright, *Work of John Frith*, 46.

79. Frith, *A disputacio[n] of purgatorye* [1531?], a 6 ʳ ("unto the Christen Reader"); See *LW* 25 (*scholia on Romans*, 1515–16): 340; *WA* 56:350; See also *LW* 35 (*The Holy and Blessed Sacrament of Baptism*, 1519): 33–37; *WA* 2:728, 731–33; *LW* 36 (*Babylonian Captivity of the Church*, 1520): 124; *WA* 6:572; *LW* 35 (*Preface to the Epistle of St. Paul to the Romans*, 1546): 371–72, 377–78; *WA DB* 7:12–13, 22–23.

80. Frith, *A disputacio[n] of purgatorye* [1531?], sig. [c 6 ᵛ]–[c 7].

81. Ibid., sig. h 2 ᵛ–h 3 ʳ.

as imputed righteousness in Christ. McGrath argues that Frith stresses the non-imputation of sin within an entirely sanative, proleptic, and Augustinian theology of justification. This claim, however, rests largely on the consideration of only one single statement, wherein Frith in a series of antitheses contrasts the inheritance of original sin with the gift of the righteousness of Christ: "Thorow Adam/Adams sinne was counted oure awne. Thorow Christ/ Christes rightwysness is reputed unto us for oure awne." McGrath argues that this contrast utilizes "Augustinian presuppositions."[82] To be sure, the Adam-sin/Christ-righteousness dialectic of Romans 5:12–21 was a favorite of Augustine with regard to his doctrine of original sin contrasted with divine grace,[83] but Frith's particular use of "reputed unto us for oure awne" is significant when interpreted in the light of other similar statements. Trueman agrees that nowhere does Frith speak explicitly of the "great exchange" occurring between the sinner and Christ in justification, but nevertheless observes that the concept of union with Christ was an intricate part of his understanding of justification: "Christ deals with God on man's behalf, and man is thus saved by virtue of this union."[84] Trueman is right to highlight the importance of union with Christ in Frith's doctrine of justification by faith, but he gives no explicit consideration to the likelihood that this was borrowed from Luther. It was the legacy of Melancthon upon later Lutheranism that more strictly described the imputation of the righteousness of Christ in justification using legal and forensic terminology whereas Luther often used the language of personal union.[85] On the basis of other statements made by Frith indicating that Christ's righteousness "clothe[s]" the Christian and that His righteous obedience unto death belongs to the sinner as if it were his or her very own, it seems just as accurate, if not more, to paraphrase Frith as saying that "God deals with man on Christ's behalf." Though perhaps not using the precise terminology of "imputed righteousness," which only becomes most prevalent in Luther in the 1530s, Frith does clearly indicate that the atoning righteousness of Christ that satisfied the wrath of God belongs completely to the Christian through faith alone as if it

---

82. Clebcsh, *England's Earliest Protestants*, 115; Knox, *Doctrine of Faith*, 44; McGrath, *Iustitia Dei*, 286 (and n.7).

83. Kelly, *Early Christian Doctrines*, 390–95.

84. Trueman, *Luther's Legacy*, 124, 133–34.

85. McGrath, *Iustitia Dei*, 182, 189–90, 199–201, 210–12.

were his or her very own. At the same time, the particular stress Luther himself placed on the reckoning of the alien righteousness of Christ in justification did not prevent him from speaking of justification using proleptic and sanative language and of the non-imputation of sin in the life of the Christian led by the Spirit.[86]

According to Frith, apart from the work of Christ, "al the repentaunce in the worlde coulde not satisfye for one synne."[87] This does not mean that Frith considered repentance unnecessary. Luther and Tyndale were both adamant that justifying faith in Christ cannot exist without following the humility of repentance under the Law, but that there is also a repentance and contrition that, without faith and hope in the Gospel, actually keeps one in bondage to sin.[88] In the context of Frith's statement, his intention is to refute the reasoning of Rastell that he perceives logically excludes the need for the work of Christ by giving repentance itself justifying power. Frith had already rejected this idea in his *A pistle to the Christen reader* in 1529. Frith describes a "repentance without fayth and is such a repentance as Judas and Rastels christen men which continue styll in synne/ haue at the later ende whych doth rather purchace them an halter then the remission of synnes." Although the only other repentance Frith identifies explicitly in this context is that which follows after justification, this is not to say that Frith ever denied the role of repentance or contrition as a necessary antecedent to justifying faith in the Gospel. In 1533, Frith received a letter from Tyndale encouraging him to avoid disputation on more complex matters involving the presence of Christ in the Lord's Supper and instead to "expounde the law truly, and open the vayle of Moses to condemne all flesh, and proue all men sinners, and all deedes vnder the law, before mercy haue taken away the condemnation therof, to be sinne and damnable."[89] The point Frith is making in his dispute with Rastell is that repentance in itself cannot satisfy the Law of God and remove the guilt

---

86. Althaus, *Theology of Martin Luther*, 226, 238–40.

87. Frith, *A disputacio[n] of purgatorye* [1531?], sig. c 3 ʳ, c 5, d–d 2 ʳ.

88. Tyndale, *Obedience* [1528], fo. xcvi ᵛ; Tyndale, *Parable of the Wicked Mammon* [1528], fo. lvii ᵛ; *LW* 25 (*scholia* on Romans, 1515-16): 240–41, 251–54, 340; *WA* 56:253–55, 254, 265–66, 350.

89. See "An other notable and worthy letter of maister William Tyndale sent to the sayd Iohn Frith, vnder the name of Jacob" (1533), in Foxe, *Whole Works*, 455. On the necessary acknowledgment of guilt, bondage, and corruption, see also Frith, *A mirroure to know thyselfe* [1536?], Aiii ᵛ.

of sin. Frith is also clear that the life of repentance that follows after faith in the Christian life cannot satisfy or remit the guilt of past sins but is only concerned with chastening the flesh out of love for God.[90]

Although Frith denies that any person can make satisfaction to God, he does believe that there is such a thing as making satisfaction to another person against whom an offense has been made. In fact, God will not forgive the offense of the guilty party "unlesse" he or she is willing to set things right. On the other hand, neither will God forgive the sins committed by the one offended unless he or she is willing to receive his or her repentant neighbor with forgiveness. Frith's comments appear to make God's forgiveness conditional upon the work of human reconciliation and forgiveness.[91] Though Frith does not explicitly elaborate the point, his theological assumptions were the same as that of Luther and Tyndale in that working toward reconciliation and peace and having a willingness to forgive others is a sign of the indwelling Spirit and of justifying favor with God through a repenting faith in Christ.[92]

Frith's response to the common objection that the evangelical gospel of justification by faith in Christ alone renders good works irrelevant is reminiscent of earlier comments made by Tyndale, and before him Luther. Although good works do not justify because Christ alone is "thy wisdome/rightwysnes/halowinge and redempcyon," they should be done for the simple fact that God has commanded them, for the good and welfare of others, drawing them to God by the means of charity, as well as for the taming of the flesh. According to Frith, good works are also a "testymonie" of belonging to God. Trueman argues that Frith is similar to Tyndale in allowing works to have a "secondary role" in assurance, but that he does not develop this as profoundly as does Tyndale in his theology of covenant conditionality. Luther also believed that works reassure Christians of the authenticity of their faith, but not just

---

90. See *An other boke against Rastel* [1537?], sig. C.v.–[C.vii.].

91. Frith, *A disputacio[n] of purgatorye* [1531?], sig. d 3– [d 4], [d 6 ʳ]. See also Trueman, *Luther's Legacy*, 139. On the necessity of making civil satisfaction for offenses against others, see also Frith, *An other boke against Rastel* [1537?], sig. [C.viii.].

92. Tyndale, *Parable of the Wicked Mammon* [1528], fo. xxiv ᵛ–xxv ʳ; Tyndale, *Obedience* [1528], fo. xciiii ᵛ–xcv. See also fo. xcvi ᵛ, xcviii ᵛ–xc ʳ; Luther, "A sermon for the second Sunday after Mary's Ascension. Preached at Wittenberg by Dr. Martin Luther, 1522," *Complete Sermons*, 2.2:296–97; *WA* 10³:278; *LW* 30 (*Lectures on I John*, 1527): 298, 309; *WA* 20:749, 768–71; *LC*, Tappert, 432–33; Kolb & Wengert, 352–54; *BSLK*, 682–85.

any works. Like Luther and Tyndale, Frith defines truly good works as characterized by selfless motivation: "Therfore must thou do thy workes with a single yie/ hauinge neither respecte vnto the ioyes of heauen/ neither yet to the paynes of hell/ but onlye do them for the profyte of thy neyghboure as god commaundeth thee/ and let hym alone wyth the resydue."[93] Frith recognizes that the intent of the Christian to do good works and to refrain from sin is always obstructed and opposed by the desires of the flesh. His description of the Christian struggle with sin is a close paraphrase of Romans 7 and hearkens back to the earlier prologues to Romans written by Luther and Tyndale. Frith asserts that God is "pacefyed" by the will and conscience that delights in and consents to His Law, hates sin, and desires to do what is right even though the old nature continues to desire the exact opposite. This does not mean, however, that love toward the Law is what justifies the sinner in the sight of God. Frith has already stated that Christ atoned the wrath of God and that the sinner is justified in Him through faith alone, but, as Luther and Tyndale both argued, God also promises that He does not impute sins to those who earnestly desire to do what is right, not giving consent in the conscience to sin despite the sinful impulses of the flesh: "pardone us oure trespaces/ and accepte oure good will for the full dede." Such a person who has these qualities is indeed already justified in the sight of God and has the Spirit of God through genuine repentance and faith in Christ.[94] For Frith, this fact removes any need for a post-mortem satisfaction of sins in purgatory. Frith also uses phrases like "consenteth to the law of god," "begynneth to loue the lawe," and "desyre to fulfylle the law of God,"[95] which are characteristic of both Tyndale and Luther.[96]

93. Frith, *A disputacio[n] of purgatorye* [1531?], sig. [d 8 ᵛ]–sig. e ʳ. On good works and resistance to sin as evidences of justifying faith, see also *An other boke against Rastel* [1537?], sig. C.ii. ᵛ– [C.iii.]. On the practical reasons for doing good works, see sig. [C.viii. ᵛ]–[D.ii.ʳ]. On faith and having a will to fulfill the Law as personal assurances of election, see Frith, *A myrroure or lokynge glasse wherin you may beholde the sacramente of baptisme* [1548?], sig. B ii ʳ; Trueman, *Luther's Legacy*, 149.

94. Frith, *A disputacio[n] of purgatorye* [1531?], sig. c 4–c 5 ʳ; Tyndale, *Romayns* [1526], sig. [b vii ʳ]; *LW* 35 (*Preface to the Epistle of St. Paul to the Romans*, 1546): 377; *WA DB* 7:22–23. See also *LW* 35 (*The Holy and Blessed Sacrament of Baptism*, 1519): 33–37; *WA* 2:728, 731–33; *LW* 36 (*Babylonian Captivity of the Church*, 1520): 124; *WA* 6:572.

95. See *An other boke against Rastel* [1537?], sig. C iiii–C v; Tyndale, *Romayns* [1526], sig. [b iiii ʳ].

96. See *LW* 35 (*Preface to the Epistle of St. Paul to the Romans*, 1546): 366–67, 375; *WA DB* 6:4–7, 18–19.

In his second book, after pointing out Augustine's own ambivalence toward the doctrine of purgatory nearly 400 years after the time of Christ, Frith then predominantly challenges More's exegesis of Scripture. Many of the passages he discusses are those already treated by Luther earlier in 1521, which actually speak of the hellish experience of the saints living on earth, including Hezekiah, David, and the saints passing through the fires of persecution in 1 Corinthians 3. Frith also follows Luther in rejecting the apocryphal book of 1 Maccabees as a valid authority on which to establish the doctrine of purgatory as an article of faith.[97]

Although exegetical arguments resurface in the third book, Frith's unique contention with Fisher in the last part of the *Disputation of Purgatory* is his use of the opinions of the Church Fathers. Frith's attack against Fisher is itself written in response to Fisher's own blast against Luther's theology. Rex argues that Fisher was the first Catholic polemicist to target the doctrine of justification by faith in Christ alone as central to Luther's thought and, thus, to identify it as his principal error. Fisher also attacked Luther's objections to making purgatory a necessary article of faith.[98] Therefore, it can reasonably be said that Frith's reply is, at least in part, written in defense of Luther and his theology of justification.

Frith's argument with Fisher on the basis of biblical exegesis and patristic testimony shows influences of his background in Humanism but it also demonstrates that two scholars could equally appropriate its methodology with different theological presuppositions and conclusions. With regard to Fisher, this was to uphold Catholic orthodoxy on the doctrine of justification and purgatory. Frith quotes from Fisher who openly acknowledged that the Fathers seldom discuss purgatory, but goes beyond him in actually using the words of Augustine, Ambrose, and Jerome on the afterlife to support his argument for its complete non-existence. Yet, this does not mean that Frith was looking to the Church Fathers as the final authority in doctrinal matters. Regardless of patristic opinion on purgatory, Frith argues that the au-

97. Frith, *A disputacio[n] of purgatorye* [1531?], sig. [e 6 ᵛ]–[e 7 ʳ], [e 8 ʳ], f, f 3 ᵛ–f 8 ʳ, g 3 ʳ–g 5 ʳ; *LW* 32 ("The Thirty-Seventh Article," *Defense and Explanation of All the Articles*, 1521): 95; *WA* 7:451–52.

98. Frith, *A disputacio[n] of purgatorye* [1531?], sig. i 4 ᵛ; *LW* 32 ("The Thirty-Seventh Article," *Defense and Explanation of All the Articles*, 1521): 95; *WA* 7:351–52; Rex, *Theology of John Fisher*, 88.

thority of the Fathers is secondary and only derivative of the supreme authority of Scripture. Although even Fisher recognized the possibility of error in the Fathers, Frith parts with Fisher in denying that the Pope acts as the rightful arbiter of truth and error in such disputed matters. Frith's response echoes Luther's own position in debate with John Eck of Ingolstadt at Leipzig in 1519. Although Frith references the words of Augustine in support of the Word of God in Scripture as alone trustworthy,[99] Frith is undoubtedly influenced by the evangelical theology of Luther and Tyndale.

Other themes in the *Disputation on Purgatory* that show the influence of Luther's evangelical theology are found in Frith's objection to the use of outward coercion in matters of the conscience where faith, the Holy Spirit, and the Word of God alone should rule,[100] as well as his identification of the "keys" in Matthew 16 as the preaching of repentance and faith, or Law and Gospel, rather than the sacerdotal imposition of penances and the exercise of power over purgatory.[101] Many of these ideas certainly might have come by Luther to Frith through the influence of Tyndale, and Frith does explicitly refer his readers to the description of "what the church of Christ is" in Tyndale's *Answer to More* (1531).[102]

In July of 1532, Frith made his second and last return to England. Why he did so continues to puzzle scholars, but some have suggested that the resignation of Thomas More as Lord Chancellor in May might have encouraged Frith to return to England to help shepherd the evangelical reform movement.[103] Whatever the reason for his return, Frith found himself a target of the policies of More still in activation under Bishop Stokesley of London, and he had to constantly elude capture. He

---

99. Frith, *A disputacio[n] of purgatorye* [1531?], sig. h 5 ᵛ–i ʳ.

100. Ibid., sig. i 5. For Luther and non-coercion in matters of faith, see *LW* 30 (*Sermons on I Peter*, 1522): 19–21; 75–79; *WA* 12:275–77, 329–33; *LW* 46 (*Against the Robbing and Murdering Hordes of Peasants*, 1525), 51; *WA* 18:358–59; *LW* 45 (*Temporal Authority: To What Extent It Should Be Obeyed*, 1522–23): 88–91, 95, 100; *WA* 11:250–52, 254–55, 258; *LW* 40 ("Letter to the Princes of Saxony Concerning the Rebellious Spirit," 1524): 49–59; *WA* 15:210–21.

101. Frith, *A disputacio[n] of purgatorye* [1531?], sig. i 6 ᵛ–i 7 ʳ; Tyndale, *Obedience*, fo. clx; *LW* 32 (*Defense and Explanation of All the Articles*, 1521): 74–76; *WA* 7:420–22.

102. Frith, *A disputacio[n] of purgatorye* [1531?], i 4 ᵛ.

103. Raynor, *John Frith, Scholar and Martyr*, 113; Clark, *John Frith: Kentish Martyr*, 12; Wright, *Work of John Frith*, 14.

was eventually arrested in October on Milton Shore in Essex, apparently in the middle of preparing to leave for the Continent with the Prior of Reading and to be reunited with his wife and children. Instead, Frith was imprisoned in the Tower of London where he would compose most of his last writings and live out the greater length of his final months before being transferred to Newgate prison and executed at Smithfield on July 4, 1533.[104]

It must have been in the tower that Frith composed the prefatory letter to his commentary on the last will and testament of William Tracy.[105] Though there has been some confusion concerning where and when the writing of the commentary actually occurred, John Day has recently provided strong evidence suggesting that it was written between March and October of 1531 during or shortly after Frith's first return to England. In the commentary itself, Frith makes no mention of Tracy's body being exhumed (October 1532), so it is likely that the commentary was written prior to this event. On the other hand, Frith does appear to refer implicitly to the sentence that was passed by Convocation against Tracy's will, which means that the commentary cannot be dated any earlier than March of 1531. Since Tyndale does refer twice to the posthumous burning of Tracy's body in his own commentary, Day concludes that Frith must have written his commentary first. However, Frith does make mention of the exhuming in the brief prefatory letter to his commentary, which Day dates separately to the time of his imprisonment in 1532. It is difficult to ascertain how Frith's commentary and prefatory letter found their way from London to Antwerp where they were later discovered in 1535 bound together with Tyndale's commentary in Frith's handwriting. Day admits that this does amount to a "strange preprinting history for Frith's contribution."[106]

Frith's commentary is so distinct in form and so much longer than Tyndale's that no direct literary relationship can be established. Nevertheless, Tyndale and Frith both equally praise Tracy for his denial of purgatory on the basis of his faith in the sufficiency of Christ

---

104. Foxe, *A&M* [1570], 1174; Wright, *Work of John Frith*, 14; Raynor, *John Frith, Scholar and Martyr*, 118.

105. For the letter, see "Jhon Frith," *The Testament of William Tracy* [1535], sig. [B iii ᵛ]-[B iiii ʳ].

106. Day, "Tyndale and Frith," in Day, Lund, and O'Donnell, *Word, Church, and State*, 162–82.

alone for his salvation. Frith attacks with biting sarcasm the canonists' greedy desire for Tracy's wealth, as well as the empty threats of purgatory they ironically nullify by their sale of half-penny pardons. Yet the faith praised by Frith is not a "dead historical faith which the devils have and tremble," but only that faith that is "formed with hope and charity" or "that worketh by cherite." The latter phrase is biblical and comes from Galatians 5:6 and it was used frequently by Augustine and other medieval theologians to stress that faith alone unaccompanied by love is not sufficient to justify, or make righteous, for acceptance with God. Frith, however, means to emphasize that acceptance with God established in justification through faith in Christ alone by its very nature results in love and not, as in Fisher's concept of "*fides caritate formata*," that love exercised in good works completes or perfects faith for justification and acceptance with God. Frith speaks of justifying faith as being the "root of the tree, and the quickening power out of which all good fruits spring." Works are vain if done without faith and they merit nothing before God. The goodness of the heart resulting from justifying faith comes before all good works, like the health of a tree before the quality of its fruit. God, the "iuste iudge," justifies the heart "inwardely," "gyuinge sentence according to faith," which is the root from which spring love and all good works. Only God can see and judge whether inward faith is truly justifying, whereas people can only judge outwardly, though fallibly, on the basis of the fruits of faith in good works, "which iustifye us before men."[107]

Clebsch wrongly interprets Frith as saying that the inability to make an infallible judgment about the justification of another person on the basis of works precludes ever speaking of works as the outward testimony of inward faith and justification. On this basis, Clebsch argues that Frith rejects the concept of "double justification" and is actually much closer to Luther on the centrality of faith than either Tyndale or Barnes. Trueman also points out Clebsch's error, although he goes on to criticize his misleading reference to the concept of "double justification," which in its formal sense developed in the context of Protestant-Catholic dialogues in the 1540s and in the proceedings of the Council of Trent.[108] Many scholars, however, see Frith as actually in implicit

---

107. *The Testament of William Tracy* [1535], sig. C ii, [C v]–[C vi r]; Rex, *Theology of John Fisher*, 118–19.

108. Clebsch, *England's Earliest Protestants*, 108–9; Trueman, *Luther's Legacy*, 140–42.

agreement with a Reformed understanding of "double justification," which supposedly owes more to the influence of Martin Bucer than to Martin Luther. In the theology of Bucer, double justification refers to the distinction between the "*iustificatio impii*" and the "*iustificatio pii*," the former referring to the gratuitous imputation of righteousness by faith alone and the latter the consequent good works and moral transformation of the Christian that testifies outwardly to faith. Although Bucer contributed to the Protestant-Catholic dialogues on justification at Regensburg in 1541, McGrath distinguishes his position from the concept of "double justification" in the most proper sense of the term, or the combined merit of imputed righteousness in Christ with the inherent righteousness of infused grace as double grounds for justification, which he argues was discussed during the proceedings of the Council of Trent.[109]

Frith, of course, never uses the phrase "double justification" nor does he ever, like Bucer, explicitly distinguish a "justification of the wicked" from a "justification of the righteous." There is no evidence of any direct influence of Bucer on his theology. The tree and fruit analogy used by Frith to explain the relationship of faith to good works was a favorite of Luther. Luther could also use "justified" in more than one sense and believed that justifying faith by its very nature produces love and good works through the presence of Christ and the power of the Spirit in that faith. In fact, Luther specified in his own writings that God justifies sinners with the proleptic view of making them new creatures, perfected only in the future resurrection, and that only the ones who struggle against sin while trusting in Christ for righteousness can rightly be said to be justified and under His grace.[110] Furthermore, Luther openly spoke of love and good works not only as self-evidences of justifying faith, even to the point of strengthening faith, but also as outward testimonies to others of justification before God.[111] Nevertheless, both Frith and Luther understood that outward works are not an infallible

---

109. Day, "Tyndale and Frith," in Day, Lund, and O'Donnell, 175–76; Trinterud, "Origins of Puritanism," 40; McGrath, *Iustitia Dei*, 199, 221–22, 242–73.

110. Althaus, *Theology of Martin Luther*, 226–27, 234–41; Peura, "Christ as Favor and Gift," 42–43; Mannermaa, *Christ Present in Faith*, 4–5, 16–7, 19, 21–22, 49–57, 66–67, 87–88; McGrath, *Iustitia Dei*, 205, 210–13.

111. For example, his sermon on Jesus' parable of the wicked mammon. *WA* 10³:281–82, 287–88. See also *LW* 31 (*Freedom of A Christian*, 1520): 357–58; *WA* 7:59–60. Althaus, *Theology of Martin Luther*, 245–50, 448–54.

reflection of the inward condition of the heart. On the one hand, only God sees the faith working through love that makes a deed truly good and, on the other, God knows whom He has justified through faith before they ever have the opportunity to put that faith to good work.

To be sure, Frith shows his admiration for the theology of Augustine by citing him throughout the commentary, and perhaps this is because he shared Tyndale's opinion that Tracy was the greatest scholar of Augustine in all of England.[112] Thus, Frith defends Tracy and the theological convictions for which he died using the writings of Augustine who was generally respected by his Catholic opponents as among the greatest of the Fathers of the ancient Church. Yet Frith's use and interpretation of Augustine does not negate the particular influence of Luther that overshadows the whole development of his evangelical theology of Law and Gospel and his understanding of the doctrine of justification by faith in Christ alone.

While in prison in 1532-33, Frith authored a number of new works. *A mirroure to know thyselfe* was written to a friend instructing him to show by his deeds a humble gratitude to God for the mercy in all His gifts. As Trueman argues, the idea of knowing oneself in relation to God is probably borrowed from Augustine and it was also used by both Zwingli and Calvin.[113] Among the gifts listed by Frith is faith itself, which he states will be taken away by God if not exercised continually in responsible action, mortification of sin, and the doing of good works: "Let us therfore with feare and tremblynge seke our helth and make stable oure vocation and eleccion/ mortifying oure membres and man of synne/ by exercisinge oureselues in Christes preceptes/ that we maye be the children of oure father that in heuen and felow heyers with oure sauioure . . ." The loss of faith seems to imply the possibility of the loss of the forgiveness of sins, since it is only "wher fayth is present" that "no synne can be imputed," yet Frith's doctrine of predestination also indicates that the elect known only to God have been given the gift of a persevering faith and are not of those who fall away beyond the reach of

---

112. Day, "Tyndale and Frith," in Day, Lund, and O'Donnell, *Word, Church, and State*, 167-68.

113. Trueman, *Luther's Legacy*, 145. Another edition with a letter by Frith was published in London in 1548-49. See *The contentes of thys boke. The fyrst is a letter . . . another treatese called the Myrrour or glasse to knowe thy selfe*.

repentance.[114] Elsewhere, in another treatise, Frith speaks of the "pure congregacion" predestined by God that can never ultimately perish in unbelief.[115] Frith also reiterates his understanding of absolute human depravity ("the unstablenes of my flesh being prone to all synne/ and rebellyous to ryghtwesnes, and that there dwelleth no goodnes in me"), justification by faith in Christ alone ("neyther of the worckes going before nor of the workes commyng after/but only of the fre fauoure of God"), and the obligation of the Christian to love his or her neighbor in fulfillment of the Law ("And the lawe of God and nature byndeth me therto/which chargeth me to loue my neyghboure as myselfe").[116] Although many of these themes also echo the sentiments of Augustine, they must be viewed in the light of the whole development of Frith's theology, which reflects the particular influence of Luther's theology of Law and Gospel and the righteousness of justification reckoned in Christ through faith alone.

That Frith was no mere admirer of Augustine is greatly illumined by his treatise on baptism, *A myrroure or lokynge glasse wherin you may beholde the sacramente of baptisme described* (1533). Frith emphasizes the spiritual meaning reflected in the sacrament of baptism over against a perceived stress in the Catholic Church on the mere performance of the external rite in mediating actual grace. He also defends his interpretation of the significance of the rite of infant baptism against both Catholic and Anabaptist extremes. Nowhere does Frith quote Augustine in this entire treatise. In fact, his argument is more focused on biblical exegesis here than anywhere else. His objections to the idea that unbaptized infants are condemned, his emphasis on the communal participation of baptism, and his understanding that the performance of the rite itself does not communicate grace but rather symbolically reflects the receiving of grace, could be argued as showing the influence of Zwingli. Indeed, Frith's arguments for infant baptism follow closely the traditional line of argument articulated by Zwingli. According to Frith, although baptism much like Old Testament circumcision signifies belonging to God and His people, it does not "testyfy" conclusively to others that one is of the invisible congregation known only to God by election: "but euerye man may know his owne thorowe his fayth and

---

114. *A mirroure to know thyselfe* [1536?], sig. [A iii ᵛ–iiii ᵛ, A v ᵛ–A vi ʳ].

115. Frith, *A myrroure or lokynge glasse* [1548?], sig. B iii ᵛ.

116. *A Mirror to Know Thyself* [1536?], sig. A iii ᵛ–A iiii ᵛ, A v ᵛ.

wil that he hath to fulfil the law of god." Even so, baptism should not be withheld from anyone who professes to believe. Neither should it be withheld from infants any more than Hebrew children were restricted from circumcision. This is on account of the fact that the promises of God are offered inclusively to the children of the congregation, Christ Himself welcomed children, and such children should be treated as among the elect when there is no reason yet to suggest otherwise.[117]

Yet Luther's theology, such as expressed in his *A Treatise on the Holy Sacrament of Baptism* (1519), could certainly be another influence behind Frith's understanding that the spiritual meaning reflected in baptism applies to the daily mortification of sin in the life of the Christian. Furthermore, Frith's opinion that the liturgical symbols surrounding the celebration of the Eucharist are theoretically indifferent to the Christian faith, so long as this is properly taught and absorbed by the congregation, is more compatible with Luther and Wittenberg than with Zwingli and Zurich. Also, the liberality with which Frith characterizes the observing of the Sabbath hearkens back to Luther's own position.[118]

Frith's treatise on baptism, then, demonstrates an important point that he was never fully "Augustinian" anymore than he was fully "Lutheran," but it does show a certain selectivity of the theological influences he chose to follow on various doctrinal themes. Frith was obviously influenced by and used a variety of sources on different theological subjects so long as they appeared to him to make the best sense of Scripture.

This is also apparent in Frith's treatment of the sacrament of the Lord's Supper, written in reply to Thomas More in 1533.[119] It was the first of its kind written by an English evangelical in thorough objec-

---

117. Frith, *A myrroure or lokynge glasse* [1548?], sig. [A vii]–[B viii].

118. Ibid., sig. B.iiii. ʳ–[B.v.ʳ], C.ii. ʳ–[C vi ʳ].

119. *A boke made by Iohn Frith* [1533]. The "fyrste little treatyse" mentioned in the full title of the work was probably written sometime between October and November of 1532 for private circulation to a friend. However, it found its way into hands of the retired More and was only later published anonymously in 1545. See *A Christen sentence* [1548]. See Wright, *Work of John Frith*, 55; Lund, "Tyndale and Frith on the Eucharist," in Day, Lund, O'Donnell, *Word, Church, and State*, 185. More's reply to the "fyrste" treatise, which then provides the basis for Frith's treatise of 1533, came into Frith's hands from his former Cambridge tutor, now Bishop of Winchester, Stephen Gardiner. See Loane, *Pioneers*, 27–35.

tion to the doctrines of transubstantiation and the Real Presence. It shows Frith to be more in line with the "spiritual feeding by faith" interpretations of the Lollards, Zwingli, Tyndale, and Oecolampadius. Wright points out the affinities of this treatise with Lollard beliefs as recounted in *Wycliffe's Wicket* (1546), but he argues that the single most influential theologian on the formulation of Frith's Eucharistic theology was the Basel reformer and patristic scholar Johann Oecolampadius (1482-1531). Augustine appears again as the most numerously cited Father throughout the treatise and is used liberally by Frith as the chief ancient authority to support his own theological interpretation of the sacrament. For example, in objection to transubstantiation, Frith quotes Augustine's interpretation of Jesus' words about "eating his flesh" and "drinking his blood" in John 6 as referring to the life of faith and not to the Lord's Supper. This interpretation, however, was also shared by Luther.[120]

With regard to Frith's use of Augustine in general, it must be remembered that Augustine was one of the most respected saints of the ancient Church. Thus, it would make more obvious sense for Frith to quote from Augustine so profusely than to reference the name of Luther, Zwingli, or Oecolampadius in argument with his Catholic opponents. Indeed, other than his early translations of Hamilton and Luther, Augustine is the only theologian that Frith borrows from so explicitly in his more original writings. His use of Augustine and the Fathers in general probably points back to his background in Humanism, although not all trained in Humanism made such frequent and explicit use of the Fathers. Tyndale is a case in point. Furthermore, not all humanists showed favoritism towards the theology of Augustine. Erasmus is a case in point. Frith's use of Augustine in his writings was obviously to reinforce his interpretation of Scripture. Nevertheless, Frith was also willing to differ openly with Augustine and other Church Fathers when they could not be squared at all with his interpretation of Scripture, and it was noted that nowhere in his treatise on the sacrament of baptism does Frith ever refer to the name or writings of Augustine. Therefore, Frith made liberal use of Augustine only when he agreed with him or, some might argue, when he could interpret Augustine in a way that

---

120. Wright, *Work of John Frith*, 58-62, 65; Lund, "Tyndale and Frith on the Eucharist," in Day, Lund, and O'Donnell, *Word, Church, and State*, 189-90; LW 36 (*Babylonian Captivity of the Church*, 1520): 19; WA 6:502.

agreed with his own theology. It cannot be simply assumed that Frith's interpretation and use of Augustine was equivalent to the actual theology of Augustine, which was obviously used on both sides of the argument. Frith was influenced by Luther's evangelical theology of Law and Gospel in the 1520s and it was through the presuppositions he inherited from Luther that he later interpreted and used Augustine.

With regard to his theology of Law and Gospel and the related themes of spiritual bondage, repentance under the Law, faith in Christ alone for justification, and the love and good works that flow from justifying faith in the life of the Christian who nevertheless remains a sinner, these all show the influence of Luther. Although elements within Frith's theology of justification and the Christian life also reflect his use of Augustine, including the contrast between powerlessness before the Law through spiritual bondage to sin and the love, righteousness, and good works that flow from justifying faith, as well the proleptic non-imputation of sin in the life of the justified, these must be interpreted in the light of other statements that clearly speak of the justifying righteousness of Christ that atoned the wrath of God and that "clothe[s]" the Christian as his or her very own in union with Christ through faith alone. It was Frith's exposure to the theology of Luther, even though this may have been significantly mediated through his acquaintanceship with Tyndale, that brought about his evangelical conversion in 1524–1525. In his own words, Frith had this to say about the legacy of Luther: "I do nether affyrme nor denye any thing because Luther so sayeth: but because the Scrypture of God doth so conclude and determe. I take not Luther for soche an auctour that I thynke he can not erre/ but I thynke verely that he both may erre and dothe erre in certayne poyntes *all though not in suche as concerne saluacyon and dampnacyon*, for in these (blessed be God) all thes whom ye [Thomas More] call heretykys [Wycliffe, Tyndale, Oecolampadius, Zwingli] do agre ryght well" (my italics).[121] Notwithstanding the possibility that Frith was simply unaware of subtler differences between him and Luther concerning the doctrine of salvation, as well as between Luther and the other reformers mentioned, his explicit and conscious endorsement of Luther's theology on this central matter in the early 1530s is a significant point that cannot be overlooked.

---

121. Frith, *A boke made by Iohn Frith*, [1533], sig. [B.6. ᵛ]–[B.7. ʳ].

In Frith's own words, it was not on account of his denial of transubstantiation that he was eventually sentenced to death in 1533, which is quite ironic in that this happened under the archbishopric of Thomas Cranmer who later espoused Frith's view, but for his conviction that tolerance should be shown to a variety of opinions so long as idolatrous reverence to the sacrament was discouraged. Even if it could be proven by Scripture and the Fathers, and Frith argues that it cannot, transubstantiation should not be constituted an article of faith compulsory for all Christians to believe on pain of persecution.[122] It seems that Frith followed Tyndale's advice in treading softly with regard to the sacrament.[123]

Despite the sympathies of Thomas Cromwell, the hard-line conservative opposition of his former Cambridge tutor, Bishop Gardiner of Winchester, eventually won the day. Frith was removed from the Tower of London to Newgate Prison in Croydon and was tried before Bishop Stokesley on account of refusal to submit to the Church's teachings on purgatory and the corporal presence of Christ in the Eucharist. Frith was burned at the stake at Smithfield on July 4, 1533.[124]

---

122. "The articles wherfore Johan Frith died which he wrote in newgate the 23. daye of June/ the yere of oure Lorde 1533," *A boke made by Iohn Frith* [1533], sig. [L vi ᵛ–vii ʳ]; Lund, "Tyndale and Frith on the Eucharist," 187–89. The subject of Frith's view of tolerance has received a lot of attention, probably due in some part to the modern ethos of religious pluralism. Wright argues that Bucer was a possible influence on Frith's more tolerant attitude to the sacrament. See Wright, *Work of John Frith*, 75–77. Rupp referred to Frith as the "Melancthon of the English Reformers." See *Studies in the Making*, 10. Dickens considered him to be a herald of the liberal element in later Anglicanism. See *English Reformation*, 204, 378. See also Hard, "The Origin and Development of John Frith's Doctrinal Adiaphora."

123. Loane, *Pioneers*, 29–30.

124. Ibid., 38–45.

8

Law and Gospel in the Theology of Dr. Robert Barnes

THE LIFE AND THEOLOGY OF ROBERT BARNES HAS RECEIVED SIGNIficantly more scholarly attention than that of John Frith,[1] and this is probably due to his prominent role at the White Horse Inn meetings of the early 1520s and the strategic part he played in Anglo-Lutheran diplomacy efforts in the 1530s. In comparison to Frith, however, Barnes left behind fewer theological writings. What he did leave behind, however, was a summary of his theological insights on a variety of matters that show not only his erudition as a scholar but a mind that was deeply influenced by the theology of Luther. Rupp argues that Barnes was the most thorough-going Lutheran of any of the English evangelical reformers. More recently, Trueman describes Barnes as "the most significant Lutheran theologian of the English Reformation" and agrees, despite

---

1. On the life of Barnes, see Trueman, "Barnes," *ODNB* 3:1006–9. The best and most up-to-date treatment is by Lusardi, "Career of Robert Barnes," in Schuster, Marius, Lusardi, and Schoeck, *Complete Works of Thomas More*, 8.3:1365–1415. For other accounts see also Clebsch, *England's Earliest Protestants*, 42–57; Loane, *Pioneers*, 49–89; Rupp, *Studies in the Making*, 31–46; Tjernagel, *Reformation Essay of Dr. Robert Barnes*, 7–19; Anderson, "The Person and Position of Dr. Robert Barnes; Tjernagel, "Dr. Robert Barnes and Anglo-Lutheran Relations." The first book-length biography was by Dallman, *Robert Barnes, Luther's English Friend*; Gardiner, "Barnes," *DNB* 1:1173–77. For the earliest accounts, see Foxe, *A&M* [1570], 1363–66, 1370–75, and "A briefe discourse of the lyfe and doinges of Robert Barnes," in Foxe, *Whole Works*. On the thought of Barnes, see Craig and Maas, "A Sermon by Robert Barnes," 542–51; Trueman, *Luther's Legacy*, 156–97; McGoldrick, *Luther's English Connection*, 59–69, 110–35, 141–46, 154–78, 184–89; Eaves, "Reformation Thought of Dr. Robert Barnes," 156–65; Anderson, "Robert Barnes on Luther," 35–66; Clebsch, *England's Earliest Protestants*, 58–77, 65–68; Knox, *Doctrine of Faith*, 63–70; Tjernagel, "Robert Barnes and Wittenberg," 641–53.

some finer qualifications, that Barnes is generally closer to Luther than either Tyndale or Frith.²

Robert Barnes was born near Lynn in Norfolk around the year 1495. John Bale, one of Barnes' later Cambridge peers, records that he entered the university order of the Augustinian friars in his youth. Earlier accounts date this to 1511–1512, but, on the basis of Barnes' own testimony that he was a resident of Cambridge for twenty years, J.P. Lusardi recently suggests that he entered the Order in 1505.³

After more than a decade at Cambridge, Barnes developed a scholarly reputation, and he was transferred to the University of Louvain from 1517 to 1521. It is generally assumed that Barnes went on to receive his Doctor of Divinity at Louvain and then later at Cambridge by incorporation in 1523. The duration of Barnes' residency at Louvain coincided with that of Erasmus, but there is no evidence that the two ever met. However, Barnes' early reforming career shows the influence of Humanism. Upon returning to Cambridge, he became prior of his Augustinian house and, with the help of Thomas Parnell who returned with him from Louvain, implemented an innovative series of lectures on the classical Latin rhetoricians Terence, Plautus, and Cicero. Future Bible translator Miles Coverdale was among the Augustinian friars who sat under Barnes' teaching.⁴ Foxe's comment that "the knowledge of good letters was scarsely entred into the Universitie" reflects the rather young influence of Humanism at Cambridge in the early sixteenth century.⁵ Nevertheless, Greek studies were significantly introduced at the university through the influence of Erasmus who described Cambridge fondly as suitable for his Greek scholarship,⁶ and Humanism had also made some significant strides at Cambridge in the co-founding of St.

---

2. Rupp, *Righteousness of God*, 39; Rupp, "Luther in English Theology," 13; McGoldrick, *Luther's English Connection*, 15; Tjernagel, *Henry VIII and the Lutherans*, viii; Trueman, *Luther's Legacy*, 17, 197.

3. *DNB* 1:1173; Lusardi, "The Career of Robert Barnes," in Schuster, Marius, Lusardi, and Schoeck, *Complete Works of Thomas More*, 8.3:1369.

4. Lusardi, "The Career of Robert Barnes," Schuster, Marius, Lusardi, and Schoeck, *Complete Works of Thomas More*, 8.3:1369; *ODNB* 3:1006; *DNB* 1:1173; Foxe, *A&M* [1570], 1363–64; Loane, *Pioneers*, 49; Rupp, *Studies in the Making*, 32 (n. 1).

5. Foxe, *A&M* [1570], 1364.

6. Marc'hadour, "Tyndale entre Erasmus et Luther," 185; Halkin, *Erasmus*, 30–40.

John's College by Bishop Fisher of Rochester and Lady Margaret of Beaufort in 1516.[7]

Foxe recounts how Barnes soon replaced the scholastic disputations of Duns Scotus with the direct reading of Paul's epistles. Yet, even despite the level of his new attention to "Christ" and "his holy worde," Foxe identifies Thomas Bilney as the one who "conuerted him wholy vnto Christ." This was possibly in the context of the White Horse Inn meetings in the early 1520s, over which Barnes soon was to preside. Foxe's narrative, however, anachronistically suggests that Barnes' 1525 sermon at St. Edward's occurred before, and in some way even instigated, these meetings.[8]

Barnes had certainly come to know of the evangelical theology of Luther even before these meetings. As a friar of the Augustinian Order, Barnes would have heard of the budding controversies surrounding his fellow friar from Wittenberg, and he was a student at Louvain when that university condemned Luther (and almost Erasmus) in 1519. The years 1520–21 saw a heightening of early tension surrounding the works of Luther in the Low Countries, and in the Augustinian monastery in Antwerp several monks began espousing his views.[9] Trueman even conjectures the possibility that Barnes attended Luther's disputation at the meeting of Augustinians at Heidelberg in 1518.[10] However, there is no evidence as to what particular influence Luther had upon Barnes' theology during the early 1520s. His participation in the White Horse Inn meetings alone does not necessarily prove that he had at this point developed any particular devotion to Luther's theology, and another member of those meetings, Stephen Gardiner, went on to oppose evangelical theology as the future Bishop of Winchester. Furthermore, Thomas Bilney is said to have converted Barnes to faith in Christ for his salvation, and though tried by association with Luther later in 1527, Bilney denied ever having learned his theology of salvation by faith from Luther, claiming instead that he first found peace of conscience

---

7. Schoeck, "Humanism in England," in Rabil, *Renaissance Humanism*, 2:6–7, 25–26.

8. Lusardi, "The Career of Robert Barnes," in Schuster, Marius, Lusardi, and Schoeck, *Complete Works of Thomas More*, 8.3:1370; Loane, *Pioneers*, 50; Foxe, *A&M* [1570], 1364.

9. Alistair Duke, "Netherlands," in Pettegree, *Early Reformation in Europe*, 143–44.

10. Trueman, *Luther's Legacy*, 18.

through his own reading of Paul in Erasmus' *Novum Instrumentum* (1519). The emphasis in his reforming preaching against images, pilgrimages, and the cult of the saints is nothing peculiar to the influence of Luther and parallels the concerns of Lollards and, to some degree, humanists as well.[11]

General criticism of the secular clergy was not even uncommon among the friars themselves, and they possessed some immunity from the jurisdiction of university and episcopal authorities.[12] This drastically changed in the case of Barnes, however, on Christmas Eve in 1525 when he preached a scathingly anticlerical sermon at St. Edward's Church, Trinity Hall, Cambridge. Barnes, probably egged on by fellow Cambridge men George Stafford and Thomas Bilney, used the opportunity to preach against clerical abuses while Latimer substituted for him as chaplain of the Augustinians.[13]

Foxe records that Barnes's sermon followed "the Scripture and Luthers postill' for that day, the fourth Sunday in Advent." Stuart Hall claims unreservedly that the sermon "wholeheartedly" expounds "Lutheran doctrines."[14] The actual sermon is not extant, but Barnes later identifies in his *Supplication* (1531 and 1534) the twenty-five articles for which he was charged in the subsequent heresy proceedings.[15] Other scholars have argued that nothing in these articles shows any obvious connection to the influence of Luther.[16] The majority of Barnes' reforming criticisms are rather conventional to the late medieval period and leveled against clerical abuses of power, such as the holding of more than one bishopric (pluralism), the temporal authority exercised by prelates, the selling of pardons, priestly absolution, clerical materialism, and the ornate opulence surrounding the clerical office and its ceremonies. Other particular articles attack superstitious legalism surrounding the keeping of Sabbaths and holidays such as Christmas and Easter, and

---

11. Marshall, *Reformation England*, 28–29, 34.
12. Anderson, "Robert Barnes on Luther," 36, 38.
13. Loane, *Pioneers*, 51.
14. Hall, "Early Rise and Gradual Decline," in Baker, *Reform and Reformation*, 114.
15. Barnes, *A supplicatyon made by Robert Barnes* [1531?], fol. xxiii ᵛ–xxviii ʳ; Barnes, *A supplicacion vnto the most gracyous prynce H. the viij*, [1534], 33–62.
16. *ODNB* 3:1006–1007; Elton, *Reform and Reformation*, 95; D'Alton, "Suppression of Heretics," 235; Tjernagel, *Henry VIII and the Lutherans*, 54–55; Clebsch, *England's Earliest Protestants*, 46; Anderson, "Robert Barnes on Luther," 37–38, 45–46.

one article objects wholesale to lawsuits involving Christians and their personal possessions on the basis of a New Testament commandment. The latter, which Stephen Gardiner considered Barnes' worst offense, caused him to be accused of Anabaptist sympathies and was of particular significance since Trinity Hall was a lawyer's college.[17] One other charge brought against Barnes was his neglect to pray to the Virgin Mary and for the souls in purgatory as was customary from the pulpit. Although he objects to this practice on the basis of Scripture, he does not openly deny the reality of purgatory itself.[18]

There is not one single article, however, that explicitly refers to being "justified by faith alone" in Christ. The closest Barnes comes to this is in reference to people and their prayers being acceptable to God, not on the basis of their works, but "allonly for christes merytes." It is not self-evident that this article was influenced by Luther's evangelical theology of justification, and it agrees with the belief expressed by Barnes' earlier spiritual mentor Thomas Bilney. Barnes acknowledges that this particular article did not receive a sentence and that those commissioned to examine him were more concerned with his anticlerical statements.[19] Although Foxe claims that Barnes followed Luther's *Postill* for that Sunday, the particular influence of Luther on Barnes' reforming criticisms in 1525 is not entirely self-evident on the basis of the articles themselves, which deal mostly with clerical abuses of power and, to a lesser extent, superstitious ritualism and devotion to saints.

After a process of hearings with university authorities, Barnes was taken into custody, and, with the help of Stephen Gardiner, was given a private hearing before Cardinal Wolsey in London prior to the commencing of his more formal trial in the days that followed.[20] Barnes

---

17. *A supplicatyon made by Robert Barnes* [1531], fol. xxiii ʳ–xxvii ʳ. Barnes expanded his discussion in 1534 to include the tale of a particular case of litigation issued just days prior to his Christmas sermon in 1525. See *A supplicacion vnto the most gracyous prynce H. the viij* [1534], 33–39; Rupp, *Studies in the Making*, 33–34. Despite the claims Barnes makes to never having universally rejected litigation altogether, "but only vncharitable sewtes," Lusardi argues that Barnes does indeed clearly adopt a more moderate position than before in his revised *Supplication* of 1534. See "Career of Robert Barnes," in Schuster, Marius, Lusardi, and Schoeck, *Complete Works of Thomas More* 8.3:1374–76.

18. *A supplicatyon made by Robert Barnes* [1531], fo. xxxv. See also *A supplicacion vnto the most gracyous prynce H. the viij* [1534], 48–49.

19. *A supplicatyon made by Robert Barnes* [1531], xxxiv ᵛ– xxxv ʳ. See also *A supplicacion vnto the most gracyous prynce H. the viij* [1534], 47–48.

20. For full details of this narrative see Barnes' own testimony in *A supplicacion vnto*

was eventually persuaded to abjure in public and to swear to whatever penance was enjoined upon him by the Bishop of Bath and Wells. After a night in prison, Barnes fulfilled his penance before Cardinal Wolsey and other prelates at St. Paul's Cross on February 11, 1526. He was also accompanied by four London Steelyard merchants recently discovered by Thomas More to be in possession of forbidden works. Barnes kneeled during the sermon of Bishop John Fisher against Martin Luther (now his second), and carried faggots around a pyre of works by Luther and other continental reformers. Barnes explains later that he made his abjuration to the Bishop of Bath and Wells thinking his examiners were genuinely concerned about his safety and that all they really desired of him was to show nominal deference to the authorities. He also gives the impression that his promise to do penance was made before being told exactly what that penance would entail. Despite being convicted under the umbrella of Lutheran heresy, Barnes objects in his *Supplication* to any such connections to "Lutherans" at this point in time.[21] Indeed, despite obvious parallels in their reforming agendas, and though such claims of disassociation from Luther during this period should always be taken with a grain of salt, it is difficult on the basis of the articles extracted from his Christmas Eve Sermon to make any substantial case for the particular influence of Luther upon Barnes' theology in 1525.

Six months later, Barnes was moved to the Augustinian house in London. He stayed here for two years and sought in vain for the official release he thought had been promised to him. During this time, Barnes' received a personal visit from two Lollards from Essex. The confession of John Tyball before Bishop Tunstall of London in April 1528 tells of "Barons" having sold to him and his associate a copy of Tyndale's superior English *New Testament* for *3s. 2d.* in the chamber of his Augustinian house. This event does not imply that Barnes had formal ties to an underground network of Lollards, nor even that Barnes himself was influenced by Lollardy. Stackhouse argues that the possibility of Lollard influence upon Barnes would cast doubts on his Lutheran inheritance. However, though it does constitute a connection between Lollards and

---

the most gracyous prynce H. the viij [1534], 50–62. See also Foxe, *A&M* [1570], 1364–65; Lusardi, "The Career of Robert Barnes," in Schuster, Marius, Lusardi, and Schoeck, *Complete Works of Thomas More*, 8.3:1376–83; Loane, *Pioneers*, 51–59; Chester, "Robert Barnes and the Burning of the Books," 211–21.

21. Barnes, *A supplicatyon made by Robert Barnes* [1531], 60–61; Doernberg, *Henry VIII and Luther*, 12.

the evangelical movement, there is no need to conclude on the basis of this encounter that Barnes himself was ever influenced by Lollardy. If anything, it appears to have been the reverse.[22]

As a result of the episode, Barnes was moved to the Augustinian house in Northampton under more scrupulous surveillance, but he staged a suicide by drowning and escaped first to Antwerp before moving on to Wittenberg.[23] Barnes' flight to Wittenberg is important in itself, and it is clear from his writings of the 1530s that his interaction with Lutherans in Germany left an indelible mark on his theology. Tjernagel might not be too far off the mark in stating that: "Louvain and Cambridge had made him a humanist scholar; Wittenberg made him a Lutheran theologian." In fact, he claims in another article that in "the entire body of Barnes' theological writings, there is no originality of interpretation or religious thinking. There is however, every evidence of a full grasp and unqualified acceptance of the teachings of Martin Luther and the Wittenberg reformers."[24] Yet Barnes' use of patristic writings in support of his biblical exegesis shows the continued influence of Humanism, and his frequent recourse to the theology of Augustine must also be taken into consideration as a possible influence.

Barnes quickly won the acceptance of the Germans. He boarded with Johann Bugenhagen ("Pomeranus") and befriended Wittenberg's leading theologians Luther and Melancthon. He assumed the name "Antony Anglus," under which he later matriculated at the University of Wittenberg in 1533 (the name Robert Barnes appears in the margin of the university rosters next to "*D. Antonius Anglus Theologiae Doctor Oxoniensis*").[25] His relationship with German Lutherans in Wittenberg, Hamburg, and Lübeck, as well as with John Frederick of Electoral Saxony and the King of Denmark, would later make him an important asset to Henry VIII in the 1530s who was then seeking political sup-

22. Stackhouse, "Native Roots," 27.

23. *L&P* 4. 2:1859; Lusardi, "Career of Robert Barnes," in Schuster, Marius, Lusardi, and Schoeck, *Complete Works of Thomas More*, 8.3:1384–86; *ODNB* 3:1007; Foxe, *A&M* [1570], 1365–66.

24. Tjernagel, *Henry VIII and the Lutherans*, 64; Tjernagel, "Robert Barnes and Wittenberg," 649–50. On the lack of originality in Barnes, see also Anderson, "Robert Barnes on Luther," 43–44.

25. Clebsch, *England's Earliest Protestants*, 48; Lusardi, "The Career of Robert Barnes," in Schuster, Marius, Lusardi, and Schoeck, *Complete Works of Thomas More*, 8.3:1387; Loane, *Pioneers*, 61–62; Rupp, *Studies in the Making*, 41.

port for his break with the papacy in his divorce from Catherine of Aragon in marriage to Anne Boleyn.[26] The opinion of Barnes among the German theologians is probably best captured by Luther, who after Barnes' martyrdom in 1540 wrote the preface to a German translation of the life and last confession of "Saint Robert."[27]

During the years 1530 and 1531, Barnes mostly focused on writing and composed his most revealing theological treatises. His first, the *Sentenciae ex doctoribus collectae, quas papistae ualde impudenter hodie damnant* (Wittenberg, 1530), was written in Latin and published in Wittenberg under the pseudonym of Antonius Anglus. The *Sentenciae* contains nineteen doctrinal propositions supported by the authority of Scripture and reinforced by the sayings of the Fathers and even canon law. A preface was written by Bugenhagen, who himself provided a German translation of the work in two editions in 1531.[28] The articles reveal how far Barnes has now come under the theological influence of Luther: 1) "Only Faith justifies"; 2) "Christ's death has made satisfaction for all sins and not only for original sin"; 3) "God's commandments cannot possibly be kept in our own strength"; 4) "freewill by its own powers is only able to sin"; 5) "the just sin in all good works"; 6) "what is the true Church and how she may be told"; 7) "God's Word, not men's powers, is the keys of the Church"; 8) "councils may err"; 9) "all should receive the Sacrament in both kinds"; 10) "priests may marry"; 11) "human ordinances cannot free sinners"; 12) "auricular confession is not necessary for salvation"; 13) "monks are not more holy than lay folks on account of cowls and monasteries"; 14) "Christian fasting does not consist in discrimination between foods"; 15) "for the Christian every day is a Sabbath day and a festal day and not only the seventh day"; 16) "unjust banning by the Pope does not disgrace the banned"; 17) "in the Sacrament of the Altar is truly (*wahrhaft*) the Body of Christ";

---

26. Lusardi, "Career of Robert Barnes," in Schuster, Marius, Lusardi, and Schoeck, *Complete Works of Thomas More*, 8.3:1391–92; Tjernagel, *Henry VIII and the Lutherans*, 151–52; Loane, *Pioneers*, 73–74.

27. Clebsch, *England's Earliest Protestants*, 55; Rupp, *Righteousness of God*, 39; ODNB 3:1009; Lusardi, "Career of Robert Barnes," in Schuster, Marius, Lusardi, and Schoeck, *Complete Works of Thomas More*, 8.3:1414. For Luther's preface, see *WA* 51:445–51.

28. A second Latin edition of the *Sentenciae* was published under Barnes own name in 1536. Lusardi, "Career of Robert Barnes," in Schuster, Marius, Lusardi, and Schoeck, *Complete Works of Thomas More*, 8.3:1387 (and n. 2)–88 (and n. 2); Tjernagel, "Robert Barnes and Wittenberg," 644–45.

18) "saints may not be appealed to as mediators"; 19) "of the origin and parts of the Mass."[29]

To a large extent the *Sentenciae* reappear again in the third part of Barnes' *Supplication* published in Antwerp in 1531, the same year as Frith's *Disputation of Purgatory* and Tyndale's *Answer to More*.[30] In the first part of the *Supplication* addressed to Henry VIII, Barnes proceeds to exonerate himself from charges of heresy and to object to the "uncheritable" treatment he and other persecuted preachers had received from Cardinal Wolsey and the bishops. Barnes deflects criticism to the magisterium, whose tyranny over the Word of God and exemption from temporal obedience to princes makes them the real traitors of the kingdom of "youre grace."[31] The second part rehearses the articles for which Barnes was charged for heresy in his Christmas Eve sermon of 1525. The final part is devoted to a more exhaustive treatment of Christian doctrine and further reveals the extent to which Luther's evangelical theology of Law and Gospel has influenced the mind of Barnes. Bishop John Fisher's sermon in condemnation of Luther provides the major literary focus of Barnes' polemic.

The very first of the "comon places" treated by Barnes is that "Only faythe Justifyeth by fore god," which he argues is the article that stands at the center of Scripture. Such paramount importance given to the article of justification by faith alone in biblical revelation agrees with the centrality Luther ascribed to it, which was affirmed also by Tyndale in both his earlier and later writings. Barnes builds his case exegetically on the basis of the gospels and the epistles of Paul, with understandable emphasis on the book of Romans. This section of his treatise is largely written as a response to Bishop Fisher of Rochester who was the first major English opponent of Luther, particularly with regard to the doctrine of justification by faith in Christ alone. In light of Fisher's use of the Fathers, Barnes' *Supplication*, much like Frith's own *Purgatory*, contains a host of patristic citations, including Augustine, Ambrose, Bernard of Clairvaux, and even Origen. Barnes' basic argument is that the Scriptures

---

29. Rupp translates the articles from Bugenhagen's *Fürnemlich Artikel der Christenlichen kirchen* (1531). See *Studies in the Making*, 39–40.

30. Actually, the work does not identify date, place, or publisher, but scholars generally agree that it was most likely published by Simon Cock of Antwerp in 1531. Lusardi, "The Career of Robert Barnes," in Schuster, Marius, Lusardi, and Schoeck, *Complete Works of Thomas More*, 8.3:1388; Loane, *Pioneers*, 62.

31. *A supplicatyon made by Robert Barnes* [1531], fo. iii ʳ–vii ʳ.

speak of Christ alone as the only Savior and Justifier, which means that there is no need for the help of any other creature or for the making of any other satisfaction for sin. For Barnes, to be of the opinion that works of any kind, either before or after faith, somehow contribute to human redemption is to deny the biblical truth about the utter gratuitousness of salvation in Christ. To deny this is to deny the very person and work of Christ Himself, which Barnes identifies, echoing Luther's antipapal response to Prierias in 1521 and translated by Frith in the *Revelation of Antichrist* (1529), as the spirit of the antichrist. For Barnes, the Scriptures clearly teach that justification, which he defines by citing Augustine as the "remission of sins" (*remissionem peccatorum*), is imputed to faith only (*Sola. Sola. Sola*). By the promise of the grace of God, Jesus Christ alone is "al oure iustice/ all oure redempcion/ all oure wysdom/ all oure holynes/ alonly the purcheser of grace/ alonly the peace maker/ bytwene god and man. Breuely al goodnes that we haue/ that yt is of him/ by him/ and for his sake only."[32] It is significant that Barnes stresses Augustine's definition of "justification" as the "remission of sins." As McGrath argues, Augustine does occasionally use justification in this sense, but he ordinarily uses *justificare* to stress being "made righteous" through love and the regenerating and renewing work of the Holy Spirit.[33] Thus, that Barnes uses Augustine to define justification as essentially the remission of sins in Christ imputed to faith alone reflects the influence of Luther upon his presuppositions.

Trueman pits Barnes and Frith against Tyndale, arguing that Tyndale more than the others "tends to emphasize Christ's work as an example rather than as an objective accomplishment of redemption,"[34] but this is a misleading distinction since Tyndale, like Luther, understood the liberation of the Christian from spiritual bondage as consisting precisely in the removal of guilt promised in the Gospel and accomplished through the righteousness of Christ. Trueman is also of the opinion that Barnes' own "doctrine of atonement in relation to the doctrine of God" is somewhat underdeveloped in comparison to that of Frith who lays more explicit stress on the propitiation of God's wrath. Although Barnes does not explicitly refer to the propitiation of

---

32. Ibid., fo. xxxvi ᵛ, xxxviii ʳ, xl ʳ, xli ᵛ, xlii ᵛ–xliii ᵛ, xlvi ʳ, xlviii.

33. McGrath, *Iustitia Dei*, 30–32.

34. See *Luther's Legacy*, 159. For the objective work of Christ in the theology of Tyndale, see his [*New Testament*, 1525], sig. B iii ʳ.

the wrath of God the Father, he does often refer to the satisfaction made for sin by the blood of Christ. It is important to remember that neither Barnes, Tyndale, nor Frith ever set out to provide a systematic and comprehensive treatment of the atonement, but it can be assumed that these reformers all shared a common belief in the objective work of Christ on the cross offered to God the Father on behalf of sinful humanity that was part of the Western medieval theological inheritance going back to Anselm and reflected through the liturgy of the Mass. The same could also be said of Luther who considered the Godward orientation of the work of Christ to be the very foundation for the liberty of the Christian from bondage to sin under the Law, death, and the Devil in justification and the new life of good works.[35]

Trueman and McGrath also argue that Barnes does not clearly set forth a doctrine of justification understood as the imputation of righteousness in Christ in the early *Supplication* of 1531. According to McGrath, Barnes' earlier treatise is "vague" on the subject and states that: "The first clear and unambiguous statement of the concept of the imputation of righteousness to be found in the writings of an English Reformer may be found in the 1534 edition of Robert Barnes' *Supplication unto King Henry VIII*."[36] Although he is certainly correct if speaking of the lack of any explicit reference to "imputed righteous in Christ" or the "imputation of Christ's righteousness," which is not even characteristic of Lutheran writings until the 1530s, it must be stressed that Barnes does clearly describe justification in terms of the forgiveness of sins "imputed" to faith "alone" (*sola*) in union with Christ and His atoning righteousness. In fact, Trueman states that Barnes' more explicit statements on imputed righteousness in the revised 1534 *Supplication*, which actually occur as a newly appended summary, are only inserted to clarify his earlier position.[37]

It is not surprising that Barnes in 1531 could anticipate objections to his doctrine of justification by faith in Christ alone, and the rationale for his response clearly reflects the influence of Luther's presuppositions though often quoting from Augustine. Works apart from grace and faith

---

35. See Althaus, *Theology of Martin Luther*, 218–23.

36. See *Luther's Legacy*, 161–64; McGrath, *Iustitia Dei*, 286; Barnes, *A supplicacion vnto the most gracyous prynce H. the viij* [1534], 85.

37. Compare fo. xxxviii ʳ with fo. xlii ᵛ–xliii ʳ in *A supplicatyon made by Robert Barnes* [1531]; Trueman, *Luther's Legacy*, 163 (n. 25).

cannot justify because they do not have the right intent and are nothing but sin. Trueman distinguishes the doctrine of faith in the theology of Barnes from that of Frith and Tyndale, arguing that the latter two stress the Holy Spirit and love in the doing of good works rather than faith. This seems like an unwarranted comparison since each of these reformers freely employed the tree and fruit analogy to stress the relationship of faith to love and good works, and Trueman himself acknowledges that Barnes stresses the sanctifying work of the Holy Spirit under his discussion of the bondage of the will.[38]

Following Luther, Barnes defines justifying faith as personal and possessive, that God is "not alonly a father, but my father." This is no general, earthly kind of faith that believes things knowable by human reason or testimony, such as the existence of a creator or the historical facts of Jesus' life. Although neither works before nor after faith justify, saving faith is a divine work that necessarily produces good works "to the honour off god/ and also to the profite of oure neyboure." A truly good work is neither done for reward nor out of fear, but after the example of Christ Himself. These good works can only be done by a justifying faith and the indwelling of Christ. Barnes states that the works of the just are all good, though not in the sense that the works of Christians are perfect. Barnes uses the familiar image of the "good tre" and its good "appylle" to describe the relationship between faith and good works. Those who respond to the promise of grace in Christ as a thief might abuse the pardon of a king are not truly among the justified who rightly do what "the kyngys pardon deseruyed." Nevertheless, in direct opposition to Bishop Fisher, Barnes argues that it is unbiblical to ascribe to love and works a meritorious role alongside faith for justification such as in the traditional Catholic notion of a *"fides caritate formata."* According to Barnes, Paul's praise of charity above faith in 1 Corinthians 13 and the faith that "worketh by charity" in Galatians 5:6 does not mean that love and faith together justify, and Barnes cites Athanasius' reference to the other kind of "faith" that works miracles, prophecies, and healings. According to Barnes, Fisher's appeal to the epistle of James does nothing for his argument, and Barnes explicitly echoes Luther's skepticism towards the apostolicity of James on account of the fact that it appears to teach justification by works and lacked the consensus of patristic

---

38. Barnes, *A supplicatyon made by Robert Barnes* [1531], xlvi ʳ; Trueman, *Luther's Legacy*, 166, 181.

acceptance as recorded by Eusebius. Nevertheless, Barnes argues that to concede the authority of James does not necessarily prove Fisher's point anyway, and he uses Augustine to demonstrate that James can be interpreted in theological agreement with Paul in praising those works that follow after faith as testimony of a justification already received. Barnes points out that a Christian who dies right after believing without having any opportunity to exercise his or her faith in a good work is yet fully justified.[39]

Though he acknowledges in the second article of his "comon places" that the word "*ekklesia*" in Scripture often refers to a local body of professing Christians in a general region or city, Barnes argues that the true, universal Church is not an outward thing, nor is it defined by the magisterium, popes, or councils that can and have erred. Rather, it is made up of all who are truly justified through inward faith in Jesus Christ. The elect are only infallibly known by God, since the justified are also still sinners and the valiant works of the wicked mask a hypocritical righteousness. Nevertheless, Barnes does not conclude that this eliminates all possibility of reasonable estimation since the "serten tokens" of preaching the pure Word of God and its positive reception among a submissive people bear witness to the likely presence of a true Christian "*ecclesia*," which Barnes translates as "churche or congregacion." The latter English word in particular was favored by Tyndale in his New Testament translation to stress, like Luther in his own use of *congregatio* ("gathering") and *Gemeinde* ("community"), the common priesthood of Christians under the rule of the Word of God. In fact, this section of the *Supplication* is reminiscent of the same discussion in Tyndale's *Answer to More*, which is interesting in the light of the fact that Barnes and Tyndale were broadsided together on this very issue in More's *Confutation of Tyndale's Answer* (1532).[40] The invisible-within-the-visible conception of the Church was taught by Augustine and was promulgated by Wyclif in the context of the doctrine of predestination,

---

39. *A supplicatyon made by Robert Barnes* [1531], xlv ʳ–xlvi ʳ, xlviii ᵛ, xlix –liv ʳ, lv ʳ, lvi ʳ, lxxxiᵛ. See also Trueman, *Luther's Legacy*, 169–71, 194–96. For the differentiation Luther develops between justifying faith and the miracle-working faith of 1 Corinthians 13, see Althaus, *Theology of Martin Luther*, 429–45.

40. *A supplicatyon made by Robert Barnes* [1531], lviii, lx, lxiii ᵛ- lxiv ʳ, lxv ᵛ–lxvi ʳ; Tyndale, *Answer to More* [1531], fo. v–viiiʳ; Lusardi, "Career of Robert Barnes," in Schuster, Marius, Lusardi, and Schoeck, *Complete Works of Thomas More*, 8.3:in Schuster, Marius, Lusardi, and Schoeck, *Complete Works of Thomas More*, 8.3:1395–96.

but Luther asserted it more recently in stressing the ultimate "hiddenness" of God's elect in the world. Barnes' admission of the fallibility of popes and councils also resonates with the thought of Luther in debate with Eck in 1519.[41]

In his third common place, Barnes argues against Duns Scotus that the preaching of the Word of God, and not sacerdotal absolution, is what is meant in Scripture by the power of the "keys" to bind and loose. Echoing the thoughts of Luther and Tyndale, the Word of God alone holds the powers of repentance, the loosing of the conscience, and the amendment of life. Though the keys of the Word of God rightly belong to all baptized Christians, who all "be Peter," there are within the "congregacion of faythefulle men" those perceived to be "most abylle and best lernyd in the word of God." These have a particular calling to serve as preachers and administers of the sacrament in the context of the regular corporate gathering.[42]

The fourth common place treated by Barnes addresses the controversy over free-will. Barnes' answer mirrors Augustine's ancient controversy with Pelagius and Luther's more recent dispute with Erasmus in arguing for the spiritual bondage of the will and the sinfulness of all works apart from grace: "he [free-will] cane neyther thynke good/ nor wylle/ nor yet performe yt . . . that man hathe lost his frewylle by synne and cane no more do vnto goodnes/ than a dede man cane do to make hym selfe a lyue agayn/ yee he cane doo nothynge but delyght in synne . . ." Barnes strongly opposes the late medieval scholastic notion of congruous merit and that the natural person can be prepared and disposed to desire grace through his or her own contrition (*facere quod in se est* and *preparare se ad graciam*): "frewylle without grace cane doo nothynge." Like Luther, Barnes asserts that sin is the property, not of the "bonys nor the synows/ nor the fleshe that hangeth there on," but of the very rational soul itself. In fact, when speaking of the mortification of the "flesh" by the Spirit of God, Barnes explicitly associates this with the suppression from within of the sinful desires that originate from

---

41. For Wyclif and Augustine on the Church as the company of the predestined, see Evans, *Wyclif*, 217–18; *LW* 44 (*To the Christian Nobility of the German Nation Concerning the Reform of the Christian Estate*, 1520): 127–31; *WA* 6:408–10; Althaus, *Theology of Martin Luther*, 287–93, 296.

42. *A supplicatyon made by Robert Barnes* [1531], fo. lxx ʳ, lxxiv ᵛ, lxxiv ᵛ–lxxvi ʳ; For Luther's theology of the ownership of the "keys" among all Christians though not all are called to the formal office of minister, see Althaus, *Theology of Martin Luther*, 316–23.

the human spirit and not with the outward control of sinful passions aroused within the physical body.[43]

Of course, Barnes is aware of the natural objections raised as to why God commands anything at all if free-will is so incapacitated and what right He has to condemn people for things they cannot possibly avoid. The answer, for Barnes, is not to look for fault in God or His Law and commandments, but "to subdewe thys presumtuous pryde of thyne/ and to bryng the to knowledge of thyne awne selfe." With this knowledge, the sinner can confess his "unabyllnes" to God and beseech the "phisician" for His mercy and for the help of His Spirit to henceforth keep the commandments. For Barnes, this is not the same thing as what scholastics like Duns Scotus called "attrition," or imperfect contrition, understood as a turning from sin out of natural fear meriting justifying grace congruously from God. As Luther objected to the theology of Gabriel Biel in his *Disputation Against Scholastic Theology* (1517), Barnes objects to Scotus and Fisher and lumps them together as Pelagians on account of their teaching that God rewards with justifying grace a soul that is penitent apart from prevenient grace. To the contrary, like Luther, Barnes states that human nature apart from grace wishes there were no God to punish sins. Furthermore, attrition did not merit grace and the remission of sins in the case of Judas.[44] Barnes' contrast of spiritual bondage to sin and the grace of God needed to help keep the Law certainly owes to his explicit use of Augustine but must be interpreted in the light of the stress in his definition of justification on the forgiveness of sins in Christ imputed to faith alone, which shows the influence of Luther's theology of Law and Gospel.

According to Barnes, God is even particular to whom He grants this special grace of repenting, believing, and willing, and it has nothing to do with foreseen cooperation on the part of individuals. The grace of election itself guarantees the conversion of the sinner. Yet God's inscrutable will in election is righteous and not open to rebuke. Barnes states that God uses the natures of both the righteous and the wicked as

---

43. Ibid., fo. lxxxi ʳ, lxxxii ᵛ, lxxxiii ᵛ–lxxxv ʳ. On the commandments as the revelation of natural and moral depravity and the inherent enmity of the natural will against them, see also fo. xci ᵛ–xcii ʳ, fo. xcixʳ. Barnes explicitly states that people are conceived with the corruption of Adam's sin. See fo. xcviii. For Luther on the corruption of the *totus homo*, see *LW* 35 (*Preface to the Epistle of St. Paul to the Romans*, 1546): 371–72; 377–78; *WA DB* 7:12–13, 22–23.

44. *A supplicatyon made by Robert Barnes* [1531], fo. lxxxvi ʳ–xcii ʳ.

"instrumentis" for His own sovereign purposes, yet He is not laid open to the charge of the fault of evil.[45]

While Barnes quotes often from Augustine throughout this section in support of spiritual bondage apart from the grace of God, his knowledge of the more recent controversy between Luther and Erasmus in 1525 must also be at the forefront of his mind. Indeed, Barnes refutes Bishop Fisher in a manner very reminiscent of the way that Luther refutes Erasmus. In fact, Barnes alludes to Luther's refutation of Erasmus in Article 4 of his earlier *Sentenciae* (1530).[46] Trueman acknowledges that Barnes made some obvious literary use of Luther's *De Servo Arbitrio* (1525), but he also distances Barnes from Luther by arguing that the latter denied "free-will" fundamentally on the "axiom of God's immutability with its implications for divine determinism."[47] It is indeed true that Luther's argument in the *De Servo Arbitrio* begins here, but that is because he is purposefully following the outline of Erasmus' own preface in the *Diatribe seu collatio de libero arbitrio* (1524). On the other hand, when Luther moves beyond direct interaction with Erasmus and proceeds to provide his own exegetical case against "free-will" he begins by discussing the universal guilt and dominion of sin, which Trueman argues is the distinguished focus of Augustine and Barnes. Furthermore, Barnes' discussion of God's sovereign use of the natures of the righteous and the wicked echoes Luther who likewise distinguished sinning by necessity of nature from sinning by compulsion as if against nature.[48]

The influence of Luther is also arguably evident in at least two of the last four common places that conclude this section of Barnes' *Supplication*. The first of the four common places advocates for the vernacular translation and distribution of the Bible among the common people.[49] As has already been mentioned, Barnes marketed a copy of Tyndale's unauthorized English New Testament to two Lollards from Essex sometime earlier between January 1526 and April 1528. Barnes' support for a vernacular Bible was not necessarily the result of the influence of either Luther or Tyndale but might have originated earlier

45. Ibid., fo. xciv ᵛ–xcvi ʳ, xcviii ᵛ.
46. Anderson, "Robert Barnes on Luther," 48–51.
47. Trueman, *Luther's Legacy*, 172, 177, 183. See also McGrath, *Iustitia Dei*, 202.
48. *LW* 33 (*Bondage of the Will*, 1525): 64–65, 246–59; *WA* 18:634–35, 756–64. See also Kolb, *Bound Choice, Election, and Wittenberg Theological Method*, 11–66.
49. *A supplicatyon made by Robert Barnes* [1531], fol. C ᵛ–C.xii ʳ.

in his associations with Humanism. To be sure, English translations of biblical texts were not even exclusively a legacy of either Lollardy or the evangelical Reformation, although these translations were scarce and based from the Latin.[50] Although vernacular lay Bibles were not entirely unknown on the continent by the fifteenth century, Luther was actually the first to translate the entire Bible from the Greek and Hebrew texts for the common German Christian. His example made an obvious impression on Tyndale's own translation work from the original languages, and this certainly was not missed by Barnes, who also wished to see an authorized vernacular English Bible.

Barnes' understanding of the "two powers" of spiritual and temporal authority is reminiscent of Luther's own concept of the "two kingdoms." The former refers to the ministry of the Gospel and the latter refers to the legitimate, though limited, authority of temporal government. In the case of the forbiddance of the English New Testament, disobedience, though not armed resistance, is obligatory for the sake of the Gospel and of the faith. This, of course, is reminiscent of Luther's advocacy of passive resistance in the case of the suppression of his own German New Testament in Ducal Saxony. According to Barnes, such passive resistance also applies in the event that ecclesiastical authorities legalistically impose upon consciences under the penalty of eternal damnation certain rites that are not commanded by God in Scripture and which constitute free or "indifferent" things: "those thynges which be of the inuencion of man do not bynde oure consciens though they seme to be of neuer so grett holynes and of humbillenes and holynes of angelles . . ." In other instances, however, such practices should be heeded if they contribute to personal or communal edification. This fundamentally echoes Luther's own understanding of the liberty of the Christian conscience with regard to matters not clearly proscribed in Scripture.[51]

Barnes' seventh common place rejects the decision of the Council of Constance and argues against Bishop Fisher that Christians should receive the sacrament of the Lord's Supper in both forms of bread and

50. Duffy, *Stripping of the Altars*, 79–80.

51. *A supplicatyon made by Robert Barnes* [1531], fol. C.xii ⱽ–C.xxiiⱽ. On Luther's view of the two kingdoms, see *LW* 45 (*Temporal Authority: To What Extent it Should Be Obeyed*, 1523): 88–96; *WA* 11:249–55. On the freedom of the conscience in relation to indifferent things, see *LW* 40 (*Against the Heavenly Prophets in the Matter of Images and Sacraments*, 1525): 128–30; 151–52; *WA* 18:110–13, 141–42.

wine. Luther raised doubts about the authority of Constance in his debate with Eck in 1519, and he advocated for the sacrament in both kinds at the very beginning of his *Babylonian Captivity* (1520).[52]

In the final common place, Barnes denounces superstitious devotion and prayers to images and saints, which was at the heart of the reforming criticisms of his earlier mentor Thomas Bilney. However, Barnes does not explicitly concede, as Tyndale and Luther both do, that images are theoretically acceptable for purposes of visual remembrance inspiring imitation. Barnes acknowledges that the saints should be revered for the glory of Christ in them and should be followed just as they followed the Lord, but he does not make an explicit connection here to any viable use of images nor does he give the impression that images constitute what he referred to before as indifferent things. Rather, he stresses that people of flesh and blood are the true images of God to whom devotion and charity must be redirected.[53] Barnes' approach to images, then, does not seem to reflect the guarded tolerance of Luther, but Luther certainly agreed in denouncing superstitious devotion to images and saints, prayers for the meritorious intercession of the saints, and the neglect of serving the saints here on earth.[54]

As in the case of Frith, Barnes balances the exegetical use of Scripture with a heavy dose of quotations from Church Fathers like Augustine to rhetorically amplify and reinforce his own theological integrity. The latter does indeed at least partly suggest the legacy of his background in Humanism, although Barnes was also a friar hermit of the Augustinian Order. Yet, as also in the case of Frith, this should not be misconstrued as dismissing a real significant indebtedness to the theological influence of Luther, and for Barnes this included intimate proximity with Luther and his colleagues in Wittenberg. Charles Anderson points out that Barnes' objection to being dismissed as a "Lutheran" in his earlier *Sentenciae* reflects his desire to win an unbiased hearing from his Catholic opponents rather than a disavowal of Luther's theol-

---

52. *A supplicatyon made by Robert Barnes* [1531], fol. Cxxiii ʳ Cxxxii ᵛ; *LW* 36 (*Babylonian Captivity of the Church*, 1520), 20–24; *WA* 6:502–5.

53. *A supplicatyon made by Robert Barnes* [1531], fol. xlvii, Cxxxiii ʳ–Cxlʳ. For Luther on images, see *LW* 40 (*Against the Heavenly Prophets in the Matter of Images and Sacraments*, 1525): 87–92; *WA* 18:69–76. For Tyndale on images, see Tyndale, *Answer to More* [1531], fo. Cxiv.

54. See Althaus, *Theology of Martin Luther*, 300–2, and n. 26.

ogy or influence.[55] Use of the Fathers by Frith and Barnes was chiefly a rhetorical and polemical strategy to reinforce the teaching of Scripture (as they interpreted it) with the ancient words of those saints generally respected by their Catholic opponents. Of course, no theologian of the early sixteenth century who wanted to gain a respectful hearing from his Catholic opponent would have zealously quoted from Luther. Even Tyndale and Frith, when liberally translating from Luther's own writings, did not openly acknowledge him as their source (what in modern times amounts to plagiarism).

Until more recently, most scholars have interpreted Barnes' early theology of 1531 as Lutheran.[56] Trueman, however, argues that upon closer inspection Barnes' treatment of the Law shows more of a synthesis of Lutheran and Augustinian influences. According to Trueman, Barnes agrees with Luther concerning the role of the Law in convicting the conscience of the sinner but not with the same extremity. Trueman also argues that Barnes does not polarize Law and Gospel to the same degree as Luther, bringing him closer to Augustine in stressing the Christian's fulfillment of the Law through the Holy Spirit.[57] Indeed, Barnes does quote Augustine repeatedly throughout the *Supplication* and this obviously impacts how his theology is expressed. However, Barnes' discussion of the role of the Holy Spirit in enabling the Christian to fulfill the Law, though quoting from Augustine, is not as uncharacteristic of Luther as Trueman assumes.[58] Furthermore, the simple fact that Barnes used Augustine does not negate the influence of Luther upon his presuppositions in reading and interpreting Augustine. Rather, his use of Augustine comes from a desire to reinforce the integrity of his interpretation of Scripture with reference to the premiere Catholic Father of the Western Christian Tradition. Trueman even acknowledges the likelihood that rhetorical and polemical strategy is at least one significant part of Barnes' heavy use of Augustine.[59]

55. Anderson, "Robert Barnes on Luther," 55 (and 65, n. 107).

56. For example, Tjernagel, "Robert Barnes and Wittenberg," 649–50; Anderson, "Robert Barnes on Luther," 46–47; Clebsch, *England's Earliest Protestants*, 67–68.

57. Trueman, *Luther's Legacy*, 179, 181–93, 198.

58. For instance, see Luther's discussion of the placement of the Creed and the Lord's Prayer after the Ten Commandments in his *German Catechism* (1529). See *LC*, Tappert, 411; Kolb and Wengert, 431; *BSLK*, 646; See also Althaus, *Theology of Martin Luther*, 267.

59. Ibid., 176.

The influence of Luther in Wittenberg was the most immediate and proximate influence shaping the theology of Barnes around the year 1530 and the writing of his most revealing theological work yet to date. Even though resourcing the sayings of the most generally respected Father and Doctor of the ancient Church, Barnes' treatment of the spiritual bondage of the will to sin under the Law apart from grace, the fruit and testimony of a living faith in love and good works, interpreted in the light of his definition of justification as essentially the remission of sins in Christ imputed to faith "alone. alone. alone" (*Sola. Sola. Sola*), bears the distinctive influence of Luther's evangelical theology of Law and Gospel.

Henry VIII received a copy of Barnes' *Supplication* along with Tyndale's *Exposition of I John* by means of Stephen Vaughn, a merchant and agent of Thomas Cromwell in the Low Countries. In a letter to Cromwell, Vaughn pointed out the potential impact of the *Supplication* upon the English people and urged that Barnes receive an invitation to speak before the *Defensor Fidei* himself. That this was even a possibility for a religious refugee results from the fact that Barnes had praised Henry's royal prerogatives in the *Supplication* and was able to obtain from Luther a response to the question of the legitimacy of the King's divorce from Catherine. Though Luther objected to the divorce,[60] Barnes' relationship to the Wittenberg theologians put him in a strategic position for the continual courting of German political support by the English crown. He returned to England under the promise of safe conduct in December of 1531, but his visit was closely scrutinized by Chancellor Thomas More. Barnes also had the opportunity to approach Stephen Gardiner, now Bishop of Winchester and a judge during his earlier heresy trial of 1525–1526. It is uncertain what transpired between Barnes and Henry VIII, and he quietly left England after only two months, probably to escape from More's antagonistic shadow. More had even accused Barnes of overstaying the period of his safe-conduct, but Frith came to his defense in his *an-*

---

60. Luther's answer was that the marriage was sin only insofar as it was a transgression of a man-made or state law, and the Mosaic laws do not apply in this situation because they were given only to the Jews. Divorce, on the other hand, is divinely prohibited for both Jew and Gentile. Elsewhere, Luther promoted a polygamous marriage to Anne as preferable to divorce. See Tjernagel, *Henry VIII and the Lutherans*, 74. In the opening of his letter, Luther addresses Barnes as "My Anthony." See *LW* 50 ("To Robert Barnes [Wittenberg, September 3, 1531]"): 31–40; *WA Br* 6:172–82.

sweringe vnto M mores lettur (1533). In the first part of his *Confutation of Tyndale's Answer*, which may have appeared before Barnes departed again for the Continent, More also attacked Barnes for rejecting the Real Presence, which Barnes effectively denied in a letter sometime in early 1532. In fact, Tyndale wrote to Frith in 1533 warning him that Barnes would be "hot against" him on account of his rejection of the Real Presence of Christ in the Eucharist. Barnes' role in the later trial and execution of John Lambert in 1538 is further proof that he remained steadfast in his understanding of the Real Presence. Despite the persistent opposition of More, Barnes crisscrossed the channel in 1533–1534, settling alternately in Hamburg and Wittenberg and establishing important diplomatic contacts in Lübeck and elsewhere, now employed as a royal diplomat and middleman between English and German emissaries. In 1534 Barnes also published a revised version of his *Supplication*, this time in London and under royal sanction to promote the prerogatives of the English Crown against the papacy.[61]

A quick glance at the overall structure of the revised *Supplication* reveals visible changes made to the previous edition of 1531. A new autobiographical section provides a detailed narration of the heresy proceedings of 1525–1526. Only three of the original eight common places remain in the new edition: justification by faith alone, the bondage of the will, and the Church. The fourth common place that supports clerical marriage is new to the revised edition, although it was derived from his earlier *Sentenciae* (1530). The fact that Barnes omitted the common place devoted to the freedom of the conscience with regard to "mennes constitucions which be not grounded in scripture" has received scholarly attention for its implications involving submission to the Royal Supremacy.[62]

Upon closer examination of the content, it is plain to see that the introduction to the *Supplication* has been rewritten and its antipapal poise even sharpened. The section describing the articles for which Barnes was condemned in the 1520s is for the most part unchanged

---

61. Lusardi, "Career of Robert Barnes," in Schuster, Marius, Lusardi, and Schoeck, *Complete Works of Thomas More*, 8.3:1390–97, 1406; Rupp, *Studies in the Making*, 41–43; Loane, *Pioneers*, 63–65, 73–74, 80–81; *ODNB* 3:1007.

62. Lusardi, "Career of Robert Barnes," in Schuster, Marius, Lusardi, and Schoeck, *Complete Works of Thomas More*, 8.3:1397–99. On the omission of the sixth common place and its significance with regard to the Act of Supremacy, see Thompson, "Sixteenth-Century Editions," 133–42.

except for a more moderate appraisal of litigation involving Christians. Barnes defends his consistency on this matter with respect to temporal authority, especially that of the King's, although Lusardi points out that he made no such allowance for it in his Christmas Eve sermon of 1525, the heresy proceedings that followed, or his *Supplication* of 1531. The common place on free-will is the least altered of all the articles, and notes taken of a sermon preached by Barnes in London in 1535 confirm the continued influence of Luther upon his understanding of the Law as the accuser of the natural conscience and its true pacification only in the forgiveness of sins promised in Christ: "when the law bryngyth us to knowledge of our selfe we have serten hobtes [obits] there and then, some hath runnyd to Jerusalem, other to S. James, other at charterhowse, other hange them selves yf christ now be not toghte per truwly toghte in remissionem peccatorum Job seyth the hevens nor the angelles ar not pur in thye syght yf thow judge them."[63] The common place on the Church has been totally revamped in the light of More's *Confutation* that attacked Barnes' previous treatise of 1531. Yet, rather than offer a direct refutation of More's counterarguments, Barnes merely restates his position using the same authorities, although improving his citations and softening his anticlericalism to the extent of acknowledging that not all secular and religious clergy are reproachable.[64]

The common place "Onely fayth iustifieth before God" is notably reduced in size compared with the earlier edition of 1531. Clebsch argues that the revised *Supplication* of 1534 displays an entirely new attitude toward good works as the outward testimony of inward justification and that this is not attributable at all to Luther.[65] As mentioned before, Trueman argues that Barnes' earlier Augustinian appraisal of the Law already distanced him from Luther, and he argues that the *Supplication* of 1534 does not reveal any real changes in this understanding.[66]

With regard to major omissions in this section, Trueman is right to point out that Barnes softens his personal invective toward the episcopacy, which he had formerly and unabashedly labeled as antichrist in

---

63. Quoted in Craig and Maas, "A Sermon by Robert Barnes," 546–48, 550.
64. Lusardi, "The Career of Robert Barnes," in Schuster, Marius, Lusardi, and Schoeck, *Complete Works of Thomas More*, 8.3:1374–76, 1397–400.
65. Clebsch, *England's Earliest Protestants*, 65–68.
66. Trueman, *Luther's Legacy*, 179, 181–83, 192, 198.

1531.⁶⁷ As for additions, Trueman identifies a paragraph on the justification of Abraham by faith,⁶⁸ although this did appear with some variation in the earlier edition. One major addition worthy of note is Barnes' expanded refutation of the notion that Paul only objects to the works of the "old law" as justifying but not works of the "new law." Whereas in the 1531 *Supplication* Barnes criticizes his opponents who associate the "old law" with the Mosaic laws and the "new law" with the laws and traditions of the Catholic Church ("workes that you haue inuented out of youre idylle brayne"), in the revised edition "old" and "new law" refer explicitly to the commandments of the Decalogue and the ethical teachings of Christ in the Sermon on the Mount respectively.⁶⁹ Thus, whereas in the earlier *Supplication* Barnes stressed justification apart from the ceremonies and practices instituted by the Church, he here clarifies this to preclude justification even by the moral laws of Scripture itself. Barnes' identification of the Ten Commandments with the Sermon on the Mount does not mean he has adopted a more legalistic position, as Trueman rightly argues against Clebsch, and Barnes' point is that Christ merely interprets the Decalogue correctly according to the commandment to love God and neighbor from the heart. This is followed by a stark contrast between the ministry of Moses and that of Christ, and Barnes argues that the latter came to fulfill what the former demanded of all people. This is completely consistent with the Law-Gospel theology of Luther and reveals his indelible influence upon the theology of Barnes in the *Supplication* of 1534.⁷⁰

Another minor addition to the text of the *Supplication* is the statement that "workes hath theyr glorye and rewarde." Luther was not against speaking about the promise of reward in heaven in the context of faithfulness in suffering, though he stressed that a good work by nature is never done with thoughts of reward nor is heaven itself a reward merited by works.⁷¹ Similarly, for Barnes, since neither the

67. Ibid., 192.

68. Ibid., 192–93; Barnes, *A supplicatyon made by Robert Barnes* [1531], xl ᵛ–xli ʳ.

69. *A supplicatyon made by Robert Barnes* [1531], fo. xl ᵛxli ʳ; *A supplicacion vnto the most gracyous prynce H. the viij* [1534], 66–68.

70. Trueman, *Luther's Legacy*, 192–93. On the difference between Moses and Christ in terms of the ministry of Law and Gospel, see *LW* 27 (*Lectures on Galatians*, 1519): 184, 226; *WA* 22:466, 494; *LW* 35 (*Preface to the Old Testament*, 1523): 241–46; *WA DB* 8:24–25, 26–27.

71. According to Luther, the glory of heaven is promised to all who believe, yet

works that are without faith nor even those that follow faith contribute to justification, he asserts unambiguously that "the glory, and prayse of iustificacion, belongeth to Christ onely."[72]

The most significant revision that occurs in the common place on justification, however, is Barnes' unhesitant exegetical use of James to prove that faith without works is really non-faith: "that fayth is a deed fayth, and of no value that hath no works. For workes shulde declare, and shewe the outwarde faythe, and workes shulde be an outwarde declaracion and a testimonie of the inwarde iustificacion . . ." Barnes nowhere expresses the same doubts he had earlier in 1531 about the apostolicity of the book. At the same time, however, he is quick to maintain that the Gospel of justification by faith alone is still most clearly explained in the epistles of Paul, which is reminiscent of Luther's own accolade of Romans, and that other scriptures must be interpreted with respect and deference to them.[73]

Trueman is right in objecting to Clebsch, who argues that this new appraisal of James moves Barnes much closer now to Martin Bucer's concept of "double justification," and observes that Barnes' theology has not substantially changed in that he openly affirmed works as the outward testimony of inward faith and justification in his previous *Supplication* of 1531.[74] Trueman argues that Barnes already shows an underlying ambivalence toward the book earlier in 1531 and that his reticence to openly accept its canonicity was due perhaps to the overshadowing influence of Luther in Wittenberg.[75] However, what Trueman and other scholars have not considered is how Barnes' decision to drop earlier doubts about the canonicity of James was politically expedient. Although Barnes' use of James is still clearly grounded on the assumption that the "rewarde" of "good workes" is "not remyssion of synnes, nor yet iustificacion," it makes more sense that he would concede its canonical integrity rather than to resurrect an antiquated discussion

---

there are different experiences of that glory in heaven. See Althaus, *Theology of Martin Luther*, 453–54, and n. 50.

72. *A supplicacion vnto the most gracyous prynce H. the viij* [1534], 70, 82.

73. Ibid., 80–81.

74. Trueman, *Luther's Legacy*, 167, 195–96; Clebsch, *England's Earliest Protestants*, 66–67. For good works as the outward testimony of inward faith in the 1531 edition of Barnes' *A supplicatyon made by Robert Barnes* [1531], see fo. liv ʳ–lvi ʳ.

75. Trueman, *Luther's Legacy*, 169–71, 194–96.

about its apostolicity in a treatise sanctioned by a Catholic royal court. Nevertheless, Luther was himself never wholly opposed to exegeting James 2 in order to stress the importance of good works as testimonies of true faith.⁷⁶ It does appear at least that Barnes revokes his earlier uncertainties that were most likely inspired by Luther, but this does not necessarily imply a conscientious break with the theology of Luther on the importance of good works or their relationship to justification. Other revisions in the *Supplication* can certainly be explained in terms of the royal sanctioning of this treatise, and Lusardi perceptively observes with regard to the new *Supplication* that: "In general, the second version of the *Supplication* remains a distinctively, indeed, militantly Protestant document, but it is less radical and uncompromising than the original version. Barnes was a staunch advocate of the revolution that was taking place in England; he wanted to see it go farther than it had, but for the time-being he was bending all his efforts to consolidate the gains already made."⁷⁷

A few other additions are worth noting, and these are surprisingly either not mentioned or not significantly explored by Trueman. As already mentioned, Trueman argues that Barnes' *Supplication* of 1531 does not develop an objective doctrine of the atonement in terms of a satisfaction made to God. However, this was most certainly implicit, and in the 1534 edition Barnes does clearly state that Christ receives all the glory for salvation for it is in His blood that there is a "satisfienge of Gods wrathe, takyng away of euerlastyng vengeaunce, purchasynge of mercy, fulfyllynge of the lawe, with all other lyke thynges."⁷⁸ Trueman also does not analyze the new conclusion appended to the article on justification in the 1534 *Supplication* where the word "imputed" appears three times, "imputative" once, and "reckened" twice. He does mention "the unequivocal statement of the doctrine" in a footnote to the *Supplication* of 1531, arguing that this is a "clarification, rather than

---

76. *A supplicacion vnto the most gracyous prynce H. the viij* [1534], 82; Luther, "A Sermon for the Second Sunday after Mary's Ascension. Preached at Wittenberg by Dr. Martin Luther, 1522," *Complete Sermons*, 2.2:291–301; See also Althaus, *Theology of Martin Luther*, 246.

77. Lusardi, "Career of Robert Barnes," 1399.

78. *A supplicacion vnto the most gracyous prynce H. the viij* [1534], 81.

a development, of his position," but he never mentions it again in his discussion of the revised 1534 edition.[79]

The conclusion discusses how faith itself is not a holy work that merits justification, but it justifies only on the basis that "it is that thynge alonely, wherby I do hange of Christe. And by my faythe alonly, am I partaker of the merites, the mercy purchased by Christes bloude, and faythe, it is alonely that receyue the promyses made in Christe." The notion that justifying righteousness is imputed to faith alone in and through union with Christ could not be stated with much greater clarity than in the statement that follows: "all the merytes, and goodnes, grace, and fauour, and all that is in Christe, to our saluacion, is imputed, and reckened vnto vs, because we hange, and beleue of hym . . . it is a iustice, that is rekened, and imputed vnto vs, for the fayth in Christ Jesus, and it is not of our deseruynge, but clerely, and fully of mercy imputed vnto vs."[80] That Barnes continues to use Augustine throughout his article on justification in the 1534 *Supplication* while explicitly stressing the imputation of righteousness in Christ to faith alone shows that he could refer apologetically to the ancient bishop with the presuppositions influenced by Luther's evangelical theology of justification.

It is quite ironic that Barnes, who had fled secretively from England as a religious refugee in 1528 or 1529, was now employed in service to the English Crown, whereas Thomas More, who had defended the English Church as a champion against heresy, was imprisoned in the Tower of London in April 1534 for his refusal to submit to the Act of Supremacy. He was beheaded a little over a year later. With More now out of the way, Anne Boleyn as Queen with evangelical sympathies, Thomas Cranmer as Archbishop, and Thomas Cromwell as Vicegerent of Spirituals, Barnes enjoyed a brief period of peace as a reforming preacher and diplomat. For the greater part of the next five years Barnes preached openly in his homeland and continued working for diplomacy between England and Germany. As a newly appointed royal chaplain, Barnes was commissioned to dissuade Melancthon from accepting an invitation to France and to come to England instead. Through an interview with Elector John Frederick, he succeeded in opening the way for negotiations between a royal embassy headed by Edward Foxe and Nicholas Heath and the German princes of the Schmalkaldic League.

---

79. See *Luther's Legacy*, 163 (n. 25).

80. *A supplicacion vnto the most gracyous prynce H. the viij* [1534], 85.

During this time, Barnes also published his history of the papacy, the *Vitae Romanorum Pontificum* (1536), which was dedicated to Henry with a preface written by Luther.[81]

With the fall of Anne Boleyn in 1536, the situation turned more precarious for the evangelicals in England. Barnes even retracted his previous invitation to Melancthon. He continued to preach and spent a brief time in the Tower of London but was released with the help of Cromwell. Thereafter, he resumed his preaching in 1537–38, was recommended to the King by Bishop Hugh Latimer of Worcester, and was praised with bequests in the last will and testament of Humphrey Monmouth. Barnes also continued performing his duties as a royal diplomat and was even urged to participate in theological discussions with a German delegation to England led by Francis Burchardt and Frederick Myconius. In 1538, Barnes was also commissioned to furrow out Anabaptists, including John Lambert who was summoned to a hearing before Archbishop Cranmer. Lambert had been with Barnes at the White Horse meetings of the early 1520s and was executed on November 22, 1538, for his more extreme views on the Eucharist.[82]

Contrary to the statement made by Foxe, Barnes was not then sent in early 1539 as the King's envoy to the Duke of Cleves to negotiate a marriage alliance. In fact, Tjernagel denies Barnes as having any direct role in forging the marriage alliance itself.[83] However, Barnes was sent to John Frederick, Elector of Saxony, and King Christian III of Denmark to garner support and to widen the political geography of the alliance.[84]

Barnes' usefulness to the King was already fading in the light of the failing negotiations between Henry and the Schmalkaldic League. In 1539–40 his security was further threatened by open conflict with

---

81. Lusardi, "Career of Robert Barnes," in Schuster, Marius, Lusardi, and Schoeck, *Complete Works of Thomas More*, 8.3:1400–403; Rupp, *Studies in the Making*, 92– 102; Loane, *Pioneers*, 75–76; For Luther's preface see WA 5:1–5. On Barnes' methodology as a historian, see also Maas, "Robert Barnes (1495–1540) as historical theologian."

82. Lusardi, "The Career of Robert Barnes," in Schuster, Marius, Lusardi, and Schoeck, *Complete Works of Thomas More*, 8.3:1403–6; Rupp, *Studies in the Making*, 115–16; Loane, *Pioneers*, 78; ODNB 3:1007–8.

83. Tjernagel, *Henry VIII and Luther*, 207. For the statement in Foxe, see A&M [1570], 1366, which is reaffirmed in *DNB* 1:1175.

84. Lusardi, "The Career of Robert Barnes," in Schuster, Marius, Lusardi, and Schoeck, *Complete Works of Thomas More*, 8.3:1406–7; Rupp, *Studies in the Making*, 120; Loane, *Pioneers*, 81–82; ODNB 3:1008.

his former acquaintance Stephen Gardiner over the doctrine of justification. Gardiner also criticized the suitability of Barnes, an abjured heretic, to serve as a royal diplomat and for his refusal to submit to the "Act of Six Articles" in 1539. It seems that Barnes' connections to Cromwell did not help his case, whose own favor with the King was in peril as a result of having spearheaded the ill-conceived marriage alliance with Anne of Cleves. After being appointed by Cranmer along with William Jerome and Thomas Garrard to preach a series of Lenten sermons at St. Paul's Cross, Barnes was attacked by Gardiner in a sermon before the King in 1540. Gardiner had preached earlier against the doctrine of justification by faith alone and was goaded by Barnes from the pulpit a month later. With the approval of the King, Gardiner held a private disputation with Barnes, the latter even momentarily appearing to concede until his colleagues soon reignited the evangelical fires from the pulpit. The three rebellious preachers were ordered by the King to preach recantation sermons, and Barnes only feigned surrender in his opening prayer. The three were then consigned to the Tower as obstinate heretics. Cromwell was soon to join them and was beheaded first at Tyburn. Without ever having a formal trial or knowing the heresies for which he was condemned, Barnes was burned along with Jerome and Garrard at Smithfield on July 30, 1540.[85]

Barnes' last confession is a testimony to the persistence of his evangelical faith. As Foxe records, Barnes went to the stake with the assurance of glory, not because of his own works but because of his trust in the atoning righteousness of Christ. As for good works, he reiterated that "they are to be done, and verely they that doo them not, shall neuer come in the kingdome of God. We must do them, because they are commaunded vs of God to shew and set forth our profession, not to deserue or merite, for that is only the death of Christ."[86]

Robert Barnes did not leave behind much of a prolific literary legacy, but his importance as a statesman during the Anglo-German negotiations of the 1530s makes him one of the most intriguing and memorable reforming figures of the early decades of the sixteenth cen-

---

85. Lusardi, "Career of Robert Barnes," in Schuster, Marius, Lusardi, and Schoeck, *Complete Works of Thomas More*, 8.3:1407–14; Loane, *Pioneers*, 78–88; Rupp, *Studies in the Making*, 44–46, 126–27; *ODNB* 3:1008–9; Foxe, *A & M* [1570], 1370–75. Barnes' last confession appears on 1372–73.

86. Foxe, *A&M* [1570], 1372.

tury. Despite the few works that Barnes' authored, the two editions of the *Supplication* bring together his thoughts on such a variety of themes as to provide a basic digest of his theology. Though often making appeal to the Fathers, especially Augustine, in addressing his Catholic opponents, the influence of Luther upon Barnes' theology is unquestionable, not least because of his proximity to Wittenberg, his personal relationship with its most influential reformers, and his extended diplomatic work throughout northern Germany on behalf of the English Crown. Although perhaps the most outstanding inheritance from Luther that sets him apart from nearly all other English evangelical reformers of his time is his retention of a belief in the Real Presence, the influence of Luther upon Barnes is also readily discernable in his treatment of the spiritual bondage of the will under the Law, the need for repentance, an articulate doctrine of justification understood as the imputation of righteousness in Christ to faith alone, and good works as the fruit and testimony of a genuine faith and new life in the Spirit. Finally, Luther's own tribute to the English friar at his death cannot be underestimated.

Conclusion

Reassessing the Influence of Luther's Theology of Law and Gospel on Early English Evangelicals

THE FATE OF ROBERT BARNES WAS IN MANY WAYS SYMBOLIC OF THE failed relationship between German Lutheranism and the English Reformation. Clebsch described Barnes as "in many ways the last Englishman to command the attention of the Lutheran party."[1] The reverse was also true, for the decade after Barnes' death in 1540 would witness increasing ties developing between the English Church and the Swiss and south German Protestants.

Luther's direct influence on the English Reformation was most significant during the 1520s and 30s, yet most recent scholarship agrees that "Lutheran" is not an entirely accurate descriptor for the three leading English evangelicals of the period. Indeed, over the last fifty years, Luther's influence on English theology has become increasingly diminished all the way down to the level of utter non-existence.

If it is true, as scholars say, that a distinctive theological legacy of Luther was the centrality he placed on the forgiveness of sins and righteous acceptance before God in justification through faith in Christ alone,[2] then this emphasis alone in the thought of the English evangelical reformers makes Luther a significant influence and is true even of Tyndale at the height of his matured theology of covenant conditionality in the *Newe Testament* of 1534. Although few early English evangelicals express having experienced quite the same intensity of *Anfechtungen* as Luther records from his memories in the Erfurt monastery, it would be wrong to imply or assume on that account that they never felt the

---

1. Clebsch, *England's Earliest Protestants*, 56.
2. McGrath, *Iustitia Dei*, 188, 220–22; Stephens, "Theology of Zwingli," in Bagchi and Steinmetz, *Cambridge Companion to Reformation Theology*, 98.

same tiredness, anxiety, or restlessness of conscience before God in the structures of late medieval Catholicism. In fact, such sobriety was highly encouraged as a further stimulant to a life of piety. This does not mean that all English people were dissatisfied with the status quo, as the evidence of popular resistance to the English Protestant Reformation shows, but there were also many, like Thomas Bilney, who genuinely welcomed the affective respite of a reformed Gospel.[3]

Although Tyndale, Frith, and Barnes define justification primarily in terms of the forgiveness of sins and the favor of God in Christ and His righteousness, scholars are right to point out that they place a significant amount of emphasis on the new obedience in good works that ensues from justifying faith in the life of the Christian. Some have attributed this to the influence of Augustine (via Humanism), the Reformed tradition, and even Lollardy. At the same time, scholars have often exaggerated the centrality in the theology of Luther of justification understood as righteousness in Christ *coram Deo* through faith alone to the degree that they fail to appreciate the regularity with which he himself substantially and positively praises the Law and stresses good works as the form of justifying faith and the rule of the Spirit in the life of the baptized and believing Christian. Luther was certainly hard against the Law and works when conceived as a means of meriting justification before God. Yet he could speak with equal adulation and urgency about the Law and good works in the context of the call upon the Christian in the light of the Gospel to mortify the flesh and to live a life of service for others in the world. Contrary to the opinions of his Catholic opponents, reforming contemporaries, and even some later Protestants, Luther was never ethically indifferent or ambivalent about morality, but he was firmly convinced that only faith alone in Christ and His perfect righteousness reckoned or imputed for justification before God could truly liberate the conscience and purify the heart through the Spirit to keep the Law with the sincerest of love in devotion to others.

It was for this reason that this book began where all previous studies have not, with a fresh look at the whole development of Luther's theology of Law and Gospel in its historical context. Indeed, Luther always perceived the chief function of the Law to be that of awakening the

---

3. See the discussion by Null of evangelical conversion in the English Reformation in "Thomas Cranmer and Tudor Evangelicalism," in Haykin and Stewart, *Emergence of Evangelicalism*, 230–38, 241–46.

conscience to the knowledge of sin and spiritual bondage in order that the repentant might believe in Christ alone for their justification before God. Yet this negative approach to the Law was not simply on account of his desire to accentuate justification as a gift to be received through faith alone in Christ and His righteousness, but it also proceeded from his conviction that the renovating presence of Christ in faith leading to the mortification of sins and the love of good works only follows a humbling encounter with the Law mitigated by filial trust in the Gospel. Of course, Luther recognized that even the works of the Christian remain imperfect on account of the weakness of faith and the opposing desires of the flesh, and it was precisely on this account that Luther stressed the continuing function of the Law in the Christian life. This refers to the ongoing work of the Law to censure sin for the sake of the increase of repentance and faith throughout the Christian life, something Luther developed and stressed even more explicitly at the end of the 1520s and into the 1530s. Yet the kindlier exhortations of Christ and the apostles were interpreted by Luther even earlier on as merely interpretations of the Ten Commandments to spur on those who have faith and possess the Spirit to good works and to battle against sin but precisely on account of the fact that they are sinners and remain sluggish in the flesh. The work of the Law in increasing repentance and as a norm of Christian obedience was fully commensurate with what Melancthon and the *Formula of Concord* more formally defined as a *tertius usus legis*. Luther openly praised the Ten Commandments as teaching the highest form of living under God in human community, and his negativity toward the Law was in rejection of works done by compulsion, "works of the Law," with the false notion that these merited justifying favor with God.

Recent scholars of early English evangelical theology have generally perpetuated these stereotypes of Luther as a reformer solely interested in the justification of the sinner *coram Deo* with little or no emphasis in his theology for the positive value of the Law and good works in the Christian life. Not only have such studies lacked serious critical interpretation and contextual engagement with the larger body of Luther's writings, but they have oversimplified his thought entirely. Therefore, it was necessary to correct this imbalance before moving on to explore the influence of Luther upon the theology of Tyndale, Frith, and Barnes.

Apart from a comparison of theological content in their writings, the identification of an historical point of contact between Luther and early English evangelicals reinforces the argument for his influence upon their intellectual formation. With regard to Tyndale and Frith, that incontrovertible point of contact is Luther's published writings. It is not insignificant that the careers of both these reformers, and Tyndale even more so, began with the publishing in English of significant portions of the works of Luther. Whether or not Tyndale or Frith ever personally met Luther or visited Wittenberg, their sojourns in and around Germany brought them deeper into the local sphere of his cultural legacy. As a younger reformer, Frith's debt to Luther was also partly mediated through his earliest associations with the elder Tyndale. As for Robert Barnes, his matriculation at Wittenberg, his close personal relationship with Luther and his colleagues, and his diplomatic services in northern Germany on behalf of the English court adds historical weight to the argument that Luther was the principal theological influence on his intellectual development. The particular relationship Tyndale, Frith, and Barnes shared with Luther, whether through his writings or his person, cannot be rivaled historically by any other single reformer of the fourteenth to sixteenth centuries.

With regard to theological content, each of these reformers stood faithfully in the tradition of Luther in affirming the necessity of preaching the Law to awaken sinners from spiritual bondage to lead them to repentance, that justification is the forgiveness of sins and favor of God in union with Christ and His righteousness through faith alone apart from works, and that a heart for the Law and good works in ongoing struggle against sin proceeds from faith through love in the power of the Holy Spirit. Though imperfect and only secondary, Luther and the early English evangelicals both described good works as further self-assurance and outward testimony to others of genuine faith, the possession of the Spirit, and the forgiveness of sins.

It cannot be denied that these reformers possessed a certain admiration for Augustine, especially Frith and Barnes who made frequent and explicit apologetic use of the bishop throughout their writings. However, their use of Augustine in the light of their theology viewed holistically and in historical correlation with Luther and his writings argues strongly in favor of the influence of Luther's evangelical theology of Law and Gospel on their presuppositions. Furthermore, it should not be assumed that the simple presence of Augustinian elements in the thought of the English evangelical reformers necessarily precludes the influence of Luther. As McGrath argues, Luther's own relationship to Augustine is "ambivalent. While one can point to elements in his thought which are clearly Augustinian, there are points—particularly his doctrine of *iustitia Christia aliena*—where he diverges significantly from Augustine."[4] The case of Barnes is particularly enlightening on this matter. His article on justification in the 1534 *Supplication* continues to reference Augustine at the same time that he expresses an even more explicit and unambiguous theology of imputed righteousness in Christ through faith alone. Recent scholars have rightly drawn attention to the varied importance of other influences, but Luther was still the principal influence that made them "evangelical" reformers and shaped their basic theological assumptions concerning the nature of justification before God in the Gospel and the obedience of the Christian life in the Law.

The influence of Luther's theology of Law and Gospel on early English evangelicals is certainly more controversial with regard to Tyndale in the light of his development of a quite distinctive rhetorical emphasis on the conditionality of God's promises of mercy in terms of the covenant. Thus, on account of this, as well as the greater prolificacy of his literary output, Tyndale naturally received an inordinate amount of attention in comparison to the others. Yet even with regard to covenant conditionality, Tyndale did not stray so far from Luther as is usually assumed. Tyndale's *Prologue to Romans* and its affirmation of the biblical centrality of justification by faith alone remains largely unchanged in the *New Testament* of 1534, and he continued to interpret Christian conversion in terms of repentance toward obedience in the Law and good works through a faith that justifies before God only in the righteousness of Christ. Tyndale's theology of covenant merely becomes his preferred way of stressing that justifying faith in Christ cannot exist where there is no repentance under the Law and earnestness for good works with intentions of showing gratitude to the mercy of God. Although Tyndale did not inherit his emphasis on the covenant as a hermeneutical principle for biblical interpretation from Luther, it was not so unlike Luther to speak of salvation in terms of covenant conditionality. Luther described the Gospel in the context of the sacrament

---

4. McGrath, *Iustitia Dei*, 205.

of baptism as an eternal covenant good for life but only for those who repent and believe and who give evidence of this in battle against sin. This was at the moment of the culmination of his evangelical "breakthrough" and reveals that his own theology of Law and Gospel was not antithetical to describing salvation in terms of covenant conditionality. This is further reflected in the many other statements in which Luther describes God's promise to not impute sin remaining in the life of the baptized who fight against sin in the Spirit while trusting in the Gospel for their righteousness and repenting again when they fall. This struggle is carried out under the grace of justification and is evidence of the beginnings of the rule of the Spirit in righteousness to be perfected by God in His eternal presence.

The influence of Tyndale, Frith, and Barnes upon the future development of the English Reformation beyond the 1540s did not extend much beyond Tyndale's Bible translations and possibly the Eucharistic writings of John Frith. Nevertheless, while it has become customary to define the English Reformation more as an achievement of politics and the enforcement of religious change from above,[5] all of which in its more comprehensive forms occurred well after the deaths of these early English evangelicals, Tyndale, Frith, and Barnes are critical to the history of the English Reformation between the years 1520 and 1540. If this is true, Luther also deserves a central place in that history.

---

5. Haigh, *English Reformations*, 12–13, 21; Scarisbrick, *Reformation and English People*, 62; MacCulloch, "England," in Pettegree, *Early Reformation in Europe*, 166.

Bibliography

Sixteenth Century Publications

Anonymous (Tyndale?). *A booke called in latyn Enchiridion militis christiani, and in englysshe the manuell of the christen knyght replenysshed with moste holsome preceptes, made by the famous clerke Erasmus of Roterdame, to the whiche is added a newe and meruaylous profytable preface.*, [Imprynted at London : By wynkyn de worde, for Iohan Byddell, otherwyse Salisbury, the. xv. daye of Nouembre. And be for to sell at the sygne of our Lady of pytie next to Flete bridge, 1533]. British Library.

Barnes, Robert. *Sentenciae ex doctrobus collectae, quas papistae valde impudenter hodie damnant* [Wittenberg, 1530].

———. *A supplicatyon made by Robert Barnes doctoure in diuinitie, vnto the most excellent and redoubted prince kinge henrye the eyght. The articles for which this forsayde doctoure Barnes was condemned of our spiritualtye, are confirmed by the Scripture, doctoures and their awne [sic] lawe. After that he disputeth certayne comon places which also he confermeth with the Scripture, holye doctoures and their awne [sic] lawe,* [Antwerp : S. Cock, 1531?]. Cambridge University Library.

———. *A supplicacion vnto the most gracyous prynce H. the viij,* [Imprinted at London : In Fletestrete by John Byddell, at the signe of our lady of Pitie, nexte to flete brydge, The yere of our lorde God. 1534. in the moneth of Nouember]. British Library.

Foxe, John. *Actes and monuments of these latter and perillous dayes touching matters of the Church, wherein ar comprehended and decribed the great persecutions [and] horrible troubles, that haue bene wrought and practised by the Romishe prelates, speciallye in this realme of England and Scotlande, from the yeare of our Lorde a thousande, vnto the tyme nowe present. Gathered and collected according to the true copies [and] wrytinges certificatorie, as wel of the parties them selues that suffered, as also out of the bishops registers, which wer the doers therof, by Iohn Foxe.* Imprinted at London : By Iohn Day, dwellyng ouer Aldersgate. Cum priuilegio Regi[a]e Maiestatis, [1563 (20 March)]. Henry E. Huntington Library and Art Gallery.

———. *The first volume of the ecclesiasticall history contaynyng the actes and monumentes of thynges passed in euery kynges tyme in this realme, especially in the Church of England principally to be noted : with a full discourse of such persecutions, horrible troubles, the sufferyng of martyrs, and other thinges incident, touchyng aswel the sayd Church of England as also Scotland, and all other foreine nations, from the primitiue tyme till the reigne of K. Henry VIII.*, At London : Printed by Iohn Daye, dwellyng ouer Aldersgate, these bookes are to be sold at hys shop vnder the gate. 1570. Harvard University Library.

———. *The vvhole workes of W. Tyndall, Iohn Frith, and Doct. Barnes, three worthy martyrs, and principall teachers of this churche of England collected and compiled in one tome togither, beyng before scattered, [and] now in print here exhibited to the church. To the prayse of God, and profite of all good Christian readers.* At London: Printed by Iohn Daye, and are to be sold at his shop vnder Aldersgate, An. 1573. Henry E. Huntington Library and Art Gallery.

Frith, John. *A boke made by Iohn Frith prisoner in the tower of London answeringe vnto M mores lettur which he wrote agenst the first litle treatyse that Iohn Frith made concerninge the sacramente of the body and bloude of, christ . . . vnto which boke are added in the ende the articles of his examinacion before the bishoppes . . . for which Iohn Frith was condempned a[n]d after bur[n]et . . . the fourth daye of Iuli. Anno. 1533.*, [Imprinted at Monster [i.e., Antwerp]: Anno 1533 by me Conrade Willems [i.e., H. Peetersen van Middelburch?, 1533]. British Library.

———. *A Christen sentence and true iudgement of the moste honorable sacrament of Christes bodye & bloud declared both by the auctorite of the holy Scriptures and the auncient doctores. Very necessary to be redde in this tyme of all the faythful* [London, 1548]. Bodleian Library.

———. *The contentes of thys boke. The fyrst is a letter which was wryten vnto the faythful followers of Christes gospell. Also another treatese called the Myrrour or glasse to knowe thy selfe. Here vnto is added a propre instruction teaching a man to dye gladly and not to feare death* [London? : W. Hill, 1548 or 1549]. National Library of Scotland.

———. *A disputacio[n] of purgatorye made by Ioh[a]n Frith which is deuided in to thre bokes. The first boke is an answere vnto Rastell, which goeth aboute to proue purgatorye by naturall phylosophye. The seconde boke answereth vnto Sir Thomas More, which laboureth to proue purgatorye by scripture. The thirde boke maketh answere vnto my lorde of Rochestre which most leaneth vnto the doctoures*, [Antwerp : S. Cock, 1531?]. British Library.

———. *A myrroure or lokynge glasse wherin you may beholde the sacramente of baptisme described. Anno. M.D.xxxiii. Per me I.F.*, [Imprinted at Lo[n]do[n] : By Ihon Daye, dwellynge in Sepulchres parishe, at the signe of the Resurrection, a litle aboue Holburne condite, [1548?]]. Cambridge University Library.

———. *A mirroure to know thyselfe* [Antwerp : M. Crom, ca. 1536?]. Bodleian Library.

———. *An other boke against Rastel named the subsedye or bulwark to his fyrst boke, made by Ihon Frithe preso[n]ner in the Tower* [London? : S.n., 1537?]. British Library.

———. *A pistle to the Christen reader. The revelation of Antichrist. Antithesis, wherin are compared to geder Christes actes and oure holye father the Popes.* At Malborow in the lande of Hesse [Antwerp]: the. xij. day of Iulye, anno. M.CCCCC.xxix. by me Hans luft [Martin de Keyser]. British Library.

———. *[Paitrikes places]* [Antwerp : S. Cock, 1531?]. Trinity College Library.

———, and William Tyndale. *The testament of master Wyllyam Tracie esquier, expounded both by Willsm Tindall and Iho[n] Frith. Wherin thou shalt perceyue with what charitie y[e] chaunceler of Worcester burned when he toke vp the deek* carkas and made asshes of hit after hit was buried, [Antwerp : H. Peetersen van Middelburch?], M.D.xxxv. [1535]. British Library.

More, Thomas. *A dyaloge of syr Thomas More knyghte: one of the counsayll of oure souerayne lorde the kyng [and] chauncellour of hys duchy of Lancaster. Wherin be treated dyuers maters, as of the veneration [and] worshyp of ymages [and] relyques, prayng to sayntys, [and] goyng o[n] pylgrymage. Wyth many othere thyngys touching the pestylent sect of Luther and Tyndale, by the tone bygone in Sarony, and by tother laboryed to be brought in to Englond*, [Enprynted at London : [By J. Rastell] at the sygne of the meremayd at Powlys gate next to chepe syde in the moneth of June, the yere of our lord. M. [and] C.xxix. [1529]]. Folger Shakespeare Library.

Tyndale, William. *An answere vnto Sir Thomas Mores dialoge made by Vvillyam Tindale. First he declareth what the church is, and geveth a reason of certayne wordes which Master More rebuketh in the tra[n]slacion of the newe Testament. After that he answereth particularlye vnto everye chaptre which semeth to haue anye apperaunce of truth thorow all his .iiij. bokes*, [Antwerp : S. Cock, 1531]. British Library.

———. *The examinacion of Master William Thorpe preste accursed of heresye before Thomas Arundell, Archebishop of Canterbury, the yere of ower Lord. MCCC. And seuen. The examinacion of the honorable knight syr Ihon Oldcastell Lorde Cobham, burnt bi the said Archebisshop, in the first yere of Kynge Henry the Fyfth.*, [Antwerp: J. van Hoochstraten, 1530]. British Library.

———. *The exposition of the fyrst epistle of seynt Jhon with a prologge before it: by W.T.*, [Antwerp: M. de Keyser, 1531]. British Library.

———. *That fayth the mother of all good workes iustifieth us before we ca[n] bringe forth anye good worke....*, [Printed at Malborowe [i.e., Antwerp] in the londe of hesse : By Hans Luft [i.e., J. Hoochstraten], the. viii. day of May. Anno M.D.xxviij] [1528]. British Library.

———. *The firste boke of Moses called Genesis newly correctyd and amendyd by W.T.*, [Antwerp: M. de Keyser], MD. XXXIIII [1534]. Cambridge University Library.

———. [*New Testament*] [Cologne: H. Fuchs, 1525].

———. *The Newe Testament dylygently corrected and compared with the Greke by Willyam Tindale, and fynesshed in the yere of our Lorde God A.M.D. & xxxiiij. in the moneth of Nouember.*, Imprinted at Anwerp [sic] : By Marten Emperowr, M.D.xxxiiij [1534]. British Library.

———. *The Newe Testament yet once agayne corrected by Willyam Tindale ; where vnto is added a kalendar and a necessarye table wherin earlye and lightelye maye be founde any storye contayned in the foure Euangelistes and in the Actes of the Apostles.*, [Antwerp : M. De Keyser for G. van der Haghen], Prynted in the yere of oure Lorde God M.D.[?].xxxo. [1530-1534?]. Bodleian Library and John Rylands University Library of Manchester.

———. *The obedie[n]ce of a Christen man and how Christe[n] rulers ought to governe, where in also (if thou marke diligently) thou shalt fynde eyes to perceave the crafty conveyance of all iugglers.*, [At Marlborow in the la[n]de of Hesse [i.e., Antwerp] : the seconde daye of October. Anno. M.CCCCC.xxviii, by me Hans luft [i.e., J. Hoochstraten], [1528]]. Bodleian Library.

———. *Pathway to the Holy Scriptures* [London: Thomas Godfray, 1536?]. Emmanuel College Library, Cambridge University.

———. [The Pentateuch]. Imprented at Malborow in the lande of Hesse [i.e., Antwerp] : By me Hans Luft [i.e., Johan Hoochstraten], M. CCCCC.xxx. the . xvij dayes of Januarij [17 Jan. 1530] Cambridge University Library.

———. *The practyse of prelates Whether the Kinges grace maye be separated from hys quene, be cause she was his brothers wyfe.*, marborch [i.e., Antwerp : Printed by Joannes Hoochstraten], In the yere of oure Lorde. M.CCCCC. [and] XXX. [1530]. Henry E. Huntington Library and Art Gallery.

———. *The prayer and complaynt of the ploweman vnto Christ writte[n] nat longe after the yere of our Lorde. M. [and] thre hu[n]dred.*, [London: T. Godfrey, ca. 1532]. Bodleian Library.

———. *The prophete Ionas with an introduccio[n] before teachinge to vndersto[n]de him and the right vse also of all the scripture, and why it waswritten, and what is therin to be sought, and shewenge wherewith the scripture is locked vpp that he which readeth it, can not vndersto[n]de it, though he studie therin never so moch: and agayne with what keyes it is so opened, that the reader can be stopped out with no sotilte or false doctrine of man, from the true sense and vderstondynge therof.*, [Antwerp : M. de Keyser, 1531?]. British Library.

———, and John Frith. *The testament of master Wylliam Tracie esquier, expounded both by Willism Tindall and Iho[n] Frith. Wherin thou shalt perceyue with what charitie y[e] chaunceler of Worcester burned whan he toke vp the deek carkas and made asshes of hit after hit was buried*, [Antwerp : H. Peetersen van Middelburch?], M.D.xxxv. [1535]. British Library.

———, and Miles Coverdale. *The Byble which is all the holy Scripture: in whych are contayned the Olde and Newe Testament truly and purely translated into Englysh by Thomas Matthew. M,D,XXXVII, Set forth with the Kinges most gracyous lyce[n] ce.*, [Antwerp : Printed by Matthew Crom for Richard Grafton and Edward Whitchurch, London, 1537]. British Library.

Modern Editions and Facsimiles of the Writings of English Evangelical Reformers

Duffield, G. E. editor. *The Work of William Tyndale*. Abingdon: Sutton Courtenay Press, 1964.

Greenslade, S. L. *The Work of William Tindale*, with an essay on Tindale and the English Language by G. D. Bone. London: Blackie & Son, 1938.

Mombert, J. I., editor. *William Tyndale's Five Books of Moses, Called the Pentateuch, Being a Verbatim Reprint of the Edition M.CCCCC.XXX. Compared with Tyndale's Genesis of 1534 . . . with Various Collations and Prolegomena*. New York: Anson D. F. Randolph, 1884.

Tyndale, William. *An answere vnto Sir Thomas Mores Dialoge*. The Independent Works of William Tyndale, Volume 3. Edited by Anne M. O'Donnell and Jared Wicks. Washington, DC: Catholic University of America Press, 2000.

———. *The Beginning of the New Testament Translated by William Tyndale, 1525. Facsimile of the Unique Fragment of the Uncompleted Cologne Edition with an Introduction by Alfred W. Pollard*. Oxford: Clarendon Press, 1926.

———. *The Prophete Jonas with an introduction before teaching to understande him and the right use also of all the Scripture by William Tyndale.* Reproduced in *facsimile. To which is added Coverdales version of Jonah, with an introduction by Francis Fray, F.S.A.* London: Willis and Sotheran; Bristol: Lasbury, 1863.

———. *Tyndale's New Testament*. Translated by William Tyndale. Edited with an introduction by David Daniell. New Haven: Yale University Press, 1989.

———. *Tyndale's Old Testament*. Translated by William Tyndale. Edited with an introduction by David Daniell. New Haven: Yale University Press, 1992.

Parker, Douglas H., editor. *A Critical Edition of Robert Barnes' A supplication Vnto the Most Gracyous Prince Kynge Henry The. VIIJ. 1534*. University of Toronto Press, 2008.

Russell, T., editor. *The Works of the English Reformers: William Tyndale and John Frith*. 3 volumes. London, 1831.

Walter, H., editor. *An answer to Sir Thomas More's Dialogue: the supper of the Lord after the true meaning of John VI. and 1 Cor. XI. And Wm. Tracy's Testament Expounded*. Cambridge: Cambridge University Press, 1850.

———. *Doctrinal Treatises and Introductions to Different Portions of the Holy Scriptures*. 1848. Reprint, Eugene, Oregon: Wipf & Stock, 2005.

———. *Expositions and Notes on Sundry Portions of the Holy Scriptures, together with the Practice of Prelates*. 1849. Reprint, Eugene, OR: Wipf & Stock, 2004.

Writings of Tindal, Frith, and Barnes. London: Religious Tract Society, 1830; reprint, Philadelphia: Presbyterian Board of Publication, 1842.

Primary Sources of the English Reformation

Colet, John. *An Exposition of St. Paul's Epistle to the Romans, Delivered as Lectures in the University of Oxford about the year 1497*. Translated by J. H. Lupton. Ridgewood, NJ: Gregg, 1965.

Ellis, Sir Henry, editor. *Original Letters Illustrative of English History*. London: Richard Bentley, New Burlington Street, 1846.

Hatt, Cecilia A., editor. *English Works of John Fisher, Bishop of Rochester (1469–1535): Sermons and other Writings*. Oxford: Oxford University Press, 2002.

Henry VIII. *Answere Unto A Certaine Letter of Martyn Lther* [London, 1528]. Amsterdam: Da Capo, 1971.

Hudson, Anne, editor. *Selections from English Wycliffite Writings*. Cambridge: Cambridge University Press, 1978.

Lawler, Thomas M. C., Germain Marc'hadour, and Richard C. Marius, editors. *The Complete Works of St. Thomas More*. Vol. 6.1. New Haven: Yale University Press, 1981.

Letters and Papers, Foreign and Domestic, of the Reign of Henry VIII, preserved in the Public Record Office, the British Museum, and elsewhere. 2nd ed. Revised and greatly enlarged by R. H. Brodie. 21 vols. 1920. Reprint, Vaduz Kraus, 1965.

Schuster, Louis A., Richard C. Marius, James P. Lusardi, and Richard J. Schoeck, eds. *The Confutation of Tyndale's Answer. Part 3. The Yale Edition of the Complete Works of Thomas More*. Vol. 8. New Haven: Yale University Press, 1973.

Strype, John, editor. *Ecclesiastical memorials, relating chiefly to religion, and the Reformation of it, and the emergencies of the Church of England, under King Henry VIII. King Edward VI. And Queen Mary I.: with large appendixes, containing original papers, records, &c.* 4 vols. Oxford: Clarendon, 1822.

Writings of Luther and the Continental Reformation

Die Bekenntnisschriften der evangelisch-lutherischen Kirche: Herausgegeben im Gedenkjahr der Augsburgischen Konfession 1930. Zwolfte Auflage. Götingen: Vandenhoeck & Ruprecht, 1998.

Calvin, John. *Institutes of the Christian Religion.* 2 vols. Edited by John T. McNeill. Translated and Indexed by Ford Lewis Battles. Library of Christian Classics Volume 20. Philadelphia Westminster, 1960.

———. *Opera quae supersunt omnia. Corpus Reformatorum* [microform]. Volumes 29–87. Edited by Guilielmus Baum, Eduardus Cunitz, and Eduardus Reuss, et al. Braunchsweig- Berlin, 1863–1900.

Chemnitz, Martin. *Loci Theologici.* Vol. 2. Translated by J. A. O. Preus. St. Louis: Concordia, 1989.

———. *Loci Theologici De Coena Domini De Duabus Naturis in Christo Theologiae Jesuitarum* [Frankfurt and Wittenberg, 1653]. A facsimile published by the Lutheran Heritage Foundation. Chelsea, MI: Sheridan, 2000.

Kolb, Robert, and Timothy J. Wengert, eds. *The Book of Concord: The Confessions of the Evangelical Lutheran Church.* Minneapolis: Fortress, 2000.

Lenker, John Nicholas, editor. *The Complete Sermons of Martin Luther.* 7 Volumes. Translated by John Nicholas Lenker, et al. Grand Rapids: Baker, 2000.

Luther, Martin. *Luther's Works: American Edition* [CD-ROM]. 55 vols. Edited by Jaroslav Pelikan and Helmut T. Lehmann. St. Louis: Concordia; Philadelphia: Fortress, 1955–1986.

———. *D. Martin Luthers Werke: Kritische Gesamtausgabe.* 63 volumes. Weimar, 1883–1987; reprint, Verlag Hermann Böhlaus Nachfolger Weimer, 2001.

Melancthon, Philipp. *Loci Communes 1543.* Translated and Edited by J. A. O. Preus. St Louis: Concordia, 1992.

———. *Melancthon on Christian Doctrine: Loci Communes, 1555.* Translated and edited by Clyde Manshreck. 1965. Reprint, Grand Rapids: Baker, 1982.

———. *Opera quae supersunt omnia. Corpus Reformatorum* [microform]. Volumes 1–28. Edited by C. G. Bretschneider and H. E. Bindsell. Halle, 1834–1860.

Pauck, Wilhelm, editor. *Melancthon and Bucer.* Translated by Lowell Satre. Library of Christian Classics 19. Philadelphia: Westminster, 1969.

Tappert, Theodore G., editor. *The Book of Concord.* Philadelphia: Fortress, 1959.

Secondary Sources and Other Writings Cited

Althaus, Paul. *The Divine Command.* Translated by Franklin Sherman with an introduction by William H. Lazareth. Social Ethics Series. Philadelphia: Fortress, 1966.

———. *The Ethics of Martin Luther.* Translated with a foreword by Robert C. Schultz. Philadelphia: Fortress, 1972.

———. *The Theology of Martin Luther.* Translated by Robert C. Schulz. Philadelphia: Fortress Press, 1966.

Amos, N. Scott, Andrew Pettegree, and Henk Van Nierop, eds. *The Education of a Christian Society: Humanism and the Reformation in Britain and the Netherlands:*

Papers Delivered to the Thirteenth Anglo-Dutch Historical Conference, 1997. Aldershot, UK: Ashgate, 1999.

Anderson, Charles S. "The Person and Position of Dr. Robert Barnes, 1495-1540: A Study in the Relationship between the English and German Reformations." ThD diss., Union Theological Seminary, 1962.

———. "Robert Barnes on Luther." In *Interpreters of Luther: Essays in Honor of Wilhelm Pauck*, edited by Jaroslav Pelikan 35-66. Philadelphia: Fortress, 1968.

Aston, Margaret. "Lollardy and the Reformation: Survival or Revival?" *History* 49 (1964) 149-70.

Aulén, Gustaf. *Christus Victor*. Translated by A.G. Herbert. London: SPCK, 1931.

Avis, Frederick, C. "Book Smuggling into England during the Sixteenth Century." *Gutenberg Jahrbuch* (1972) 180-87. Mainz: Gutenberg Gesellschaft,

———. "England's Use of Antwerp Printers, 1500-1540." *Gutenberg Jahrbuch* (1973) 239-40. Mainz: Gutenberg Gesellschaft.

Bagchi, David, and David C. Steinmetz, editors. *The Cambridge Companion to Reformation Theology*. Cambridge: Cambridge University Press, 2004.

Bainton, Roland. *Erasmus of Christendom*. New York: Scribner, 1969.

Baker, D., editor. *Reform and Reformation: England and the Continent c. 1500—c. 1750*. Oxford: Blackwell, 1979.

Baker, J. Wayne. *Heinrich Bullinger and the Covenant: The Other Reformed Tradition*. Athens: Ohio University Press, 1980.

Barth, Karl. *Community, State and Church: Three Essays*. Translated by A.M. Hall with an introduction by Will Herberg. Garden City, NY: Doubleday, 1960.

Bayer, Oswald. *Martin Luther's Theology: A Contemporary Interpretation*. Translated by Thomas H. Trapp. Grand Rapids, Michigan: Eerdmans, 2008.

Beeke, Joel R. *The Quest for Full Assurance: The Legacy of Calvin and His Successors*. Carlisle, PA: Banner of Truth Trust, 1999.

Bierma, Lyle D. *German Calvinism in the Confessional Age: The Covenant Theology of Caspar Olevianus*. Grand Rapids: Baker, 1996.

Bornkamm, Heinrich. *Luther in Mid-Career 1521-1530*. Edited with a foreword by Karin Bornkamm. Translated by E. Theodore Bachmann. London: Darton Longman, & Todd, 1983.

———. *Luther and the Old Testament*. Translated by Eric W. and Ruth C. Gritsch. Edited by Victor I. Gruhn. Philadelphia: Fortress, 1969.

Bouman, Walter R. "The Concept of the 'Law' in the Lutheran Tradition." *Word & World* 3 (1983) 413-22.

Bozeman, Theodore Dwight. *The Precisianist Strain: Disciplinary Religion and Antinomian Backlash in Puritanism to 1638*. Published for the Omohundro Institute of Early American History and Culture, Williamsburg, Virginia. Chapel Hill: University of North Carolina Press, 2004.

Braaten, Carl. "Reflections on the Lutheran Doctrine of the Law." *Lutheran Quarterly* 18.1 (1966) 72-84.

———, and Robert W. Jensen, editors. *Union with Christ: The New Finnish Interpretation of Luther*. Grand Rapids: Eerdmans, 1998.

Bray, Gerald. "Luther's Legacy to the English Reformation." *Evangel* 15.2 (1997) 42-50.

Brecht, Martin. *Martin Luther: His Road to Reformation, 1483-1521*. Translated by James L. Schaaf. Minneapolis: Fortress, 1985.

———. *Martin Luther: The Preservation of the Church, 1533–1546*. Translated by James L. Schaaf. Minneapolis: Fortress, 1993.

———. *Martin Luther: Shaping and Defining the Reformation, 1521–1532*. Translated by James L. Schaaf. Minneapolis: Fortress, 1990.

Bridston, K. R., "Law and Gospel and Their Relationship in the Theology of Luther." PhD diss., University of Edinburgh, 1949.

Bring, Ragnar. "Does Lutheran Theology Recognize a 'Third' Use of the Law?" In *Faith and Action*, edited by H. H. Schrey, 113–18. Edinburgh: Oliver & Boyd, 1970.

———. "Gesetz und Evangelium und der dritte Gebrauch des Gesetzes in der lutherischen Theologie." *Zur Theologie Luthers: Aus der Arbeit der Luther-Agricola Gesellschaft in Finnland*. Schriften der Luther-Agricola Gesellschaft in Finnland 4. Helsinki: Ackademische Buchhandlung, 1943.

Brown, Colin, editor. *The New International Dictionary of New Testament Theology*. Volume 2. Translated, with additions and revisions, from the German *Theologisches Begriffslexikon Zum Neuen Testament*, edited by Lothar Coenen, Erich Beyreuther, and Hans Bietenhard. Grand Rapids: Zondervan, 1986.

Buechner, Quinten A. "Luther and the English Reformation." *History Today* 22 (1972) 799–805.

Chester, A. G. "Robert Barnes and the Burning of the Books." *Huntington Library Quarterly* 14 (1951) 211–21.

Clark, F. L. *John Frith: Kentish Martyr 1503–1553*. Sevenoaks: Private Publishing, 1978.

Clark, R. Scott. "Calvin versus the Calvinists: A Bibliographic Essay." *Modern Reformation* 18.4 (2009) 16.

Clebsch, William A. *England's Earliest Protestants 1520–35*. New Haven: Yale University Press, 1964.

Craig, John, and Korey Maas. "A Sermon by Robert Barnes, c. 1535." *Journal of Ecclesiastical History* 55 (2004) 542–51.

Collinson, Patrick. *The Reformation: A History*. New York: Modern Library, 2004.

Dallman, William. *Robert Barnes, Luther's English Friend*. Third Printing. St. Louis: Concordia, n.d.

D'Alton, Craig W. "The Suppression of Lutheran Heretics in England, 1526–1529." *Journal of Ecclesiastical History* 54 (2003) 228–53.

Daniell, David. *The Bible in English*. New Haven: Yale University Press, 2003.

———. *William Tyndale: A Biography*. New Haven: Yale University Press, 1994.

Davis, J. F. "Lollardy and the Reformation in England." *Archiv für Reformationsgeschichte* 73 (1982) 217–37.

Day, John T., Eric Lund, and Anne M. O'Donnell, editors. *Word, Church, and State, Tyndale Quincentenary Essays*. Washington, DC: Catholic University of America Press, 1999.

Demaus, Robert, and Richard Lovett. *William Tindale: A Biography: Being a Contribution to the Early History of the English Bible*. Rev. ed. London: Religious Tract Society, 1925.

Dick, John A. R., and Anne Richardson, editors. *William Tyndale and the Law*. Sixteenth Century Essays & Studies 25. Kirksville, MO: Sixteenth Century Journal Publishers, 1994.

Dickens, A. G. *The English Reformation*. London: Schocken, 1964.

---. *Lollards and Protestants in the Diocese of York, 1509–1558*. Oxford: Oxford University Press, 1959.

Dictionary of National Biography. 22 vols. Founded by George Smith. Edited by Sir Leslie Stephen and Sir Sidney Lee. Oxford: Oxford University Press, 1885–1901; reprint, 1971.

Doernberg, Erwin. *Henry VIII and Luther*. Stanford: Stanford University Press, 1961.

Dowling, Maria. *Humanism in the Age of Henry VIII*. London: Croom Helm, 1986.

Duke, Alistair. *Reformation and Revolt in the Low Countries*. Ronceverte, WV: Hambledon, 2003.

Duffy, Eamon. *Stripping of the Altars: Traditional Religion in England 1400–1580*. New Haven: Yale University Press, 1992.

Duhamel, Albert P. "The Oxford Lectures of John Colet: An Essay in Defining the English Renaissance." *Journal of the History of Ideas* 14 (1953) 493–510.

Eaves, Richard G. "Reformation Thought of Dr. Robert Barnes, Lutheran Chaplain and Ambassador to Henry VIII." *Lutheran Quarterly* 28 (1976) 156–65.

Ebeling, Gerhard. *Luther: An Introduction to His Thought*. Translated by R. A. Wilson Philadelphia: Fortress, 1970.

---. "On the Doctrine of the *Triplex Usus Legis* in the Theology of the Reformation." In *Word and Faith*, 62–78. Translated by James W. Leitch. Philadelphia: Fortress, 1963.

Elert, Werner. "Eine Theologische Falschung zur Lehre vom *tertius usus legis*." *Zeitschrift für Religions- und Geistesgeschichte* 1.2 (1948) 168–70.

---. *Law and Gospel*. Translated by Edward H. Schroeder. Minneapolis: Fortress, 1967.

Elton, G. R. *Luther in der Neuzeit*. Gutersloh: Gutersloher Verlagshuas Mohn, 1983.

---. *Reform and Reformation: England, 1508–1558*. Cambridge: Harvard University Press, 1979

Evans, G. R. *John Wyclif: Myth and Reality*. Downers Grove, IL: InterVarsity, 2005.

Fagerberg, H. *A New Look at the Lutheran Confessions (1529–1537)*. Translated by G. Lund. St. Louis: Concordia, 1972.

Forde, Gerhard O. "Justification and the Law in Lutheran Theology." In *Justification by Faith*, edited by H. Anderson, T. Murphy, and J. Burgess, 278–303. Lutherans and Catholics in Dialogue 7. Minneapolis: Augsburg, 1985.

---. *The Law-Gospel Debate: An Interpretation of its Historical Development*. Minneapolis: Augsburg, 1969.

---. *On Being a Theologian of the Cross: Reflections on Luther's Heidelberg Disputation*. Grand Rapids: Eerdmans, 1997.

Fowler, David C. "John Trevisa and the English Bible." *Modern Philology* 58.2 (1960) 81–98.

---. *The Life and Times of John Trevisa, Medieval Scholar*. Seattle: University of Washington Press, 1995.

Fulop, R. E. "John Frith (1503–1533) and His Relation to the Origins of the Reformation in England." PhD diss., Edinburgh University, 1956.

Gairdner, James. *Lollardy and the Reformation in England: An Historical Survey*. 4 vols. London: Macmillan, 1908–13.

Gleason, John B. *John Colet*. Berkeley: University of California Press, 1989.

Godfrey, W. Robert. "John Colet of Cambridge." *Archiv für Reformationsgeschichte* 65 (1974) 6–18.

Greaves, R. L. "The Origins and Early Development of English Covenant Thought." *The Historian* 31 (1968) 21–35.
Green, Lowell C. *How Melancthon Helped Luther Discover the Gospel: The Doctrine of Justification in the Reformation.* Fallbrook, CA: Verdict Publications, 1980.
Greenman, Jeffrey P. and Timothy Larsen, editors. *Reading Romans Through the Centuries: From the Early Church to Karl Barth.* Grand Rapids: Brazos, 2005.
Greschat, Martin. *Melancthon neben Luther: Studien zur Gestalt der Rechtfertigungslehre zwischen 1528 und 1537.* Untersuchungen zur Kirchengeschichte 1. Witten: Luther-Verlag, 1965.
Hagan, Kenneth G. "The Testament of a Worm: Luther on Testament and Covenant." *Consensus* 8.1 (1982) 12–20.
Haigh, Christopher. *English Reformations: Religion, Politics, and Society under the Tudors.* Oxford: Oxford University Press, 1993.
———, editor. *The English Reformation Revised.* Cambridge: Cambridge University Press, 1987.
Haikola, Lauri. *Usus Legis.* Uppsala: A. B. Lundequistica Bokhandeln, 1958.
Halkin, Léon-E. *Erasmus: A Critical Biography.* Oxford: Blackwell, 1992.
Hammond, G. "William Tyndale's Pentateuch: Its Relation to Luther's German Bible and the Hebrew Original." *Renaissance Quarterly* 33 (1980) 351–85.
Hard, David C. "The Origin and Development of John Frith's Doctrinal Adiaphora." PhD diss., Westminster Theological Seminary, 1997.
Haykin, Michael A. G., and Kenneth J. Stewart, eds. *The Emergence of Evangelicalism: Exploring Historical Continuities.* Nottingham: Apollos, 2008.
Heal, Felicity. *Reformation in Britain and Ireland.* The Oxford History of the Christian Church. Oxford: Oxford University Press, 2003.
Heino, O. Kadai, editor. *Accents in Luther's Theology: Essays in Commemoration of the 450th Anniversary of the Reformation.* St. Louis: Concordia Publishing House, 1967.
Heintze, Gerhard. *Luthers Predigt von Gesetz und Evangelium.* Munich: Kaiser, 1958.
Hesselink, I. John. *Calvin's Concept of the Law.* Princeton Theological Monograph Series 30. Allison Park, PA: Pickwick, 1992.
Holl, Karl. "Die Rechtfertigungslehre in Luthers Vorlesung über der Römerbrief mit besonderer Rücksicht auf die Frage der Heilsgewissheit." In *Gesammelte Aufsätze zur Kirchengeschichte*, 1:111–58. 3 vols. Tübingen: Mohr/Siebeck, 1928.
Hudson, Anne. *Lollards and Their Books.* Ronceverte, WV: Hambledon, 1985.
———. *The Premature Reformation: Wycliffite Texts and Lollard History.* Oxford: Clarendon, 1988.
———, editor. *Selections from English Wycliffite Writings.* Cambridge: Cambridge University Press, 1978.
Hughes, Paul L., and James F. Larkin, editors. *Tudor Royal Proclamations.* Vol. 1: *The Early Tudors (1485–1553).* New Haven: Yale University Press, 1964.
Jacobs, Henry. *The Lutheran Movement in England During the Reigns of Henry VIII and Edward VI: and its literary monuments.* Rev. ed. Philadelphia: General Council Publication House, 1908.
Janz, Dennis R. *Luther and Late Medieval Thomism: A Study in Theological Anthropology.* Waterloo, ON: Wilfried Laurier University Press, 1983.
Joest, Wilfried. *Gesetz und Freiheit: Das Problem des Tertius Usis Legis bei Luther unde die neutestamentliche Parainese.* Göttingen: Vandenhoeck & Ruprecht, 1951.

Kelly, J. N. D. *Early Christian Doctrines*. Rev. ed. San Francisco: Harper & Row, 1978.
Kjeldgaard-Pederson, Stephen. *Gesetz, Evangelium, und Busse: Theologiegeschichtliche Studien zum Verhaltnis Zwischen dem jungen Johann Agricola (Eisleben) und Martin Luther*. Acta theological Danica 16. Leiden: Brill, 1983.
Klug, Eugene. "Luther on Law, Gospel, and the Third Use of the Law." *Springfielder* 38 (Summer 1974) 155–169.
Knappen, M. M. "William Tindale: First English Puritan." *Church History* 5 (1936) 201–15.
Knox, D. B. *The Doctrine of Faith in the Reign of Henry VIII*. London: James Clarke, 1961.
Kolb, Robert. *Bound Choice, Election, and Wittenberg Theological Method: From Luther to the Formula of Concord*. Grand Rapids: Eerdmans, 2005.
———. *Martin Luther: Confessor of the Faith*. Oxford University Press, 2009.
———, and Charles P. Arand. *The Genius of Luther's Theology: A Wittenberg Way of Thinking for the Contemporary Church*. Grand Rapids: Baker Academic, 2008.
Lake, Peter, and Maria Dowling, editors. *Protestantism and the National Church in Sixteenth Century England*. London: Croom Helm, 1987.
Lancel, Serge. *St. Augustine*. Translated by Antonian Nevill. London: SCM, 2002.
Laughlin, P. A., "The Brightness of Moses; Face: Law and Gospel, Covenant, and Hermeneutics in the Theology of William Tyndale." PhD diss., Emory University, 1975.
Leader, D. R. *A History of the University of Cambridge 1: The University to 1546*. Cambridge: Cambridge University Press, 1988.
Leininger, Jeffrey W. "How Lutheran was William Tyndale?" *Lutheran Theological Review* 15 (2002–3) 54–72.
Lewis, C. S. *English Literature in the Sixteenth Century Excluding Drama*. Oxford History of English Literature. Edited by F. P. Wilson and Bonamy Dobrée. Oxford: Clarendon, 1954.
Lillback, Peter A. *The Binding of God: Calvin's Role in the Development of Covenant Theology. Texts & Studies in Reformation and Post-Reformation Thought*. Grand Rapids: Baker Academic, 2001.
Lindberg, Carter. "Do Lutherans Shout Justification But Whisper Sanctification?" *Lutheran Quarterly* 30 (1999) 1–20.
———. *European Reformations*. Oxford: Blackwell, 1996.
Litzenberger, Caroline. *The English Reformation and the Laity: Gloucestershire, 1540–1580*. Cambridge: Cambridge University Press, 1997.
Loane, Sir Marcus. *Masters of the English Reformation*. Edinburgh: Banner of Truth Trust, 2005.
———. *Pioneers of the Reformation in England*. London: The Church Book Press Room, 1964.
Lohse, Bernard. *Martin Luther's Theology: Its Historical and Systematic Development*. Translated and edited by Roy A. Harrisville. Minneapolis: Fortress, 1999.
Lund, Norman J. "Luther's Third Use of the Law and Melancthon's *tertius usus legis* in the Antinomian Controversy with Agricola (1537–1540)." PhD diss., University of St. Michael's, 1986.
Lutton, Richard. *Lollardy and Orthodox Religion in Pre-Reformation England: Reconstructing Piety*. London: Boydell, 2006.

Maas, K. D. "Robert Barnes (1495–1540) as Historical Theologian." DPhil diss., Oxford University, 2005.

———. "Thomas Bilney: 'Simple Good Soul'?" *Tyndale Society Journal* 27 (July 2004) 8–20.

Mannermaa, Tuomo. *Christ Present in Faith: Luther's View of Justification*. Edited and introduced by Kirsi Stjerna. Minneapolis: Fortress, 2005.

Mann, Jeffrey K. "Melanchthon's Response to Antinomianism: How the 'Antinomian Question' Shaped the Development of His Theology." *Concordia Journal* 26 (2000) 305–25.

———. *Shall We Sin? Responding to the Antinomian Question in Lutheran Theology*. American University Studies, Series VII, Theology and Religion 226. New York: Lang, 2003.

Marc'hadour, Germain. "William Tyndale entre Erasmus et Luther." In *Actes du Colloque International Erasme* (Tours, 1986), edited by Jacques Chomarat, Andre Godin, and Jean Claude Margolines, 185–98. Geneva: Droz, 1990.

Marshall, Peter and Alec Ryrie, editors. *The Beginnings of English Protestantism, c. 1530–1700*. Cambridge: Cambridge University Press, 2002.

Marshall, Peter, editor. *The Impact of the Reformation in England*. Readers in History Series. London: Edward Arnold, 1997.

———. *Reformation England, 1480–1642*. London: Edward Arnold, 1997.

Mayote, Judith Moberly. "William Tyndale's Contribution the Reformation in England." PhD diss., Marquette University, 1976.

Meyer, Carl S. "Henry VIII Burns Luther's Books." *Journal of Ecclesiastical History* 9 (1958) 173–87.

McConica, James Kelsey. *English Humanists and Reformation Politics under Henry VIII and Edward VI*. Oxford: Clarendon, 1965.

McDonough, Thomas M., O.P. *The Law and Gospel in Luther: A Study of Main Luther's Confessional Writings*. Oxford: Oxford University Press, 1963.

McGiffert, Michael. "William Tyndale's Conception of Covenant." *Journal of Ecclesiastical History* 32 (1981) 167–84

McGoldrick, J. E. *Luther's English Connection: The Reformation Thought of Robert Barnes and William Tyndale*. Milwaukee: Northwestern Publishing, 1979.

———. *Luther's Scottish Connection*. London and Toronto: Associated University Press, 1989.

———. "Patrick Hamilton: Luther's Scottish Disciple." *Sixteenth Century Journal* 18 (1987) 81–88.

McGrath, Alister. *Intellectual Origins of the European Reformation*. Grand Rapids: Baker, 1993.

———. *Iustitia Dei: A History of the Christian Doctrine of Justification*. 2nd ed. Cambridge: Cambridge University Press, 1998.

———. *Luther's Theology of the Cross*. Oxford: Blackwell, 1990.

McKeon, Richard, editor. *The Basic Works of Aristotle*. Translated by W. D. Ross. New York: Random House, 1941.

Moeller, Jens G. "Beginnings of Puritan Covenant Theology." *Journal of Ecclesiastical History* 14 (1963) 46–67.

Modalsi, Ole. *Das Gericht Nach Den Werken: Ein Beitrag zu Luthers Lehre vom Gesetz*. Göttingen: Vandenhoeck & Ruprecht, 1963.

Moynahan, Brian. *God's Bestseller: William Tyndale, Thomas More, and the Writing of the English Bible—A Story of Betrayal*. New York: St. Martin's, 2003.

Mozley, J. F., *William Tyndale*. London: SPCK, 1937.

Mullett, Michael W. *Martin Luther*. London: Routledge, 2004.

Oberman, Heiko A. *The Harvest of Medieval Theology: Gabriel Biel and Late Medieval Nominalism*. Rev. ed. Grand Rapids: Baker Academic, 2000.

Olin, John, James D. Smart, and Robert E. McNally, eds. *Luther, Erasmus and the Reformation: A Catholic-Protestant Reappraisal*. New York: Fordham University Press, 1969.

Osslund, Richard. "*Imputatio iustitiae Christi, Liberum arbitrium in renatis*, and *tertius usus legis* in Melancthon's later *Loci*." ThD diss., Concordia Theological Seminary, 1986.

Oxford Dictionary of National Biography. 60 vols. In Association with the British Academy. From the Earliest Times to the Year 2000. Edited by H. C. G. Matthew and Brian Harrison. Oxford: Oxford University Press, 2004.

Ozment, Steven. *Age of Reform 1250–1550: An Intellectual and Religious History of Late Medieval and Reformation Europe*. New Haven: Yale University Press, 1980.

———. *Homo Spiritualis: A comparative study of the Anthropology of Johannes Tauler, Jean Gerson and Martin Luther (1509–16) in the Context of Their Theological Thought*. Leiden: Brill, 1969.

Pearce, E. George. "Luther and the English Reformation." *Concordia Theological Monthly* 31 (1960) 597–606.

Pesch, Otto H. "Gesetz und Evangelium: Luthers Lehre im Blick auf das moraltheologische Problem des ethischen Normenzerfalls." *Theologische Quartalschrift* 149 (1969) 313–35.

Pettegree, Andrew, editor. *The Early Reformation in Europe*. Cambridge: Cambridge University Press, 1992.

Porter, H. C. "Introduction." In *Erasmus and Cambridge: The Cambridge Letters of Erasmus*. Translated by D. F. S. Thompson. Introduction, Commentary and Notes by H. C. Porter. Toronto: University of Toronto Press, 1963.

Preus, Robert, editor. *A Contemporary Look at the Formula of Concord*. St. Louis: Concordia, 1978.

Rabil, Albert, Jr., editor. *Renaissance Humanism: Foundations Form, and Legacy. Volume II: Humanism Beyond Italy*; and *Volume 3: Humanism and the Disciplines*. Philadelphia: University of Pennsylvania Press, 1988.

Raynor, B. *John Frith, Scholar and Martyr: A Biography*. Otford, UK: Pond View, 2000.

Reed, Arthur W. "The Regulation of the Book Trade Before the Proclamation of 1538." *Transactions of the Bibliographical Society* 15 (October 1917 to March 1919; London: Blades, East & Blades, 1920) 157–84.

Rex, Richard. "The Crisis of Obedience: God's Word and Henry's Reformation." *The Historical Journal* 39 (1996) 863–94.

———. "The English Campaign Against Luther in the 1520's." *Transactions of the Royal Historical Society*. Fifth Series, 39 (London, 1989) 85–106.

———. "The Early Impact of Reformation Theology at Cambridge University 1521–1547." *Reformation and Renaissance Review* 2 (1999) 38–71.

———. *The Lollards*. Houndmills, UK: Palgrave, 2002.

———. "New Light on Tyndale and Lollardy." *Reformation* 8 (2003) 143–71.
———. *The Theology of John Fisher*. Cambridge: Cambridge University Press, 1991.
Richardson, Anne. "Tyndale's Quarrel with Erasmus." *Fides et Historia* 25.3 (1993) 46–65.
Richter, Matthias. *Gesetz und Heil: Eine Untersuchung zur Vorgeschichte und zum Verlauf des sogennanten Zweiten Antinomistichen Striets*. Göttingen: Vandenhoeck & Ruprecht, 1996.
Rogge, Joachim, "Innerlutherische Streitigkeiten um Gesetz und Evangelium, Rechtfertigund und Heiligung." In *Leben und Werk Martin Luthers von 1526 bis 1546: Festgabe zu seinem 500. Geburtstag*, edited by H. Junghans, 187–204. Göttingen: Vandenhoeck & Ruprecht, 1983.
Rupp, E. G. "Luther in English Theology." *Lutheran World* 2.1 (1955) 12–23.
———. *The Righteousness of God: Luther Studies*. Birbeck Lectures in Ecclesiastical History, 1947. London: Hodder & Stoughton, 1953.
———. *Six Makers of English Religion 1500–1750*. London: Hodder & Stoughton, 1957.
———. *Studies in the Making of the English Protestant Tradition*. Cambridge: Cambridge University Press, 1947.
Ryrie, Alec. *The Gospel and Henry VIII: Evangelicals and the Early English Reformation*. Cambridge: Cambridge University Press, 2003.
———. *The Origins of the Scottish Reformation*. Manchester, UK: Manchester University Press, 2006.
———. "The Strange Death of Lutheran England." *Journal of Ecclesiastical History* 53 (2002) 64–92.
Scaer, David P. "Formula of Concord Article VI: the Third Use of the Law." *Concordia Theological Quarterly* 42 (April 1978) 145–55.
———. "The Law and the Gospel in Lutheran Theology." *Grace Theological Journal* 12 (Fall 1991) 163–78.
———. "Sanctification in Lutheran Theology." *Concordia Theological Quarterly* 49 (Apr-Jul 1985) 181–97.
Schott, Erdmann. *Fleisch und Geist nach Luthers Lehre, unter besonderer Beruksichtigung des Begriffs "Totus Homo."* 1930. Reprinted, Darmstadt: Wissenschaftliche Buchgesellschaft, 1969.
Schuetze, Armin W., "On the Third use of the Law: Luther's Position in the Antinomian Debate." In *No Other Gospel: Essays in Commemoration of the 400th Anniversary of the Formula of Concord, 1580–1980*, edited by Arnold J Koelpin, 207–27. Milwaukee: Northwestern Publishing House, 1980.
Schurb, Ken "The Law Always Accuses: The Augsburg Confession and the Apology." *Concordia Journal* 23 (1997) 199–200, 347–49.
———. "Philip Melancthon, the Formula of Concord, and the Third Use of the Law." PhD diss., Ohio State University, 2001.
Seebohm, Frederic. *The Oxford Reformers: Colet, Erasmus and More*. London: Dent & Sons, 1914.
Silcock, Jeffrey G. "Law and Gospel in Luther's Antinomian Disputations, with Special Reference to Faith's Use of the Law." ThD diss., Concordia Seminary, 1995.
Slavin, Arthur J., editor. *Humanism, Reform, and Reformation in England*. New York: Wiley & Sons, 1969.

Smeeton, Donald Deen. *Lollard Themes in the Reformation Theology of William Tyndale.* Sixteenth Century Essays & Studies 6. Kirksville, MO: Sixteenth Century Journal Publishers, 1986.
Smithen, F. J. *Continental Protestantism and the English Reformation.* London: James Clarke, 1927.
Stackhouse, Ian. "The Native Roots of Early English Reformation Theology." *Evangelical Quarterly* 66 (1994) 19–35.
Steinmetz, David C. *Luther in Context.* 2nd ed. Grand Rapids: Baker Academic, 2002.
Stephens, W.P. *The Theology of Huldrych Zwingli.* Oxford: Clarendon, 1986.
Thielicke, Helmut. *Theological Ethics. Volume 1: Foundations.* London: Adam & Charles Black, 1968.
Thomson, J. A. F. *The Later Lollards, 1414–1520.* London: Oxford University Press, 1965.
Thompson, W. D. J. "The Sixteenth-Century Editions of *A Supplication unto King Henry the Eighth* by Robert Barnes, D.D.: a footnote to the history of the Royal Supremacy." *Transactions of the Cambridge Bibliographical Society* 3 (1960) 133–42.
Tjernagel, N. S. "Dr. Robert Barnes and Anglo-Lutheran Relations, 1521–40." PhD diss., University of Iowa, 1955.
———. *Henry VIII and the Lutherans: A Study in Anglo-Lutheran Relations from 1521–47.* St. Louis: Concordia, 1965.
———. *The Reformation Essay of Dr. Robert Barnes Chaplain to Henry VIII.* London: Concordia, 1963.
———. "Robert Barnes and Wittenberg." *Concordia Theological Monthly* 28 (1957) 641–53.
Trinterud, L. J. "A Reappraisal of William Tyndale's Debt to Martin Luther." *Church History* 31 (1962) 24–45.
———. "The Origins of Puritanism." *Church History* 20 (1951) 37–57.
Trueman, Carl R. *Luther's Legacy: Salvation and English Reformers, 1525–56.* Oxford: Clarendon, 1994.
Vasilev, Georgi. *Heresy and the English Reformation: Bogomil-Cathar Influence on Wycliffe, Langland, Tyndale and Milton.* London: McFarland, 2008.
Wagner, Walter H. "Luther and the Positive Use of the Law." *Journal of Religious History* 11 (1980) 45–63.
Wannenwetsch, Bernd. "Luther's Moral Theology." In *The Cambridge Companion to Martin Luther,* edited by Donald K. McKim, 120–35. Cambridge: Cambridge University Press, 2003.
Watson, Philip S. *Let God Be God! An Interpretation of the Theology of Martin Luther.* Philadelphia: Muhlenberg, 1947.
Wengert, Timothy J. *Law and Gospel: Philip Melancthon's Debate with John Agricola of Eisleben over poenitentia.* Texts and Studies in Reformation and Post-Reformation Thought. Grand Rapids: Baker, 1997.
———. "Luther and Melancthon, Melancthon and Luther." *Lutherjahrbuch* 66 (1999) 55–88. Göttingen: Vandenhoeck & Ruprecht.
Werrell, Ralph S. "John Trevisa and William Tyndale." *Tyndale Society Journal* 24 (April 2003) 22–26.
———. *The Theology of William Tyndale.* Cambridge: James Clarke: 2006.

———. "Tyndale's Disagreement with Luther in the Prologue to the Epistle to the Romans." *Reformation and Renaissance Review* 7.1 (2005) 57–68.

Wicks, Jared. "Luther on the Person Before God." Review of *Ontologie der Person bei Luther* by Wilfried Joest. *Theological Studies* 30 (1969) 289–311.

Williams, C. H. *William Tyndale*. Stanford: Stanford University Press, 1969.

Wingren, Gustaf. *Luther on Vocation*. Translated by Carl C. Rasmussen. 1957. Reprint, Eugene, OR: Wipf & Stock, 2004.

The Works of John Wesley. 3rd ed. Vol. 1: *Journals from October 14, 1735 to November 29, 1745*. 1872. Reprint, Grand Rapids: Baker, 2007.

Wright, N. T. "New Perspectives on Paul." Rutherford House, Edinburgh: 10th Edinburgh Dogmatics Conference: 25–28 August 2003. Online: http://www.ntwrightpage.com.

———, editor. *The Work of John Frith*. Courtenay Library of Reformation Classics 7. Appleford, UK: Courtenay, 1983.

Yost, John K. "The Christian Humanism of the English Reformers, 1525–55: A Study in English Renaissance Humanism." PhD diss., Duke University, 1965.

———. "Reappraisal of how Protestantism Spread During the Early English Reformation," *Anglican Theological Review* 60 (1978) 437–46.

———. "William Tyndale and the Renaissance Humanist Origins of the English *Via Media*." *Nederlands Archief voor Kerkgeschiedenis* 51.2 (1971) 167–86.

www.ingramcontent.com/pod-product-compliance
Lightning Source LLC
Chambersburg PA
CBHW071146300426
44113CB00009B/1102